A
History *of*
New Mexico
Since Statehood

A
History *of*
New Mexico
Since Statehood

Richard Melzer,
Robert J. Tórrez,
and
Sandra K. Mathews

UNIVERSITY OF NEW MEXICO PRESS
ALBUQUERQUE

Contents

List of Illustrations

Chapter 3

Chapter 4

Chapter 5

Chapter 6

Chapter 7

Chapter 8

Chapter 9

Maps

Preface

Welcome, new historians! The authors of this textbook are excited to have you join us on a journey that we began many years ago—learning about New Mexico history! Like many historians, we love history and hope that after reading this book, you will enjoy it, too.

Some people think that learning history means memorizing names, dates, places, and events. You will learn some, but you will also learn a lot about the stories behind them—because history is a collection of stories pieced together from many different places (archives, oral traditions, books, images, and much more). In order to find the stories that accompany those names, dates, places, and events, the authors of this textbook spent a lot of time doing research, collecting and then synthesizing information into a logical format, and finally writing (and rewriting) the story in a way that brings these facts together in an interesting manner.

The first step in "doing" history is figuring out what story needs to be told. Sometimes that involves asking questions like "Why do people say Governor Clyde Tingley liked power too much?" or "How did Frijoles Canyon become Bandelier National Monument?" The next step is doing background research. Kind of like on the new show *History Detectives* (on PBS), historians first have to know something about the event or person about which (or whom) they want to write. Historians have to know a basic story line so they will know where to begin looking for information to tell the story. Asking thoughtful questions is important, questions such as: Which people were most important to New Mexico's history and why? What events were turning points in New Mexico or had some impact on how people lived? How did people interact with others who came from different cultures? How did people live? Once historians have questions and know what story they want to tell, they must find out where to look for information that will help tell that story.

What kind of information do historians use? We use secondary sources such as books, academic journal articles, and pamphlets, as well as informational brochures about places or people. Historians also must use primary sources (written documents or oral history told by people who actually witnessed the events). Some primary sources we used to write this book included stories that people told us or wrote down many years ago (oral history); letters between family, friends, and acquaintances; letters between officials of the church, military, and governmental agents; newspaper articles; government reports; laws; wills; and other government documents like the census, land-grant records, or legislative and other governmental official records. And believe it or not, we even used political cartoons! Historians use a wide variety of sources to help us tell the story. We do not find information in just one place and begin writing. A good historian must make sure the information is correct by corroborating it with other sources.

Having a wide variety of sources is very important because historians have to make sure they are not just telling one side of the story. Imagine finding a document from the first half of the 1700s about the establishment of outlier towns (such as Abiquiú or Belén) and the author wrote about the "marauding and dangerous nomadic tribes such as the Navajo, Ute, and Comanche" who constantly raided, killed, and stole from the Spanish people. Is this true? Is there another point of view? Why did the author write this? What is the author's training, background, or bias? As important, why does it matter today how the nomadic tribes were perceived three hundred years ago? These are some of the many questions researchers must ask to make sure the story they tell is as unbiased as possible. Using a solid combination of primary and secondary sources, as well as sources from many different views, is the goal of good historians—and should be yours, too.

Once historians have collected all this information about the story by doing research (research should take up about 80 percent of your time in preparing a research paper), they have to figure out how to piece the story together. Chronological organization is often the key to presenting information in the most coherent fashion but not always. Most important, however, is the ability of the researcher to make history relevant and meaningful to those who read it. Why does it matter where the CCC camps were located and what they did? How does that affect students today? Just because Los Alamos became a secret scientific facility that developed the first atomic bomb and was important in the 1940s, why should students today have to study about it? Does it really matter that Bruce King served more than one term as governor? What did he accomplish, and why is that important to students now? Does it really matter if students in Hobbs know where Mount Taylor is or if students in Farmington know where Carlsbad Caverns are? Why is it significant that Pres. Theodore Roosevelt made Taos Pueblo's sacred Blue Lake part of the national forest system only to have the lake returned to Taos Pueblo during Pres. Richard M. Nixon's administration? What did each of those decisions hope to achieve, and what was the end result?

Research oftentimes emanates from a question researchers might have (or from an assignment their teacher gave them). No single history book will answer every single question about a particular topic. As you read through this textbook, think about what questions you might want to ask about New Mexico history. When you read about Gov. Clyde Tingley, did you wonder about his relationship with his wife, Carrie Tingley, and what they did after he did not win a third term as governor? What did he do? That could be an interesting research paper. Historians not only try to answer questions about an individual's political career but also about their personal lives. By doing so, historians make the individual seem more relevant to the reader. More important, historians try to do research to find out why people make the decisions they do. Many decisions people make are based on their own past, their family life, their heritage, or something they learned along the way. Therefore, it is important for historians to look at far more than just what a governor did in office and try to see the character behind the man. Also, historians must look beyond male political leaders—they must understand the points of view of women and minorities, environmental issues or concerns, and local and national issues as well. In other words, studying history means studying everything from politics to geography, science to cultural studies, and agronomy to immigration. Good history is multifaceted, well balanced, and broadly supported. Good history can be really fun to read. Most important, though, learning history is important. Perhaps Spanish philosopher George Santayana said it best: "Those who cannot remember the past are condemned to repeat it."

Introduction
The Struggle to Become a State

☼ Introduction

New Mexico had been part of the Spanish empire for more than two hundred years (1598–1821) and part of the independent country of Mexico for another twenty-five years (1821–46) before the United States conquered it in the Mexican-American War of 1846–48. Almost as soon as **Brigadier General Stephen Watts Kearny** led his U.S. Army of the West into Santa Fe on August 15, 1846, many New Mexicans looked forward to the day their homeland would become a state of the United States.

New Mexicans were made to wait another sixty-six years before finally achieving statehood on January 6, 1912. Incredibly, twenty western territories achieved statehood during the sixty-six years New Mexico was made to wait for this higher political status within the United States. The only legal requirements to become a state were that a territory have a population of at least 60,000 residents, write a state constitution, and be approved by a majority vote in the U.S. Congress. New Mexico had a population of 61,547 in 1850, the first year it had applied for statehood. Further, New Mexico's population was much higher than many other territories, like Montana and Wyoming, when they became states between 1846 and 1912.

Since the territory was often confused with Old Mexico, New Mexicans went so far as to consider changing its name to increase their chances for statehood. At one time or another, New Mexicans considered changing the territory's name to Acoma, Sierra, or Lincoln, among several suggestions. Fortunately, New Mexico's name has never changed.

TIMELINE

1846
The U.S. Army invades and captures New Mexico in the Mexican-American War

1847
U.S. forces suppress the Revolt of 1847

1848
The Mexican-American War ends with the signing of the Treaty of Guadalupe Hidalgo

1850
As part of the Compromise of 1850, New Mexico becomes a territory of the United States

1861
The Civil War begins; Confederate troops occupy southern New Mexico

1862
Confederate troops advance into northern New Mexico, but, once defeated at Glorieta Pass, retreat home to Texas

1863
Kit Carson defeats the Navajos, who are then forced on the Long Walk to Bosque Redondo

1865
Mescalero Apaches held at Bosque Redondo flee to their homeland to the south

1868
The disastrous reservation at Bosque Redondo is closed as the Navajos sign a new treaty and return to their homeland in northwestern New Mexico

1871
The San Carlos Indian reservation is founded in southeastern Arizona; thousands of Apaches will be forced to relocate to this distant location far from their homeland

1878
John Tunstall is killed, starting the Lincoln County War

1880
The Atchison, Topeka, and Santa Fe Railroad builds the first tracks into New Mexico

1881
Sheriff Pat Garrett kills Billy the Kid, essentially ending the Lincoln County War

1898
New Mexicans prove their loyalty to the United States by serving heroically in the Spanish-American War, especially as members of a cavalry unit known as the Rough Riders

1906
Arizona voters reject a plan to enter the Union as a single state with New Mexico

1912
New Mexico achieves statehood at last

What had prevented New Mexico from becoming a state? Despite consistent efforts by New Mexico leaders and the support of most residents, there were five main reasons for New Mexico's long, frustrating delay.

First, early efforts were hampered by a general ignorance about the territory and unfair suspicion about its citizens. People in other parts of the United States often opposed statehood because New Mexico's largely Hispanic and Native American population was considered too "foreign" in language, culture, and religion to ever be a state in the Union. People also asked whether New Mexicans, who had lived under Spanish and Mexican rule for so long, would be loyal to the United States, especially if the United States ever went to war against New Mexico's former governing countries.

Second, territorial politics also hurt New Mexico's chances of becoming a state. A corrupt band of politicians and businessmen dominated the territory's government and economy for most of the late 1800s. Observing this corruption, leaders in other parts of the country (where corruption was, ironically, as bad, if not worse) criticized New Mexico and did everything in their power to prevent New Mexico from reaching statehood.

Third, national politics often interfered in New Mexico's progress in becoming a state. National issues that often had little to do with New Mexico took priority at key moments, often delaying New Mexico's goal of statehood for years at a time.

Fourth, New Mexico took so long to become a state because its Indian wars were so costly and so long, perpetuating the territory's image as a place dominated by a largely violent, "primitive" population. While the U.S. Army had defeated Indian resistance in most of the West by the 1870s, Native American warriors like **Geronimo** fought off thousands of U.S. troops in the Southwest until 1886. The *Chicago Tribune* declared that New Mexico's Indians "can never be eligible to . . . become citizens. It would [be ridiculous] to allow . . . them to form a state . . . on the same level as the more prosperous and enlightened [states of the East]."

The Difference Between a Territory and a State

Most New Mexicans wanted their homeland to become a state in the Union rather than remain a territory after 1850 because as a territory

- the governor was appointed by the president, rather than elected by New Mexicans;
- judges were appointed by the president, rather than selected by New Mexicans;
- only the territorial legislature was elected by New Mexicans;
- New Mexicans were represented in the U.S. Congress by a **congressional delegate** who could do everything a congressman did, but could not vote on New Mexico's behalf in the U.S. House of Representatives;
- New Mexico had no representation or vote in the U.S. Senate.

In short, New Mexico enjoyed far less democracy at home and representation in Washington, D.C., as a territory than it would have as a state.

Finally, New Mexico's chances of becoming a state were hurt by the territory's image as one of the last lawless enclaves of the "Wild West." When Easterners read about New Mexico in newspapers, magazines, and novels, they usually read of notorious outlaws like Billy the Kid— hardly responsible, law-abiding citizens of a potential state. An editorial in the *New York Times* went so far as to call New Mexico "the heart of our worst civilization."

The purpose of this introduction is

- to teach more about the five main reasons why it took New Mexico so long to become a state;
- and to reveal how these problems were largely overcome, leading to final victory and statehood in 1912.

 ## The U.S. Invasion and the "Revolt of 1847"

First, let's consider the question of New Mexico's loyalty to the United States in the mid-1800s.

Brig. Gen. Stephen Watts Kearny and his U.S. Army of the West swept into New Mexico and captured Santa Fe without firing a shot in 1846. Kearny raised the U.S. flag in Santa Fe and declared that all New Mexicans were now citizens of the United States. This hardly meant that everyone in New Mexico was pleased by the Americans' bloodless conquest of their homeland, though. New Mexicans were, after all, still citizens of the Republic of Mexico, and their country was still at war with the United States in the **Mexican-American War**. By December 1846, rumors of a rebellion were serious enough that **Charles Bent**, the first U.S. governor of New Mexico, had several suspected rebel leaders arrested.

Despite the arrests, planning for an uprising continued. On January 19, 1847, a large group of New Mexicans converged on Governor Bent's home in Taos. Before the day was over, Bent and several other Anglos and individuals sympathetic to the new U.S. government lay dead. A second group of rebels killed at least five Americans in Mora, on the east side of the Sangre de Cristo Mountains. More than a thousand insurrectionists advanced toward Santa Fe, intent on recapturing New Mexico from the Americanos.

Within days, the insurrection, referred to as the **Revolt of 1847**, had spread through much of northern New Mexico. On January 23, a force of nearly four hundred U.S. troops, accompanied by Anglo friends of Bent and the others who had been killed, marched north to quell the uprising and seek revenge. Between January 24 and January 28, this large force met and defeated New Mexican forces in battles at Santa Cruz de la Cañada and Embudo.

By February 1, more than six hundred New Mexican insurgents had retreated to the Pueblo of Taos where they fortified their position in the old Spanish mission church and awaited the advancing American army. The American assault on the pueblo began on February 3. After a fierce two-day battle, the Americans succeeded in destroying the walls of the church and routing the New Mexicans. When the smoke cleared, at least two hundred New Mexicans lay dead, and most survivors were captured.

San Geronimo ruins after the battle in Taos Pueblo

Meanwhile, residents of Mora had managed to repulse an attack by U.S. troops sent from Las Vegas. The soldiers returned with reinforcements and began an artillery attack that soon forced Mora's defenders to abandon their town. The troops proceeded to level Mora to the ground.

Crushing defeats at Taos and Mora ended the brief Revolt of 1847. The day after the fighting ended, a series of so-called treason trials began. A military court was organized to try Pablo Montoya, Tomás Romero, and several dozen other men captured following the desperate battle at Taos Pueblo.

Montoya and Romero had been identified as leaders in the insurrection and were scheduled to be tried together. But Tomás Romero was shot and killed by a guard who claimed Romero had tried to escape. So on February 6, Montoya stood alone before Judge Charles Beaubien, whose son was among those killed in Taos, with Ceran St. Vrain, the late Governor Bent's former business partner, serving as the official interpreter in the proceedings. The biased court found Montoya guilty and sentenced him to hang for his "rebellious conduct" against the United States. Pablo Montoya was hanged the following day. By the time the court adjourned, at least seventeen men had been hanged in Taos.

Following these executions in Taos, court convened at Santa Fe, where a grand jury indicted Antonio María Trujillo and three other men for treason. On March 12, Trujillo was tried, convicted, and sentenced to hang, but his sentence was never carried out. Immediately following his conviction, Trujillo's attorney filed an appeal that questioned the authority of an American court to try a Mexican citizen for treason while the United States was still at war with Mexico.

General Kearny's superiors in Washington agreed. Just because General Kearny had announced that New Mexicans were citizens of the United States when he occupied the territory in August 1846 did not make it so. Granting citizenship is a right reserved to Congress, and, since the United States and Mexico were still at war, Congress had not yet granted that right. New Mexicans were, therefore, still citizens of the Republic of Mexico. The court had no jurisdiction to try anyone for treason, and Trujillo was released.

If Antonio Trujillo was not a rebel, then the battles he and his fellow New Mexicans fought against the United States could not be called a rebellion. For years, though, many U.S. citizens still thought of the events of early 1847 as a rebellion and proof that New Mexicans could not be trusted as loyal American citizens. This perception lingered throughout New Mexico's prolonged fight for statehood. As late as 1902, a congressional committee in Washington, D.C., met to review the "rebellion" and use it against the territory in its struggle for statehood.

☼ Ending the Mexican-American War and the Treaty of Guadalupe Hidalgo

While U.S. troops occupied New Mexico and suppressed the so-called Revolt of 1847, the Mexican-American War raged in Mexico to the far south. In March 1847, ten thousand U.S. troops landed at the Mexican port of Veracruz and, after a series of bloody but decisive battles, reached Mexico City by late summer. On September 13, U.S. troops stormed the citadel of Chapultepec (the "Halls of Montezuma" referred to in the U.S. Marine Corps song), and by the following day Mexico City was in American hands. The war was over. Now it was time to negotiate the peace.

U.S. Pres. James K. Polk appointed Nicholas P. Trist to negotiate a peace treaty with Mexico. After several months, Trist succeeded in negotiating an agreement in the community of Guadalupe Hidalgo, a suburb of Mexico City. The U.S. and Mexican governments officially signed the agreement, known as the **Treaty of Guadalupe Hidalgo**, on May 30, 1848.

The Treaty of Guadalupe Hidalgo did much more than end the Mexican-American War. It also had a tremendous impact on New Mexico's international boundary with Mexico, the issue of citizenship, and the question of land ownership in the Southwest.

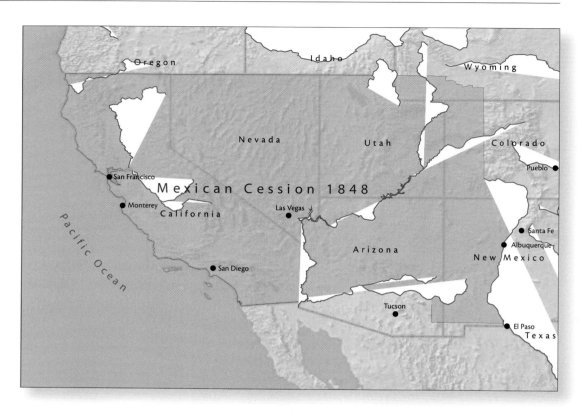

International borders: Mexico and its lost northern territories

....

The treaty established a new boundary between the United States and Mexico, forever changing the map of North America. The new boundary began at the Gulf of Mexico and proceeded west and north along the Rio Grande to a point approximately where Truth or Consequences (Hot Springs) is located today. The boundary then went west to the Gila River and on to California and the Pacific Ocean. As a result of the treaty, Mexico **ceded**, or transferred ownership, of nearly half its territory to the United States. This territory included all or part of the current states of New Mexico, Arizona, California, Colorado, Nevada, and Utah.

The treaty also allowed Mexican citizens in the ceded territories to keep their Mexican citizenship, even if they remained in the United States. The treaty also allowed Mexican citizens who did not want to stay in the ceded territories to move to Mexico if they chose to do so. Several hundred families moved to the Mesilla Valley and northern Chihuahua, where they received land grants from the Mexican government. Doña Ana, Mesilla, Refugio, and Santo Tomás were among the new settlements established by those who chose to leave.

The Treaty of Guadalupe Hidalgo included a controversial extension called the **Protocol of Querétaro**. This extension seemed to protect the

The Protocol of Querétaro

In the city of Querétaro on the 26th month of May 1848 at a conference between Their Excellencies Nathan Clifford and Ambrose H. Sevier Commissioners of the United States of America, . . . and His Excellency Don Luis de la Rosa, Minister of Foreign Affairs of the Republic of Mexico, it was agreed, after adequate conversation respecting the changes alluded to, to record in the present protocol the following explanations. . . .

First.

The American Government by suppressing the IXth article of the Treaty of Guadalupe and substituting the III article of the Treaty of Louisiana did not intend to diminish in any way what was agreed upon by the aforesaid article IXth in favor of the inhabitants of the territories ceded by Mexico. Its understanding that all of that agreement is contained in the IIId article of the Treaty of Louisiana. In consequence, *all the privileges and guarantees, civil, political and religious*, which would have been possessed by the inhabitants of the ceded territories, if the IXth article of the Treaty had been retained, will be enjoyed by them without any difference under the article which has been substituted.

Second.

The American Government, by suppressing the Xth article of the Treaty of Guadalupe *did not in any way intend to annul the grants of lands* made by Mexico in the ceded territories. These grants, notwithstanding the suppression of the article of the Treaty, preserve the legal value which they may possess; and the grantees may cause their legitimate titles to be acknowledged before the American tribunals. . . .

And these explanations having been accepted by the Minister of Foreign Affairs of the Mexican Republic, he declared in name of his Government that with the understanding conveyed by them, the same Government would proceed to ratify the Treaty of Guadalupe as modified by the Senate and Government of the United States. In testimony of which their Excellencies the aforesaid Commissioners and the Minister have signed and sealed in quintuplicate the present protocol.

[Seal] A. H. Sevier

[Seal] Nathan Clifford

[Seal] Luis de la Rosa

property rights of former Mexican citizens who had received land grants from the Spanish or Mexican governments. A protocol does not have the same force of law as a formal treaty, however. As a result, all former citizens of Mexico who had land grants in New Mexico had to prove ownership of their land before a court established by the United States. Proving ownership was difficult to do, and many individuals and communities eventually lost their land once New Mexico became a part of the United States.

The Santa Fe Ring

Despite the Treaty of Guadalupe Hidalgo and the Protocol of Querétaro, Hispanic New Mexicans often lost their land grants, frequently to Anglo lawyers and businessmen known as the **Santa Fe Ring** during the U.S. territorial period.

Under Spanish and Mexican rule, disputes over land ownership were usually settled locally, according to local custom. Under U.S. law, land disputes required more exacting proof of ownership. To resolve these disputes in U.S. courts, Hispanics often hired Anglo lawyers, including such men as Thomas Catron, Stephen B. Elkins, and Samuel Axtell. If lacking cash,

Thomas Catron

Hispanic clients paid these attorneys with portions of the very land the lawyers had been hired to defend. In this way, attorneys became owners of vast amounts of land, creating bitterness among Hispanics, who argued that much of their land grants had been stolen from them. Attorney Thomas Catron, the suspected leader of the Santa Fe Ring, became the largest landowner not only in New Mexico but also in the entire United States. By the end of the 1800s it is estimated that Hispanic land owners had lost as much as two-thirds of the land they had been granted under Spanish or Mexican rule.

Political cartoon of
the Santa Fe Ring

☀ New Mexico Becomes a U.S. Territory

A convention of representatives met to write a New Mexico state constitution to submit to Congress for approval just two years after the Treaty of Guadalupe Hidalgo was signed. On June 20, 1850, the citizens of New Mexico overwhelmingly ratified the new constitution by a vote of 8,371 to 39. Elections held at the same time selected Henry Connelly as governor and Manuel Alvárez as lieutenant governor. That summer a "state legislature" met in Santa Fe to draw up laws for the new state of New Mexico.

The U.S. Congress, though, rejected every action taken in New Mexico. The federal government ruled that New Mexico had acted without proper authority and would have to wait for official permission from

Congress before it could organize a state government. New Mexico's future status would have to wait until Congress negotiated an important national agreement called the **Compromise of 1850**.

The Compromise of 1850 resolved several major issues, including some regarding New Mexico. The most serious was slavery. In 1850, slavery was still legal in the United States, although many who opposed slavery fought to limit its expansion into the new Western territories, including New Mexico. Pro-slavery southerners fought just as hard to allow slavery to expand into Western territories that might someday become states. New Mexicans joined the debate, although there were few Black slaves in New Mexico, mostly servants of Southern officers temporarily stationed in Southwestern forts.

The second issue regarded Texas's claims to eastern New Mexico. Texas had won its independence from Mexico and established the Republic of Texas in 1836. The Republic of Texas claimed that its western border

The Lincoln Canes

New Mexico's Pueblo Indians supported the United States during the Confederate invasion of the territory. In fact, Isleta Pueblo lent the federal government $18,000 in gold to help pay Union soldier salaries during the war. To reward the Pueblos for their support, Pres. Abraham Lincoln gave each Pueblo governor an impressive ebony cane with a silver head and inscription with the year, 1863, the words "A. Lincoln, Pres. USA," and the name of the pueblo to which it was presented. There is even a false report that Lincoln traveled to New Mexico and personally presented the canes to the governors of Acoma, Cochití, Isleta, Jémez, Laguna, Nambé, Picurís, Pojoaque, Sandia, San Felipe, San Ildefonso, San Juan, Santa Ana, Santa Clara, Santo Domingo, Taos, Tesuque, Zia, and Zuni.

The **Lincoln canes** served another important purpose. During Spanish and Mexican times canes had been given to the Pueblos to recognize their separate authority and land-grant rights. The Lincoln canes served the same purpose under U.S. rule.

Today Pueblo governors often appear at official functions carrying a brightly decorated bundle with as many as five canes from the Spanish, Mexican, and U.S. periods. In recent years, canes have been presented to Pueblos to help celebrate important events in their proud history. Of all the canes the governors have received, however, the Lincoln canes remain the most famous and most often displayed.

The Lincoln cane and others of Zia Pueblo

extended to the Rio Grande, meaning that Texas claimed all of New Mexico east of the river. Texas went so far as to send a military force to secure its claim to much of New Mexico, although this small army was easily defeated in 1841.

The Compromise of 1850 helped settle these national and regional issues. The U.S. government agreed to pay Texas $10 million to drop its claim to New Mexico land east of the Rio Grande. In another part of the compromise, Utah and New Mexico (which included Arizona from 1850 to 1863) were admitted as territories and allowed to decide

The Civil War in New Mexico

In 1861, the United States faced its greatest challenge as a nation when eleven states seceded from the Union over slavery, states' rights, and slavery in the western territories to form a new country called the Confederate States of America. Texas was among the states that chose to join the Confederate cause.

The first military action of the Civil War in the far West was directed at New Mexico. The Confederacy saw New Mexico as a land bridge to California, with its valuable ports and gold fields to the west, and Colorado, with its gold and silver mines to the north.

In the summer of 1861, a force of Texas volunteers invaded southern New Mexico. By the end of 1861, the Confederacy was in firm control of southern New Mexico and Arizona. The region was organized as the "Confederate Territory of Arizona," with its capital at Mesilla.

In early 1862, a force of more than three thousand Texans under the command of Gen. Henry H. Sibley marched northward up the Rio Grande Valley. The commander of the Union forces in New Mexico was Col. Edward R. S. Canby. He commanded more than four thousand U.S. soldiers as well as more than two thousand New Mexico volunteers and militia. Thirteen

hundred Colorado volunteers, known as the Colorado Column, rushed to New Mexico to help fight the Tejanos. Another fourteen hundred volunteers, known as the California Column, headed to New Mexico from the West Coast.

On February 20, 1861, the Union and Confederate armies met about sixty miles south of Socorro in the Battle of Valverde. By the end of a bloody, two-day battle, the rebel army claimed victory, causing Union forces to retreat to nearby Fort Craig. Despite this victory, the Confederates found themselves with many casualties and dangerously few supplies. They continued north, though, occupying Albuquerque and Santa Fe en route to Fort Union, a U.S. military post filled with valuable supplies, northeast of Las Vegas.

The battle that ended Confederate ambitions in the far West began on March 26, 1862, when Union and Confederate forces met at Glorieta Pass, between Santa Fe and Las Vegas. By the second day of the battle, the Confederates seemed ready to crush Union forces. A group of Colorado volunteers, though, guided by Lt. Col. Manuel Chávez of the New Mexico volunteers, discovered the Confederate supply train and destroyed the Confederates' last store of supplies.

for themselves whether to allow slavery within their borders when and if they became states at some future date.

Eleven years after the Compromise of 1850 was reached, the United States was torn apart in the bloodiest conflict in our history, the Civil War. Unfortunately, New Mexico's chance at statehood had been lost as Congress dealt with a national issue, Black slavery, which had little real importance in New Mexico. This was the first of many times that New Mexico's chance for statehood was lost in the shuffle as the United States dealt with larger national events and crises first.

Sibley and his Confederate invaders realized they were in no position to continue the battle, much less win their campaign. Exhausted and without supplies, the Confederates withdrew from Glorieta Pass and made a hurried retreat south, back toward Texas. A Confederate defeat at the Battle of Peralta south of Albuquerque marked the end of the Confederate campaign to capture California and Colorado by way of New Mexico. Ragged and quite hopeless, the Confederates returned to Texas in mid-1862, never to return to the Southwest in the Civil War.

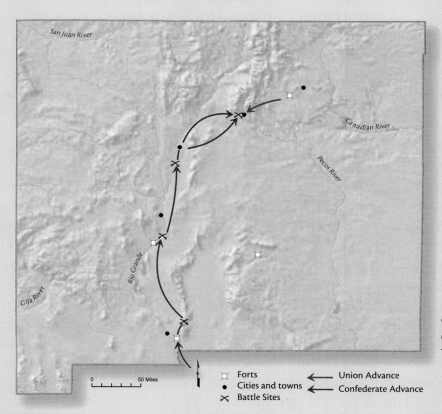

Confederate invasion and Colorado Column routes

Elkins's Handshake

In 1874, New Mexico's Congressional Delegate Stephen B. Elkins submitted a new request for the U.S. Congress to consider New Mexico statehood. Elkins's official request pointed out that New Mexico's population had reached 135,000, more than twice the 60,000 required for a territory to become a state. Well aware of the question of New Mexico's loyalty, Elkins emphasized his territory's loyalty to the Union in the Civil War. He also mentioned the territory's improved schools and healthy climate.

Elkins received strong support in Congress for his statehood proposal, and it appeared the territory was on the verge of finally achieving full membership in the American Union. Just then, a "fateful handshake" intervened.

One day in March 1876, members of the U.S. House of Representatives were engaged in a heated debate over an issue regarding the outcome of the Civil War. Congressman Julius Caesar Burrows of Michigan was speaking in support of a measure the northern states supported and the South strongly opposed. Burrows's words reportedly "grilled the Southerners from head to foot."

As Burrows was ending his speech, New Mexico delegate Elkins walked onto the floor of the House. Unaware of how Burrows's words angered southern congressmen, Elkins applauded the speech and rushed to the head of the line to shake Burrows's hand. Seeing Elkins's handshake, southern congressmen assumed that Elkins—and therefore all New Mexicans—favored the north rather than the south on all issues that still divided the nation more than a decade after the Civil War had ended. Southerners quickly withdrew their support for New Mexico statehood, and the territory's latest bid for higher political status went down in defeat. A national issue, division between the north and the south, had interfered with New Mexico's statehood chances—again.

The Indian Wars in New Mexico

New Mexico's Indian wars began as early as 1598 when the Acoma Indians had attempted to defy Spanish rule in rebellion with disastrous results for Acoma Pueblo and its people. Less than a century later the Pueblo Indians of New Mexico united in the Rebellion of 1680 to kill more than four hundred Spanish colonists and expel two thousand Spanish survivors. The Spaniards regrouped to reconquer New Mexico after twelve years in dismal exile.

Nomadic Indian raids plagued the pueblos and white settlements throughout the Spanish, Mexican, and early U.S. territorial periods. Realizing the death and destruction of these frequent raids, General Kearny had promised the people of New Mexico that the U.S. Army would defeat the raiding tribes once New Mexico was made part of the United States.

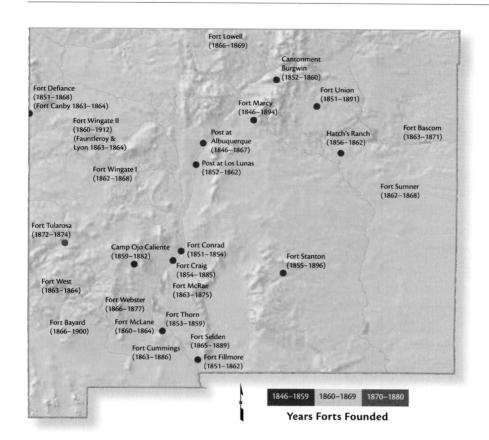

The U.S. government attempted to defeat the warring Indians using two principal strategies. First, the federal government built military forts throughout the territory to help the U.S. Army respond to raids more quickly, before the raiding warriors could retreat to their familiar home-lands. Next, the U.S. government created a series of Indian agencies located at or near where the Indians lived. Indian agents assigned to these outposts stayed in contact with the various tribes, providing them with goods and services and making it less likely they would resort to raiding to meet their needs. As of 1857 a superintendent of Indian affairs was put in charge of dealing with all the Indian tribes in the territory, including the nomadic Navajos, Utes, and Apaches.

Defeat of the Navajos and Mescalero Apaches

The American strategies worked to a large degree, creating a general peace with most of the Ute and Jicarilla Apache tribes. Navajo warriors, by contrast, continued their raids on New Mexico's western frontier. The

U.S. Army sent troops to defeat the raiders as early as two months after General Kearny's entry into Santa Fe, but this and later campaigns proved frustratingly futile through the 1850s.

It was not until the following decade that Gov. Henry Connelly and military commander Gen. James H. Carleton devised a plan to pacify the Navajos. In early 1863, the government delivered a powerful message: the Navajos had until July to surrender peacefully or face U.S. troops and New Mexico volunteers under **Col. Christopher "Kit" Carson**, who would be ordered to destroy all Indian crops and livestock.

When the Navajos did not surrender, Carson's forces attacked Navajo settlements in western New Mexico and at Canyon de Chelly, the tribe's stronghold in eastern Arizona, destroying their dwellings, burning their crops, and chopping down their fruit orchards. The starvation policy was so complete and, in Indian memory, so unmerciful that by early 1864, more than two thousand Navajo had surrendered and been rounded up at Fort Canby, Arizona. The government's goal was to take the Navajos far from their homeland, strip them of their traditional culture, and force them to accept American ways while living as farmers in a distant valley. The vain hope was that with these changes Navajos would lead peaceful lives, ending their frequent raids and warfare.

On March 5, 1864, Navajo prisoners formed a long, thin column and began the five-hundred-mile trek from their homeland to **Bosque Redondo**, a small piece of land on the Pecos River in eastern New Mexico. The historian William A. Keleher described the trek as a "funeral-like procession, in twos and fours, silent, grim and gloomy." No one knows for certain how many hundreds of Navajos died from disease, starvation, and broken hearts. Soldiers reportedly shot some people if they grew sick and fell behind. The trek, known as the **Navajo Long Walk**, unfairly punished men, women, and children, most of who had never participated in raids, much less taken up arms against the U.S. Army.

The Bosque Redondo experiment was a disaster. Poor funding, fraud, crop failures, lack of shelter, and bad weather contributed to this tragedy. Of the approximately eight thousand Navajos held at Bosque Redondo, many died of disease and starvation. Problems were made worse by the government's decision to place about 525 imprisoned Mescalero Apaches alongside Navajos at Bosque Redondo. Conflicts between these traditional enemies confined in a small space made life miserable for members of both tribes. On November 3, 1865, the Mescalero Apaches escaped from Bosque Redondo, heading south. Eight years later Pres. Ulysses S. Grant established the Mescalero Indian Reservation in the tribe's traditional homeland in the Sacramento Mountains.

Navajos on the
Long Walk, 1864

By 1868, the U.S. government realized that its attempt to **Americanize** the Navajos at Bosque Redondo had failed. After entering into a new treaty, in which they promised to never raid again, the Navajos began their return trek to their homeland to the northwest on June 18, 1868. Navajo tears of agony in 1864 had turned to tears of joy in 1868.

The treaty of 1868 established a reservation of more than 3 million acres, making it the largest reservation in the country to this day. True to their word, the Navajos stopped their raids and returned to their traditional ways, focusing on raising livestock, especially sheep, and making crafts, especially rugs and jewelry.

Other Apache Tribes of the Southwest

In addition to the Mescaleros, other Apache tribes lived in the Southwest. These included the Jicarillas, the Lipans, and the Chiricahuas of southwest New Mexico and northern Chihuahua. Each tribe was divided into clans of about a hundred families who hunted, raided, and migrated in the rugged terrain of their region. Individual clans, rather than the entire Apache tribe, waged war against the U.S. Army until the late 1800s.

After many years of fighting, the U.S. Army forced about four thousand Apaches to relocate to a reservation in southeastern Arizona called **San Carlos**. The goal was the same as at Bosque Redondo: strip the Indians of their native cultures and impose white culture in their

Above: Geronimo; right: Buffalo Soldiers at Diamond Creek

place. Living in this barren wasteland, nicknamed Hell's Forty Acres, the Apaches at San Carlos experienced many of the same hardships the Navajos and Mescalero Apaches had faced at Bosque Redondo. Suffering under these terrible conditions, some Apaches fled San Carlos, led by warriors like Victorio and Geronimo.

Returning to their homeland, fleeing Apaches raided white settlers who had come to the region to mine, farm, and ranch. White settlers attempted to defend themselves with the help of U.S. cavalry units, often manned by Black troopers, nicknamed the **Buffalo Soldiers**. Each side displayed great acts of bravery, but each also committed terrible atrocities; an estimated four thousand whites, Blacks, and Apaches were killed in a thirty-year period. After many years of combat, the last band of Apache warriors, under Geronimo, finally surrendered to U.S. forces on September 4, 1886.

The Indian wars hurt New Mexico's statehood chances because many easterners mistakenly thought of the Southwest as a vast battleground populated by "wild, primitive" Indians who attacked innocent white settlers, hardly the image most Americans had of a peaceful territory ready for statehood. Sensational newspaper reports, magazine articles, and cheap novels reinforced this image even after Geronimo's surrender in 1886.

Law and Disorder in the Territory

Newspapers, magazines, and novels of the late 1800s also portrayed New Mexico as a lawless territory filled with Wild West gunslingers like **William "Billy the Kid" Bonney**. These accounts fired the popular imagination but damaged New Mexico's reputation among potential settlers, investors, and those who might have favored statehood in Congress.

Violence was rampant in many parts of the American West after 1865. Murders, bank robberies, stagecoach holdups, and cattle rustling were common in western states and territories alike. Historians have revealed complex reasons for this violence, including rapid population growth, ethnic diversity, the easy availability of alcohol, a prevailing gun culture, and social instability in new expanding communities, known as **boomtowns**.

All these elements were present in New Mexico from the 1870s through the 1890s. The territory experienced a rapid increase in population after the Civil War. Its major towns sprouted saloons and dance halls at every corner, and nearly every male carried a gun. While almost all newcomers to the territory were peaceful men and women who came to make better lives for themselves, by the 1870s, a much rougher crowd had also made its way into the territory. New Mexico's lawmen, courts, and jails were nearly overwhelmed by a wave of violent crimes.

Individual bad men or infamous gangs caused much of this lawlessness. By the 1880s, however, violence had escalated to the point that whole counties were at war, with competing political and economic factions arming themselves to win absolute local control.

In the most famous of these conflicts, known as the **Lincoln County War**, competing leaders sought control of profitable contracts to supply the military posts and Indian reservations of southeastern New Mexico. Newcomer **John T. Tunstall**, an Englishman who had established a ranch and a mercantile business in Lincoln, led one side of the conflict. The powerful local boss **Lawrence G. Murphy**, a suspected member of the Santa Fe Ring, dominated the other faction. According to a U.S. special agent sent to New Mexico to investigate the conflict, each side recruited the "most desperate cut-throats in the territory." Among those Tunstall hired was the soon-to-be-famous William "Billy the Kid" Bonney. The war began when Tunstall was murdered on February 18, 1878, and ended only after Sheriff Pat Garrett killed Billy the Kid at Fort Sumner on July 14, 1881.

Billy the Kid

Opponents to New Mexico statehood asked how the territory could be governed with the rule of law if whole counties were split by lawless factions, as in Lincoln. Further, how could New Mexico be fit for statehood when its citizens had so little trust in its courts that they resorted to lynching at least sixty-nine suspected outlaws in the 1880s alone? Clearly, New Mexico would have to control its spreading lawlessness and guarantee law and order if it were ever to become a state.

※ Overcoming the Obstacles to Statehood

Five major obstacles caused New Mexico's statehood struggle: the territory's poor image, political corruption, national politics, Indian wars, and lawlessness. How, then, was New Mexico able to largely overcome these considerable obstacles and finally win its long battle for statehood?

First, New Mexico's image as a "foreign," distant region of the United States began to change with the coming of the railroad to the territory in 1880. The **Atchison, Topeka, and Santa Fe Railroad** tied New Mexico to the rest of the country with faster, vastly improved transportation and communication. Travelers from outside the territory began to learn more about New Mexico and its value as a potential state. Other Americanos moved to New Mexico by train, often imposing Anglo culture, values, religion, and language on the territory. These changes gradually impressed those who had previously thought New Mexico was too different from the rest of the nation to ever become a state.

New Mexico also dealt with its image as a "foreign" region of the United States by proving its loyalty to the country in the **Spanish-American War** of 1898. When the United States declared war on Spain on April 20, 1898, **Gov. Miguel A. Otero** began receiving telegrams from other parts of the country asking whether Hispanics in New Mexico would be loyal to the United States or to their former ruling country, Spain, in the new conflict. Outraged that their loyalty would be questioned, the governor and most New Mexicans were quick to respond. Appearing at one of many patriotic rallies held in the territory, Governor Otero spoke for most Hispanic New Mexicans when he proclaimed, "I am a New Mexican, and in saying that I am saying that I am an American. We have a war on our hands now, and we want [nothing] to interfere with its successful prosecution. Let us all be Americans." The rally came to a rousing close as a military band played "The Star Spangled Banner."

Hundreds of New Mexicans also proved their loyalty to the United States by volunteering to serve in the U.S. Army. **Maximiliano Luna** and other young men joined the most famous fighting unit in the war, a cavalry regiment best known as the **Rough Riders**. New Mexicans fought bravely throughout the conflict and returned to a heroes' welcome that included a private visit with Pres. William McKinley in Washington, D.C. Few now doubted whether New Mexico would be a loyal state, if admitted to the Union.

The issue of political corruption in New Mexico was largely overcome after 1900 with the decline of the once-dominant Santa Fe Ring. By the early 1900s most leaders of the ring had been exposed, had retired, or had passed on. Charges of corruption still surfaced in the territorial government but it was nothing like it had existed before.

Next, national politics did not interfere with New Mexico's chances for statehood in the first decade of the twentieth century. Furthermore, New Mexico's congressional delegates were careful not to alienate factions or regions of the nation divided on issues having little to do with the territory. In other words, they avoided additional Elkins's handshakes or similarly costly political mistakes.

New Mexico's Indian wars were less of an obstacle to statehood by the beginning of the twentieth century following Geronimo's surrender in 1886 and death in 1909. If Geronimo reminded Americans of Indian warfare in New Mexico, his confinement in Oklahoma and newspaper photos of his gradual aging reminded the public that this once-great warrior was no longer a threat to anyone in the Southwest.

Finally, violence in New Mexico subsided by the early twentieth century with improvements in the territory's legal system. Many outlaws were captured and punished, often in New Mexico's first penitentiary, opened in Santa Fe in 1885. Respect for the law increased, as reflected in a sharp decline in the number of lynchings, from sixty-nine in the 1880s to eight in the 1890s, and a significant rise in the number of legal executions, from only three in the 1870s to fourteen in the 1890s.

Gov. Miguel A. Otero

 ## The Final Climb to Statehood

Despite these promising developments, New Mexico still faced stiff opposition to statehood from 1900 to 1910. Indiana **Senator Albert Beveridge**, the chairman of the U.S. Senate's key Committee on Territories, opposed New Mexico statehood so much that he once hid in an

Political cartoon of
Arizona rejecting
New Mexico, 1906

attic rather than let his committee meet and possibly approve statehood for the territory. Not even his committee's ten-day tour of New Mexico in 1902 changed Beveridge's stubborn mind.

Trying a new strategy, most New Mexicans favored joining with Arizona and applying for statehood as a single state, to be called Arizona. Known as the **jointure** movement, this idea was presented to the citizens of New Mexico and Arizona in an election held in 1906. The voters of New Mexico approved the proposition by a two-to-one margin, but the voters of Arizona defeated it by an equally large majority. After this disappointing effort to enter the Union as one, the neighboring territories would have to enter statehood separately or not at all.

So the territories pursued statehood on their own. By 1910, the political path was sufficiently cleared of obstacles to allow both New Mexico and Arizona to begin their final preparations for statehood in early 1912. The long struggle for statehood had ended in triumph at last.

1. List five main reasons why it took New Mexico so long to become a state.

2. Explain how the so-called Revolt of 1847 hurt New Mexico's chances of becoming a state.

3. Explain how political corruption and the Santa Fe Ring hurt New Mexico's chances of becoming a state.

4. Explain how national political issues like slavery hurt New Mexico's chances of becoming a state.

5. Explain how the Indian wars hurt New Mexico's chances of becoming a state.

6. Explain how crime and lawlessness hurt New Mexico's chances of becoming a state.

7. Explain how New Mexico was eventually seen as less "foreign" and how this change in perception helped the territory become a state.

8. Explain how the coming of the railroad helped New Mexico become a state.

9. Explain how New Mexico's political corruption was largely overcome, allowing New Mexico to become a state.

10. Explain how national issues became less of an obstacle to New Mexico's chances of becoming a state.

11. Explain how the end of the Indian wars helped New Mexico's chances of becoming a state.

12. Explain how a decline of lawlessness helped New Mexico's chances of becoming a state.

Statehood at Last

1910–15

☀ Introduction

After sixty-six years and more than fifty attempts, New Mexico finally achieved statehood in 1912. New Mexicans had cause to celebrate. Before the celebration could begin, though, a **state constitution** had to be written, and our first state leaders had to be elected. Once admitted as our nation's forty-seventh state, New Mexico was more eager than ever to create a modern image of itself to attract more tourists and settlers, draw new investments, and otherwise benefit from its brand-new political status.

The purpose of this chapter is to teach you about

- how New Mexico's state constitution was written;
- what the constitution guarantees;
- who were chosen as our first state officials;
- how New Mexico tried to promote itself in its new role as a full member of the United States;
- how homesteaders attempted to create new farms;
- and how some New Mexicans felt the sting of racism in direct and indirect ways.

☀ Becoming a State

The State Constitution of 1910

New Mexico's **Enabling Act of 1910** required New Mexicans to write a state constitution in preparation for the day their territory would become a state. New

TIMELINE

1898
Indian Day School, the first movie made in New Mexico, is produced by a Thomas Edison company

1901
Blackdom is founded by Francis Marion Boyer

1908
Folsom is flooded; George McJunkin finds prehistoric bison bones

1909
Spanish-American Normal School is founded in El Rito

1910
Congress passes New Mexico's Enabling Act
The New Mexico state constitution is written at the state constitutional convention in Santa Fe

1911
The citizens of New Mexico approve the state constitution, 31,742 to 13,399
Pres. William Howard Taft and the U.S. Congress approve New Mexico's state constitution

1912
President Taft signs New Mexico's statehood bill
New Mexico's first state governor, William C. McDonald, is inaugurated
New Mexico's first congressmen and senators are sworn into office in Washington, D.C.
D. W. Griffith films *The Pueblo Legend*, starring Mary Pickford, at Isleta Pueblo
Black boxing champion Jack Johnson defeats Jim Flynn in a controversial nine-round Las Vegas bout

1915
Opening of the Panama-California Exposition in San Diego

1916
Elephant Butte irrigation project completed and dedicated

1919
Julián and María Martínez create their first black-on-black pottery

1921
The first Black student is admitted to the University of New Mexico (UNM)

1927
Archeologists discover Folsom Man, based on George McJunkin's earlier discovery of prehistoric bison bones outside Folsom

1929
Blackdom is abandoned

1934
Clara Belle Williams is the first Black student admitted to New Mexico A&M

1910 constitutional convention

Mexicans had had some experience in writing state constitutions, having written three previous documents in 1850, 1872, and 1889. Each had been written to help prove New Mexico was ready to rule itself as a state. None of these earlier constitutions had been approved. Now, however, with New Mexico on the eve of statehood, its leaders knew they must write a "safe and sane" constitution not only to rule their future state, but also to avoid Washington's rejection when statehood had never been so close at hand.

New Mexicans prepared to write their constitution by holding a **constitutional convention** in Santa Fe. A hundred delegates were elected, representing every county in the territory. The vast majority (seventy-one) of delegates were Republican, with fifty-five of them known as Old Guard, or conservative members of their political party. Twenty-eight delegates were Democrats, and one, G. P. Patterson of Chaves County, was a socialist, although his fellow delegates so shunned Patterson that they declared he had smallpox and insisted he be quarantined in isolation for the rest of the convention.

The remaining politically acceptable delegates included some of the richest, most powerful citizens of New Mexico. The greatest number of delegates were lawyers (thirty-two), ranchers (twenty), or merchants (fourteen). Other delegates included bankers, doctors, newspaper editors, a college president, and at least one saloonkeeper. With thirty-five Spanish speakers, all proceedings at the convention were conducted in Spanish as well as in English. All delegates were either Hispanic or Anglo males, meaning that women, Native Americans, Blacks, and other minorities were not directly represented.

The convention began at noon on October 3, 1910. Although Charles A. Spriers of San Miguel County officially presided over the convention, **Solomon Luna** of Valencia County was clearly the most powerful member of the political gathering. By 1910, Luna was the wealthiest sheep rancher in New Mexico and a dominant figure in the Republican Party on the local, territorial, and even the national levels. An Old Guard Republican, Luna chaired the constitutional convention's most important committee, the Committee on Committees. This committee oversaw twenty-seven other convention committees, each of which wrote a section of the final constitution. Luna was said to be so powerful that he influenced each committee's work and only had to raise an eyebrow to dictate the results of votes taken on the convention floor. Other Republican leaders included Thomas B. Catron, the oldest delegate at seventy years of age, and Thomas J. Mabry, the youngest at twenty-five. **Harvey B. Fergusson** of Albuquerque led the Democratic minority.

The delegates worked for seven weeks, until eleven fifteen on the night of November 21, 1910. Predictably, the constitution they wrote was very conservative, very long (more than twenty-one thousand words, compared to about seven thousand in the U.S. Constitution), and, under Luna's leadership, very protective of Hispanic rights. The constitution guaranteed two Hispanic rights in particular. Regarding voting rights, Article 7, section 3, of the constitution protected the right of every citizen to vote regardless of his "religion, race, language or color" and regardless of his inability to speak the Spanish or English language. Regarding education, Article 12, section 10, stated that "children of Spanish descent" would never be denied admission to public schools nor ever be "classified in separate schools, but shall forever enjoy perfect equality with other children in all public schools." Hispanic children were never to experience **segregated**, inferior schools like most Black children faced in southern public schools.

To protect Hispanic voting rights and education, convention delegates created what are called the ironclad clauses in the state constitution. According to these clauses, to change any part of the constitution regarding Hispanic voting rights and education, three-quarters of the voters in the state as a whole and two-thirds of the voters in every county would

Solomon Luna

The Spanish-American Normal School at El Rito

In an effort to train Hispanic men and women to become good teachers and educational leaders, the territorial legislature created the **Spanish-American Normal School** in 1909. Located in El Rito, the school and its mission were considered so important that it was made a permanently funded state institution in the state constitution of 1910. The school was created to train Spanish-speaking teachers to teach Hispanic children not only Spanish, but also English, especially in preparation for work in the business world.

Just as important, students at the Spanish-American Normal School learned about their Hispanic culture. In the words of Erlinda Gonzales-Berry, now a University of New Mexico professor of Spanish, the school instilled "a strong sense of cultural identity and pride" in her and her fellow students when she attended in the 1950s.

Today, the El Rito school is part of Northern New Mexico College.

A Safe and Sane Constitution

New Mexico's original state constitution was safe, sane, and conservative in several ways, including:

- state governors served four-year terms, without the possibility of reelection;
- the state government was led by a **plural executive**, meaning that the governor and other leaders of the executive branch (such as the lieutenant governor) were each elected separately, weakening the strength of the governor to appoint and dismiss fellow members of the executive branch;
- the legislature only met in thirty-day sessions, weakening the strength of the legislative branch by limiting the time it had to pass new laws each year;
- the constitution limited women's suffrage, or right to vote, to school board elections, unless a percentage of the male voters in a county voted to deny women even this limited right.

Each of these sections of the constitution has been altered by constitutional amendments since 1912. Now:

- state governors serve four-year terms, but can be reelected once;
- the state government is still led by a plural executive, but since 1964 the governor and lieutenant governor run for election and serve in office as a team;
- since 1966 the state legislature meets for thirty-day sessions in even-numbered years (like 2012) and for sixty days in odd-numbered years (like 2013);
- women citizens can vote and run for all offices in all local, state, and national elections.

Madeline Mills Raised the U.S. Flag

On January 6, 1912, Madeline Mills was the sixteen-year-old daughter of New Mexico's last territorial governor, William J. Mills. Sixty years later Madeline recalled the events of the day New Mexico learned it had become a state:

> My father [called from] his office [in the capitol building] . . . to the Executive Mansion [where our family lived]. I was at home, and it was about one o'clock [p.m.]. He told me to come right over and hoist the [U.S.] flag because President Taft had [just] signed the statehood bill.

Former governor Miguel A. Otero had had a [U.S. flag with forty-seven stars] made years before in anticipation of [our] statehood. It had been tenderly and hopefully cherished . . . and now it [was the flag I] raised over the Capitol. . . . How very happy it made me.

(Quoted on the sixtieth anniversary of statehood in the *Carlsbad Current-Argus*, February 15, 1972, the *Tucumcari Daily News*, February 16, 1972, and the *Lincoln County News*, February 17, 1972.)

have to approve. With Hispanic voters representing more than a quarter of all voters in the state and as many as 90 percent of the voters in some counties, the odds of these rights ever being lost were close to zero. As suggested by their name, it was as if these clauses of the constitution were protected with nothing less than iron.

New Mexico welcomed to the Union cartoon, 1912

Several modern political reforms, such as women's **suffrage**, **prohibition**, and the election of state judges, were debated at the constitutional convention but quickly defeated. The Constitution of 1910 was clearly "safe and sane" because without "radical" political ideas the odds of congressional approval were very good. After two months of public debate, the voters of New Mexico approved their new constitution by a great majority, 31,742 to 13,399, on January 21, 1911; voters approved a small change in the amending process, known as the Blue Ballot, later that year. New Mexico sent its "safe and sane" document to **Pres. William Howard Taft**, who approved it on February 24, and then to the U.S. Congress, where it was approved without major opposition in August 1911.

Statehood celebration parade in Albuquerque, 1912

Only one step remained before statehood would be achieved. Surrounded by New Mexican leaders, President Taft officially signed New Mexico's statehood bill at exactly 1:35 p.m. on January 6, 1912. As he signed the long-awaited bill, Taft declared, "Well it is all over. I am glad to

Interviews on Statehood

Moments after President Taft signed New Mexico's statehood bill, a reporter from the *Albuquerque Evening Herald* asked several leading citizens what statehood meant to them. Here are some of their enthusiastic replies:

- Nestor Montoya, a Spanish-language newspaper editor and author said, "There is no question that New Mexico will now enter upon an era of prosperity. Capital will come here for investment, and business will pick up right away";
- T. N. Wilkerson, attorney, said, "Well, we will have our own [elected] officials [at last]";
- M. Marshall, an Albuquerque merchant, confidently declared, "Statehood is the best thing that ever happened to New Mexico."

(Quoted in the *Albuquerque Evening Herald*, January 6, 1912.)

give you life. I hope you will be healthy." New Mexico's long wait—and struggle—for statehood had ended at last.

First State Leaders

New Mexico's first state leaders entered office within weeks after President Taft signed our statehood bill. On January 8, 1912, New Mexico's first two Congressmen, Republican **George Curry** and Democrat Harvey B. Fergusson, took their oaths of office in the U.S. House of Representatives. Although the press reported that Curry and Fergusson were greeted with "generous applause," as the newest members of Congress New Mexico's representatives were assigned to desks in the last row of the House chamber.

New Mexico's first two U.S. senators were sworn in in Washington, D.C., on April 2, 1912. Before the Seventeenth Amendment of 1913 allowed for the **direct election** of senators, the New Mexico state legislature had elected Thomas B. Catron and **Albert B. Fall**. It had taken eight ballots and much discussion before Catron and Fall were finally chosen from a field of thirteen Republican and Democratic contenders. Fulfilling a lifelong goal, Catron would serve in the Senate until 1917; Fall served until 1921.

New Mexico's first state governor, Democrat William C. McDonald, was sworn into office with great fanfare on January 15, 1912. Elected in November 1911 over his main rival, Republican H. O. Bursum,

Governor William C. McDonald

New Mexico's first state governor was born and raised in New York before arriving in the gold-mining town of White Oaks, New Mexico, in the spring of 1880. After ten years in mining, he entered the cattle business, eventually owning his own ranch under the "Bar W" brand. Rising through the ranks of the Democratic Party, McDonald ran as his party's first candidate for state governor in 1911. Winning 31,035 votes and a majority in 65 percent of New Mexico's twenty-six counties, he was inaugurated and served a four-year term in office, 1912 to 1916.

According to attorney and historian William A. Keleher, who knew many governors in his fifty-year career, McDonald was "in my estimation, the nearest approach to an ideal governor" largely because he was so honest.

(William A. Keleher, *New Mexicans I Knew: Memoirs, 1892–1969* [Albuquerque: University of New Mexico Press, 1983], 138.)

Gov. William C. McDonald's inauguration, 1912

McDonald arrived in Santa Fe on a special train from his home in southern New Mexico.

As many as seven thousand New Mexicans greeted McDonald when his carriage, escorted by the New Mexico Mounted Police and the First Regimental Army Band, approached the capitol building on January 15. Seeing McDonald, the crowd broke into "deafening cheers," according to a reporter on the scene. Although a winter day, the weather was comfortably mild as McDonald took the oath of office at exactly 12:29 p.m. Seven former territorial governors sat in attendance to witness the great event.

Governor McDonald's inaugural address was brief, but it is significant that he identified public school education as the new state's "first concern." New Mexico's future leaders could only be wise and successful if they were well educated as children. In the governor's words, "The past is history, the present is the dawn of the future. It is to the future we look and that future will be what we make it."

As Governor McDonald concluded his remarks, the crowd shouted, "Three cheers to the stars and stripes!" In the words of an eyewitness, "The flag of the nation waved from the dome of the capitol, directly over the actors in this great political drama. The band burst into an exultant strain of patriotic music." Prolonged cheers and happy laughter filled the air. A gala ball, with music, dancing, food "in plenty," and women in beautiful gowns, lasted into the night. Hundreds of congratulatory telegrams poured into Santa Fe from every part of the state and the country. According to former territorial governor L. Bradford Prince, "The new state was born. The territory was no more."

Working to Improve New Mexico's State Image

New Mexicans had worked hard to be seen as both modern and prosperous during their struggle for statehood. Now that the territory had become a state, they continued their efforts to impress individuals who might help advance New Mexico's political and economic fortunes. Their efforts met with mixed results.

Early Movies

Moviemakers have long been welcome in New Mexico and the Southwest. They have been fascinated by the region's beautiful scenery, mild climate, low costs, and, perhaps most important, varied cultures. In fact, a film company owned by the inventor of modern motion pictures, Thomas Edison, shot New Mexico's first movie at an Indian pueblo. *Indian Day School* was filmed at Isleta Pueblo in 1898. Lasting only fifty seconds, it showed a group of Isleta children being led out of and back into their school—twice.

The next movie made in New Mexico was filmed shortly after statehood was achieved in 1912. The film crew included the most famous producer of his time, D. W. Griffith, and perhaps the most famous movie actress of all time, **Mary Pickford**. Twenty minutes long, *A Pueblo Legend* featured Pickford as a Hopi maiden who heroically saved her Pueblo Indian friends in battle. Unfortunately, few of the Native American characters in the film were played by Native Americans, and Griffith made little effort to accurately portray Pueblo Indian culture during the week he shot the film at Isleta Pueblo.

Romaine Fielding arrived in New Mexico with his movie crew the following year. Brimming with talent and energy, Fielding directed, produced, and acted in movies he wrote as they were being filmed. Fielding filmed as many as a dozen short and feature-length silent movies in New Mexico, including *The Golden God* in Silver City and *The Rattlesnake* in Las Vegas.

Tom Mix, the most famous cowboy star of his day, filmed about two dozen silent movies in Las Vegas from 1914 to 1916.

Tom Mix

The citizens of Las Vegas so admired Mix that they experienced a "Mix craze" while he starred in the movies he made in town. Everything, from Mix scarves to Mixed drinks, was named in his honor. New Mexico children enjoyed Tom Mix cowboy films so much they "went to see him [with] every dime [we] could get," in the words of author Max Evans.

Early movie making helped New Mexico by bringing new business to the state, at least while films were in production. More important, movies made in the Southwest gave moviegoers across the country an opportunity to see and appreciate New Mexico's beauty and economic potential. Ironically, the same cultures that had attracted moviemakers to New Mexico were seldom portrayed fairly or accurately, a problem that persists in many movies to this day.

New Mexico at the Panama-California Exposition of 1915–16

Built with American skills and finances, the Panama Canal was considered one of the greatest engineering achievements in all of history when it opened on August 15, 1914. Thanks to the new canal, ships

Movie Making in New Mexico

The movie industry that began in New Mexico in the late nineteenth century has expanded and prospered ever since. Starting with Mary Pickford and Tom Mix, other famous movie actors and actresses who have worked in New Mexico include:

Kevin Costner	Katharine Hepburn	Sean Penn
Billy Crystal	Dennis Hopper	Christopher Reeve
Bette Davis	Jennifer Lopez	Jimmy Stewart
Clint Eastwood	Jack Nicholson	John Travolta
Henry Fonda	Edward James Olmos	John Wayne

Some movie producers have said New Mexico's landscape and cultures are so important to their films that New Mexico itself is like another star actor in their movies.

As might be expected, most of the movies filmed in New Mexico have been Westerns, but other popular films have been made here as well. Some of the most famous Western—and other—movies made in New Mexico include:

could travel from the Atlantic Ocean to the Pacific without sailing around South America's dangerous Cape Horn, cutting eight thousand miles and thirty days off the average trip from New York City on the East Coast to San Francisco on the West Coast. To celebrate this remarkable accomplishment, the city of San Diego, California, planned an international exposition with large exhibits from several Latin American countries and southwestern states.

When New Mexico was invited to participate in the **Panama-California Exposition**, Governor McDonald jumped at the opportunity. The governor knew that this would be an ideal chance to promote New Mexico's resources and cultures. Having won the prize for the best exhibit at the Louisiana Purchase Exposition, held in St. Louis in 1904, New Mexicans were confident they could create an equally impressive exhibit in San Diego.

New Mexico's exhibit building in southern California was certainly unique. To celebrate the state's Spanish and Indian cultures, exhibit planners designed a structure to resemble the Spanish colonial mission church at Acoma Pueblo. Inside, the building was decorated with art by some of the best-known artists in the state. The exhibit's director, anthropologist **Edgar Lee Hewett**, stressed historical and cultural

Billy the Kid (1930)
The Salt of the Earth (1954)
Lonely Are the Brave (1962)
Easy Rider (1969)
Butch Cassidy and the Sundance Kid (1978)
The Ballad of Gregorio Cortez (1982)
The Milagro Beanfield War (1988)
Indiana Jones and the Last Crusade (1989)
Lonesome Dove (1989)
Young Guns I (1988) *and II* (1990)
City Slickers (1991)
The Avengers (2012)

New Mexico has been the site of so many Western movies that a whole western town has been built as a permanent movie set. Located south of Santa Fe and built in just five months in 1969, the Eaves Ranch is said to be so realistic that visitors have to be reminded the place is not a real western town preserved since the 1870s. Tours of the set are available to the public.

Movie making has become so important in New Mexico that it brought more than a billion dollars into the state's economy during 2006 alone. Sixty-four movies of all kinds were filmed in New Mexico in just three years, from 2003 to 2006.

New Mexico's State Flag and Song

New Mexico was such a new state that it had yet to create a state flag when the San Diego Panama-California Exposition opened in 1915. Lacking a flag to fly over the New Mexico exhibit at the exposition, Santa Fe attorney Ralph Emerson Twitchell designed one. It had five main features: a U.S. flag in the upper left-hand corner to stress the state's loyalty to the nation; the New Mexico state seal in the bottom right-hand corner; the number forty-seven (representing New Mexico's status as the forty-seventh state) in the top right-hand corner; the name "New Mexico" running from the bottom left-hand to the top right-hand corner; and all on a field of turquoise to remind people of New Mexico's famous blue skies. The state legislature officially adopted this design on March 19, 1915.

By 1920, many New Mexicans sought to create a new state flag to better represent the state's unique character and several cultures. A contest was held for the best new design. Dr. Harry P. Mera of Santa Fe won the competition with a flag that featured the ancient Zia sun symbol in red on a field of gold, with red and gold representing the colors of Spain, New Mexico's original ruling country. Mera's design, sewed by his wife Reba Mera, was adopted by the state legislature exactly ten years after New Mexico's first flag had been adopted in 1915.

New Mexico's flag is considered to be one of the most beautiful state flags in the United States, but it has created controversy. The state legislature never asked Zia Pueblo for permission to use their sacred sun symbol

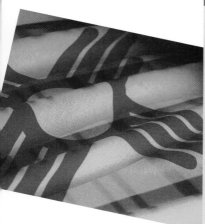

New Mexico's state flag

New Mexico's exhibit building in San Diego

accuracy in all murals, paintings, and architectural models on display. A specially produced movie with scenes from as far north as Ratón and as far south as Deming was shown more than 630 times in 1915 alone. Thousands viewed the production and, most important, learned more about New Mexico than they had ever known before.

New Mexicans were also well represented at another unique exhibit called the Painted Desert. Here, Native Americans from several tribes, including the Navajo, the Apache, and at least five pueblos, lived and on the state flag. In fact, many companies and organizations have used the sun symbol on their products without permission and with no thought of compensating Zia Pueblo in any way. Most recently, pueblo leaders have suggested that the state pay Zia as much as $45 million for having used their sun symbol on the state flag for more than eighty-five years.

In the same year that New Mexico adopted its first state flag, **Elizabeth Garrett** composed "O, Fair New Mexico." Blind from birth, the daughter of Sheriff Pat Garrett once said, "My father tried to bring peace and harmony to our country with his guns. I would like to do my part with my music." In 1917, the state legislature adopted "O Fair New Mexico" as the state's official song. The song's first verse and chorus are as follows:

Under a sky of azure,	O, Fair New Mexico
Where balmy breezes blow,	We love, we love you so,
Kissed by the golden sunshine	Our hearts with pride o'erflow,
Is Nuevo Méjico.	No matter where we go.
Land of the Montezuma,	O, Fair New Mexico,
With fiery hearts aglow,	We love, we love you so,
Land of deeds historic,	The grandest state to know
Is Nuevo Méjico.	New Mexico.

worked in a living exhibit designed to foster a better understanding and appreciation of Indian cultures. Indians performed their native dances, cooked their native foods, and made their native arts and crafts. While many visitors learned from the exhibit, others did not, describing what they saw as "queer customs" and refusing to respect Indian beliefs, such as the one that their spirits would be lost if Indians were photographed before performing certain ceremonies. Many Native Americans from the exhibit, however, saw parts of the country they had never seen before, including the Pacific Ocean. Others, like **María and Julián Martínez** of San Ildefonso Pueblo, shared their strikingly beautiful art with thousands of new admirers.

New Mexico's display at the Panama-California Exposition was such a success that it received five awards, including a prize given to the best state exhibit. New Mexico's exhibit building has long since been

María Martínez

María Martínez was born and raised in San Ildefonso Pueblo. As a young married woman she learned the fine art of pottery making, an art that had almost been lost in New Mexico's pueblos with the use of more modern enamelware.

Quite by accident, María and her husband Julián developed a new black-on-black pottery design in 1919, a unique design that soon made the couple world famous. Unlike many artists, María gladly shared her art and methods with others, including her neighbors at San Ildefonso, her children and grandchildren, and countless visitors at world's fairs in St. Louis (1904), San Diego (1915), and Chicago (1934). Although she became well known and might have lived in Santa Fe or anywhere else in the world, María remained true to her roots, her values, and her art by living her long life in her Pueblo Indian home in San Ildefonso.

María Martínez and members of her family with some of their pottery

remodeled in what is now San Diego's Balboa Park, but the structure became the model for Santa Fe's Fine Arts Museum when it was constructed and opened in November 1917. The museum remains a major landmark on the northwest corner of the Santa Fe plaza, where it continues to draw thousands of visitors to promote a most positive image of New Mexico.

Homesteading

As a result of good publicity and the availability of open land, many newcomers moved to New Mexico to farm in the first two decades of the twentieth century. Thousands came to **homestead** on the eastern plains, one of the last large areas of public land in the West. To acquire land, homesteaders simply had to pay a small filing fee and "prove up," meaning they had to live on the land and work it for five years.

A homesteading family

Living on the eastern plains and working it for five years was no easy task, though. Families found little wood to build homes, much less to make fences or use as fuel. Crops were difficult to grow with little rain, frequent dust storms, and regular invasions of insects, mainly grasshoppers. Few farmers could afford to dig deep wells, and many had to haul water from long distances, making fire a constant danger. Schools were few and literally far between. Neighbors lived miles apart, and social activities were rare, leading to feelings of extreme isolation. Towns with stores, doctors, and lawmen were usually days away.

Homesteading in a Boxcar

The Collins family moved from Oklahoma to Union County in northeastern New Mexico to homestead in 1915. With little wood or other building materials, the family resorted to living in a deserted boxcar. Sisters Lula and Ruth Collins later wrote of life in their unique rural home:

> Trying to fit a family of seven into a boxcar house took some doing, but Mother was ingenious. Soon three iron bedsteads were fitted into the corners—one, a double bed for Mother, Daddy, and Baby Louise; and two small ones where two children would sleep on each. . . . A big cook stove, a homemade table, some trunks, a water stand made from a box, a dressing table (also a box), and a small mirror on the wall above the dressing table: these comprised the necessary furnishings. . . .
>
> [But our] most precious possessions were our books. . . . We were delighted when Mama had time to read to us. . . . Our books added not only physical beauty to our stark [boxcar home], but they also added enrichment to our simple lives. . . .

(Lula Collins Daudet and Ruth Collins Roberts, *Pinto Beans and a Silver Spoon* [Ardmore, PA: Dorrance and Company, 1980], 5–9.)

Conditions were so difficult that homesteaders often believed the government was betting they *could not* survive for five years on public land. So many farmers failed to prove up that their deserted farm buildings on the open plains reminded observers of gravestones or memories of now-dead dreams. Many former homesteads reverted to open range or became parts of larger cattle ranches. The population of most eastern counties dropped drastically between the census of 1910 and the census of 1920. In Roosevelt County alone, the population fell from 12,064 citizens in 1910 to only 6,548 in 1920. Furthermore, what was true for white homesteaders was also true for Blacks.

☀ Blackdom

New Mexico's African-American population was small, but significant, in the first years of statehood. Numbering only 1,628, or less than 1 percent of the population in 1910, Blacks were never protected with ironclad clauses in the state constitution of 1910. Nor was Black culture ever mentioned in New Mexico's state exhibit in San Diego. Most Blacks in New Mexico lived and labored quietly, simply glad to be free from slavery and far from the South, where Blacks faced discrimination, segregation, and racial violence on a daily basis.

A Black homesteading family

In fact, some Black families fled to New Mexico to escape the prejudice they had experienced in other parts of the nation. While thousands journeyed to the North and many moved to other parts of the West in what was known as the Great Migration, several Black families came from the South to create an all-Black community on the eastern plains of New Mexico. Called **Blackdom**, the settlement had been founded in 1901 by **Francis Marion Boyer**, who had first walked from Georgia to New Mexico in 1896. Boyer recruited as many as twenty-five Black families to homestead on open land sixteen miles south of Roswell. With a peak population of three hundred residents, Blackdom eventually boasted a school, a store, a Baptist church, and, from 1912 to 1919, a U.S. post office.

Elephant Butte Irrigation Project

Farming and ranching in the arid lands of southern New Mexico and west Texas became far more possible and profitable with the building of the **Elephant Butte** dam and reservoir from 1911 to 1916. Building the 301-foot-high, 1,674-foot-long concrete dam required amazing engineering skill, performed by an army of able New Mexico workers.

Sadly, a small community (San José) and an old military fort (Fort McRae) were abandoned, submerged, and lost forever beneath the forty-mile long lake. Once the project was dedicated on October 19, 1916, however, it helped countless others with needed irrigation and flood control.

The Elephant Butte project created the country's largest man-made reservoir and the world's largest dam to that date in history.

(Robert Julyan, *The Place Names of New Mexico* [Albuquerque: University of New Mexico Press, 1998], 121, 135, 315; interpretive signs at Elephant Butte State Park.)

Elephant Butte Dam under construction

George McJunkin and the Discovery of Folsom Man

George McJunkin

George McJunkin, a former slave, migrated to northeastern New Mexico from his native state of Texas in 1868 while he was still a teen. Hired as a cowhand on a ranch near Folsom, New Mexico, McJunkin became so respected for his hard work and cowboy skills that he was eventually made ranch foreman.

A disastrous flood in August 1908 left normally three-foot-deep arroyos more than ten feet deep in and around Folsom. Checking these arroyos for possible survivors of the flood, McJunkin found larger bison bones than he had ever seen before. Collecting and examining the bones, the ranch foreman tried to convince others he had made an important discovery of an unusual prehistoric animal. No one, though, would listen to an uneducated former slave.

Five years after George McJunkin died in 1922, archeologists took a closer look at the cowhand's collection of bones and found something remarkable. There, between two of the ancient animal's ribs, they discovered the imprint of an arrowhead made by ancient man and used to kill this large prey. Archeologists concluded that based on the age of the bison bones, humans must have lived in New Mexico twenty thousand years ago, much earlier than scientists had previously thought. George McJunkin had helped to discover what became known as Folsom Man, in one of the most significant finds in archeological history.

The people of Blackdom enjoyed working on their own farms and living in peace as a separate community. In the words of a woman resident, the town was "filled with good neighbors and . . . beautiful New Mexico sunshine." What it was not filled with, however, was accessible, life-giving water. Facing terrible drought conditions, most residents moved on. Even Francis Boyer left Blackdom to found a new Black settlement at Vado in the better-irrigated southern Rio Grande Valley. By 1929, the noble racial experiment at Blackdom had been abandoned, a failure caused by nature far more than a lack of human will.

Jack Johnson Fights Jim Flynn in Las Vegas

Blacks in New Mexico experienced more direct forms of prejudice. **Jack Johnson** won the heavyweight championship of the world when he defeated Tommy Burns on December 6, 1908, becoming the first Black boxing champion in history. Upset that a Black man had defeated a white champion, racist whites searched for a "great white hope" to win the crown from Johnson.

Jim Flynn, a Colorado fireman, was signed to fight Johnson in Las Vegas, New Mexico, on July 4, 1912. While most states had banned boxing matches by 1912, New Mexico had not yet created a state law banning the sport just six months after achieving statehood. Governor McDonald and many other New Mexicans were embarrassed by this neglect; in the words of a minister in Belén, hosting a boxing match in New Mexico was against "the best interests of this state materially, morally, and spiritually." Dozens of petitions opposing the bout arrived in the governor's office, including a petition from the citizens of Laguna Pueblo pointing out the irony that "white men tell us not to fight and then fight themselves and set a bad example for our people."

Despite these protests, the fight went on as scheduled. The match drew unfavorable attention not only because Johnson was Black, but also because his wife was white at a time when miscegenation, or interracial marriages, was illegal in most parts of the United States.

Johnson in training camp at 2008 North Gonzales St., Las Vegas, New Mexico

The Johnson-Flynn fight took place in Las Vegas before a crowd of five thousand spectators, including several hundred "disgraceful 'ladies.'" Flynn was no challenge for the champ, however, and disappointed those who thought he might be their long-awaited great white hope. Although the fight was scheduled to go many more rounds, Governor McDonald had previously ordered a state lawman to mercifully stop the match in the ninth round before it became a bloodbath. Johnson left New Mexico, never to return, but not before feeling the sting of racism when a Santa Fe newspaper described him as "grinning like an ape" early in the fight. Mercifully for New Mexico, the contest received little press attention or criticism outside the state.

▲▲▲▲▲▲▲▲▲▲▲▲▲▲▲▲▲▲▲▲▲▲▲▲▲

Racism in New Mexico Schools

Other forms of racism against Blacks occurred in scattered events during the first years of the twentieth century. At Albuquerque High School three Black students were about to graduate in 1907 when prejudiced city residents objected to school officials. Rather than cause a confrontation, school authorities had the three girls transferred to a high school attached to the University of New Mexico, where they graduated without further opposition.

Faced with such prejudice, Black leaders organized the Albuquerque Independent Society in 1912, which became a branch of the new National Association for the Advancement of Colored People (NAACP) in 1914. With the new organization's influence, Birdie Hardin became the first Black student to graduate from Albuquerque High, in 1914. The local NAACP branch raised money to help pay Birdie Hardin's tuition to attend UNM, but the university denied her admission. With NAACP persistence, UNM finally admitted its first Black college student in 1921. It took another thirteen years before Clara Belle Williams was admitted as the first Black student at New Mexico A&M, now New Mexico State University. Three years later Williams became the college's first Black graduate; a building on the NMSU campus is named in her honor.

 ## Conclusions

New Mexicans had struggled to finally achieve statehood by 1912. Their representatives at the constitutional convention of 1910 wrote a "safe and sane" constitution and proceeded to select our first state leaders, from our first state governor, William C. McDonald, to our first U.S. senators, Albert B. Fall and Thomas B. Catron.

New Mexicans knew, however, that much more work needed to be done after 1912 to promote their new state and attract new settlers, investors, and visitors. They succeeded in promoting their state, especially at the Panama-California Exposition, and in attracting many new settlers, especially homesteaders on the eastern plains.

New Mexico suffered several setbacks as well, especially with natural disasters, like draughts, and human failings, including a prizefight clouded by racism. Having celebrated statehood with great joy and anticipation, New Mexico's first steps as a new state proved small, slow, and often controversial.

1. How well were the people of New Mexico represented at the state constitutional convention of 1910?

2. Who benefited most directly from the new state constitution of 1910? Who did not benefit as directly?

3. Why was the state constitution of 1910 considered a "safe and sane" document?

4. Who had to approve New Mexico's state constitution before it could be used?

5. How did New Mexicans react to the achievement of statehood?

6. Was New Mexico promoted accurately and well in early movies by Mary Pickford, D. W. Griffith, Romaine Fielding, and Tom Mix?

7. What did homesteaders need to do to prove up? Were most homesteaders successful? Why or why not?

8. Why did Francis Marion Boyer found Blackdom? Was the town a success? Why or why not?

9. How did Jack Johnson feel the sting of racism in New Mexico? How did George McJunkin feel the sting of racism? How did Black students feel the sting of racism? How did Native Americans feel the sting of racism at the Panama-California Exposition?

10. What aspects of New Mexico would you have been proud of if you had lived in these first years of statehood? Why?

11. What aspects would you have been less proud of if you had lived in these first years of statehood? Why?

12. What lessons can we learn from these first years of New Mexico's statehood?

New Mexico in World War I

1916–18

TIMELINE

1910
The Mexican Revolution begins

1914
World War I begins in Europe

1916
Pancho Villa raids Columbus

Gen. John J. Pershing leads the American Punitive Expedition into Mexico

1917
Zimmermann Telegram intercepted

American Punitive Expedition withdraws from Mexico

United States enters World War I

First U.S. Army draft since the Civil War

1917–18
Camps Cody and Funston train thousands of American troops

1918
Millions of American troops of the American Expeditionary Force arrive in Europe to fight the last major campaigns of World War I

Private Marcelino Serna becomes the first Hispanic to earn a Distinguished Service Cross, having single-handedly captured twenty-four German soldiers

Spanish flu epidemic claims more than a thousand lives in New Mexico and 21 million victims in the world

☀ Introduction

The world was rife with violence during New Mexico's early years of statehood. To the south, Mexico suffered through years of chaos and bloodshed in a revolution that spanned a decade, 1910 to 1920. In Europe, the First World War that began in 1914 engulfed countries and peoples around the globe.

At first the United States was able to avoid direct involvement in these terrible conflicts. Pres. Woodrow Wilson was actually reelected in 1916 largely because he had steered the country on a neutral course. A banner in Socorro and many other communities in the United States urged voters to support Wilson because "He Kept Us Out of War."

However, world events swept the United States into conflicts in both Mexico and Europe. The purpose of this chapter is to describe New Mexico's role in:

- a major event of the Mexican Revolution;
- the First World War;
- and a terrible pandemic that struck the state and the rest of the world in 1918.

☀ The Mexican Revolution and Pancho Villa's Raid on Columbus

The Mexican Revolution had begun in 1910 with the overthrow of Mexico's ruler, **Porfirio Díaz**. Dictatorial, corrupt, and supported by powerful foreign companies, Díaz had caused much misery and injustice during his

Exiles from the Mexican Revolution

Caught in the midst of revolutionary bloodshed and chaos, thousands of Mexican men, women, and children fled from their homes, desperately hoping to find safety elsewhere in their country or in the United States. The great Mexican author Mariano Azuela captured the horror of this war and exodus by describing the plight of one small group of characters in his famous novel, *The Flies*:

> [It] was said that the enemy was committing every kind of atrocity, with no respect for women, children, or old people! They carried a flag with the skull and crossbones on it! They were killing people as one would step on ants! . . .
>
> Ahead it was worse. Carts and carriages piled high with trunks, mattresses, furniture, and humanity were moving in all directions. Public buildings were being emptied. Government clerks were . . . dazed, unable to sense the magnitude of the catastrophe. . . .
>
> At the railroad station, which they neared at long last, the tide of humanity washed up to their feet. On every hand they saw ragged and sick-looking soldiers, women all skin and bones, angry and despairing faces. Soon they could push their way through the boiling mass of people with difficulty.

(Mariano Azuela, *Two Novels of Mexico: The Flies, The Bosses* [Berkeley: University of California Press, 1972], 44, 60.)

Pancho Villa

thirty-four years as president, from 1876 to 1910. Revolutionary generals like Emiliano Zapata in the south and **Pancho Villa** in the north fought each other with countless casualties and no clear outcome for years.

The United States managed to avoid direct involvement in the Mexican Revolution until April 1914. American naval forces landed in Veracruz, Mexico, in an attempt to weaken Victoriano Huerta, a particularly brutal revolutionary general who had seized power in 1913. The United States withdrew from Mexico in November 1914 when Huerta was overthrown.

A far more direct threat to the United States occurred fewer than two years later. In the early morning hours of March 9, 1916, Pancho Villa's revolutionary army crossed the international border and attacked the small border town of Columbus, New Mexico.

Columbus in ruins after the raid

Although no one saw Pancho Villa that day, nearly 500 of his men raided Columbus, burning businesses and homes and killing 11 civilians. U.S. soldiers based in a camp south of town fought the Villistas, finally driving them across the Mexican border with the loss of 8 American soldiers and an estimated 190 Mexican lives. Much of Columbus lay in ruins, especially its central business district.

Upset by the news of this tragedy, Americans across the United States asked what had caused this sudden attack, the first by a foreign force on American soil since the War of 1812.

There are several possible explanations for Villa's raid on Columbus. One is that Villa was angry at the United States for aiding one of his revolutionary enemies in a key battle that Villa had lost in 1915. In a much stranger explanation, some say that Germany paid Villa to raid Columbus in order to draw the United States into the Mexican Revolution and prevent America from entering the world war against Germany and its allies in Europe. A third explanation, which most residents of Columbus believed, involved revenge against a local merchant who had reportedly cheated Villa in a business deal for war goods and supplies.

We will probably never know the real reason for Villa's raid on Columbus, but in 1916, the American public sought justice against their foreign attacker. Organized under **Gen. John J. "Black Jack" Pershing**, an **American Punitive**

Heroine Susie Parks

Susie Parks was only twenty years old when Pancho Villa raided her hometown of Columbus. As the town's only telephone operator, Parks stayed at her telephone station, dutifully calling for help while the battle raged outside. With bullets flying around her, Parks sheltered her infant daughter in her arms and bravely did what she could to save her neighbors and her town. Parks was one of the true heroes of that most tragic day in Columbus.

The American
Punitive Expedition
in Mexico, 1916–17

Expedition entered Mexico to chase, capture, and with luck punish Villa for his misdeeds. Meanwhile, the New Mexico National Guard joined thousands of other national guardsmen and U.S. troops in securing the U.S.-Mexican border against additional raids.

Corrido: "La Persecución de Villa"

While most Americans were outraged by Pancho Villa's raid on Columbus, many Mexicans were outraged by the American Punitive Expedition's search for Villa in their country. Reflecting these feelings, the following translation of a Mexican corrido, or ballad, portrays Villa as a hero for his ability to elude the invaders, despite their numbers and modern machines:

[In 1916 Mexican President Venustiano]
    Carranza let
[Thousands of] American soldiers
And [many] airplanes
Come search for Villa.

Carranza told them, If you are brave and
Want to fight, I'll gladly
Grant you permission to die
Searching for Villa
Throughout the whole country.

The expedition began,
The airplanes flew all over,
They looked everywhere
To kill Pancho Villa.

Those soldiers from [America]
Couldn't find Pancho Villa,
After [many] boring hours
They just wanted to go home. . . .

When they thought Villa dead
They all shouted with glee,
Now we can all go back [home]
With honor and glory.

But they found that Villa lived,
That they couldn't catch him,
Unless they wanted to visit him
Deep inside the rugged mountains. . . .

(Quoted in David Dorado Romo, *Ringside Seat to a Revolution* [El Paso: Cinco Puntos Press, 2005], 133.)

With its base in Columbus, the American Punitive Expedition traveled four hundred miles into northern Mexico, searched in all directions, and fought a small battle without ever finding Villa in a region he had known and traveled through since childhood. One reporter said the U.S. Army chasing Pancho Villa in northern Mexico was as impossible as an El Paso city policeman chasing a jackrabbit in Kansas.

Pershing and the American Punitive Expedition finally withdrew from Mexico in February 1917. Although the expedition had failed in its primary goal, it had some important achievements. For the first time in its history, the U.S. Army had experimented with the use of airplanes and land motor vehicles in combat conditions. The army experienced problems with both of these new forms of transportation but gained valuable knowledge that would be applied on other fronts in the near future. General Pershing and thousands of his soldiers, including New Mexico National Guardsmen, also benefited from valuable field experience in preparation for later combat in the world war that had been raging in Europe for nearly three years.

In a strange twist of fate, Columbus itself benefited from the Punitive Expedition. Serving as the expedition's headquarters, the small town recovered from Villa's raid and enjoyed an economic boom like none other in its history. The raid was no less tragic: precious lives had been lost, and battle scars on the terrain are still visible in parts of Columbus today.

New Mexico on the Eve of World War I

The United States entered the First World War two months after the American Punitive Expedition's return from Mexico. The nation was forced to abandon its neutrality and enter the international conflict because Germany refused to respect American rights as a neutral nation. In President Wilson's famous words, the United States also fought to "make the world safe for democracy."

There were other reasons the United States entered the war, one of which directly involved New Mexico. In January 1917, a coded telegram sent by the German foreign minister, Arthur Zimmermann, was intercepted before it reached its destination in Mexico. Known as the **Zimmermann Telegram**, this German message proposed that if the United States entered the war in Europe, Mexico should become Germany's ally. Germany hoped that with Mexico as its ally the United States would have to fight on two fronts, making it a far less dangerous enemy in Europe.

How would Mexico benefit from such an alliance with Germany? The Zimmermann Telegram stated that if Mexico were Germany's ally and they won the war, Mexico would be rewarded by receiving all the land it had lost to the United States in the U.S.-Mexican War of 1846–48. This large territory included New Mexico and all the American Southwest.

The Zimmermann Telegram outraged Americans in the Southwest and throughout the nation when its contents were revealed. The telegram never reached Mexico, and the Mexican government never responded to it, but Americans bristled at the thought that Germany would tamper with American land, people, and resources. The telegram did not cause American entry into World War I, but it helped deepen resentment against Germany in the months before April 1917.

New Mexicans were also eager to fight in World War I because their loyalty to the United States was questioned again, as it had been during the Civil War and the Spanish-American War. One author even suggested that New Mexicans might readily assist an invading enemy army in the Southwest. Outraged, Senator Albert B. Fall called these charges a "fantastic mixture of ignorant, malicious, and false statements." Patriotic New Mexicans agreed, expressing their desire to once again prove their state's loyalty with strong actions as well as words.

☼ New Mexicans on the Home Front in World War I

New Mexico's Hispanic State Governors

New Mexicans have elected six Hispanic governors since statehood in 1912. They are

- Ezequiel C de Baca, January 1 to February 18, 1918
- Octaviano A. Larrazolo, 1919–21
- Raymond S. "Jerry" Apodaca, 1975–79
- Toney Anaya, 1983–87
- William B. "Bill" Richardson, 2003–10
- Susana Martinez, 2011– .

New Mexico's lieutenant governor, **Washington E. Lindsey** of Portales, assumed office on the day after Governor C de Baca's death. Lindsey had hardly settled into his new job when the United States entered World War I.

Governor Lindsey acted with decisive leadership. Lindsey called a special week-long session of the state legislature, which assigned $750,000 in state funds for public defense. A statewide Council of Defense, with leaders from towns from Los Lunas to Roswell, was created to coordinate all war efforts. Smaller councils were created in each of the state's thirty-six counties.

Coordinating New Mexico's war efforts was not easy. With 423,649 residents scattered over 78 million acres (making New Mexico the nation's fourth largest state in area), it was difficult to communicate war needs quickly and efficiently. New Mexicans spoke many different languages and, with the exception of newspapers and movie theaters in larger towns, there were no regular means of mass communication.

New Mexico's leaders dealt with their state's communication problems in several ways. Twice a month a publication called *New Mexico War News* was printed in both Spanish and English. More than eleven hundred posters illustrated how New Mexicans could contribute their time, energy, and money to the war. Students staged patriotic school plays, while theaters showed movies with titles like *The Beast of Berlin*, referring to Germany's leader, Kaiser Wilhelm II. Singers formed Liberty choruses, and 250 speakers delivered forty-five hundred speeches in small and large communities alike. Promising to limit their remarks to just four minutes at public gatherings, these speakers were appropriately known as the **Four-Minute Men**. New Mexicans responded to these calls for help far beyond expectations. Asked to purchase more than $11 million in **Liberty Bonds** to help the national government pay for the war, New Mexicans bought almost $18 million worth of bonds. Corporations like the Santa Fe Railroad, workers like underground coal miners, and students like those at the Albuquerque and Santa Fe Indian schools purchased bonds and gave what they could to help other worthy causes, like the Red Cross. Twenty-one students at Albuquerque High School gave persuasive speeches to urge fellow students to buy Liberty Bonds; senior Helen Drury gave the best speech and won a fifty-dollar Liberty Bond.

Asked to use less food so there would be more for our troops and factory workers, a third of all New Mexico families signed pledge cards to serve "loyalty menus," observing at least one meatless and one wheatless day per week. About three thousand families also grew small backyard gardens, known as **victory gardens**, with good practical advice from the New Mexico College of Agriculture and Mechanics, now New Mexico State University.

Farmers and ranchers did their share as well. New Mexican farmers, who had produced 2.1 million bushels of wheat in 1916, grew 3.3 million bushels in 1918. Ranchers increased their herds from 1.5 million head of cattle in 1915 to 1.9 in 1918. The number of sheep had grown to more than 3 million by early 1918. As a speaker at a wartime meeting of the New Mexico Cattle and Horse Growers Association told his audience, it was the job of "every patriotic citizen . . . to produce as much as he can."

Main Countries at War in World War I

The Allied Powers:
United States, England, France, Russia, Italy, and Japan

The Central Powers:
Germany, Austria-Hungary, Bulgaria, and Turkey

A Recipe for Wheatless Days

Newspapers encouraged New Mexicans to conserve wheat for the war effort by preparing wheatless recipes, such as the following from the *Albuquerque Journal* (April 21, 1918):

Corn Meal Bread
2 cups milk
1½ cups cornmeal
1 tablespoon flour
4 teaspoons baking powder
1 teaspoon salt
1 tablespoon melted fat
1 egg

Mix and sift dry ingredients. Combine milk, egg, and fat and add to the dry ingredients. Mix well and pour into oiled muffin tins or shallow pans. Bake in a hot oven. Serve hot.

Fuel production also rose to meet climbing wartime demands. Coal companies in Colfax, McKinley, and Santa Fe counties mined record amounts of coal in 1918. With wartime demand far outreaching supply, New Mexico producers of essential raw materials earned greater profits than ever before. With such high demand for its valuable products, the state soon experienced a wartime labor shortage. The University of New Mexico started classes in October so students could work longer through the summer, especially in agricultural jobs. Governor Lindsey even pardoned some inmates at the state penitentiary so they could fill in for the labor shortage. Further, many families who had fled the chaos of the Mexican Revolution found new jobs and peace in border states like California, Arizona, and New Mexico. American employers welcomed Mexican immigrants, sometimes transporting them by the trainload to work sites like the coal fields of Colfax County.

A recruiting poster for the Women's Land Army

New Mexico women helped fight the war by playing both traditional and nontraditional roles. In addition to conserving food and fuel in their homes, many women rolled bandages, knit clothing, created "comfort kits" for soldiers, and helped sell Liberty Bonds. In a less traditional role, women formed the Women's Land Army to help farmers in particular need of labor. To save the hay crop in Grant County, women in the Land Army mowed, raked, and stacked hay. To save the fruit crop, fifty women volunteers worked tirelessly in the orchards of Otero County.

New Mexicans clearly proved their loyalty on the home front, but some New Mexicans went too far. In their zeal to win the war, New Mexicans sometimes pressured people to buy Liberty Bonds, suggesting that those who did not buy bonds must not be true Americans. Four miners who refused to buy bonds were tarred and feathered in northern New Mexico. A woman in Roswell wrote to Governor Lindsey to turn in her German-American neighbor who, she suspected, must be a spy because he did not fly an American flag outside his house each day. At least twice, crowds forced suspected German sympathizers to demonstrate their loyalty to the United States by kissing the American flag. Teaching the German language was banned at the University of New Mexico, although only two students were enrolled in the university's sole German class. The *Santa Fe New Mexican* newspaper supported shooting suspected traitors without trial. In Congress, New Mexico's Representative William Walton declared that those who criticized the government "ought to be shot within twenty-four hours after their crime is discovered!"

▲▲▲▲▲▲▲▲▲▲▲▲▲▲▲▲▲▲▲▲▲▲▲▲▲▲▲▲▲▲▲▲▲

Liberty Mania

Americans expressed their overzealous patriotism in an intolerance of anything identified with the German enemy:

- German shepherds became known as the more patriotic liberty dogs;
- German measles became known as the more patriotic liberty measles;
- sauerkraut became known as the more patriotic liberty cabbage;
- playing German music was banned or discouraged;
- and drinking German beer—and all kinds of alcohol—was banned with the passage of the Eighteenth Amendment to the U.S. Constitution.

Some New Mexicans had let their emotional support for the war become extreme. The loss of freedom, especially the freedom of those identified with the enemy, is always a tragic cost of war. This was especially ironic in World War I, which was fought to "make the world safe for democracy" and its freedoms. Facing threats to their freedom in New Mexico and many other states, German-Americans reacted by showing their loyalty whenever and wherever possible. Many purchased more than their share of Liberty Bonds, grew victory gardens, volunteered for the military, and applied for American citizenship, if they had not already done so before the war. It was good that German-Americans participated in the war effort, but tragic that they felt forced to do so for their own protection.

☀ New Mexicans in the American Armed Forces

More than fifteen thousand New Mexicans helped win the war by serving in the American armed forces during World War I. Of these men, more than eight thousand were inducted in the nation's first **draft** since the Civil War. Another seven thousand volunteered for service in the army, navy, or marines. Volunteers in New Mexico included cowhands, farmers, miners, railroad workers, medical doctors, draftsmen, carpenters, salesmen, bookkeepers, and at least one newspaper editor, a playwright, a chauffeur, and a movie-picture camera operator. More than 70 percent of all male students at UNM and the entire Lobo football team enlisted by the fall of 1917. So many male students volunteered at New Mexico A&M that

Soldiers' Letters Home from Europe

September 8, 1918

France

Dear Brother [Milford Attabery],

Well finally we are near the business part of France for us. Last night we finished three days and nights of travel. . . . Now we are close to a rather quiet front and fully expect to hike to our [battle] stations tomorrow. . . .

We buy Velvet tobacco for 6 cents . . . and candy is cheap when we can get it. Good wines are not very plentiful and U.S. soldiers are really not supposed to get any. We get small mail editions of New York and Chicago [newspapers] published in Paris that give us part of the news.

This is a great country and I can see why they put up such an awful fight [for it]. Everyone is glad to see us and will do anything they can for us. . . . Hope I will soon be able to pull the trigger for [the] defense of France and America.

I have not seen anyone from home as yet.

Harold [Attabery]

(As printed in the Silver City Enterprise, October 11, 1918.)

George E. McCown mentioned a "field card" in his letter home in 1918. These postcards had been in use since early in the war in an effort to encourage soldiers to write home but also limit the information they gave that might be of aid to the enemy.

A typical field card had several printed remarks, allowing soldiers to simply check off the comments that pertained to him, such as:

____ I am quite well.
____ I have been admitted into the hospital.
____ Wounded, but am getting on well.
____ I received your recent letter.
____ I have received no letter from you for a long time.

(Santa Fe New Mexican, August 9, 1917.)

the graduating class of 1918 had only seven members, and most of them were female. So many cadets volunteered at the New Mexico Military Institute in Roswell that the school's commander urged students to finish their military education so they could be better soldiers once they went off to war. Several Rough Riders from the Spanish-American War enthusiastically offered to fight for their country again but were turned down because they were considered too old. Motivated by both loyalty and self-interest, a group of convicts won their early release from the state penitentiary in exchange for service to their nation. All races and ethnicities, including Hispanics, Native Americans, Anglos, and Blacks, were represented in the ranks of those who volunteered. New Mexico's volunteer rate was among the highest in the United States.

France

Dear Mother and Father,   [October 1918]

This sure is a beautiful country. The towns resemble the towns in [New Mexico] to some extent except that the houses instead of being made of adobe are all of solid rock. Most of the towns I have seen are torn up to a large extent. When one of these big shells hit a house there is not much left of it except a pile of rock.

I sent you a field card the other day. They are easy to use as they are printed when you get them and all you have to do is to scratch out what you don't want [to say]. This sure is a hard place to write a letter as when you do see anything you cannot tell about it or where it is.

We have traveled over quite a bit of France since we landed [on May 30, 1918] and I have seen all I want to see while I am in the army. . . . [J]ust now I would rather see the good old U.S.A. . . .

The Americans are doing good fighting and taking prisoners every day. You ought to hear the fireworks when a big bombardment is on. It sounds alright when you are a long way off in a good dugout but when you are close up and out in the open it [doesn't] sound so good. . . .

Going across the country you find shell holes everywhere. They are from two to four feet across and from 18 inches to three feet deep. There are barbed wire entanglements everywhere the Germans have been. . . .

Fritz [an American nickname for German pilots] was flying around a good deal last night. We were in our pup tents and it was rather uncomfortable to hear him up over us not knowing when he would drop a bomb. We have got the best of him tonight for we have a dugout even if it is full of fleas and cooties. This sure is a muddy place when it rains and it don't have to rain very much.

Write me a long letter soon, and tell all the boys [in Hurley] hello for me. . . .

George [E. McCown]

(As printed in the *Silver City Enterprise*, November 1, 1918.)

New Mexico had few "slackers," or men who refused to serve, because most young men were eager to serve in this national emergency. Some men were exempted from service because they had physical disabilities or worked in essential work industries, like mining or the railroad. Even these men often joined the military rather than face embarrassing questions about why they were not serving in uniform. Often accused of being cowards, some discovered that their front doors had been painted yellow. As with those who were mistakenly identified with the enemy, these young men suffered unfair pressure and loss of freedom during a war that was fought to protect freedoms in the United States and around the world.

Once drafted or enlisted, New Mexicans joined millions of their peers in training camps across the United States. New Mexico had two main

Soldiers training at
Camp Cody

training camps. The U.S. Army built **Camp Cody** on twenty thousand acres west of Deming because its location—near the Southern Pacific and Santa Fe Railroads—made for easy troop transport and cargo shipments and because the weather there was so mild that soldiers could train outdoors most of the year. Unfortunately, few of the more than thirty thousand soldiers from Nebraska, Iowa, Minnesota, and the Dakotas who trained at Camp Cody appreciated southern New Mexico's strong winds, desert sand, and high daytime temperatures. After several months at Camp Cody, members of the 34th Infantry Division actually christened themselves the Sandstorm Division.

While many New Mexican soldiers trained in camps out-of-state, about one out of ten trained at **Camp Funston**, built on the outskirts of the University of New Mexico campus. The campus was transformed as fifteen hundred soldiers from Battery A of New Mexico's National Guard marched, dug trenches, and competed for the bragging rights of having the highest-rated company each week. In the words of UNM historian Dorothy Hughes, the campus was soon "khaki-clad," and, with all its military activity, Camp Funston "made the war seem real in New Mexico."

New Mexico sent its young men off to war with great fanfare. In September 1917, Governor Lindsey and three thousand men, women, and children saw twenty draftees off at the Santa Fe train depot. A month later an equally large crowd bid farewell to members of Battery A, presenting them with gifts of nine thousand apples and oranges to eat as snacks on their long train trip ahead. In Silver City, the local newspaper reported that forty-eight "strapping specimens of young manhood all

Atanacio Springer García in France

Two-thirds of the 5 million American soldiers and sailors who served in World War I were drafted. Atanacio Springer García of Los Duranes of Albuquerque registered for the draft on June 5, 1917, and was drafted a few months later. Thanks to the research of **genealogist** Henrietta M. Christmas, we can learn who Atanacio was and what became of him once he entered the military to serve his country.

Using information recorded on his draft registration card, Christmas discovered that Atanacio was born in Los Barelas in 1894. Doing additional genealogical research, Christmas found that Atanacio was a direct descendent of several founding families who had come to New Mexico with Juan de Oñate in 1598. A farm laborer, Atanacio was tall, of medium build, with brown hair and dark eyes.

Once in the army, Atanacio was assigned to the 356th Infantry Regiment and was trained at Camp Funston, Kansas, before shipping out from New York in mid-1918. In Europe he fought on the western front in the offensive of Meuse-Argonne. A fellow member of the 356th recalls their stopping

at a place the boys called "mud valley"... within easy range of [German] artillery and great precautions were taken not to show fires at night.... Every man slept in a hole regardless of mud and water. It was here we learned to sleep [as] next door neighbors to big guns and not lose any sleep.... [I]n a few days we went "over the top."

Four days after these words were written, Atanacio Springer García was killed in battle. Along with thousands of other American troops, he was buried in France. Three weeks later the First World War ended, and those who were fortunate enough to have survived went home.

(Henrietta M. Christmas, "Albuquerqueans Mourn Native Sons, Heroes of World War I," *Herencia: The Quarterly Journal of the Hispanic Genealogical Research Center of New Mexico* 14 [April 2006]: 30–34.]

eager to 'do their bit'" left for training in California with much encouragement in May 1918; another seventy-six left two weeks later. Similar scenes were repeated in large and small towns alike.

Like millions of American soldiers, sailors, and marines, those from New Mexico arrived in the war zones of Europe by the spring of 1918. They arrived just in time to make the critical difference in several major military campaigns, including at Champagne-Marne, Alsne-Marne, and Meuse-Argonne. Whether serving in support roles or in muddy trenches on the front lines, New Mexico's members of the **American Expeditionary Force (AEF)**, led by Gen. John J. Pershing, helped defeat

▲▲▲▲▲▲▲▲▲▲▲▲▲▲▲▲▲▲▲▲▲▲▲▲▲▲▲▲▲▲▲▲

The USS *New Mexico*

One of the most modern war ships of World War I was named for New Mexico. A 33,400-ton battleship, the USS *New Mexico*, was launched at the New York navy yard on April 23, 1917, christened by former Gov. Ezequiel C de Baca's daughter, Margaret. Although the ship proudly bore our state's name, few, if any, of its 1,323-man crew were New Mexicans. To remind the crew of New Mexico and its culture, the state contributed a collection of books by New Mexico authors and a silver setting engraved with images of New Mexico, from the state seal to a Native American home. The ship's commander accepted these gifts, a military band played patriotic tunes, and all present gave three cheers for New Mexico, "with enthusiasm," according to an eyewitness at the scene.

Back in New Mexico, local residents proudly read of the *New Mexico*'s launching. The *Santa Fe New Mexican* even offered its readers thirty-six-inch felt pennants with the image of "the newest and most modern warship in the world."

The USS *New Mexico* saw no action in World War I but was very active in World War II, playing important roles in the invasions of the Gilbert Islands, the Marshall Islands, the Philippines, Guam, and Okinawa.

Dismantled after World War II, the battleship's bell remains on display in a place of honor outside Zimmerman Library on the University of New Mexico campus. A shell casing from the *New Mexico* is on display in the Raton Historical Museum.

A new $2.5 billion submarine, called the USS *New Mexico*, was christened in December 2008. Its first commander was Robert Dain, a proud native New Mexican and a St. Pius X High School graduate. The ship is the nation's newest and most advanced nuclear-powered submarine. Emilee Sena of St. Pius High School designed the ship's crest in a contest among 180 high school students.

the German military and cause the enemy to finally surrender on November 11, 1918.

New Mexicans could boast of a proud record in the war. Only four New Mexican soldiers deserted, while 501 died in combat or from disease. Many New Mexicans earned military medals for their acts of bravery and honorable service to their country. Army **Private Marcelino Serna** of Albuquerque became the first Hispanic in the nation's history to earn a Distinguished Service Cross, having single-handedly captured twenty-four German soldiers on September 12, 1918.

New Mexicans welcomed news of the end of the war with joyous celebrations. The *Santa Fe New Mexican* reported that on November 11,

USS *New Mexico*

known as Armistice Day, citizens in the capital city "were whistled out of bed at 6 o'clock this morning to celebrate the end of the world war. By 6:30 scores were parading in the streets and by 7:00 there were hundreds carrying flags, cheering and shouting in a frenzy of delight."

Similar excitement reigned in other New Mexico towns. Far to the south, the *Deming Graphic* described Armistice Day as a "perfect day" in which "the town went mad. Sane and ordinarily sedate men and women rushed about the streets, shouting, laughing, crying, beating each other on the back, waving flags. . . . Every motor horn in town needed throat medicine [by noon]." In Las Cruces a large parade was held on Main Street with the Aggie marching band and a character dressed as the kaiser, whom the crowd condemned for "every thinkable crime" against humanity.

☀ The Spanish Flu Epidemic

Just as news of the war's end arrived in New Mexico, a far smaller, though more deadly, enemy appeared to threaten the state, the nation, and the entire world. The most deadly flu epidemic of all time, misnamed the **Spanish flu**, struck New Mexico and nearly every part of the globe in the fall of 1918. The flu was dangerous and mysterious because it was

▲▲▲▲▲▲▲▲▲▲▲▲▲▲▲▲▲▲▲▲▲▲▲▲▲▲

Spanish Flu Poem

As reflected in the following poem from Ratón, people did every-thing possible to avoid catching the dreaded Spanish flu:

The flu has got my nanny;
I'm skeered as skeered can be;
If I meet a guy a-sneezin'
I just quiver like a tree.

I've had three shots of serum,
And I'm searin' of the mask,
But if I hear the people coughin'
I fairly hustle for the flask. . . .

I've lined out several boxes
For victims of the flu,
And you bet your bottom dollar
It makes a fellow blue. . . .

So if there is a remedy
That overlooked have I,
Please give it to me quickly,
For I do not want to die.

(Anonymous poet, *Raton Range*, January 16, 1919.)

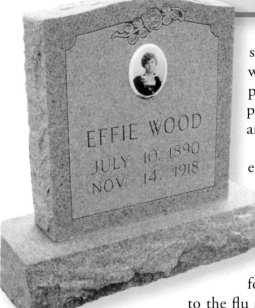

The headstone of a victim of the Spanish flu

so fast—many victims caught the flu in the morning and were dead by nightfall—and because it was most fatal for people between the ages of twenty and forty-five, when previous flu epidemics had usually affected the very young and very old the most.

New Mexicans tried to prevent catching the flu in several ways. Taos and other communities required residents to protect themselves by wearing surgical masks over their mouths and noses, using the same gauze material Red Cross volunteers had just recently used to roll bandages for the wounded overseas. In other towns, strangers were not allowed to disembark from trains for fear they might be carrying the flu germ. Referring to the flu as a "crowd disease," state officials closed down schools, churches, courthouses, movie theaters, lodges, and dance halls for weeks at a time.

Sadly, few preventive measures worked. Those who caught the disease tried various remedies, although most could not be taken seriously. The *Deming Graphic*, for example, recommended eating lemons as an effective cure, with consuming onions as an alternative treatment. Manufacturers of patent medicines with strange names like Wizard Oil and Dr. Pierce's Pleasant Pellets used newspaper ads to make exaggerated claims about their ability to cure the flu. A more serious serum was developed at the Mayo Clinic in Minnesota, but there was hardly enough, and it arrived too late to help many New Mexicans fight the flu.

Annie Dodge Wauneka and the Spanish Flu

Annie Dodge Wauneka was only eight years old in the fall of 1918. A Navajo student at the Fort Defiance Indian School, Annie was one of 250 students who caught the Spanish flu within the first ten days of the epidemic at her school. Fortunately, Annie survived, but many other children did not. In Annie's words, "pretty soon they [were] just dying like flies." Annie helped the best she could, assisting the school's only nurse and spoon-feeding soup to students too weak to feed themselves.

No one could stop the disease, though. Annie recalled that five to ten children died in her school's dorms each night. Running out of coffins for all the dead, "they used to just pile them up like a bunch of wood and haul them away" to be buried in mass graves. As many as twenty-five hundred people died of the flu or its complications on the Navajo Reservation.

Although she could do little to save her fellow students at Fort Defiance, Annie remembered this service to others as a major turning point in her life. After several similar experiences, she decided to dedicate her life to helping Native Americans in the health field. Never satisfied she had done enough for others, Annie became famous for her sincere vow, "I'll go and do more," just as she had done in the Spanish flu epidemic.

(Carolyn Niethammer, *I'll Go and Do More: Annie Dodge Wauneka, Navajo Leader and Activist* [Lincoln: University of Nebraska Press, 2001], 27–30.)

By the end of November 1918, more than a thousand New Mexicans had died of the flu or its complications, meaning that more than twice as many New Mexicans died in the epidemic as had been killed in the world war. One out of every five families had at least one family member die of the flu, and sometimes whole families perished. So many people died that carpenters could not build coffins fast enough, and the dead were often buried in mass graves. Church bells rang day and night, announcing new deaths by the hour. Fatalities were especially bad on the Navajo Reservation and in small or crowded towns like Chilili and Dawson. By the end of October, thirteen out of every thousand soldiers at Camp Cody were dying of the flu or pneumonia each week.

Then the epidemic passed, almost as quickly as it had begun. New Mexicans joined other Americans across the nation and people around the world in breathing a great sigh of relief. Both World War I and the Spanish flu epidemic were behind them. All hoped that after many months of tragic war and terrible disease, peace and good health might be enjoyed at last.

Conclusions

New Mexicans hoped to prove their loyalty to the United States by helping to defend the nation's border during the Mexican Revolution and by fighting in Europe during World War I. Citizens of the new state made every sacrifice requested of them by buying war bonds, conserving resources, working hard, and serving bravely in the military.

As in every war, of course, the cost of victory in World War I was high in lives, money, and freedoms, especially for those identified with the German enemy. We must never forget these great costs whenever our country considers going to war, especially if we lose freedoms at home during a war that is fought to save freedoms somewhere else, as happened during World War I.

1. Why did Pancho Villa raid Columbus, New Mexico, in 1916?
2. How successful was the Punitive Expedition during its campaign in Mexico of 1916 to 1917?
3. Why were New Mexicans so eager to fight in World War I?
4. How did state leaders overcome problems of communication during World War I?
5. What did New Mexicans sacrifice on the home front to help win the war?
6. How were those identified with the enemy treated in New Mexico? Why is this ironic and sad?
7. What groups of New Mexicans served in the military during World War I?
8. What did New Mexicans sacrifice by serving in the military during World War I?
9. How did New Mexicans attempt to prevent catching the Spanish flu in 1918? Were they successful?
10. What aspects of New Mexico would you have been proud of if you had lived in the state during World War I? Why?
11. What aspects of New Mexico would you have been less proud of if you had lived in the state during World War I? Why?
12. What lessons can we learn from the history of New Mexico in World War I?

The 1920s
Artists, Authors, Lungers, and Dudes

Introduction

The 1920s was an exciting decade, full of changes and challenges in New Mexico. Many businesses prospered as new people arrived, often with money to spend and talents to share. Art colonies thrived. New Mexico's health industry expanded. Tourism grew. For the first time in the state's history, companies pumped oil and gas from New Mexico wells.

Yet there was still widespread poverty in New Mexico. After enjoying great success in World War I, farmers, ranchers, and miners experienced major setbacks in the 1920s, forcing some to look for work in other parts of the West or move from New Mexico forever.

The purpose of this chapter is to teach you about New Mexico's

- new art colonies;
- expanding health industry;
- increased tourism;
- new oil and gas fields;
- and new, or renewed, difficulties in agriculture and mining.

New Artists Arrive

Artists have honed their skills and created great works of art in New Mexico for centuries. Thousands of petroglyphs on rocks across the state remind us that Native American artists were active long before the arrival of European settlers in the sixteenth century. Hispanic *santeros* have created beautiful images of Roman Catholic saints since the eighteenth century.

☀ Creating the Taos Art Colony

Anglo artists joined the ranks of creative New Mexicans in the late nineteenth century. Two were especially important in helping to develop new art colonies in the Southwest. **Bert Geer Phillips** and **Ernest Blumenshein** were young artists en route from Denver to Mexico in search of new subjects to paint and new cultures to enjoy in mid-1898. The pair had traveled as far as the road between Questa and Taos in northern New Mexico when a wheel on their wagon broke.

Phillips and Blumenshein flipped a coin to see who would carry the broken wheel into Taos to have it fixed. Blumenshein lost the coin flip and set off for town. As he waited for the wheel to be repaired, Blumenshein wandered through Taos, observing its beauty and cultures. When he returned to Phillips with the repaired wheel, Blumenshein announced that they had gone far enough in their search for new subjects and cultures. As Blumenshein later remembered, "For the first time in my life I saw whole paintings right before my eyes. Everywhere I looked I saw paintings perfectly organized, ready to paint."

Blumenshein and Phillips stayed in Taos to live and work, first in the summers and, eventually, year-round. Enthusiastic about what they

Ernest Blumenshein by his broken wagon

had discovered, Blumenshein and Phillips told other artists about Taos and urged them to visit and, perhaps, join them as permanent residents. Several did. **E. Irving Couse** visited in 1902 and painted in Taos each summer after 1906. **Joseph Henry Sharp** bought a home in Taos in 1908. **William Herbert "Buck" Dunton** arrived in 1912. Each new artist bought or rented a studio, often hiring local residents to serve as models and work as handymen. So many artists moved to the area that a thriving art colony had evolved by World War I.

Artists were drawn to Taos for several reasons. First, they were attracted by the beautiful natural scenery and diverse cultures of northern New Mexico. Depending on an artist's interests, he could paint landscapes in the Taos Valley, on the high mesa, or in the nearby Sangre de Cristo Mountains. Many artists were fascinated by Hispanic, ranch, and Native American cultures. Some painters devoted their entire life's work to capturing and preserving the beauty of Taos Pueblo, fearing that the pueblo's ancient culture was threatened by forces of modern change.

Artists were also attracted to New Mexico for its incredible light and good weather. With many cloudless days and a vast, largely unobstructed sky, the sun's light created sharp contrasts of bright rays and dark shadows; colors were more vivid and exciting. New Mexico's mild climate was another advantage. Painters could take their easels outdoors to work for hours at a time, during nearly every month of the year.

Finally, artists came to Taos in increasing numbers to live and work in the growing art colony. As friends and neighbors, artists usually enjoyed each other's company and visited for hours, talking about their shared interests. The cost of living was lower in Taos than in most other art colonies in the world, making it possible for struggling artists to subsist longer, while more successful artists enjoyed greater shares of their hard-earned profits.

The Taos Society of Artists

So many exceptional artists had gathered in Taos by 1915 that a group of six, including Blumenshein and Phillips, decided to organize themselves as the **Taos Society of Artists**, or **TSA**. Although able to market their paintings individually, the six were confident they could do much better if they showed their works together in traveling exhibits. Group exhibits would also lessen the need for artists to show their paintings to tourists, who often interrupted the artists' work by dropping by their studios at all hours of the day and night. One TSA member even warned off

The Taos Society of Artists' Constitution and Purpose

The Taos Society of Artists was founded as an organization with a constitution, bylaws, annual meetings, annual dues—a dollar—and an application process for new members. Article 3 of the TSA's constitution explained the society's purpose:

> This Society is formed for *educational purposes*, to develop a high standard of art among its members, and to aid in the diffusion of taste for art in general. To promote and stimulate the practical expressions of art—to preserve and promote the native art.
>
> To facilitate bringing before the public through *exhibitions* and other means, tangible results of the work of its members—to promote, maintain and preserve high standards of excellence in painting, and to *encourage* sculpture, architecture, applied arts, music, literature, thnology, and archaeology, solely as its pertains to New Mexico and the States adjoining.

(Robert R. White, *The Taos Society of Artists* [Albuquerque: University of New Mexico Press, 1998], 17–18; emphasis added.)

Some original members of the Taos Society of Artists

bothersome tourists by placing a sign on his studio door that read, "Keep Out! TNT Explosives!" The sign worked but did nothing for the possible sale of the artist's paintings.

Not every artist could join the TSA. As the most elite artists' organization in New Mexico, the TSA only allowed new members who had won major artistic awards and had stayed and painted in Taos at least three times. Two-thirds of all old members had to approve each new member. Given these strict requirements, TSA membership never exceeded a dozen active members. Of these, **Catharine Carter Critcher** became the only female member of the TSA when she was elected unanimously in 1926.

TSA exhibits traveled by railroad to enthusiastic buyers as far east as Boston and as far west as San Francisco. By 1927, however, personal differences and individual successes caused the group to disband after twelve profitable years. The TSA and its members' art had helped make the Taos art colony and native Taos cultures famous far beyond the horizons of northern New Mexico.

☀ Mabeltown

Another famous member of the Taos art colony never won a major prize for her art, much less belonged to the TSA. **Mabel Dodge Stern** first visited Taos in 1917. Touring Taos Pueblo, she became fascinated by Pueblo culture as explained by her Indian guide, **Tony Luján**. Moving to Taos, Mabel married Tony Luján in 1923, although Mabel always spelled Luján with an *h* to help her Anglo friends correctly pronounce the name.

Together, Mabel and Tony built a large adobe house, modeled after Taos Pueblo, called **Los Gallos**. Eager to help preserve Native American culture and have others appreciate it as she did, Mabel invited artists and authors to stay at Los Gallos and spend their time in town depicting Taos on canvas and in words.

Many artists and authors accepted Mabel's invitations, living in her guest rooms for short or long periods of time. Among the talented people who stayed at Los Gallos were authors Mary Austin, Witter Bynner, Willa Cather, and Thornton Wilder. Artists included **Ansel Adams**, the most famous landscape photographer in American history, and a young painter named **Georgia O'Keeffe**.

Ansel Adams was so excited about what he saw in New Mexico that he wrote some friends of "Such MOUNTAINS! . . . Pines; aspens; snow;

Mabel Dodge Luhan's First Memories of Taos Pueblo

Mabel Dodge Luhan described her first trip to Taos Pueblo and her first encounter with Tony Luján in her autobiography, *Edge of Taos Desert: An Escape to Reality*:

> I wanted to see the Indians [of Taos Pueblo], to know them, for, as they passed up and down the road outside the house [we stayed at in Taos] . . . I searched their faces and tried to penetrate their infinitely unfamiliar souls. . . . [And so we drove to the pueblo.]
>
> Just inside the Pueblo, across from the little Catholic church, there was a group of houses. . . . The doors were open . . . and a couple of small children ran up to us in a friendly way. Then a beautiful woman stepped to one of the open doors. . . . Near the door, I stopped, for I heard a low singing and the soft beat of a drum. [In the room a] man sat beside the fireplace. . . . A thin, gray blanket came over his shoulders and fell in folds around his moccasined feet, and he tapped lightly on a little water-drum that rested on the floor between his knees. He was singing in a low, far-away murmur . . . and he didn't look up, even when we came crowding in. . . .
>
> The woman motioned to the low, white bedrolls with a gesture that was grave and quiet and respectful to the song, and we tiptoed in and sat, in an atmosphere that was new to me.
>
> The room was impregnated with a fullness of life. It had a rich, slow peacefulness. . . . I had never felt more satisfied and at ease. . . .
>
> And as I was thinking so, the man stopped singing and raised his head and looked at me for the first time, with a quick glance that penetrated to the depths with an instantaneous recognition. . . . He bowed slightly. . . .
>
> "I sang you a little song," he said gently.
>
> "Thank you ever so much!" I answered . . . [but soon said] we must be going. . . .
>
> I hated to go . . . and leave that good and lively feeling behind me in the room, for not in any room I have ever . . . lived in had I achieved such a plentiful and active sense of living. . . .
>
> The moment we were all in the car together again, the ease was gone. . . .

(Mabel Dodge Luhan, *Edge of Taos Desert: An Escape to Reality* [New York: Harcourt, Brace and Company, 1937], 92–95.)

Mabel and Tony Luján

clouds; burros; swell people. . . . You gotta see this place before you die." Adams returned to photograph scenes in northern New Mexico many times. On October 31, 1941, he took New Mexico's most famous photograph, "Moonrise, Hernandez, New Mexico."

▲▲▲▲▲▲▲▲▲▲▲▲▲▲▲▲▲▲▲▲▲▲▲
Taking "Moonrise, Hernandez, New Mexico"

Photographers take hundreds of photos over many months before they take one they are pleased with enough to develop and show. In the following excerpt taken from his autobiography, Ansel Adams describes October 31, 1941, "one of those unproductive days" until about four in the afternoon, when he saw an image that was to become the most famous photo in New Mexico history:

> One bright autumn afternoon found [my son and a fellow photographer at work] in the Chama River Valley. . . . I struggled with several [photos] . . . and decided it was just one of those unproductive days. We unanimously agreed to call it quits and return to Santa Fe.
>
> Driving south along the highway, I observed a fantastic scene as we approached the village of Hernandez. In the east, the moon was rising over distant clouds and snowpeaks, and in the west, the late afternoon sun . . . blazed a brilliant white upon the crosses in the church cemetery. I steered the station wagon into the deep shoulder along the road and jumped out, scrambling to get my equipment together, yelling at [my son and friend] to "Get this! Get, that . . . ! We don't have much time!" With the camera assembled and the image composed and focused, I could not find my Weston exposure meter! Behind me the sun was about to disappear behind the clouds, and I was desperate. [I did the calculations in my mind as quickly as I could and took the picture], for I instinctively knew I had visualized one of those very important images. . . . [A]s I pulled out the slide the sunlight left the crosses and the magical moment was gone forever.

(Ansel Adams, *Ansel Adams: An Autobiography* [Boston: Little, Brown and Company, 1996], 231.)

Adams was, of course, wrong, for he had captured his "magical moment" for all future generations to enjoy.

Georgia O'Keeffe was also inspired by what she saw. After touring northern New Mexico with Tony Luján, O'Keeffe was so captivated that she returned many times, first during summers at **Ghost Ranch** and later as a permanent resident of Abiquiú. By the time of her death at ninety-eight, her striking paintings of landscapes, adobe gateways, flowers, and animal skulls made her the most successful woman artist in the United States.

D. H. Lawrence was undoubtedly the most noted author to visit Los Gallos, joining what he called a "rendezvous of bizarre and interesting people" from around the world. An Englishman best known for

Getting Georgia O'Keeffe to Taos

Mabel Dodge Luhan was so eager to have artists and authors visit and admire Taos that she even resorted to a bit of trickery to make sure they accepted her invitations. In 1929, when Georgia O'Keeffe and a friend were visiting New Mexico, they met Mabel at an Indian dance. Mabel invited the pair to Taos, but O'Keeffe's friend hesitated because she knew what a "difficult hostess" Mabel could be.

Mabel was not deterred. When O'Keeffe and her friend did not arrive in Taos, Mabel simply had their luggage taken to Los Gallos so they had no choice but to follow their belongings north.

(Lois Palken Rudnick, *Mabel Dodge Luhan: New Woman, New Worlds* [Albuquerque: University of New Mexico Press, 1984], 235–36.)

Georgia O'Keeffe's house in Abiquiú

his scandalous novel, *Lady Chatterley's Lover*, Lawrence arrived in Taos with his wife Frieda in 1922. Like so many creative people, Lawrence sincerely admired Taos and its cultures, writing about and even painting what he saw and felt. Unfortunately, like most creative people who visited Los Gallos, Lawrence grew tired of Mabel Dodge Luhan's tendency to meddle in his life. As one observer put it, Mabel liked to "collect people and arrange them like flowers." Lawrence soon acquired some land Mabel owned on a mountain north of Taos. Lawrence and Freida built a ranch on the mountain, staying there in quiet isolation whenever they returned to Taos before finally moving to Europe, where Lawrence died of tuberculosis in 1930.

Despite her flaws, Mabel Dodge Luhan helped make Taos and Taos Pueblo famous by serving as a generous **patron of the arts** and by writing several books about her life and times.

▲▲▲▲▲▲▲▲▲▲▲▲▲▲▲▲▲▲▲▲▲▲▲▲▲▲▲▲▲▲▲▲▲▲▲▲▲

D. H. Lawrence Letter from New Mexico

Shortly after arriving at Los Gallos in Taos, D. H. Lawrence wrote to a friend in Europe:

October 19, 1922

> *Well, we have been here for five weeks, and are more or less getting used to it. We have a gay little adobe house on the edge of the desert. . . . The Indian pueblo is about two miles off, and Taos Plaza one mile. We don't see much of the "world"—save Mabel . . . and her visitors.*
>
> *The land I like exceedingly. You'd laugh to see Frieda and me trotting on these Indian ponies across the desert, and scrambling wildly up the slopes among the piñon bushes, accompanied by an Indian, John Concha, or a Mexican, José. It is great fun. Also we go to a hot spring and sit up to our necks in the clear, jumping water.*
>
> *Of course, humanly, America does to me what I knew it would do: it just bumps me. I say the people charge at you like trucks coming down on you—no awareness. But one tries to dodge aside in time. Bump! Bump! Go the trucks. And that is human contact. One gets a sore soul, and at times yearns for the understanding mildness of Europe. Only I like the country so much.*

(Quoted in Keith Sager, ed., *D. H. Lawrence and New Mexico* [Salt Lake City: Gibbs M. Smith, 1982], 13.)

D. H. Lawrence in Taos

She became such a dominant figure in Taos that observers kiddingly called her adopted community Mabeltown and referred to her as nothing less than the Empress of Mabeltown.

☀ The Santa Fe Art Colony and Cultural Preservation

Artists and authors were also attracted to many other parts of New Mexico in the first decades of the twentieth century. Starting with artists like **Carlos Vierra**, **William Penhallow Henderson**, and **Gerald Cassidy** before World War I, artists and authors began to settle in Santa Fe for many of the same reasons that artists and authors had been drawn to Taos

▲▲▲▲▲▲▲▲▲▲▲▲▲▲▲▲▲▲▲▲▲▲▲▲▲▲▲▲

Laughing Boy and Slim Girl

Oliver LaFarge's award-winning novel, *Laughing Boy*, focused on the tension between traditional Indian culture and modern ways. In the following scene, Laughing Boy speaks to his respected, traditional uncle about marrying Slim Girl, who had gone to an Indian boarding school, lives by the railroad, and is no longer allowed to participate in Navajo dances.

Laughing Boy went to his uncle's hogan, or Navajo house, to discuss his relation to Slim Girl:

> "My uncle."
>
> "Yes, my child." [His] old-fashioned, round silver earrings shimmered faintly. . . .
>
> "I have been thinking about a wife."
>
> "You are old enough. It is a good thing." . . .
>
> "You know that Slim Girl? The one who wears so much hard goods? She danced the first two nights."
>
> "She is a school-girl." The tone was final. "She was taken away to [an Indian boarding school], for six years."
>
> "That is all right. I like her."
>
> "That is not all right. I do not know how she came to be allowed to dance. They made her stop. . . . She is bad. She lives down by the railroad. She is not of the People any more[;] she is American. . . ."
>
> "I do not know what you mean, but I know her, that girl. She is not bad. She is good. She is strong. She is for me." . . .
>
> "And what makes you think you can go out and pick a wife for yourself like this? The next thing I know, you will jump into the fire. I tell you, she is all bad. . . ."

(Oliver LaFarge, *Laughing Boy* [Boston: Houghton Mifflin, 2004], 24–25.)

since 1898. By the 1920s a new art colony had developed, with both aspiring and already established artists living side-by-side on streets like Canyon Road and Camino del Monte Sol.

Although no organization matched the fame or success of the TSA, several Santa Fe artists attempted to market their work in groups, as had been done in Taos. The **Santa Fe Painters** included painters from both Santa Fe and Taos. **Los Cinco Pintores** (the Five Painters) consisted of five free-spirited young friends who attempted to build adobe houses along Camino del Monte Sol. More successful in their art skills than in their building skills, **Will Shuster**, **Fremont Ellis**, **Willard Nash**, **J. G. Bakos**, and **W. E. Murch** were locally known as "the five little nuts in five adobe huts."

▲▲▲▲▲▲▲▲▲▲▲▲▲▲▲▲▲▲▲▲▲▲▲▲▲▲▲▲▲▲▲▲

Willa Cather's *Death Comes for the Archbishop*

Of the many books and articles written in Santa Fe in the 1920s, Willa Cather's *Death Comes for the Archbishop* was the most controversial. *Death Comes for the Archbishop* was a historical novel about the life of New Mexico's first bishop, Jean Baptiste Lamy, in the nineteenth century. Cather's book reflected her admiration of Lamy, a French churchman with modern ideas for New Mexico's Roman Catholic Church, but had few kind words for the native Hispanic culture and priests, especially Padre Antonio José Martínez of Taos. When Cather's Lamy (called Bishop Latour in her novel) told Padre Martínez of his planned reforms, the New Mexico priest replied:

> You are a young man, my Bishop . . . and you know nothing about Indians or Mexicans. If you try to introduce European civilization here and change our old ways . . . I foretell an early death for you. I advise you to study our native traditions before you begin your reforms. . . . You cannot introduce French fashions here.

Latour refused to heed Martínez's warning and saw mostly evil in the padre's ways: he "snored like an enraged bull," and he "hated the Americans. The American occupation meant the end of men like himself. He was a man of the old order, . . . and his day was over."

(Willa Cather, *Death Comes for the Archbishop* [New York: Alfred A. Knopf, 1927], 147–53.)

Artists and authors in the Santa Fe art colony worked to preserve Native American and Hispanic culture by other means in the 1920s. Led by **Mary Austin**, **Frank Applegate**, and **John Gaw Meem**, they helped to create new organizations like the Indian Arts Fund, the Spanish Colonial Arts Society, and the Old Santa Fe Association. Artists also encouraged Indian and Hispanic artists, including María Martínez and **Eliseo Rodríguez**, who had worked for Los Cinco Pintores as a youth and is sometimes known as the sixth *pintor*. Santa Fe's first annual **Indian Market** began in 1922; the **Spanish Market** was organized in 1926. Both events continue to draw thousands of art collectors, eager to purchase the best new Hispanic and Native American art each year. Some collectors even camp out in front of their favorite artists' booths so they can be first in line when the market opens. According to one observer, "It's like they're waiting in line for tickets to a rock concert."

Members of the art colonies joined native New Mexicans in preserving ancient adobe architecture in organizations like the Society for the

Archeologists and Historians

Artists and authors were not alone in their efforts to help preserve the cultures of New Mexico. As a pioneering anthropologist of the Southwest, Edgar Hewett was largely responsible for the passage of the federal **Antiquities Act** of 1906, banning the looting of archeological sites in the United States. The Antiquities Act states:

> Be it enacted by . . . Congress . . . , that any person who shall appropriate, excavate, injure, or destroy any historic or prehistoric ruin or monument, or any object of antiquity, situated on lands owned or controlled by the Government of the United States, without the permission of the . . . Government . . . shall, upon conviction, be fined in a sum of not more than five hundred dollars or be imprisoned for a period of not more than ninety days, or shall suffer both fine and imprisonment. . . .

Hewett also helped organize the School of American Archaeology, later known as the School of American Research in Santa Fe.

By the 1920s, a new generation of scientists had become active, opening Santa Fe's important Laboratory of Anthropology in 1929. Many of these professional anthropologists were talented young women. Fortunately, archeologists like **Marjorie Ferguson Lambert** and **Bertha Dutton** ignored male sexism, as expressed by a male archeologist who said, "There's no point in teaching women archeology. They're only going to get married."

Historians helped preserve the past by creating the Museum of New Mexico, in rooms of the old Palace of the Governors, and by collecting valuable primary sources for a New Mexico history archives. In addition to writing a five-volume history of New Mexico entitled *The Leading Facts of New Mexican History* and serving as a leader in the Historical Society of New Mexico, historian Ralph Emerson Twitchell went so far as to rescue New Mexico's archives from a fire that completely destroyed the new territorial capitol building in 1892. As with New Mexico's anthropologists, a new generation of historians began work by the 1920s, including New Mexico's foremost colonial historian, France V. Scholes, a former health seeker who began to teach at UNM in 1925.

Preservation and Restoration of New Mexico Missions. Adobe architecture was so admired that it inspired the remodeling of old buildings, like the Palace of the Governors, and the design of new buildings, like the new Museum of Fine Arts in Santa Fe. Despite some early criticism, the University of New Mexico began remodeling existing buildings and designing new ones in adobe-style early in the twentieth century. (One critic asked if the university's buildings were built in Indian-style, would the school's president and faculty be expected to wear Indian blankets and headdresses on campus?) In Santa Fe, town leaders discussed the need to build "the town architecturally in harmony with its ancient character" for both historical and financial reasons. As early as 1910, a visitor from Boston had urged that "if you are to make Santa Fe attractive [to tourists] in the future you must preserve the old traditions. Don't be afraid to keep your old buildings."

A new generation of architects used adobe architecture to design hundreds of new structures across the state. The most successful architect of this group and in all of New Mexico history, John Gaw Meem used what is known as **Pueblo Revival** or **Santa Fe style** architecture to design a wide

John Gaw Meem with a model of Pueblo Revival architecture

range of buildings, including schools, hotels, banks, a hospital, a theater, a dude ranch, a church, at least 150 private homes, and 30 buildings on the UNM campus, where he became the university's official architect in 1934. When the La Fonda Hotel expanded from 46 to 156 rooms in 1929, Meem designed the addition, while **Mary Colter**, one of the most accomplished designers in the nation, designed the interior, using Spanish furniture, fixtures, and decorations to make every room unique. Colter designed many other hotels in the Southwest, relying on Native American as well as Spanish art to enhance her work.

☀ Health Seekers Flock to New Mexico

Thousands have come to New Mexico to recover their health. Suffering from ailments from asthma to arthritis, they arrived in such large numbers that New Mexico began to call itself the Wellness Country. By the 1920s, most patients who traveled to New Mexico suffered from one terrible disease in particular. **Tuberculosis**, also known as TB, the white plague, or consumption, was the major cause of death in the United States by the early twentieth century. Nicknamed **lungers** because they coughed so much, many men and women afflicted with this disease believed the odds of recovery were much greater if they moved to the Southwest on a temporary or permanent basis.

▲▲▲▲▲▲▲▲▲▲▲▲▲▲▲▲▲▲▲▲▲▲▲▲▲▲▲▲▲▲▲▲▲

Tuberculosis

An infectious disease . . . caused in humans by the bacterium *myco-bacterium tuberculosis*. Tuberculosis was once common worldwide and was a major killer in childhood and early adult life. . . .

Infection is passed from person to person in airborne droplets (produced by coughing or sneezing). The bacteria breathed into the lungs then multiply to form an infected "focus." In a high proportion of cases, the body's immune system then checks the infection and healing occurs, leaving a scar.

In about 5 percent of cases, however, the primary infection does not resolve. Spread occurs via the vessels of the lymphatic system to the lymph nodes. Sometimes at this stage bacteria enter the bloodstream and spread to other parts of the body. . . .

Because tuberculosis usually affects the lungs, the main symptoms include coughing (sometimes bringing up blood), chest pain, shortness of breath, fever and sweating (especially at night), poor appetite, and weight loss. . . .

[As of the mid-twentieth century] modern drugs are very effective against tuberculosis. . . . Provided the full course of treatment is taken, the majority of patients are fully restored to health and suffer no recurrences.

(Charles B. Clayman, ed., *The American Medical Association's Home Medical Encyclopedia* [New York: Random House, 1989], 2:1013–14.)

As a result, nearly every train that arrived in large towns like Albuquerque and Santa Fe had at least one lunger aboard. The newly arrived represented every social class and every occupation, from artists and authors to doctors and lawyers.

Lungers flocked to New Mexico mainly because many doctors told them that the best cure for TB was clean, fresh air. If patients rested properly, kept to a strict diet, and spent most of their days breathing fresh air, they could eventually expect good results. Few states in the nation could offer not only so much clean air, but also so many days of mild temperatures, allowing lungers to be outdoors doing what they needed to do most: breathe and rest. New Mexico's good weather and bright sunshine also brightened patients' dispositions during a generally dismal stage of their lives.

In addition, lungers were attracted to New Mexico because by the 1920s, the state had many doctors and medical facilities that specialized in the treatment of TB. **Frank Mera** in Santa Fe, **LeRoy Peters** and **A. G. Shortle** in Albuquerque, **Carl Gellenthien** of Valmora (near Las Vegas), and others were counted among the best TB specialists in the

A Lunger's Schedule in Chasing the Cure

As reflected in the strict schedule prescribed in a booklet given to all new patients at the Valmora Sanatorium, TB patients focused on rest, light recreation, and a proper diet:

7:00 a.m.	awaken; take temperature; wash upper body with cold sponge
8:00 a.m.	breakfast
9:00 a.m.	light exercise when ordered by doctor, mostly walking
10:00 a.m.	rest; take temperature
11:00 a.m.	recreation
12:00 p.m.	dinner
1:00 p.m.	rest; take temperature; reading, but no talking allowed
2:00 p.m.	rest; reading, but no talking allowed
3:00 p.m.	rest; take temperature and pulse
4:00 p.m.	light exercise when ordered by doctor, mostly walking
5:00 p.m.	rest
6:00 p.m.	supper
7:00 p.m.	recreation; take temperature
9:00 p.m.	wash lower body with cold sponge; go to bed; no talking

Total number of hours resting:	5	(about 20 percent of the day)
Total number of hours eating meals:	3	(about 12 percent of the day)
Total number of hours light exercise (if ordered by the doctor)	3	(about 12 percent of the day)
Total number of hours of recreation:	3	(about 12 percent of the day)
Total number of hours of sleep:	10	(about 40 percent of the day)

Other rules at the Valmora Sanatorium included the following:

- You are not at Valmora to be amused, and since all amusements demand more or less energy, mental as well as physical, it is advisable to get along with as little [amusement] as is consistent with your [condition].
- Patients are required to use individual sputum cups.... Every evening the paper sputum boxes or pocket cups must be burned.
- Do not eat between meals unless otherwise instructed. Drink little with your meals, but drink 6 to 8 glasses of water during the day.
- [Because breathing clean air is essential] your room should never, even when you are dressing or disrobing, be entirely closed.
- Never hurry.
- Never kiss.

(Patients' Booklet, Valmora Sanatorium, New Mexico Health Historical Collection, Health Sciences Library and Information Center, University of New Mexico, Albuquerque, New Mexico.)

Sunmount Sanatorium
cottage exterior
....

New Mexico's sanatoriums
....

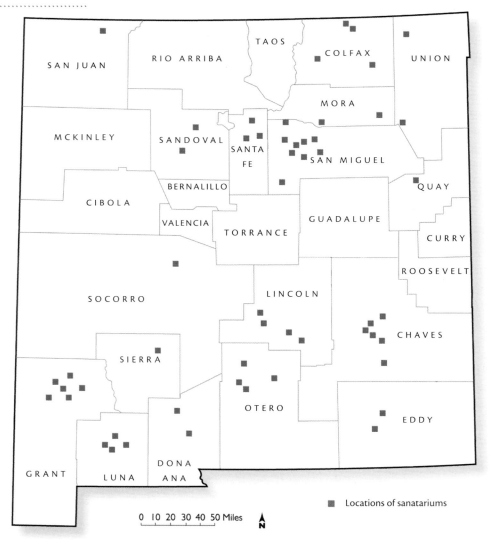

Sunmount Sanatorium cottage interior

nation. **Sanatoriums**, or hospitals devoted to the treatment of tuberculosis, were also prevalent in towns and cities across New Mexico. St. Vincent Hospital in Santa Fe and St. Joseph's and Presbyterian Hospitals in Albuquerque were originally founded as sanatoriums, or **sans**, as they were commonly called. A san was created for merchant marines at Fort Stanton, while soldiers stricken with TB could receive care at Fort Bayard.

Most sans included not only a large main building but also many small, one-room cottages where individual lungers lived and, it was hoped, recovered. With large, screened windows and sleeping porches, these cottages offered maximum access to fresh air twenty-four hours a day. When not in their cottages, lungers spent much of each day on chaise lounges, "chasing the cure." Nurses took their temperatures and frequently checked on their progress. Tray boys, hired from local communities, delivered their meals, prepared according to strict diets their doctors prescribed.

Not everyone could afford to be treated in sans. Fortunately, New Mexico's low cost of living made it possible for poorer lungers to chase the cure outside of sans. Long streets, like Walter or Ash in southeast Albuquerque, offered boardinghouses with sleeping porches, meal trays, and comfortable backyards where lungers could sit to breathe clean air. One little girl saw so many female lungers sitting in attractive pajamas and nice robes in her neighborhood that she vowed she would become a lunger when she grew up.

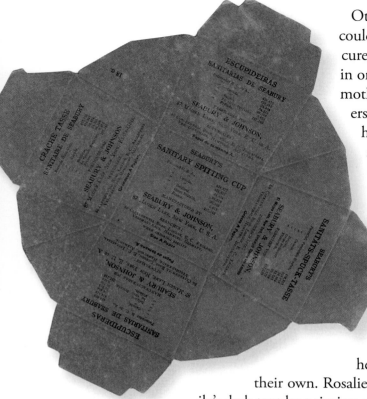

An unassembled
spitting cup

Other lungers rented or purchased houses so they could stay with their families while chasing the cure. As a girl, Lilian Kineline remembers living in one such Albuquerque neighborhood while her mother recovered from TB. With so many lungers living on her street, seeing doctors visit and hearing neighbors coughing at all hours were normal parts of daily life for Lilian and her childhood friends. To prevent spreading the disease, Lilian's family followed strict health rules; no one in the family could ever eat from the same plates or drink from the same glasses as their mother.

Lungers who could not afford sans, boardinghouses, or homes of their own sometimes resorted to chasing the cure while living in tents or wagons. Almost every large town had a "tent city" where poor health seekers gathered and chased the cure on their own. Rosalie Doolittle's mother tried to brighten her family's drab tent by painting colorful murals on its interior canvas walls.

So many health seekers had arrived in New Mexico by the 1920s that they had developed their own lunger subculture. Socializing with fellow lungers, they entered contests, made arts and crafts, traveled to events (from wrestling matches to Indian dances), read issues of Albuquerque's *Health City Sun*, vacationed in nearby TB resorts, and lent each other emotional support during their darkest moments. Often shunned by people who feared catching TB, lungers enjoyed each other's company, often becoming good friends for the duration of their stay in New Mexico and, sometimes, for life. Some even found romance, marrying fellow lungers and creating new families.

So many health seekers came to New Mexico that a high percentage of each large town or city's population consisted of lungers or their relatives. In Silver City, 60 percent of all households had at least one TB patient. In Santa Fe, an estimated third of all artists and authors had suffered from TB when they first arrived in New Mexico. In Albuquerque, the number of lungers was so great it was said that if someone put a tent over the city, Albuquerque would have been one giant san. There were so many sans along Central Avenue and so many lungers who walked along its sidewalks that the street was nicknamed TB Avenue or, sometimes, Lungers Alley. For the state as a whole, 10 percent of the population either suffered from TB or had at least one relative who did.

Businesses on Central Avenue and elsewhere profited handsomely from the lungers' trade. Many doctors, nurses, tray boys, and other staff members earned their livings in the sans. Drugstores, clothing stores (specializing in pajamas, robes, and slippers), stationery stores, bookstores, banks, insurance companies, construction companies, real estate companies, taxis, and, unfortunately, mortuaries and cemeteries are a few of the seemingly countless businesses that profited directly or indirectly. Ads appealing to the lungers' business could be found in daily newspapers, especially in classified advertisements.

Conditions were not always ideal for the health seekers. While lungers were at first welcomed to Wellness Country, some New Mexicans began to fear TB as a public health menace. New Mexicans worried about the impact TB might have on themselves, their families, or, in the case of businesses, their healthier customers. Signs began to appear outside stores and restaurants, warning, "Lungers Not Allowed." Now, scattered among newspaper ads that advertised rooms for rent to lungers, other landlords' ads banned health seekers with the code words "no sick." Some jobs were restricted to "healthy" men and women. New UNM professors had to prove they did not have TB before they could begin their teaching career; new dorms were built on campus so that fewer students would be exposed to TB in boardinghouses in town.

Despite such precautions, New Mexicans began to catch TB, a highly contagious, airborne disease. So many New Mexicans caught TB by the 1930s that a state-operated sanatorium was built north of Socorro and a Native American sanatorium was built in Albuquerque. So many students caught TB at the Albuquerque Indian School that school officials added sleeping porches to campus dorms to help treat ill children. One study revealed that the death rate among Hispanic lungers was three or four times as high as for Anglo health seekers. Hispanic women who worked as housekeepers in boardinghouses or sans were especially vulnerable to the disease.

While many lungers recovered from TB, a good many suffered relapses or finally died of the disease. By 1929, TB was the number one cause of death in New Mexico, causing 13 percent of all deaths in the state.

A Typical Lunger's Newspaper Ad

Attention Healthseekers

"Villa Mari," an exclusive convalescent home now open, newly built, thoroughly modern, beautifully furnished. Beautyrest mattresses, excellent food, tray service, nurse care, bed patients welcome. Phone 2421-J.

(*Albuquerque Journal*, November 17, 1929.)

A Typical "No Sick" Newspaper Ad

The Alhambra

Most modern apartments. Close-in. Everything furnished, including Frigidaire and maid service. No sick. Phone 3556-W.

(*New Mexico State Tribune*, April 28, 1930.)

The Tale of Two Lungers

Anne Ellis was a health seeker from Colorado who chased the cure at sans in Albuquerque during the 1920s. She fondly remembered her fellow patients, especially a young man named James:

> James, a Southerner, handsome, virile, charming, rather aloof, could have had many callers, but so earnest and determined was he to get well that he [focused only on chasing the cure]. . . . He had been "chasing" for years, and finally was so much better that he arranged to go to the [University of New Mexico] to finish his engineering course. . . . I . . . was thrilled the morning he started—looking so clean, well-dressed and beaming. . . .
>
> [But the] moment James returned [from his first day in class] he went to bed. This was natural, but the next morning I noticed that he did not step as briskly. . . .
>
> Then one morning [a few weeks later] he didn't go up the hill to the university, but instead went down the hill to town, where he saw his doctor. The examination showed that there was new "activity" [or trouble with his TB]. Again he was put to bed for months, perhaps years. . . .
>
> In the daytime when he was alone [James] whistled defiantly, but in the night, when he thought no one was listening, he gave up to his grief. As I listened I worried, and damned and wondered why things were as they were. But sick, disappointed, hurt as he was, James cheerfully carried on without one complaint.

(Anne Ellis, *Sunshine Preferred* [Lincoln: University of Nebraska Press, 1984], 59–61.)

Like James, Clinton P. Anderson was a young man, just starting out in life, when his doctor told him he had TB in 1917. Years later he described that moment and some wise advice that saved his life:

> It was the lowest moment of my life. I was only 21. A few weeks before, I had been well on my way in the newspaper business in my hometown in South Dakota, and was eagerly anticipating getting married. Now, confined to bed in a tuberculosis sanatorium in New Mexico, I had nothing to look forward to, I thought, but death.
>
> The doctor had wired my father to come within five days if he wanted to see me alive. . . .
>
> Then I realized that someone was standing beside me. It was Joe Maas, an old "lunger." The words he spoke literally saved my life. They have come back repeatedly in moments of crisis and helped pull me through.
>
> "Remember this, son," Joe said in the husky whisper of the advanced TB case. "What you got will never kill you if you keep it in your chest. But if you let get up here," and he tapped his temple significantly, "it's fatal. Worrying kills more patients than TB itself ever did."
>
> The veteran's words made my young heart leap. . . . I sent for my typewriter and had it suspended from the ceiling on a pulley. Each morning, propped up on a pillow, I lowered the machine onto my lap. Throughout my eight months in bed I laboriously pecked out sketches, poems and short stories. . . . And every day . . . I wrote a letter to the girl I was going to marry, and received a letter from her. I never doubted that I'd get well. . . .
>
> By contrast, there were patients with only mild cases who lived in perpetual fear. Some of them eventually succumbed, more, I believe, because of abandoning hope than because of physical illness. . . .
>
> [Joe's advice] can bring peace of mind to anyone who will use it.

(Clinton P. Anderson, "The Best Advice I Ever Had," *Reader's Digest*, vol. 62 [July 1953]: 51–52.)

Clinton P. Anderson recovered to became a reporter, a businessman, a U.S. congressman, a U.S. secretary of agriculture, and, from 1949 to 1973, a U.S. senator representing his new home state of New Mexico.

Despite these poor odds of recovery, other lungers survived, especially if they had arrived in New Mexico and chased the cure at an early stage of their illness. There is no proof the Southwest's sunshine and clean air cured these more fortunate patients, but sunshine and clean air could not have harmed them and, with the good care lungers received in its sans and from TB specialists, New Mexico was usually a better place to recover than in crowded Eastern cities, where many health seekers had lived and had first been diagnosed.

Of those who recovered, most returned to their home states. Others chose to remain in New Mexico, however, because they had grown to think of the state, with its healthy climate, its beauty, and its interesting cultures, as their new home. Many of the recovered health seekers who stayed in New Mexico made major contributions to their adopted state and its residents. Will Shuster and Carlos Vierra became famous artists in Santa Fe, while **France V. Scholes** became an esteemed New Mexico historian, Katherine Stinson-Otero and John Gaw Meem became noted

Katherine Stinson-Otero, the Schoolgirl Flyer

Katherine Stinson-Otero was one of New Mexico's most famous lungers. Before coming to New Mexico, she had become internationally known as the "Schoolgirl Flyer" because she had flown at such an early age and broken so many records in her teenage years. Some of her records were

- only the fourth woman to earn a pilot's license in the United States, in 1912, at age sixteen;
- the first woman pilot to fly an airmail route;
- the first woman pilot to fly a solo flight at night;
- the first woman pilot to fly a loop-the-loop.

Katherine Stinson-Otero

Katherine became so admired as a brave young pilot that she inspired other women to fly, both professionally and for sport.

Denied permission to fly for the U.S. Army during World War I, Katherine drove an ambulance in Europe to do what she could to help win the war. After the war she contracted TB and came to New Mexico to chase the cure. Once recovered, she married a fellow pilot, World War I veteran Miguel Otero, Jr., and began a new career in another male-dominated profession, architecture. She was a success in her new field, winning awards and surviving to the age of eighty-one.

A Los Alamos Ranch School Letter by Student Jay Rice

The **Los Alamos Ranch School** was founded in 1917, specifically for wealthy boys who sometimes suffered from poor health. The school became famous not only for its high academic standards but also for its rigorous outdoor activities, from hiking and camping to riding and hunting. All students belonged to Boy Scout Troop 22. Most boys excelled in their new environment.

Jay Rice of St. Louis, Missouri, was a typical student at the Los Alamos Ranch School in the 1920s. Like other boys at the school, he was interested in horses, hunting, grades, girls, and radios, a relatively new invention. He was also concerned about his health. In a typical letter home he wrote:

> [1928]
>
> Dear Family,
>
> I had my physical exam last night and, to my great disappointment, most of my growing was in height. I've grown an inch since I've been here and gained only 4 1/2 lbs. However, I'm as hard as rocks and far healthier than I've ever before been. . . .
>
> Love,
>
> Jay

Jay Rice continued to enjoy good health at Los Alamos, graduating from the Ranch School in 1930 and going on to graduate from Harvard University. He served in the U.S. Army during World War II, married, had one son, and was a successful St. Louis businessman. He died in 1984.

(J. G. Rice's Los Alamos Ranch School Correspondence, 1928–30, Los Alamos Historical Society Archives, Fuller Lodge, Los Alamos, New Mexico.)

Los Alamos Ranch School for boys

architects, **Bronson Cutting** and **Clinton P. Anderson** became U.S. senators, **William Randolph Lovelace** and Carl Gellenthien became trusted physicians, and **Carrie Tingley** became the first lady of New Mexico when her husband, Clyde, served as governor of the state in the 1930s. These and many other health seekers lived long, productive lives in New Mexico; the average age at death for Shuster, Vierra, Scholes, Stinson-Otero, Meem, Cutting, Anderson, Lovelace, Gellenthien, and Tingley was seventy-eight.

It would be hard to imagine New Mexico today without its important health industry, which began with the treatment of health seekers in communities across the state. Major health centers, including Presbyterian Hospital, St. Joseph's Hospital, and the Lovelace Medical

Center, began either as TB sanatoriums or as a clinic founded by a former health seeker, like Dr. William Randolph Lovelace.

Cars, Tourism, and Western Dudes

New Mexico has long been a destination for travelers, especially with the building of the Santa Fe Railway into New Mexico in 1880. Tourists arrived in ever greater numbers in the 1920s, traveling by train and, increasingly, by car.

Introduced in New Mexico in 1897, cars were at first considered a luxury for the few wealthy New Mexicans who could afford to not only purchase but also maintain this most modern form of transportation. Not even the governor of New Mexico could afford a car in those early years. Having bought a new Ford for $2,400 ($49,255 in today's money) in 1904, Gov. Miguel Otero complained that the vehicle was incapacitated so often that it cost him $275 ($5,644 in today's money) a month to operate; he claimed to have done more walking, to search for help for his often-broken car, than in any other period of his life. After just four months, Otero was relieved to sell his Ford to a man from Albuquerque for $400 ($8,208 today), at a loss of $2,000 ($41,047 today). In his memoirs, *My Life on the Frontier*, the governor recalled "experiencing a feeling of great relief when [the buyer] finally drove it out of [my] yard" and home to Albuquerque. Counting Governor Otero's secondhand vehicle, there were only thirty-two cars in Albuquerque by 1910.

New Mexico's First Car

Albuquerque's R. L. Dodson purchased New Mexico's first car in Denver, Colorado. Roads for cars were so poor between Denver and Albuquerque that it took Dodson five days to drive his new vehicle home in November 1897. A bicycle-shop owner, Dodson wanted a car not only for his own use but also to train himself to fix other cars as the number of cars in New Mexico increased. The only mechanic in New Mexico, Dodson charged $15 a day ($332 in today's money) in addition to expenses, since he often had to travel by railroad to get to broken cars in need of repair.

Two early cars

La Bajada

One of the steepest roads in New Mexico lies eleven miles south of Santa Fe on the main route to Albuquerque. La Bajada means "gradual descent" in Spanish, but the one-and-a-half-mile descent was hardly gradual in the 1920s. The road was so steep it had no fewer than twenty-three hairpin turns. To negotiate these sharp curves, drivers had to slowly maneuver their cars and trucks back and forth as they turned, placing rocks behind their wheels before inching forward.

Drivers going up La Bajada found it was often more efficient to back up the hill, using their cars' more powerful reverse gears. Even then male passengers often had to ride on their cars' running boards and, in the words of one teenager, "jump off and push with all our might" to clear the steepest sections of the road.

Some travelers became so frightened by the experience of driving up or down La Bajada that they abandoned their cars halfway through the trip, walking the rest of the way and announcing that they refused to drive one more curve.

Accidents occurred on a regular basis. An article in the *Albuquerque Journal* of December 30, 1929, reported:

An automobile containing two Albuquerque girls, Miss Dora Barela and Miss Eloisa Baca, plunged over a hairpin curve on La Bajada. . . . The girls, both under 20, were returning to Albuquerque after a weekend visit to relatives in Santa Fe. They had just started downward when their car lost control and swerved over the side of the road, rolling down [the] rocky hillside. The fact that they were riding in a closed car is believed to have saved their lives, [although] both [girls suffered] severe cuts and bruises.

La Bajada near Santa Fe

LA BAJADA GRADE NEAR SANTA FE N.M.

Cars became less of an expensive luxury and more of an affordable necessity by the 1920s. The price of cars like the Ford Motor Company's Model T actually declined in the 1920s, making them accessible to more and more New Mexicans. By 1928 New Mexico had 67,118 licensed vehicles, with the most (9,330) in Bernalillo County and the fewest (528) in Catron County.

Car owners still faced many problems. Often referred to as "devil wagons," cars scared livestock and humans alike with their strange appearance and loud noise. Dirt roads were so rough that a driver could expect to experience two or three flat tires in an average fifty-mile trip. When not fixing tires, drivers were often busy pushing their vehicles out of sand or mud, often with the help of a local farmer's horse. Gasoline stations were rare, causing motorists to run out of gas or suffer breakdowns (like Governor Otero's) without much hope of immediate rescue. Road signs and maps were also scarce, causing out-of-town drivers to get lost for hours, if not days, at a time.

Thanks to the use of convict labor and a good roads movement in New Mexico, car owners drove on increasingly better roads throughout the state. **U.S. Route 66** opened in 1927, running from Chicago in the East to Los Angles in the West and going through several New Mexico towns, including Tucumcari, Albuquerque, and Gallup.

Route 66 had not always gone directly east-to-west through Albuquerque and Gallup. Several routes through New Mexico competed for the new highway's permanent route when it was created in the 1920s. Gov. Arthur Hannett made the final decision to build the highway through Tijeras Canyon into Albuquerque and on to Gallup (Hannett's hometown) in the last days of his term in office in 1926. Residents of towns bypassed by the new main road were so angered by the decision they attempted to stop the road-building project. According to the project's chief engineer, "Saboteurs appeared. Gas tanks on the tractors were fed sugar. Sand appeared in the engines. The . . . tractor drivers rolled their beds in the snow and slept alongside their machines [to protect them at night]." Despite such efforts at sabotage, the new road was completed in 1927 and was officially designated as part of Route 66 a decade later.

Early postcard showing Route 66 through downtown Albuquerque

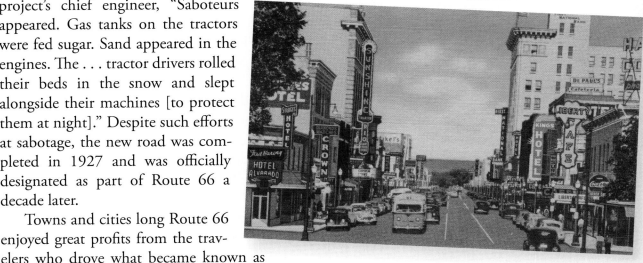

Towns and cities long Route 66 enjoyed great profits from the travelers who drove what became known as the Mother Road or the Main Street of America. "Auto camp grounds," "motor hotels" (motels), diners, and "filling stations" lined the highway to serve thousands of motorists who drove the highway for business or pleasure each month.

Top: map showing Route 66; above left: Albuquerque signage commemorating Route 66; above right: Route 66 sign near Carnuel, New Mexico.

Tourists came to New Mexico by train and by car for many of the same reasons artists and health seekers had come to the state. Vacationers enjoyed New Mexico's mild climate, clean air, low costs, and beautiful scenery. Many were drawn to natural wonders like Carlsbad Caverns, which opened as a national monument in 1923; White Sands, a national park as of 1933; and the Gila Wilderness, the state's first national forest as of 1924. Natural spas in Hot Springs, Jémez, and Ojo Caliente were also favorite destinations.

Other tourists were attracted to New Mexico by the state's native cultures, past and present. Large numbers learned of ancient Indian cultures when they visited Chaco Canyon, a national monument as of 1907, and Frijoles Canyon, known as Bandelier when it became a national monument in 1916. Tourists interested in contemporary Indian life visited reservations, witnessing Indian dances and buying Native arts and crafts, like pottery and turquoise jewelry. Other tourists bought traditional arts and crafts from Indians who displayed their work at busy New Mexico train depots.

Dude ranches were opened for easterners who cared to experience western ranch hospitality and culture by "roughing it," at least in small, safe ways. Popular western novels and movies featuring cowboy stars like Tom Mix helped promote 355 dude ranches in the West,

Burma Shave Signs

▲▲▲▲▲▲▲▲▲▲▲▲▲▲▲▲▲▲▲▲▲▲▲▲

The Burma Shaving Cream Company became famous by advertising its product with the help of six-line jingles along roads like Route 66. Each line of the jingle was painted on a small wooden sign, with signs placed about a hundred feet apart. Travelers looked forward to reading the signs and completing each jingle as a diversion on long trips. Here are some examples of typical Burma Shave jingles:

Burma Shave signs

The answer to	He played a sax
A maiden's	Had no B.O.
Prayer	But his whiskers
Is not a chin	Scratched
Of stubby hair.	So she let him go.
Burma Shave	Burma Shave

Burma Shave jingles also gave good driving advice:

If you dislike	Past
Big traffic fines	Schoolhouses
Slow down	Take it slow.
'Till you	Let the little
Can read these signs.	Shavers grow.
Burma Shave	Burma Shave

including 26 in New Mexico, by the 1930s. Ranch names varied, from the Kickapoo Kamp in Mora County to the Rancho de Días Alegres (Happy Days Ranch) near Las Vegas and the mysterious-sounding Ghost Ranch near Abiquiú.

In 1926, the Santa Fe Railway opened a new business, using both railroad and car transportation. Known as the **Southwestern Indian Detours**, the railway provided guided tours of from one to eight days. Led by specially trained young women known as couriers, these excursions allowed tourists to come to New Mexico by train and then travel in Harvey Coaches to visit natural wonders, historical sites, and Indian communities throughout the Southwest. Schedules were arranged so that guests often ate their meals at Santa Fe's Harvey Houses and often spent their nights at these same fine resorts. Artists helped promote the tours by painting Indian scenes used on popular Santa Fe Railway calendars.

Whole towns developed special events to help celebrate their local cultures and, it was hoped, draw tourist dollars. Las Vegas held its **Cowboy Reunion**, an annual rodeo featuring nearly a hundred cowboys who competed in bronco busting, bull riding, calf roping, and

Jim White and Carlsbad Caverns

Jim White at
Carlsbad Caverns

Jim White was a teenage cowhand when he first explored Carlsbad Caverns in 1901. Years later he wrote of his first experience in the caverns after watching thousands of bats fly from "the biggest and blackest hole I had ever seen":

> The more I thought of it the more I realized that any hole in the ground which could house such a gigantic army of bats must be a whale of a big cave. I crept between cactus until I lay on the brink of the chasm, and looked down. . . . There was no bottom in sight! I shall never forget the feeling of aweness it gave me. . . .
>
> A couple of days later . . . I gathered up a kerosene lantern, several coils of rope, sire, and a hand axe. I got to the cave about mid-afternoon [and used my rope to climb down to a tunnel]. . . . Standing at the entrance of the tunnel I could see ahead of me a darkness so absolutely black it seemed a solid. The light of my lantern was but a sickly glow. Nevertheless, I forged ahead, and with each step the tunnel grew larger, and I felt as though I was wandering into the very core of the Guadalupe Mountains.
>
> (Jim White, *The Discovery and History of Carlsbad Caverns* [Carlsbad: Carlsbad Caverns Guadalupe Mountains Association, 1998], 2–4.)

Twenty-one years later Jim White took the first scheduled sightseeing party into the caverns when he lowered thirteen local residents down into the depths before leading them as their guide. White charged nothing for this historic tour on September 10, 1922. More than a half million visitors explored the caverns in 1996 alone. Adults now pay six dollars each (equal to about sixty-five cents in 1922) for the adventure.

horse-racing events. Crowds of up to ten thousand enjoyed this athletic competition as well as western dances, trick rope shows, and spectacular fireworks.

Not to be outdone, in September 1922, promoters in western New Mexico organized the first Gallup **Inter-Tribal Ceremonial** to celebrate Native American culture and attract new tourist trade. Native Americans from the nearby Navajo Reservation, the pueblos, and other western tribes were invited to compete for cash awards in races, dances, parades, and arts and crafts. Thousands of tourists arrived to witness these annual events, traditionally started with a long, colorful parade

Dude Ranches

Dude ranches became increasingly popular in New Mexico in the 1920s. The Vermejo Park Ranch, on the old Maxwell land grant in northeastern New Mexico, catered to wealthy guests, including movie star Douglas Fairbanks, businessman Harvey Firestone, and Pres. Herbert Hoover. Guests had access to thousands of acres of land, filled with good riding, fishing, and hunting. Membership in the exclusive Vermejo Club (limited to 150 members) cost $5,000 ($54,000 in today's money).

Tex Austin, a cowboy and rodeo promoter known as the King of the Rodeo, operated another famous dude ranch near Pecos, New Mexico. Opened in 1925, Austin's 5,500-hundred-acre Forked Lightning Ranch featured a nine-bedroom guesthouse designed by the famous architect John Gaw Meem. Dudes paid $125 a week ($1,500 a week in today's money) to enjoy all the comforts of home while living on a working ranch. The ranch is now part of the Pecos National Monument.

The state's most famous dude ranch covered twenty-one thousand beautiful, rugged acres in northwestern New Mexico. Ghost Ranch was owned and operated by Arthur Peck and his family for about twenty years. Georgia O'Keeffe, the ranch's most famous guest, was hardly a "dude," having spent many summers on the ranch painting the surrounding landscape until she finally moved to nearby Abiquiú in 1949.

Other guests were clearly novices to the Southwest. Arthur Peck wrote of a lady who, when asked whether she preferred an Eastern saddle or a Western one, seemed unsure, and inquired . . . what was the difference. [Slim, a resident cowhand,] replied patiently that a Western saddle had a horn while the Eastern saddle did not. "I think I'll take the Eastern saddle," she replied. "I don't think we will be meeting much traffic."

(Arthur Newton Peck, *We Called It Ghost Ranch* [Abiquiú: Ghost Ranch Conference Center, 1966], 61.)

Dude ranch magazine advertisement

▲▲▲▲▲▲▲▲▲▲▲▲▲▲▲▲▲▲▲▲▲▲▲▲▲▲▲▲▲

Sample Southwestern Indian Detour Schedule

Southwest Indian Detour guests could enjoy tours of various lengths, costs, and destinations. A three-day, $57.50-tour in 1928 included the following schedule on day two:

8:00 a.m.	Breakfast, Alvarado Harvey House Hotel, Albuquerque
9:00 a.m.	Leave Alvarado by Harvey car
10:45–11:45 a.m.	Santo Domingo Pueblo
1:00 p.m.	Arrive at La Fonda Harvey House Hotel, Santa Fe
1:30 p.m.	Lunch at La Fonda
3:30 p.m.	Drive through Santa Fe, visiting the Governor's Palace, museums, San Miguel Church, and other historic sites
6:00 p.m.	Dinner at La Fonda
8:00 p.m.	Informal Lecture about the Southwest
Overnight at La Fonda	

(D. H. Thomas, *The Southwestern Indian Detours* [Phoenix: Hunter Publishing Co., 1978], 183.)

Pueblo Indians greeting tourist train

through downtown Gallup. The ceremonials are still enormously popular and profitable. They represent the longest ongoing public celebration of Native American culture in the United States.

Other towns created their own special events, but none surpassed the **Santa Fe Fiesta** for its size and mass appeal. Started in 1919 to celebrate the 1693 Spanish reconquest of New Mexico, the annual fiesta soon became a celebration of all groups and all periods of New Mexico history. Organized by the Santa Fe Chamber of Commerce with the help of volunteers from the local art colony, the event became so popular by the late 1920s that every hotel room in the city was booked and dorm rooms at the Santa Fe Indian School and the State School for the Deaf were used to accommodate out-of-town guests. The fiesta featured the burning of **Zozobra**, street dances, Indian dances, a formal ball, arts and craft sales, a historical-hysterical parade for adults, and a pet parade for children.

Clearly, many communities and groups benefited from tourism in the 1920s. Tourism also created its share of problems for the state and its citizens, however. Some businessmen charged unfair prices or

A Ceremonial Organizer's Letter

Native American and Gallup leaders volunteered countless hours to make the Inter-Tribal Ceremonials a success in the 1920s and since. The following letter from Packy Powers to Vera Powers describes some of the work done by early volunteers, especially Homer Powers. Packy was Homer's cousin; Vera was Homer's wife.

April 5, 1967

Dear Vera,

I have thunk and thunk about the early days of the Ceremonial, but it was a long time ago — too long. I worked on [the Ceremonial] with Homer for seven years [1926–33]. . . .

When I first started, [the Southwest Indian Detours] would pick up the dancers at the various pueblos and meet me in Albuquerque. . . . At that time the only paved road was to Los Lunas, and for 20 miles east of Gallup. The trip . . . took about six or seven hours . . . , and we generally got into Gallup for a late supper after dark. We housed the Pueblo dancers in a series of rooms of adobe. We gave them [each] a steel cot, mattress, and two blankets. Things weren't so complicated or sophisticated in those days. All of the Pueblo Indians were housed here, and we fed them — except the old governor of Acoma and his family. They came in their own Cadillac, and we quartered them at the Harvey House. . . .

The Indians dressed out twice a day — in the morning for the parade, and again for the night performance. . . . The first couple of years my only job was to take care of the dancers and smooth out their complaints (very few — they were nice people to work with). I had to see that they were fed, and that they got to the parade and back, and were ready for the evening performance. . . .

We always had a couple of dance teams standing by in the afternoons, so if there was a lull in the program we could put on a dance. [Homer and I] took great pride in the fact that there was never a drag or dull moment. We each carried a sack of silver dollars and paid off the contestants on the spot. . . .

Vera, I don't imagine anyone knows or appreciates the thought and time Homer put into the Ceremonial, and the weeks, each year, he spent on his own going to the pueblos and reservations signing up the dancers. In those days it couldn't be done by mail. . . . The people of Gallup may not commemorate Homer with a plaque, but you and I know how much of himself he contributed.

Love,

Packy

(Quoted in Sally Noe, *Our Gallup, New Mexico, U.S.A.*, Story [Virginia Beach, VA: Donning Company, 1997], 116–21.)

provided inferior goods or services, leaving tourists with bad memories of their time spent in New Mexico. Special event participants, including some Native Americans at the Inter-Tribal Ceremonials, felt they were unfairly compensated and complained that their living quarters were subpar and unsanitary.

Zozobra

Zozobra

Many Santa Fe artists participated in the Santa Fe Fiesta each year, but two in particular used their creative talents to make a lasting contribution to the annual event. In 1926, Will Shuster and Gustave Baumann created the first Zozobra, or Old Man Gloom, a twenty-foot-high puppet filled with firecrackers and papers bearing bad news, such as divorce decrees and debts. When lit, the giant figure made awful noises and moved his arms in agony as firecrackers exploded and human dancers circled the scene. Hundreds cheered from a safe distance. The excitement was over in less than ten minutes. When consumed by flames, Zozobra symbolically destroyed all gloom, making way for the joyful fiesta to follow.

The burning of Zozobra has been a Santa Fe Fiesta tradition, and the fiesta's most popular event, for more than eighty years. The ritual is essentially the same as it was at the first burning on September 1, 1926, although the monster puppet now stands as high as fifty feet and has sometimes resembled our nation's current enemies, as with Hitler in World War II and, most recently, with the al-Queda terrorist Osama bin Laden. Nationally famous, Zozobra has appeared in paintings, in movies, on T-shirts, and even in an award-winning float at the Rose Bowl Parade in Pasadena, California, in 1950. The bogeyman's annual destruction is one of the oldest community events in the United States.

Tourists caused many problems themselves. Coming from other states and from mainstream American culture, they did not always respect native cultures, customs, or values. Some tourists cheated unsuspecting natives when purchasing pottery, rugs, and other arts and crafts. Souvenir hunters searched for arrowheads, pottery shards, and other cultural artifacts to collect and take home, essentially stealing small bits of New Mexico history and culture. Some—but not all—archeologists confiscated larger pieces of New Mexico culture, including Indian bodies and artifacts taken from reservation cemeteries, for museum collections elsewhere in the country.

Not understanding native culture, some tourists returned home only to criticize what they had seen and heard in the Southwest. Anglos questioned the morality of certain Indian cultural practices, especially Indian dances. Many used words like "vulgar," "obscene," "pagan," and "devilish" to describe misunderstood Pueblo dances. Government officials used

Town Festivals Today

Festivals are still popular and lucrative for many towns today. Each event celebrates a location's history, culture, or special products. In addition to the New Mexico State Fair, county fairs, the Santa Fe Fiesta, and the Inter-Tribal Ceremonials, there are, among others:

Albuquerque International Hot Air
   Balloon Fiesta
Deming Duck Race
Billy the Kid Pageant in Lincoln
Lizard Races in Lovington
Festival of Cowboy Poets in Silver City
Hatch Chile Festival
Hillsboro Apple Festival
Indian Market in Santa Fe
Juneteenth in Hobbs

Miners' Day in White Oaks
Old-timers Day in Magdalena
Pancho Villa Day in Columbus
Route 66 Festival in Santa Clara
Smokey Bear Days in Capitán
Spanish Market in Santa Fe
Taos Film Festival
UFO Festival in Roswell
Whole Enchilada Festival in
   Las Cruces

The Arguments For and Against Indian Dances

The controversy over Indian dances began long before the 1920s. As early as 1897, a U.S. Army officer described Pueblo Indian dances as "the origin of great outrages." Capt. Charles E. Nordstrom claimed the Indians danced for every reason:

Is rain wanted? They dance. If there is a flood? They dance. . . . [If] the floods fail to subside, they immediately cast about them for a scapegoat, who is arrested and threatened as a witch. . . . whom they devote to torture. . . .
   The government [must stop these dances] through the strong arm of its arbitrary powers. Force [must be used to convince the Indians that] the government is in earnest.

(*Santa Fe New Mexican*, July 26, 1897.)

Almost twelve years later the editor of the *Santa Fe New Mexican* expressed a far different opinion of Indian dances when he announced that

on August 4, [1909,] one of the finest Pueblo dances to be witnessed will take place at Santo Domingo, about 40 miles south of Santa Fe. It is a gorgeous spectacle that is worth coming many miles to see and should be witnessed . . . by all those who can possibly make the trip, for the Pueblo dance is distinctly a pageant of the past.

(*Santa Fe New Mexican*, July 27, 1909.)

Witter Bynner and the Changes Caused by Tourism

Witter Bynner came to Santa Fe as a health seeker and stayed to become a leading member of the Santa Fe art community. Artists and authors gathered at his large adobe home almost every afternoon. Most admired Santa Fe but worried that the town had been compromised by tourists and businessmen interested in profit and spectacle, not history and culture, in the 1920s. Bynner wrote an article entitled "A City of Change" to criticize new trends and express his concerns about Santa Fe's future:

> We Americans from the outside have quickly made of Santa Fe the city of our discontent. It must be boosted, paved, enlarged, it must be Americanized.... The streets which were rough and made us go slowly are smooth now and make us go fast.... The little adobe houses near the Plaza have [been removed for] a bulk of garages, ... inviting blatant vehicles which hurry people's errands and harden their faces.... The outlying views are flecked and flanged now with billboards. There are campgrounds for the tourists.... Spanish gives way to English on the streets....
>
> To "attract and amuse the tourists," to make a show of our town, are we cutting down and withering its beauty? Are we killing ... the best qualities of Santa Fe, in order that a long line [of tourists] may come and look?

(Quoted in Sharyn R. Udall, *Spud Johnson and Laughing Horse* [Albuquerque: University of New Mexico Press, 1994], 264–70.)

similar terms. In 1923, the U.S. Indian commissioner in Washington, D.C., urged Native Americans to spend more time on their farms and less time at "dances, pow-wows, ceremonies, handling poisonous snakes, [and] torturing your bodies in these useless and harmful performances." Influenced by such remarks, "moral" reformers worked to ban Indian dances in the name of "civilized morality."

Artists, authors, and other defenders of Native American rights fought reformers with every literary weapon at their command. Magazine articles, poems, and letters to newspapers argued that Indians had every right to perform their dances as essential parts of their native cultures and religious beliefs. The fervor to ban Indian dances eventually cooled, but this misguided campaign represented yet another attempt to suppress Native American customs and Americanize southwestern Indians.

The New Oil and Gas Industry

Oil had been discovered in New Mexico as early as 1901 when a water well was being dug south of Carlsbad. No major discoveries were made until April 1924, however, when

> [oil] drillers decided that the well [they were working on] needed a stimulus. The practice of "shooting" in a well using explosives was common in the early days of the "oil patch." . . . Tex Thornton, a well-known "shooter" from Amarillo, was brought to the well . . . and he prepared three canisters of nitroglycerin to do the job. The residents of . . . Artesia heard that the well was to be "shot," and most of the town turned out for the event.
>
> [Tex] carefully lowered the first two canisters . . . into the well. As the third canister was being lowered, suddenly from deep within the earth came a roar, and the well came in—a gusher! The oil rushed up the drill hole. Recognizing the danger to the crew and spectators, Thornton quickly removed the third canister, which was just a few feet into the hole. The other two canisters, unexploded, were in the process of being brought up the drill hole by the rising head of oil. . . . [Tex] coolly reached into the flow of oil as it cleared the well head and caught the nitroglycerin canister. . . . He turned back to the flow in time to catch the second canister. The emergency was calmed without mishap, and the crowd cheered . . . as the oil flowed across the prairie of southeast New Mexico.

Other drilling followed. One of the most valuable oil fields in the entire country was discovered with the drilling of the Midwest State No. 1 well, on June 13, 1928, outside Hobbs. Midwest State No. 1 and its surrounding oil field proved to be so successful that Hobbs grew from a tiny community to become the fastest-growing town in the United States in 1930. According to an eyewitness at the time,

> Overnight the town sprung up. They came in Model T's, and other automobiles, they came in airplanes, and trucks and busses. Some even came on foot. . . . Where six months before only prairie had met the eye, a noisy raggle-taggle town of raw lumber store buildings, shacks and tents shot up.

Other valuable strikes in southeastern and northwestern New Mexico made oil and gas one of the most profitable industries in New Mexico. By 1929, New Mexico had become one of the major oil-producing states in the nation.

And what was good for the oil and gas industry was good for New Mexico state revenues, or income. The state government collected its first revenues from the oil and gas industry in 1924. By 1938, oil and gas revenues represented 82 percent of all state government income.

(Paige W. Christiansen, *The Story of Oil in New Mexico*. [Socorro: New Mexico Bureau of Mines and Mineral Resources, 1989], 23, 26–30.)

☼ Poverty

While art, tourism, the health industry, and oil and gas companies prospered in New Mexico in the 1920s, other parts of the economy did not. This was particularly true in the coal-mining industry. Mining communities in Colfax, McKinley, and Santa Fe counties did well during World War I when they profited from the great demand for coal to fuel the nation's factories and railroads. The demand for coal declined in the 1920s, though, with the end of the war and the competition of more modern fuels, especially oil and gas. Coal production in Dawson, one of the largest coal camps in New Mexico, dropped by half from 1917 to 1929.

Oil and gas regions of
New Mexico
....

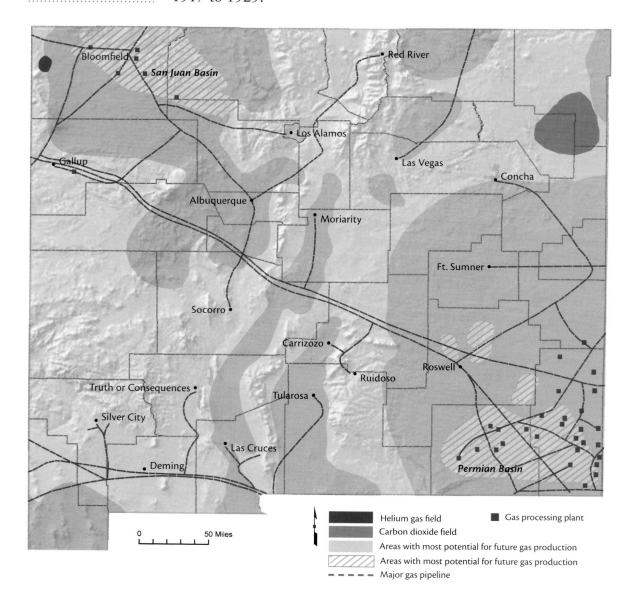

■ Helium gas field	■ Gas processing plant
Carbon dioxide field	
Areas with most potential for future gas production	
▨ Areas with most potential for future gas production	
– – – – Major gas pipeline	

0   50 Miles

▲▲▲▲▲▲▲▲▲▲▲▲▲▲▲▲▲▲▲▲▲▲▲▲▲▲▲▲▲▲▲▲▲▲

Two Tragedies in Dawson

The Phelps Dodge Corporation owned and operated the Dawson coal mines and camp from 1905 to 1950. The camp was a thriving community, with a great mixture of immigrant groups and generally safe working conditions.

Unfortunately, Dawson is probably best known for two mining disasters that struck almost exactly ten years apart. The first mine explosion occurred on October 23, 1913, when 265 men lost their lives in the second worst tragedy of its kind in U.S. history. (An explosion in a West Virginia mine had taken 362 lives in 1907.)

Tragedy struck Dawson again on Thursday, February 8, 1923. Celso Chávez, a student, later recalled that at 2:30 in the afternoon,

> I was in manual training class at the Downtown School when we heard the blast. R. Dye was our teacher. Several of the boys in the class, [including] Henry Dupont [and] Terence Scanlon . . . had fathers up at the mine, so there was worry. Right away we jumped into Mr. Dye's car. . . . When we got to the entrance of the mine, there were people moaning and all. But Mr. Dupont was out there directing traffic [and Mr. Scanlon] was in the electrician's office, so he was okay, too.
>
> (Quoted in Toby Smith, *Coal Town: The Life and Times of Dawson, New Mexico* [Santa Fe: Ancient City Press, 1993], 67–68.)

The Dupont and Scanlon families were fortunate. There were 120 miners who never made it to safety, although rescue crews from as far away as Wyoming worked to free them for twenty hours. Only two miners were rescued. The bodies of the remaining 120 men were laid out for identification at the Dawson Opera House before they were taken in mule-drawn wagons to the town cemetery for burial.

Today Dawson is abandoned, but row after row of white crosses at the cemetery remain to remind us of the hundreds of men lost in 1913 and 1923.

Farmers and ranchers also suffered after a brief period of high profits during the war. By the 1920s, many men from small Hispanic villages migrated as far away as California and Montana to find jobs as farm laborers, as sheep herders, or in whatever other work was available. Away for many months of the year, the men sent money home to their families and lived on what little was left.

Other farmers and ranchers faced additional problems with drought and lower crop prices. Homesteaders who had proven up were often forced to leave the land they and their families had worked so hard to obtain. Some moved to large towns or cities, like Albuquerque, while others left the state, never to return.

Ranchers and Farmers Suffered

Agnes Morley and her family had lived on a cattle ranch in southern New Mexico for thirty-five years before they faced especially hard economic times in the 1920s. Agnes described her family's plight in her famous memoir, *No Life for a Lady*:

> Cattlemen everywhere overstocked their ranges—an irresistible temptation since [the demand was so great and] three-year-old steers brought 60 to 80 dollars a head [during World War I. But] then, without warning, . . . the cattle boom collapsed. This disaster was followed by a protracted drought, and everybody's ranges became a very tragic spectacle. Mass starvation [of cattle] is not pleasant to contemplate. . . .
>
> The New Mexico Cattle and Horse Growers Association, of which [my brother] Ray was then president, decided on a drastic move. They sent Ray . . . to negotiate [an agreement] with Mexico, whereby the starving herds of the Southwest could be sent over the border into Chihuahua, where grass was knee-high and scarcely an animal left to eat it. [The plan was to bring the

cattle back when conditions improved in New Mexico.] But deep in our hearts . . . we really didn't believe it, and we were right.

Homesteaders were no better off in the region west of the Morleys' ranch, near Pie Town, New Mexico. Agnes recalled that

> I watched the homesteaders as they trekked by. They came in family groups, in any sort of conveyance that would roll. . . . "On to Pie Town," Ray would say as the slow caravans passed [by our ranch. But, having arrived, each of these pioneers] soon . . . had to face the hard fact that his [land] could not support his family. His bean crop failed far too frequently, his little patch of corn wilted with too great regularity under prolonged drought. Beaten, he gave up and moved on, or back to where he had started from. . . . "Back from Pie Town," we said, and felt compassionate as we watched the sad little parade retracing its steps.

(Agnes Morley Cleaveland, *No Life for a Lady* [Lincoln: University of Nebraska Press, 1977], 308–12, 332–33.)

Conclusions

New Mexico had become a state of great contrasts by the 1920s. On the one hand, many New Mexicans enjoyed relative success and prosperity, especially as artists, authors, health providers, those involved in the tourist business, and those who developed new oil and gas fields. On the other hand, many New Mexicans suffered little or no growth, especially farmers, ranchers, and coal miners.

As in most parts of the world, most modern change took place in New Mexico's few cities, or urban centers, while fewer changes and greater poverty characterized more rural sections of the state. It was as if the state were divided into two groups, with one traveling at one speed while the other traveled at a slower speed, for better or worse. New Mexico has traveled at these different rates of speed, with radically different results, ever since.

1. What attracted artists to New Mexico to form art colonies in Taos and Santa Fe?
2. How did the Taos Society of Artists succeed, and what was its impact on New Mexico?
3. Why did Mabel Dodge Luhan invite artists and authors to her home in Taos?
4. How did artists and authors help preserve and encourage New Mexico's cultures?
5. How did anthropologists and historians help preserve New Mexico's cultures?
6. What male-dominated professions did women enter in at least small numbers by the 1920s? Give four examples of these professions and the women who entered them.
7. What attracted lungers to New Mexico?
8. Why did New Mexico invite lungers to chase the cure in the Southwest?
9. How successful were lungers in chasing the cure in New Mexico?
10. What life lessons can we learn from the experiences of lungers like Clinton P. Anderson and Katherine Otero-Stinson?
11. What made automobile travel so difficult in the early years of the twentieth century?
12. What attracted tourists to New Mexico?
13. How did New Mexico benefit from tourism?
14. What problems did tourism cause in New Mexico, especially for Native Americans?
15. How did the new oil and gas industry help New Mexico? What problems might it have caused?

16. What parts of the economy suffered the most losses in the 1920s? Why? What did workers in these sectors of the economy often do to survive?
17. List the new groups of people who arrived in New Mexico in increasing numbers during the 1920s. Now list the groups of people who often left New Mexico in increasing numbers in this decade. What was the overall impact of these movements?
18. Which of the following groups can be said to have helped other groups in the 1920s? Which groups did they help? How? Why?

artists   lungers
authors   Native Americans
businessmen   tourists
Hispanics

19. Which of the following groups can be said to have exploited (taken advantage of) other groups in the 1920s? Which groups did they exploit? How? Why?

artists   businessmen
authors   tourists

20. What aspects of New Mexico would you have been proud of if you had lived in the 1920s? Why?
21. What aspects of New Mexico would you have been less proud of if you had lived in the 1920s? Why?
22. What lessons can we learn from the history of New Mexico in the 1920s?

The 1920s
Minority Rights, Prohibition, and a National Scandal

TIMELINE

1919

New Mexico ratifies the Eighteenth Amendment

The Eighteenth Amendment, establishing national Prohibition, is added to the U.S. Constitution

1920

New Mexico ratifies the Nineteenth Amendment, and it is added to the U.S. Constitution later that same year

1921

An amendment to the New Mexico state constitution guarantees women the right to run for all public offices

1922

New Mexico's "Monkey Trial" is held in Fort Sumner

Nina Otero-Warren is the first woman in New Mexico to run for the U.S. Congress

Soledad Chávez de Chacón is elected as New Mexico's first woman secretary of state

Bertha M. Paxton is the first woman elected to the New Mexico House of Representatives

The Bursum Bill is introduced in the U.S. Senate but later defeated

The All Pueblo Council is founded

1924

The Indian Citizenship Act is passed by the U.S. Congress

Louise Holland Coe is the first woman elected to the New Mexico State Senate

Soledad Chávez de Chacón becomes the first woman governor of New Mexico for sixteen days

1927

Taos Pueblo leaders sign a Cooperative Use Agreement regarding Blue Lake

1929

Louise Holland Coe is the first woman to serve as president pro tempore in the New Mexico State Senate

Albert B. Fall is convicted of taking a bribe

1933

National Prohibition is repealed

Introduction

New Mexico had clearly experienced major social, economic, and cultural changes in the 1920s. The state also experienced considerable political change, starting with some hard-fought victories in the struggle for women's rights. Unfortunately, while much was gained, much remained the same, as many Hispanics, Blacks, and Native Americans still suffered from unfair, often cruel discrimination. In other unfortunate developments, the "noble experiment" known as Prohibition failed, and a famous New Mexico leader became the center of national attention in the country's worst political scandal of the early twentieth century.

The purpose of this chapter is to teach you

- how women won the right to vote and hold all political offices;
- how minorities, including Blacks, Hispanics, and Native Americans, still suffered racism;
- why Prohibition did not work;
- and how the Teapot Dome scandal affected New Mexico and led to the downfall of a famous New Mexico citizen.

Women's Suffrage

By 1914, eleven far western states, and much of the rest of the nation, had amended their state constitutions to guarantee women the right to vote, or suffrage. New Mexico was the only far western state that had not yet taken this vital step. The New Mexico state constitution of 1910 had allowed women to vote in local school board elections, but even this limited right could be denied if a majority of male voters in a county voted to eliminate it.

Why was New Mexico one of the last states to guarantee this most basic right of citizenship? Many male—and female—opponents of women's suffrage came from Hispanic and Anglo families with very traditional ideas about the proper role of women in the home and in society. According to these conservative values, women should remain at home where their high sense of morality could be protected against the tarnished, corrupt world of politics and business. With their moral standards protected, women could raise their children to be good future citizens, while positively influencing their husbands, who would, in turn, vote on behalf of their entire families. In the words of John J. Kenney of Santa Fe, women were far "more refined, more virtuous, [and] more spiritual" than men. If a woman entered the political arena and voted, she would inevitably compromise her natural goodness. As Kenney put it in 1917, "What touches mud is stained." According to Kenney and those of a similar mind, women should "point the way" with high moral standards at home, while men must go off to "scale the perilous cliff" in the dangerous realm of politics.

Not all women—or men—agreed with these ideas, especially John Kenney's sister-in-law, **Nina Otero-Warren**. Born into the powerful Otero family of Los Lunas, Nina had spent most of her life in Santa Fe, where she became a strong proponent of women's rights. Bilingual and

Nina Otero-Warren

Women's suffrage float in Silver City parade

well educated, Nina was in an ideal position to pressure law-makers because her uncle was the most powerful leader at New Mexico's state constitutional convention of 1910. Influenced by his young niece, Solomon Luna was largely responsible for including article 7, section 1, of the state constitution, which allowed women at least limited suffrage and the right to hold office in local school board elections.

Nina Otero-Warren and other reformers were not satisfied with this partial victory. Over the next decade, they continued to **lobby** political leaders in Santa Fe and Washington, D.C. It was an uphill climb. New Mexico's conservative U.S. Senator Thomas Catron was so opposed to women's suffrage that women who went to argue their case in his office usually left feeling that their only purpose in life was "to stay home, have children, have more children, cook, and wash dishes."

Progress was slow in the New Mexico state legislature as well. A bill to grant women the right to vote was defeated in 1917 but by a slim four votes. Encouraged by national suffrage leaders like Alice Paul, Otero-Warren worked hard to have the **Nineteenth Amendment** to the U.S. Constitution **ratified**, or approved, by New Mexico's state legislature. Never resorting to hunger strikes or other extreme measures that might well have alienated conservative males, Otero-Warren and her fellow activists preferred to quietly, but persistently, convince legislators to vote for ratification. Although no American—male or female—should have to earn his or her rights, suffragettes strengthened their argument by reminding male leaders of the great contributions women had made in World War I. Only women like Otero-Warren, who knew New Mexico's cultures and traditional values, could have argued so well and used their political skills so wisely.

To the suffragettes' relief, New Mexico state legislators passed the Nineteenth Amendment in February 1920, making New Mexico the thirty-second state in the Union to approve this major reform. Six months later the amendment was officially ratified when 75 percent of the states had approved it, as the U.S. Constitution required.

Women in New Mexico finally cast their first votes in local, state, and national elections in November 1920. The total number of New Mexico citizens who voted in the 1920 presidential election represented a 58 percent increase over the number who had voted in the presidential election of 1916. While not all of these additional voters were women, such an increase shows that a great number of women in New Mexico exercised their long-awaited right to vote with serious intent and enthusiasm.

The Nineteenth Amendment to the U.S. Constitution

The Nineteenth Amendment to the U.S. Constitution reads:

> The right of citizens of the United States to vote shall not be denied or abridged by the United States or by any State on account of sex.

Having won the right to vote, women were also eager to win the right to serve in all public offices. An amendment to the New Mexico state constitution, extending this basic right to women, was passed by a vote of 26,744 to 19,751 in a special election in 1921. Nina Otero-Warren became the first woman to run for the U.S. Congress from New Mexico, although she was defeated following a hard-fought campaign in 1922. That same year, thirty-two-year-old **Soledad Chávez de Chacón** was elected as New Mexico's first female secretary of state. Two years later, when **Gov. James F. Hinkle** was out of state and his lieutenant governor had died in office, Chávez de Chacón became the first woman governor in New Mexico history. She also became the first Hispanic woman to ever serve as a state governor anywhere in the United States. Her term in office lasted only sixteen days, until Governor Hinkle's return, but it was a large step forward for women's rights.

While many applauded Chávez de Chacón's brief service, some were not ready for even this limited change. Five days after Chávez de Chacón's short term began, the editor of the *Alamogordo News* wrote that a woman in public office was likely "to be mannish and lacking in many feminine qualities." Such criticism served as a reminder that while women had achieved much in the 1920s, there was still much to be done to secure their full rights as American citizens.

Soledad Chávez de Chacón

☀ Civil Rights

Segregated Schools

Blacks

Much also needed to be done to protect Black **civil rights** in the 1920s. Instead of making progress in this decade, most Black New Mexicans experienced increased discrimination, especially in public schools. Although the state constitution of 1910 banned segregation in New Mexico schools, the ban affected "children of Spanish descent" only. Black students were clearly not protected by the constitution when the state legislature passed

Women Firsts in New Mexico Political Office

- In 1922, Republican Nina Otero-Warren of Santa Fe became the first New Mexico woman to run for the U.S. Congress, although she lost to Democrat John R. Morrow;
- In 1922, Democrat Soledad Chávez de Chacón of Albuquerque became the first woman to be elected as New Mexico's secretary of state. This important office has been held by women ever since;
- **Bertha M. Paxton**, a Democrat representing Doña Ana County from 1923 to 1924, was the first woman elected to the New Mexico State House of Representatives;
- In 1924, the secretary of state, Soledad Chávez de Chacón, became New Mexico's first female governor when Gov. James Hinkle was out of state and his lieutenant governor had died; her term in office lasted sixteen days, until Governor Hinkle's return;
- **Louise Holland Coe**, a Democrat, was the first woman elected to the New Mexico State Senate. At various times she represented parts of Lincoln, Otero, Torrance, and Socorro counties, serving from 1925 to 1941;
- Louise Holland Coe was also the first—and only—woman to serve as president pro tempore of the New Mexico State Senate, 1929–41;
- **Georgia Lee Witt Lusk**, a Democrat from Carlsbad, was the first woman elected to the U.S. House of Representatives from New Mexico. She served one term in Congress, from 1947 to 1949. It would be another fifty years before another woman, Republican Heather Wilson, was elected to represent New Mexico;
- **Petra Jiménez Maes**, one of the first two Hispanic women to graduate from the University of New Mexico's law school (in 1973), became the first woman to serve as the chief justice of the New Mexico Supreme Court when she was unanimously elected by her fellow Supreme Court judges in January 2003;
- **Diane Denish**, a Democrat from Hobbs, was elected as New Mexico's first female lieutenant governor in 2002. Reelected by a wide margin in 2006, she frequently served as governor while Gov. Bill Richardson was out of state;
- **Susana Martinez**, a Republican, became New Mexico's first elected female governor in 2011. She also became the first elected Hispanic female governor in American history.

new **Jim Crow** laws in the 1920s, allowing local school boards to provide "separate rooms for the teaching of pupils of African descent." Defending this law, one state legislator declared in 1923, "It is disgraceful . . . to put the Negroes on an equality with the whites. . . . When the Negroes try to push themselves up to the level of our fair women I think they should be pushed back further than they were in the days of slavery."

▲▲▲▲▲▲▲▲▲▲▲▲▲▲▲▲▲▲▲▲▲▲▲▲▲▲▲▲▲▲▲

Octaviano A. Larrazolo and Other State Governors of the 1920s

Octaviano A. Larrazolo, Republican, 1919–21

Born in Allende, Mexico, Octaviano A. Larrazolo came to the United States to attend school in Arizona and New Mexico when he was only ten years old. Later, while a lawyer practicing in Las Vegas, New Mexico, he entered politics and became well known as a great orator in both Spanish and English. In fact, when he was elected New Mexico's second Hispanic state governor (and the first Mexican-born governor in New Mexico history), he delivered his inaugural address in English and then in Spanish. Recalling his own road to success, he told young listeners at his inaugural:

> Be not disheartened by the circumstance of birth; . . . within the pale of law, you all stand on an equal plane, with equal rights and privileges and with equal opportunities. . . . [In] the land of the stars and stripes there are no privileged classes, [as] the avenues to place and distinction are open equally to all.
>
> (Inaugural address quoted in Paul F. Larrazolo, *Octaviano A. Larrazolo: A Moment in New Mexico History* [New York: Carlton Press, 1986], 103.)

Octaviano Larrazolo was later elected to the U.S. Senate, becoming the first Hispanic senator in American history. Devoted to creating opportunities for the young, just as educational opportunities had been created for him in his youth, Larrazolo worked hard to limit child labor, establish compulsory education, create a bilingual education program, and encourage vocational education in New Mexico.

New Mexico's five other governors in the 1920s were

- Merritt C. Mechem, Republican, 1921–22
- James F. Hinkle, Democrat, 1923–24
- Soledad Chávez de Chacón, Democrat, sixteen days in 1924
- Arthur F. Hannett, Democrat, 1925–26
- Richard C. Dillon, Republican, 1927–30

While most towns in the state did not exercise their option and segregate Black children, many in the southern and eastern parts of the state did. Separate schools were created in Alamogordo, Carlsbad, Clovis, Hobbs, Las Cruces, Roswell, Tucumcari, and Vado. Sadly, members of Frank Boyer's family, the same family that had journeyed thousands of miles to create Blackdom and escape racism in the South, now faced racism and segregated schools in their new home in Vado.

Albuquerque schools were not officially segregated, but Black students were seldom treated equally with other children. They were often

Jim Crow Laws

Jim Crow laws enforced the segregation of public facilities "from cradle [when we are born] to grave [when we die]," including the following facilities:

- public bathrooms
- beauty and barber shops
- buses
- cemeteries
- hospitals
- hotels and motels
- lunch counters

- many stores
- movie theaters
- restaurants and bars
- schools
- swimming pools
- trains
- water fountains

Excluding the Negro

Extreme racists called for action beyond the segregation of Blacks and whites in New Mexico. An editorial in the *Ratón Range* asserted:

All of the peace officers on the eastern borders of the state have had a constant problem in the worthless and "bad" negroes [*sic*]. . . . The good negro is a useful member of the community . . . , but unfortunately his coming is always attended by the arrival of bad negroes, an element of [the] population which is not good for any town. It is hard to tell which [negro] is good and which is bad, at first sight. The safer plan is to keep them all out.

(Editorial, *Ratón Range*, November 26, 1931.)

Fortunately, no one in Ratón or the rest of the state followed this unfair, unjust, racist advice. Unfortunately, racism in hiring Blacks and other minorities still existed, as shown in the want ads of many state newspapers:

```
Wanted—A white
woman for house-
work and cooking.
Bandy Ranch.
(New Mexico State
Tribune, April 28,
1930.)
```

```
Wanted—Dishwasher;
white girl. Brown
Bobby Inn. Apply
in person.
(Santa Fe New Mexi-
can, June 4, 1930.)
```

```
Wanted—Colored man
to wash cars; must
have some experi-
ence. Apply Philips
Petroleum Co.
(Santa Fe New Mexi-
can, June 5, 1930.)
```

Far worse, racism sometimes led to Blacks being found guilty of crimes they may not have committed. Two Black men were executed in New Mexico's electric chair (in 1933 and 1947) for the murders of white women, although historians now doubt their guilt, based on a lack of evidence and the racism of the era in which they lived.

made to sit in the back of their classrooms, and, at graduation, they were deliberately placed in the center of the procession line so they were never in a position to lead their graduating class either in or out of the assembly hall. Even the Albuquerque High School yearbook was "segregated": photos of Black graduates were always placed last in yearbooks from 1919 until 1942.

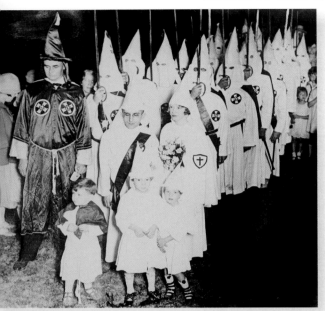

Ku Klux Klan parade with children

As in much of the United States, racism in New Mexico was largely fueled by the Ku Klux Klan (KKK). While never as large or as powerful as in other states, the KKK in New Mexico held secret meetings and recruited new members by posing as a highly patriotic, strictly moral organization. The Klan intimidated individuals and burned crosses in scattered parts of New Mexico, including on a hill overlooking Albuquerque where a twenty-five-foot-high cross burned for nearly an hour in early September 1923. Fortunately, most New Mexicans recognized the KKK for what it was: a hate-filled, destructive enemy of American civil rights. Brave New Mexicans denounced the KKK; in the words of Gov. Merritt C. Mechem in 1921, "I am absolutely opposed to the Ku Klux Klan and [its] law-breaking methods." An anti-Klan bill was enacted in 1923, although the new law was rather weak and had no impact on stopping the spread of racism and ending the practice of segregation in public facilities, especially in public schools in the eastern portion of the state.

Segregated Schools

Hispanics

Hispanics also felt the sting of racism, especially in education. Although legally protected against segregated schools by the New Mexico state constitution, Hispanic children were often separated and made to feel inferior because of their language, their culture, and their ethnicity.

Mari-Luci Jaramillo's experiences were sadly typical. Born in 1928, she lived in East Las Vegas, a largely Anglo community. Wearing a dress made of material from a flour sack, Mari-Luci went to her first day of school "speaking absolutely no English." As she later recalled in her autobiography, she could not afford to buy school milk and was embarrassed by her lunch sandwiches made with tortillas rather than with bread. Worse, she and other Hispanic children were separated in different rooms from

One Hundred Percent Americanism

Teachers of the 1920s insisted that Hispanic children learn English so they could succeed not only in class but also at work when they were old enough to be employed. Some educators also believed that everyone should speak English to be good American citizens at a time when many citizens in the United States insisted on nothing less than **100 percent Americanism**. To be anything less than 100 percent American in language and culture was to be unpatriotic in an age of intolerance not unlike the extreme intolerance of World War I.

Both Hispanic and Anglo teachers used the **"direct method"** to teach English in the 1920s. According to this method, Spanish speakers were segregated in the first grade, where they heard and spoke only English, until they had mastered enough English to proceed into regular first grade classes.

The direct method worked for some children but often at the expense of the students' dignity, leaving them at least one year behind their peers at the very beginning of their school lives. Educators like Nina Otero-Warren attempted to restore student dignity by celebrating Hispanic culture in New Mexico's schoolbooks. On one of the first pages of her book, *Old Spain in Our Southwest*, Otero-Warren wrote:

> The Spanish descendant of the conquistadores may be poor, but he takes his place in life with a noble bearing, for he can never forget that he is a descendant of the conquerors.

(Nina Otero-Warren, *Old Spain in Our Southwest* [New York: Harcourt, Brace and Company, 1936], 9.)

Books like *Old Spain in Our Southwest* were, however, too few and were often read too late to salvage lost pride for a generation of Hispanic children.

their Anglo peers. By the sixth grade Hispanic children were even kept on "their side" of the school building at recess. Anglo children joined Anglo clubs, while "most Spanish Americans didn't join any clubs." Teachers were particularly mean to Hispanic boys, hitting them with rulers and sometimes not letting them go to the bathroom. Students were punished for speaking Spanish, and even Mari-Luci's favorite teacher urged her to deny that she was Hispanic. In Mari-Luci's words, "There was no overt pride or joy in being a Spanish-American."

Such treatment severely affected Hispanic children. Many fell behind in their studies or simply dropped out of school, closing the gate to a wide range of opportunities in their lives. Other children survived discrimination, especially if they had strong, proud parents. Mari-Luci remembers

Hispanic Mutual Aid Societies

Hispanic citizens of New Mexico often defended their interests and rights by organizing or joining *sociedades mutualistas* (**mutual aid societies**). As they had done since Spanish colonial days, Hispanics banded together to assist one another, especially in times of personal need. When a member died, for example, mutual aid societies helped pay for a dignified funeral and helped his widow and children with low-cost life insurance. Societies also helped defend members' rights against forces of modern change, like the railroad, that often threatened their traditional rural lives and culture.

Mutual aid societies were especially popular in the early twentieth century when Hispanics felt an increased need to unify and cooperate in their own best interests. In 1900, Hispanics organized the Sociedad Protección Mutual de Trabajadores Unidos, which soon became one of the largest, most influential societies in the Southwest, with sixty-five local *concilios* (lodges) in New Mexico, Colorado, and Utah. National societies, like the Alianza Hispano-Americana, helped empower members and defend Hispanic culture against movements like 100 percent Americanism.

her shoemaker father "teaching us children to be sure of ourselves, become educated, and be proud of who we were. His love and pride in his culture . . . rubbed off on us and I never felt inferior to the Anglo kids in school." Strengthened by this confidence, Mari-Luci finished high school, graduated from college, taught school, became a vice president at the University of New Mexico, and served as the U.S. ambassador to Honduras. She declared that "while once I was afraid to eat a tortilla in public, now I had spoken as an equal with world leaders."

Although confronted with obstacles, Mari-Luci and many Hispanic children drew strength from their proud heritage to become successful, fulfilled adults. Children who are not taught the value of their traditions often stuggle with their cultural identity, facing frustrations their entire lives.

Indian Rights

The Bursum Bill

Pueblo Indian rights were directly threatened in several ways in the 1920s. Native American children were still forced to attend boarding schools, where their cultures were suppressed as part of an ongoing effort to make them "100 percent American." Reformers attempted to ban Indian dances, criticizing them as pagan and "uncivilized." Further, in 1924, the U.S. Congress granted U.S. citizenship to all Native Americans, guaranteeing their right to vote, in all states but two, New Mexico and Arizona. Provisions in the New Mexico state constitution still limited Indian suffrage to Native Americans who lived off of their tribal reservations.

In yet another threat to Native American rights, New Mexico's U.S. Senator H. O. Bursum proposed a new federal law in 1922. Known as the **Bursum Bill**, the law would have given title of much Pueblo land to non-Indians who had long occupied property on pueblo borders. Learning that the Bursum Bill was about to be passed by the Senate in early 1923, more than sixty artists, authors, and anthropologists shot off round after round of literary protests. Alerted of the bill's progress in the Senate, Pueblo leaders like Tony Luján in Taos organized the **All Pueblo Council** to battle Bursum's plans.

Using every peaceful means at their command, from petitions to testimony in Washington, D.C., Pueblo leaders and their allies argued that, if passed, the Bursum Bill would destroy not only Indian resources but also Indian culture based on land and its spiritual importance. As a result of these well-coordinated efforts, the Bursum Bill was defeated in Congress to the great relief of Pueblo communities throughout New Mexico. The Pueblos had defended their rights and, in the process, developed new political and organizational skills they could use in future political struggles.

The Struggle for Blue Lake

Tribal leaders in Taos Pueblo attempted to use these political skills in defending **Blue Lake**, a place of great spiritual importance in their native religion. Blue Lake, located high in the Sangre de Cristo Mountains, is considered the source of all life for the people of Taos Pueblo. In the words of tribal leaders in 1927, the lake was "like a church to us," where Taos Indians went to pray and worship in private, much as other worshipers attended church without outside interference in their freedom of religion.

Taos Pueblo's ownership of Blue Lake was suddenly compromised in 1906, however, when the U.S. government made most of the Sangre de Cristo Mountains part of the Carson National Forest. Ironically, while national forests were created to help preserve forests and the natural resources found within them, the creation of the Carson National Forest served to threaten the Taos Indians' most precious spiritual resource, Blue Lake. As part of the national forest, the lake was now available to campers, hikers, and hunters who frequently contaminated the lake's water, left trash, and interrupted Indian religious services, especially during the important summer months.

Tribal leaders finally signed a Cooperative Use Agreement with the National Forest Service in 1927. According to this agreement, the Forest Service pledged to protect Blue Lake from pollution and only allow non-Indian visitors into the area if they had written permission. These promises meant little in reality, though. To the horror of Taos Pueblo Indians, in 1928, the Forest Service cut trees and built a log cabin, an outhouse, garbage pits, and horse corrals within a short distance from Blue Lake. That same year as many as a hundred non-Indian visitors received written permission to visit the area, often interrupting private Indian ceremonies. Taos Pueblo's religious rights were no better protected than before the 1927 agreement had been negotiated and signed. The issue of Blue Lake was hardly resolved by the end of the 1920s.

The women's temperance movement in the United States had a long history, as reflected in this 1874 Currier and Ives print

Prohibition

In addition to the Nineteenth Amendment, a second, equally controversial amendment was added to the U.S. Constitution at the outset of the 1920s. The **Eighteenth Amendment**, or Prohibition, prohibited the manufacture and sale of alcohol. Like the women's suffrage amendment, Prohibition had been enacted in many states before it became a national statute, the product of a long history of heated debates.

Few denied the potential evils of alcohol. Most people agreed that excessive drinking could cause the loss of health, values, income, jobs, family, friends, and life itself. The **Women's Christian Temperance Union (WCTU)**, the most powerful temperance organization in the nation, identified saloons, like Albuquerque's infamous Bucket of Blood, as centers of vice and violence. Drinking had to be eliminated in the name of Christian morality and modern civilization. While some extremists resorted to breaking up saloons with hatchets, most reformers in New Mexico used more peaceful methods of persuasion, like those used in the fight for women's suffrage. New Mexico ratified the Eighteenth Amendment, which created national

Rumrunner's car

Prohibition, on January 20, 1919. Prohibition officially began a year later, on January 16, 1920.

Creating Prohibition and enforcing it were, of course, two different matters in New Mexico. Many Hispanic residents, as well as immigrants from countries like Germany and Italy, had been making beer or wine as a cultural tradition for generations; they seldom drank to excess and saw no need to stop consuming alcohol, especially during cultural holidays. Also, with ingredients and equipment easily obtainable, many people entered the business of making and selling liquor as a new source of badly needed income. Mexico's nearby location made it easy to bring liquor across the border packed in or on every form of transportation, from cars and trucks to airplanes and pack mules.

Prohibition drew both ordinary and infamous outlaws to New Mexico. In the most famous arrest of the Prohibition era, a man calling himself Franklin Turner was apprehended near Alamogordo and charged with transporting liquor from Mexico by car in early 1927. Closer investigation revealed that Franklin Turner was none other than the notorious "Machine Gun" Kelly. Kelly quickly posted bail and was on his way. Alphonse "Al" Capone, the most famous bootlegger in the entire United States, often vacationed in Jémez and at Fenton Lake, accompanied by an army of personal bodyguards. A special FBI agent was assigned to keep an eye on the Chicago-based outlaw, although there is no evidence that Capone engaged in any illegal business activities during his leisurely visits to New Mexico.

Prohibition was especially hard to enforce in New Mexico because, as the nation's fourth largest state, stills to make illegal liquor could be hidden in any number of far-off, isolated locations. Innovative New Mexicans built stills not only on farms and ranches but also on mountains, on mesas, and in valleys. At least one still was found in Carlsbad Caverns. So much moonshine, or illegally produced liquor, was manufactured in an

▲▲▲▲▲▲▲▲▲▲▲▲▲▲▲▲▲▲▲▲▲▲▲▲▲▲▲▲▲

Prohibition Lingo

Drys:	men and women who supported Prohibition
Wets:	men and women who opposed Prohibition
Stills:	equipment used to produce illegal liquor, especially whiskey
Moonshine:	illegally produced liquor, especially whiskey
White lightning, white mule, or mula:	illegally produced liquor, especially strong whiskey
Bathtub gin:	home-made gin, produced in bathtubs
Rumrunners:	men and women who transported illegally produced liquor
Bootleggers:	men and women who sold illegally produced liquor
Speakeasies:	illegal bars that sold illegally produced liquor
Revenuers:	government agents who investigated violators of Prohibition

isolated canyon in Catron County that the place became known as Moon-shine Canyon.

While many prospered from the manufacture and transport of liquor, others profited from its sale. Bootleggers made convenient home deliveries or were so well known that even strangers were able to purchase liquor within an hour of their arrival in cities like Albuquerque or Santa Fe; bellboys at the Alvarado Harvey House were known to be especially helpful in identifying local sources of liquor. Saloons closed, but speakeasies, or illegal bars, that became fashionable hangouts for drinkers from all levels of society quickly replaced them.

Many New Mexicans—and other Americans—spoke of the virtues of Prohibition, while regularly ignoring its rules. Even judges, governors, and senators drank in private and, discreetly, at public gatherings. While Senator Bronson Cutting's newspaper, the *Santa Fe New Mexican*, had stated in 1917 that Prohibition would make New Mexicans "happier . . . and more prosperous," Cutting was known to keep one of the finest wine cellars in the entire Southwest in the 1920s. Artists and authors attended daily "teas" at poet Witter Bynner's elaborate home in Santa Fe, while guests at Mabel Dodge Luhan's home in Taos seldom suffered from thirst at her frequent social gatherings. Artists like Will Schuster kept stills in their own backyards for easy access to their homemade whiskey supply.

To make matters worse, Prohibition was difficult and often dangerous to enforce. Local lawmen seldom attempted to enforce the unpopular law, claiming that residents in their communities recognized them

The Still in Apache Canyon

Tomás Brown and two of his teenage friends had heard rumors about a still located in an isolated place called Apache Canyon. Young Tomás told about his adventure in Apache Canyon in his memoirs:

> One morning the three of us took off bareback on our horses for a day of exploration [in the canyon]. We hadn't searched in ... the canyon more than a couple of hours before we could detect an odor not related to either piñon or cedar.... [C]onvinced that we must be very near to the hidden still we dismounted and hid our horses.... Continuing on foot and following the origin of the odor of fermenting corn we soon found the camouflaged entrance of a well-hidden cave.
>
> We ... slowly entered a place far different from any we had ever seen before. In the semidarkness we were able to see vats, ... jars, whiskey barrels, and all sorts of equipment unfamiliar to any of us. Lawrence suggested lighting a match, but Lee said something about there being sufficient alcohol fumes in the cave to cause [a major] explosion if ignited.
>
> After being inside a short time we heard, or imagined we did, the sound of approaching hoof beats.... As we started to quietly slip out of the cave one of us overturned a piece of equipment, causing a thunderous roar that I'm sure could be heard outside for a mile in every direction. We all ran wildly for our horses....
>
> After that, when hearing people talk of the mysterious still, we three would glance at one another knowing we knew something most people didn't know about that particular mystery.

(Tomás Brown, *Heritage of the New Mexico Frontier* [New York: Vantage Press, 1985], 86–88.)

long before they could get anywhere near enough to stills and speakeasies to make arrests. Only eleven federal Prohibition agents were assigned to New Mexico, far too few to be effective; their movements were easily followed, making it possible to warn illegal operators when "revenuers" were headed in their direction. Further, federal agents who were too diligent in their duties could face dire consequences. Prohibition agent Ray Sutton disappeared while working a case in northeastern New Mexico; only his car was found on an isolated stretch of rural road in 1930.

By the early 1930s, many New Mexicans joined thousands of their fellow Americans in questioning whether Prohibition could ever be properly enforced. Critics began to call for the **repeal** of Prohibition, arguing that it not only caused crime but also created a lack of respect for law and order in general. In 1926, Prohibition agents made 571 arrests in New Mexico; in 1927 there were 773. Courts were so jammed that special "bootlegger days" had to be held to help clear court dockets. Uninspected liquor was sometimes lethal, and the number of driving while intoxicated (DWI) cases increased each year. Perhaps most disturbingly, New Mexicans noted a dangerous increase in the drinking of alcohol by younger and younger children. Ironically, instead of stopping

▲▲▲▲▲▲▲▲▲▲▲▲▲▲▲▲▲▲▲▲▲▲▲▲▲▲▲▲▲▲▲▲▲▲▲▲

Prohibition Agent Howard S. Beacham

Howard S. Beacham was the most committed federal Prohibition agent in New Mexico in the 1920s. He was so devoted to catching moonshiners, rumrunners, and bootleggers in southern New Mexico that he took a photo of every crime scene at which he made an arrest. Agent Beacham was even said to have a sixth sense about suspicious circumstances. In his most famous arrest, he was standing outside his house in Alamogordo in February 1928

> when a very unusual load of lumber [loaded on a truck] came by. . . . The lumber was of good quality, without knots, a fact that struck [Beacham] as odd, since lumber from the nearby Sacramento Mountains is never free of knots. . . .
>
> Beacham followed the lumber truck on its way out of town and stopped it near La Luz. [The lawman] found that it was a rumrunner's truck, cleverly camouflaged with a load of lumber [embedded in a space cut into the load of wood]. The driver of the truck, D. E. Sherry, was running his goods out of Mexico. The load contained 972 pints of American whiskey, 60 quarts of Gordon's gin, 60 quarts of tequila and cognac, 9 one-gallon cans of alcohol, and a 10-gallon keg of whiskey. It was valued at $7,000 ($75,000 in today's money).

(David A. Townsend and Clif McDonald, "Howard S. Beacham: Otero County's Eliot Ness," *Southern New Mexico Historical Review* 7 [January 2000]: 49.)

the use of alcohol and controlling its evils, Prohibition seemed to have only made matters worse. Most people agreed that it had been a "noble experiment" in the 1920s, but a majority of Americans voted to repeal the Eighteenth Amendment in 1933. Prohibition officially ended in the United States on December 5, 1933.

The Teapot Dome Scandal

It was a proud day for New Mexico when Pres. Warren G. Harding appointed New Mexico's U.S. Senator Albert B. Fall to serve as the nation's secretary of the interior in 1921. As the *Sierra County Advocate*'s editor wrote, "His appointment bestows great honor on the Sunshine State."

As secretary of the interior, Fall oversaw all federal lands and resources, as well as the Bureau of Indian Affairs. With so much federal land and so many Indian reservations within its borders, New Mexico could hope to benefit from having one of its leading citizens in such a key government position.

Creation or Evolution?

Americans have long debated whether public school teachers should be allowed to teach Charles Darwin's theory of evolution. In 1925, a Tennessee teacher named John T. Scopes was tried in court for teaching evolution to his high school students when a just-passed Tennessee state law had forbidden it. The famous Scopes Trial (also known as the Great Monkey Trial) drew national attention to the issue. A jury found Scopes guilty and fined him $100. The Tennessee law remained in effect until 1967.

Three years before John Scopes went on trial in Tennessee, a principal at Fort Sumner High School in New Mexico was not rehired because he had refused to follow a local school board order that he fire any teacher who taught evolution to high school students. R. E. Dean defended his controversial stand in a series of letters to his town's newspaper, the *Fort Sumner Review*. According to Dean, "all of modern science . . . is written from the evolutionary point of view." He argued that "evolution is more than half of modern thought" (*Fort Sumner Review*, August 12, 1922).

A local citizen named L. S. Smith replied to Dean's defense of Darwin by writing to the newspaper that "nine-tenths of evolution is sheer nonsense, not founded on observation and wholly unsupported by facts." Smith believed that only the biblical story of creation should be taught to the students of Fort Sumner (*Fort Sumner Review*, August 19, 1922).

The Fort Sumner case received attention in various parts of New Mexico, although by the time it was over observers claimed that the incident had "been the cause of men making monkeys of themselves" (*Fort Sumner Review*, September 2, 1922).

Of course, neither the biblical nor Darwinian theory of creation considered traditional Native American beliefs. Nearly every tribe has its own creation story, based on the tribe's history and unique culture. Blue Lake, for example, is the source of all life for Taos Pueblo. Some argue that if all theories of creation are to be considered, Indian beliefs must be respected and taught as well.

Albert B. Fall

Albert B. Fall had come to New Mexico in the mid-1880s, largely to recover from poor health and find new economic opportunities. Finding what he was looking for in southern New Mexico, Fall became a lawyer, a judge, a legislator, and, in 1898, a captain in the Spanish-American War. A Republican leader at the state constitutional convention of 1910, he went on to become one of the state's first two senators in 1912. He and his family lived on his huge Three Rivers Ranch south of Carrizozo.

No one could have guessed that in becoming secretary of the interior Albert B. Fall was about to be involved in one of the biggest political scandals in American history. Soon after entering office, Fall

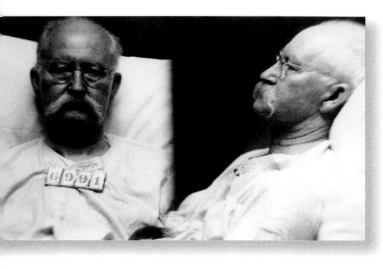

Albert B. Fall's prison
photos

illegally leased oil reserves on federal land in Teapot Dome, Wyoming, and in Elk Hills, California. To make matters worse, Fall was charged with taking a $100,000 bribe to lease the reserves to his powerful friends in the oil industry.

Although he argued that the money was simply a loan to finance improvements on his ranch, Fall was put on trial in 1929 and convicted of taking a bribe. As punishment, he was sentenced to serve a year and a day in prison and to pay a $100,000 fine. He became the highest-ranking federal official ever convicted of a felony crime.

Ill, Fall was allowed to serve his sentence at the state penitentiary in Santa Fe, rather than at a distant federal prison, to be closer to his family. Given his poor health, he remained in the prison's infirmary and was granted an early release in May 1932, after nine months and nineteen days in prison. Low on funds, he soon lost his Three Rivers Ranch but claimed his innocence to his dying day in 1944. Fall's many friends in New Mexico stood by him to the end, although others had strong doubts about his innocence. All agreed that what had begun as a "great honor" for New Mexico had ended with great misfortune, if not disgrace.

☀ Conclusions

Important political changes occurred in New Mexico in the 1920s as women won the right to vote, federal agents enforced Prohibition, and Albert B. Fall served as the country's secretary of the interior.

Unfortunately, tragic setbacks often outnumbered positive gains. Prohibition failed, Fall was convicted in a major political scandal, and, while women won new rights, Blacks, Hispanics, and Native Americans sometimes lost many of their civil rights.

These mixed developments were not unique to New Mexico in the 1920s. In fact, the state reflected some of the same advances and reversals as the rest of the country, from racial discrimination to unworkable Prohibition and major scandals, of which Teapot Dome was only the most famous.

New Mexico had become a state in the United States and, in the process, had grown to look and act like the rest of the nation, often for the better, but at other times for the worse. ✦

1. What obstacles did women have to overcome in order to win the right to vote in New Mexico? How did they overcome these obstacles and finally win the right to vote?

2. What racism did Blacks experience in New Mexico in the 1920s?

3. What racism did Hispanics experience in New Mexico in the 1920s?

4. How did Native Americans deal with threats to their land in the Bursum Bill?

5. How did the Indians of Taos Pueblo react to threats to Blue Lake?

6. Why did many New Mexicans originally favor Prohibition?

7. Why was it so difficult to enforce Prohibition in New Mexico?

8. Why did a majority of New Mexicans favor the repeal of Prohibition by 1933?

9. What theory, or theories, of creation do you think should be taught to students in public schools? Biblical? Darwinism? Native American? Others?

10. Why was the Teapot Dome scandal such a tragedy for Albert B. Fall? For New Mexico?

11. What aspects of New Mexico would you have been proud of if you had lived in the state during the 1920s? Why?

12. What aspects of New Mexico would you have been less proud of if you had lived in the state during the 1920s? Why?

13. What lessons can we learn from the history of New Mexico in the 1920s?

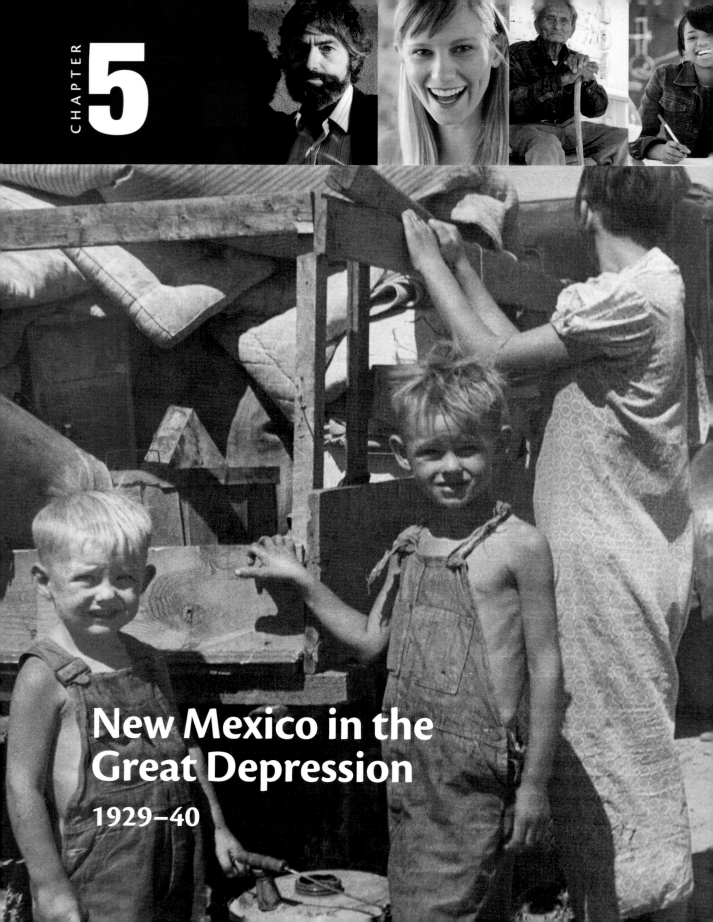

New Mexico in the Great Depression

1929–40

TIMELINE

1929
Stock market crash

1932
Franklin Delano Roosevelt elected president

Dorothy Dunn opens the Santa Fe Indian School Art Studio

1933
The New Deal begins

Gallup coal strike

John Collier appointed the U.S. Commissioner of Indian Affairs

1934
Clyde Tingley elected governor of New Mexico

Indian Reorganization Act (IRA) passed by Congress

Taylor Grazing Act passed by Congress

U.S. Senator Bronson Cutting defeats Dennis Chavez in controversial election

1935
Bronson Cutting killed in plane crash

Dennis Chavez appointed U.S. senator

Camp Capitán created for young women

Bosque Farms created as a Farm Security Administration project

Sheriff Mac Carmichael killed in Gallup riot

Dust Bowl's Black Sunday, April 14, 1935

1937
Carrie Tingley Hospital opens in Hot Springs (now Truth or Consequences)

1938
Works Progress Administration scandal

1939
Congress passes the Hatch Act

1940
Publication of *New Mexico: Guide to the Colorful State*

1941
United States enters World War II

☀ Introduction

The United States suffered the worst economic crisis in its history in the 1930s. Starting with the **stock market crash** of late 1929, the **Great Depression** lasted until the eve of World War II. The country had never experienced such economic turmoil, widespread unemployment, and personal misery. Businesses closed, banks failed, and stores shut down for lack of customers. Some observers worried that **capitalism**, our free market economy, would never be the same. Others worked hard to save our economic system, our democratic form of government, and, most of all, the millions of people who endured this most trying decade of the twentieth century.

The purpose of this chapter is to consider

- how bad the Great Depression was in New Mexico;
- how a new federal government policy, known as the **New Deal**, attempted to end the Great Depression;
- what impact the New Deal had on the state;
- and how New Mexicans managed to survive the Great Depression.

☀ The Great Depression Hit New Mexico Like a Storm

Already a poor state, New Mexico was especially hard hit by the Great Depression. Every part of the state's economy was adversely affected. It was as if a prolonged,

125

powerful storm had hit the state, leaving vast destruction and human suffering in its wake.

The mining, oil, and gas industries were especially hard hit by this storm. Coal production, valued at more than $8 million in 1929, fell to less than $3 million by 1933. Half of McKinley County's two thousand coal miners lost their jobs, and, of those who remained employed, none worked full-time. The production of copper, zinc, gold, and silver, valued at more than $24 million, plummeted to less than $5 million in the same four-year period. The price of oil dropped to as low as ten cents a barrel, making "even a producing oil well just an expensive hole in the ground," according to historian Paige Christiansen. The population of Hobbs plummeted from twenty thousand to one thousand residents almost overnight.

Railroad business also declined. The Santa Fe Railroad lost a third of its business income from 1930 to 1931 alone. Faced with such losses, the Santa Fe laid off almost 40 percent of its workers. Those left on the railroad's payroll worked only four and a half days a week, rather than their usual six. Wages fell by 25 percent for workers fortunate enough to have jobs with the railroad or in any other business in New Mexico.

Unemployment reached unheard of levels. While the nation's unemployment reached 25 percent for *all* workers in 1933, the unemployment rate in New Mexico was so high that 25 percent of the state's *skilled* workers were jobless that year. Job seekers placed want ads in newspapers, and newspapers like Albuquerque's *New Mexico State Tribune* offered to run such ads without charge. When the Albuquerque city government opened an employment office in April 1930, one hundred unemployed workers applied for help in finding jobs in the first week alone.

Unemployment was especially high for women, the young, and Mexican immigrants. Married female teachers, for example, often lost their jobs to unemployed male teachers so that the men could earn money to support their families. Many women who had entered male-dominated professions by the 1920s now lost the jobs they had worked so long and hard to attain.

☀ Unemployed Youth

Young people often dropped out of school for lack of funds and to help support their destitute families. With no education, training, or experience they were seldom able to secure jobs, much less keep them for long.

Even the educated few faced probable unemployment. Bill Whitley called his graduation day from Dawson High School in 1934 "the

▲▲▲▲▲▲▲▲▲▲▲▲▲▲▲▲▲▲▲▲▲▲▲▲▲▲▲▲▲▲▲▲▲▲▲

Newspaper Classified Ads of the Great Depression Era

Middle aged man, active, handy and very reliable needs a job badly. [Inquire via] Independent [office]. (*Gallup Independent*, June 4, 1930.)

Refined lady, 60, plain cook, good to children, wishes good home. $15.00 per month. Address L. Gross, General Delivery, Gallup, N.M. (*Gallup Independent*, June 4, 1930.)

NOTICE

Anyone wishing to employ laborers please call the City Inspector phones 251 or 812. There are a great many men in town who need the work and any job will be appreciated. (*Santa Fe New Mexican*, June 14, 1930.)

WANTED

A sober, industrious young man desires work as an all-around cook at Hotel, Café or Mining Camp. Address Box 264, Farmington, New Mexico. (*Farmington Times-Hustler*, December 25, 1931.)

WANTED

Work of any kind by colored man. Experience in coal mining, farm, and laundry work. Tom Jones, 241 Garcia St. (*Ratón Range*, February 16, 1932.)

Anyone having second-hand bedsprings for full sized beds wishing to give to charity call Santa Fe County Welfare mornings. Phone 949-W (*Santa Fe New Mexican*, July 3, 1930.)

FOR SALE

Diamond ring worth $250.00 for $125.00. Lady from Oklahoma needing funds. Inquire [at the] Independent [office]. (*Gallup Independent*, August 15, 1930.)

blackest day of my life" because there were no jobs in town for older, experienced workers, much less for young, inexperienced boys like Bill and his classmates. It took Bill two years to land his first job, but he always feared losing it because the last hired were usually the first fired in economic hard times.

At least Bill Whitley had had a school to attend. With little or no incomes, families were often unable to pay their taxes, and, with few revenues, state and local governments were forced to reduce public services. Education was often the first public service to suffer. The school year, normally lasting nine months, was cut back to just seven, six, or five months in many school districts. In early 1933, an editorial in the *Farmington Times-Hustler* reported that "some [schools] have been closed entirely."

Without schools to attend or jobs to work, many young New Mexicans left home, joining thousands of other youths from across the nation who had already taken to the road. Some found work and sent money home to help their families. Most found no permanent employment and simply traveled on freight cars or on foot, often not returning home to their families for months or years. The same *Farmington Times-Hustler* editorial of early 1933 concluded, "The army of vagabond youth . . . is [creating] an alarming situation."

Mexican Immigrant Labor

Of all groups, Mexican migrant workers faced the worst discrimination in the 1930s. Usually drawn to the United States to help harvest crops, migrants had arrived from Mexico in record-breaking numbers in the 1920s. Few Americans objected to such migration in the 1920s because Mexican workers were needed as a main source of cheap labor that could be easily exploited, given their illegal status and lack of legal means to defend their best interests. Mexican workers represented as much as 75 percent of the farm work force in the Southwest in the 1920s.

American attitudes changed drastically with the onset of the Great Depression, though. No longer needed for their cheap labor when unemployed Americans were now willing to take low-paying jobs, thousands of Mexican immigrants were rounded up and suddenly deported back to Mexico; estimates on the number tricked or forced into deportation range from four hundred thousand to 2 million. Not waiting to be deported, many other immigrants returned home to Mexico voluntarily. At least half of all deported men and women were American citizens, including an unknown number of Hispanic New Mexicans found working in other states without documentation to prove that they were U.S. citizens, much less members of families that had, in many cases, resided in New Mexico for hundreds of years.

Seasonal Labor for New Mexicans

Seasonal employment in other states became increasingly hard for New Mexicans to find. Before 1929, men from rural Hispanic communities regularly left home for from four to seven months a year to work as sugar-beet harvesters, sheepherders, railroad workers, and miners in Colorado, Utah, Wyoming, and Nevada. The wages they mailed back

▲▲▲▲▲▲▲▲▲▲▲▲▲▲▲▲▲▲▲▲▲▲▲▲▲▲▲

A Deportees' Corrido

The deep feelings of Mexican immigrants deported in the 1930s are clearly reflected in a corrido (ballad) entitled, "Deported":

Los gringos son muy maloras,	The gringos are very unkind.
Se valen de la ocasión,	They take advantage of the chance
Y a todos los mexicanos . . .	To treat all the Mexicans . . .
Nos tratan sin comapasión.	Without compassion.
Hoy traen la gran polvadera . . .	Today they are rounding [us] up . . .
Y sin consideración,	And without consideration
Mujeres, niños y ancianos	Women, children, and old folks
Los llevan a la frontera	Are taken to the border
Los echan de esa nación.	And expelled from [the United States].
Adiós, paisanos queridos . . .	So farewell, dear countrymen,
Ya nos van a deportar	They are going to deport us now,
Pero no somos bandidos . . .	But we are not criminals,
Venimos a camellar.	We [only] came to work.
Los espero allá en mi tierra . . .	I'll wait for you there in [Mexico],
Ya no hay más revolución;	Now that there is no revolution;
Vámonos cuates queridos	Let us go, brothers dear,
En nuestra bella nación.	In our own beautiful land.

(Quoted in María Herrera-Sobek, *Northward Bound: The Mexican Immigrant Experience in Ballad and Song* [Bloomington: Indiana University Press, 1993], 127–28.)

home often represented the most important single source of income for the workers' families and their impoverished villages.

These out-of-state opportunities ended almost overnight with the onset of the Great Depression. A study of poverty in several northern New Mexico communities showed that in villages like Trampas every man traveled out of state each year of the 1920s, but by 1935 only one man could find work elsewhere. In some cases employers were simply not hiring. In other cases, New Mexicans may have not wanted to risk the real possibility of confusion and deportation to Mexico. In either case, the residents of many rural settlements were deprived of a major source of annual income.

Many rural New Mexicans suffered terribly. With an average farm of less than twelve acres in northern New Mexico, most New Mexicans could not survive on income from the sale of crops alone. As many

Shirley Vogt

Like so many brave New Mexico wives whose husbands had left home to find work during the Great Depression, Shirley Vogt coped, playing traditional as well as nontraditional female roles in her husband's absence. In her letters to her husband Evon, Shirley told of dealing with broken water pumps, leaky roofs, runaway colts, mites in the chicken coop, and days when she had "no horse. No car. [And it was] too hot to walk to the post office." Somehow Shirley managed, keeping her family alive and well until the happy day when her husband returned and the Vogt family was united once more.

(Quoted in Barbara Vogt Mallery, *Bailing Wire and Gamuza: The True Story of a Family Ranch Near Ramah, New Mexico, 1905–1986* [Santa Fe: New Mexico Magazine, 2003], 81–83.)

Poverty at Si Porter's Farm Family near Corona

The Great Depression caused increased poverty on farms and ranches as well as in towns and cities. Leonard "Si" Porter recalled conditions on his family's farm near Corona, New Mexico:

There were nine [of us] kids in the Porter family tree: four girls and five boys. I was number seven, a tall skinny guy, sixteen years, but not old enough to get a job even if there had been one in or near our small town of Corona. We had a small farm, but we couldn't make a living on it anymore. . . .

We mostly ate pinto beans and venison at our house. . . . Some of our neighbors were somewhat better providers for their families. We sometimes visited them at the right time and learned what beef tasted like, but in our house it was almost unknown. . . .

My youngest brother, Jack, had a bad heart condition and my dad was in bad health. Dr. Barry would always get by our house on his rounds to check on my dad and Jack. He never did bill my folks for house calls or medications. One type of medicine he gave my dad was a powder and [Dad] was supposed to take what he could pile on a dime. My dad didn't have a dime so he used two nickels.

(Quoted in Richard Melzer, ed., "Leonard W. 'Si' Porter's Memories of Life in the Civilian Conservation Corps Camps in Southern New Mexico, 1936–39," *New Mexico Historical Review* 80 [Fall 2005]: 419–20.)

▲▲▲▲▲▲▲▲▲▲▲▲▲▲▲▲▲▲▲▲▲▲▲▲▲

Angelica Gurulé Chávez's Memories of the Great Depression

Angelica Gurulé Chávez described her Hispanic family's problems during the Great Depression. With one exception, Angelica faced these problems with a most positive attitude:

> I was the sixth of thirteen children born to Jacobo and Valentina Gurulé. Two of my siblings died as infants. . . .
>
> When I was very young we moved from Belén to Albuquerque. We traveled by covered wagon and stopped to sleep that night in Isleta Pueblo, and the Indians there were so nice to us. In Albuquerque we lived in a two-room shack. It was papered with newspapers to cover all its cracks. It was kind of fun to read all those words on the newspapers so I didn't mind that the shack was papered with newspapers. . . .
>
> At night we would all gather around one [oil] lamp. [It] didn't give off much light, but we thought [it] did at the time. . . .
>
> When we lived in Albuquerque, my older sisters worked as maids and my dad would buy and sell things. My sisters and I picked wild asparagus by the river and bundled them up to sell them to the Anglo people for five cents a bunch. . . . We felt so rich. . . .
>
> When we ate beans and chile we didn't need any silverware. We made our own silverware out of tortillas by making palitas (little shovels) and using them to dip into the beans and chile. We had less silverware to wash that way. . . .
>
> We had one pair of shoes each. In the summertime we kids would go bare footed a lot [which we liked]. . . . When it came time for our first Holy Communion, mother made our white dresses and veils, but we couldn't afford to buy shoes. So my parents bought us some white high-top tennis shoes and mother cut off the tops and put bias tape around the raw edges of each tennie. So we wore fancy dresses and veils and tennies. It was a letdown.

(Oral history quoted in Richard Melzer, ed., *When We Were Young in the West: True Stories of Childhood* [Santa Fe: Sunstone Press, 2003], 74–86.)

as 70 percent of the residents of some villages received relief, or what we would call welfare. Some New Mexicans resorted to making illegal liquor as a way to make money while Prohibition was still enforced in the early 1930s. Men often hunted and fished out of season simply to put food on the table for their families. Teenager Barbara Vogt watched her father send money-making ideas and job applications to companies and government agencies across the United States. In one letter Evon

Vogt suggested an ad for Palmolive Soap, which, he wrote, "cleanses, cheers and rests" ranchers' hands better than any other soap available. With most of his suggestions rejected, Vogt even considered selling his ranch near Ramah until he finally found work scouting for gold mines in Colorado and Nevada. Like so many families in New Mexico, the Vogt family survived, but only with great sacrifice, hard work, and devotion.

Other Transient Labor

Youths and rural males were hardly the only workers traveling in search of steady labor. Thousands came to New Mexico following every rumor of possible employment, especially in the warm Southwest where job seekers could hope to survive out-of-doors far longer than they could live in the harsher climates of the North.

There were not enough jobs in New Mexico for New Mexicans, much less for other workers. The situation became so bad in Albuquerque by August 1930 that any nonresident found without money, employment, or a place to stay was escorted out of town by the local police. The chief of police, Pat O'Grady, estimated that about a hundred transient workers arrived daily, mostly by freight trains, each of which was searched upon arrival in the city's train yards.

Dust Bowl scene in Clayton, 1937

Tomás Wesley Brown Weathers a Dust Storm

Seventeen-year-old Tomás Wesley Brown told the adventure of traveling through a dust storm in northeastern New Mexico during the mid-1930s:

The morning I left Maxwell the wind must have been blowing fifty miles per hour. . . . There was so much dust in the air I was unable to see the mountains I had planned to help me in my navigation. . . . Visibility was so poor that at times I could hardly see the team of horses pulling [my] wagon. In order to help filter out the dust I was wearing a bandanna over my nose. There were times when I might just as well have had it over my eyes also. . . .

Sometime around noon . . . I was able to distinguish the outline of a ranch house and windmill barely visible through the thick dust. Being eager to check my location I tied up the team and went to the door and knocked. . . . A rugged, weather-beaten rancher . . . opened the door. [He] apologized for the place being such a mess, and muttered something about his wife having gone back to her folks. Said she could no longer put up with living in this dust bowl. I noted that there was at least a quarter of an inch of dust over everything in the kitchen. . . .

[Discussing the storm,] I asked him if the wind blew that way all the time around there. I'll never forget his slow Texas drawl . . . as he replied, "No, son, it will blow like this sometimes for up to two or three days, and then it will start in and blow like hell." . . .

(Tomás Wesley Brown, *Heritage of the New Mexico Frontier* [New York: Vantage Press, 1995], 167–68.)

Many other transients traveled by car or truck with whole families en route to California on U.S. Route 66. Thousands of these families were victims of a 150,000-square-mile drought-stricken area appropriately called the **Dust Bowl**. Starting in the mid-1930s, violent wind storms blew dust everywhere. Dense, dark dust clouds measured as high as a mile and a half in the sky. Roads, fences, farm equipment, cars, trucks, and whole fields of crops lay buried under layers of dirt. "Black blizzards" blew day and night, causing sunless days and making it impossible to keep anything—including oneself—clean from the dust that blew through even the smallest cracks in walls and windows. People and livestock grew ill from breathing the fine dust; many died, including men, women, and children who could not drive to medical care over flatland roads covered by dust. People prayed for relief. Some resorted to buying rain-making machines from dishonest salesmen. Nothing worked.

Woody Guthrie's Dust Bowl Songs

As with many human crises, the Dust Bowl of the 1930s stimulated much creativity, resulting in some of the greatest fiction, poetry, photographs, and music of the twentieth century. Some of the most creative music of the Depression era was composed and sung by Woody Guthrie, probably the most famous folksinger in American music history. Two of Guthrie's most memorable songs of this era were entitled "Dust Storm Disaster" and "Dust Bowl Refugee":

"Dust Storm Disaster"

On the 14th day of April of 1935,
There struck the worst of dust storms that ever filled the sky.
You could see that dust storm comin', the cloud looked deathlike black,
And through our mighty nation, it left a dreadful track.

From Oklahoma City to the Arizona line,
Dakota and Nebraska to the lazy Rio Grande,
It fell across our city like a curtain of black rolled down,
We thought it was our judgement, we thought it was our doom.

The radio reported, we listened with alarm,
The wild and windy actions of this great mysterious storm;
From Albuquerque and Clovis, and all New Mexico,
They said it was the blackest that ever they had saw. . . .
The storm took place at sundown, it lasted through the night,
When we looked out next morning, we saw a terrible sight.
We saw outside our window where wheat fields they had grown
Was now a rippling ocean of dust the wind had blown.

It covered up our fences, it covered up our barns,
It covered up our tractors in this wild and dusty storm.
We loaded our jalopies and piled our families in,
We rattled down that highway to never come back again.

"Dust Bowl Refugee"

'Cross the mountains to the sea,
Come the wife and kids and me.
It's a hot old dusty highway
For a dust bowl refugee.

Hard, it's always been that way,
Here today and on our way
Down that mountain, 'cross the desert,
Just a dust bowl refugee. . . .

Unable to survive in such adverse conditions, much less grow crops and make a living, as many as 350,000 Dust Bowl farmers and their families packed up their most essential belongings and headed west to California. They had heard that farming was better in California, especially in the San Joaquin Valley where migrant workers were needed to harvest fruits and vegetables, often taking jobs left vacant by the thousands of Mexican laborers who had been deported. Sadly, many more Dust Bowl victims went to California than were needed, driving wages down and leaving most families as bad—if not worse—off than they had been before their long trek west began.

Most New Mexicans treated Dust Bowl families kindly as these travelers crept along the highway in ancient pickup trucks piled high

John Steinbeck's *The Grapes of Wrath*

In 1939, John Steinbeck wrote *The Grapes of Wrath*, the most famous novel of the Great Depression era. Steinbeck's novel described the plight of the Joad family as they fled their Oklahoma farm in the Dust Bowl and traveled through New Mexico toward California in search of work. In the following scene at a transient camp somewhere in New Mexico, the Joads meet a man who is traveling in the opposite direction with a story about what he had found in California. Unfortunately, his story was true for thousands of Okies like this tragic fictional character:

The ragged man said slowly, "Me—I'm comin' back . . . I been there [and nearly starved]."

The faces turned quickly toward him. . . .

Pa said, "What the hell you talkin' about? I got a han'bill says they got good wages . . . and need men [in California]."

"Look," said the man. "[If a big farmer in California] wants eight hundred men . . . he prints up five thousand [handbills] an' maybe twenty thousan' people see 'em. An' maybe two [to] three thousan' folks gets movin' account a this here han'bill. Folks that's crazy with worry [about their families' future]. . . .

["But when those people get to California the farmer only pays them twenty cents an hour because] the more fellas he can get, an' the hungrier [they are, the] less he has to pay. . . ."

The circle [of men] was quiet. . . . The men breathed shallowly, and watched. The ragged man looked around at the circle, and then he turned and walked quickly away into the darkness, . . . his head hanging down and his hands in [his] coat pockets.

(John Steinbeck, *The Grapes of Wrath* [New York: Penguin Books, 1951], 208–10.)

An Albuquerque Family's Generosity

Priscilla Montoya of Albuquerque recalls that during the Great Depression

[My mother often gave travelers] food . . . or lodging for the night out in the garage. . . . Everyone wanted to chop wood or milk the cows or whatever—just for a meal. It was very sad.

[Years later a man] stopped at my dad's house and gave him $300. My dad said, "What is this for?" [The man answered,] "You remember during the Depression that people were [always] stopping over here and you fed them? . . . I [had] made a sign in front of your house on a post to let people know that [you and your wife were kind and generous]. . . . I have been very successful and I want to come and thank you for the people [you helped]."

(Quoted in Kathryn Sargeant and Mary Davis, *Shining River, Precious Land: An Oral History of Albuquerque's North Valley* [Albuquerque: Museum of Albuquerque Press, 1986], 123–24.)

Harvey House Generosity

Bob O'Sullivan was just a boy when his mother and sister drove through Albuquerque on their way to California. Although they had little money, the small family stopped at the Alvarado, Albuquerque's famous Harvey House. Seeing that the children were hungry, the manager of the Harvey House ordered a large meal for them, while their mother insisted that she only wanted coffee to drink. When her children finished eating, Bob's mother attempted to pay for the food, but

the [Harvey Girl] pushed [the money] back with a smile.

"Oh, no, ma'am. You're Mr. Harvey's guests," she said and placed two bags in front of my mother.

"The manager said I was to wrap up what you didn't eat, so you could take it along. . . ."

In the car my mother and my sister looked in the bags, which clearly contained a greater volume of food than we'd had for dinner.

"What's in them?" I asked.

"Loaves and fishes," she said. "Loaves and fishes."

(Quoted in Lesley Poling-Kempes, *The Harvey Girls: Women Who Opened the West* [New York: Paragon House, 1989], 187.)

Going Back to Pie Town

Although many homesteaders had abandoned their claims near Pie Town in the 1920s, conditions in the 1930s became so desperate that some Dust Bowl–stricken farmers attempted to settle and work the soil again. Some of these families were en route to California, but had suffered car trouble, poor health, or simply the lack of enough money to continue their trip west.

In a typical Pie Town experience, Doris Caudill and her small family struggled to survive in a one-room dugout on a farm outside of town. The family's brave efforts became the focus of pictures by a famous photographer, Russell Lee, and a later book entitled *Pie Town Woman.*

with mattresses, boxes, and odd pieces of luggage. Some towns along Route 66 gave each destitute family five dollars for gasoline, either out of human kindness or to make sure the families did not stay and become an economic burden on local communities. Individual New Mexicans offered what little food or shelter they could spare, given their own dire straights. Gas station owners sometimes offered help fixing broken car parts or overheated engines. Motel owners lowered prices or charged the most destitute families nothing at all. Travelers offered to pay for goods and services with their last dollars or with what few possessions they could offer as **barter**. Most New Mexicans would refuse to take the travelers' money, much less items they really needed, like spare tires and kitchen utensils. When some exiles could go no further, many created shantytowns, or temporary slums, on the outskirts of towns like Albuquerque. Most of the **Okies**, as they were called, continued on, eventually reaching their destination and the new problems that awaited them in far-off California.

 ## A New Deal For the Country— and New Mexico

As the Great Depression worsened, Americans turned to their state and national governments for assistance. Unfortunately, most state governments, including New Mexico's, lacked the resources to be of much help, especially when many citizens could not afford to pay their taxes. The federal government was no better able to provide aid, much less lasting

▲▲▲▲▲▲▲▲▲▲▲▲▲▲▲▲▲▲▲▲▲▲▲▲▲▲▲▲▲

Blaming Hoover

So many Americans blamed Pres. Herbert Hoover for either causing the Great Depression or not doing enough to end it that they began to name certain vehicles and places in his "dishonor." Old pickup trucks used by families to flee the Dust Bowl became known as Hoover wagons. Shantytowns, like the one built over an old dump outside Albuquerque, became unofficially known as Hoovervilles.

solutions to the deepening crisis. An increasing number of Americans rightly or wrongly blamed the Depression on **Pres. Herbert Hoover** because the economic emergency had begun during the first months of his term in office in 1929. Many also blamed the Republican administration for not doing more to end the Depression, although Hoover did more than any previous president faced with a similar economic crisis.

Few other depressions had lasted so long or had caused so much misery. Bold new strategies would be needed to deal with this new economic disaster before it grew any worse.

Franklin Delano Roosevelt, the Democratic Party's presidential candidate in 1932, offered fresh ideas in what he called a New Deal for the American people. Eager for such a new approach, voters elected Roosevelt with 59 percent of the popular vote to Herbert Hoover's 41 percent. Roosevelt's victory in New Mexico was even more impressive. Roosevelt won 63 percent of the popular vote, the largest margin of victory in a presidential election in New Mexico state history.

Pres. Franklin D. Roosevelt

Once sworn into office on March 4, 1933, Roosevelt became one of the most active, most popular presidents in American history. As promised, his New Deal attempted to end the Depression with reforms to correct the causes of the crisis, recovery to help end the crisis, and relief for those who still suffered through the crisis. The new administration created hundreds of new government programs with an air of optimism that helped sweep away the gloom that had settled over the country for so long. In the most famous statement of his political career, Roosevelt asserted his positive and "firm belief that the only thing we have to fear is fear itself."

Bringing the New Deal to New Mexico

New Mexicans were fortunate to have two strong leaders who became closely tied to Franklin Roosevelt and his New Deal plans. **Clyde Tingley** and **Dennis Chavez** worked hard to help New Mexico recover and, in many ways, grow, despite the Great Depression.

Gov. Clyde Tingley

Clyde Tingley first came to New Mexico in 1911, following his fiancée Carrie who had come to the Southwest in search of a cure for her tuberculosis. Clyde entered Albuquerque city politics in 1916 and soon dominated city government from his position as chairman of Albuquerque's city council. Nominated as the Democratic Party's candidate for governor in 1934, Tingley won the election with 52 percent of the vote; he won reelection with a record 56 percent two years later. Soon after his victory in 1934, Tingley wrote to President Roosevelt,

Clyde Tingley's Political Style

Mary Lou Heaphy, whose family knew and admired the Tingleys in Albuquerque, remembers that

> Clyde's warm, commanding voice caught people's attention. . . . His down-home, common man routine was exaggerated for effect [but] he was genuinely interested in people and their problems. Everyone waved and spoke to him as he passed. He loved it. . . .

In what were known as Tingleyisms, Clyde often confused word meanings, murdered pronunciation, or generally used poor grammar. When his political advisors urged him to stop saying "ain't" in his speeches, he replied, "I ain't goin' to quit saying ain't."

Many places in Albuquerque are named for Clyde Tingley, including Tingley Drive near the Rio Grande, Tingley Coliseum on the State Fair Grounds, and Tingley Beach near Old Town. Tingley might best be remembered, though, for bringing two thousand Chinese elms to the city and distributing them free to the public to provide both shade and beauty for whole neighborhoods. While many city residents appreciated this effort, others became allergic to the trees and suffered from their illness much of the year. Some still believe that Albuquerque's many elms were first brought to the city by a Chinese mayor named Ting Lee!

(Mary Lou Heaphy, *A Cliffie Experience: Tales of New Mexico, 1902–1940* [Albuquerque: Diamond Press, 2005], 142, 153–54, 165.)

New Mexico's governors in the 1930s were

- Arthur Seligman, Democrat, 1931–33
- Andrew Hockenhull, Republican, 1933–35
- Clyde Tingley, Democrat, 1935–39
- John E. Miles, Democrat, 1939–43

vowing "to carry out the purposes of everything that you have in mind" for the nation—especially as it might benefit New Mexico.

Tingley traveled to Washington, D.C., as many as twenty-three times to meet with federal government officials and secure New Deal funding for important public projects in New Mexico. Effective and popular, Tingley was elected for a second term in 1936, the same year Roosevelt was elected for a second term as president. Although worlds apart socially, the two leaders supported each other enthusiastically, to New Mexico's great political and economic advantage.

Dennis Chavez was equally devoted to Franklin Roosevelt and his New Deal reforms. Elected as New Mexico's sole congressman in 1930, Chavez ran as the Democratic Party's challenger to New Mexico's powerful Republican senator, Bronson Cutting, in 1934. In one of the closest, most controversial elections in New Mexico history, Cutting won the senate seat by less than 1 percent of the final vote. Convinced that the election had not been fairly run, Chavez officially contested the vote but to no avail.

Senator Bronson Cutting

Bronson Cutting boarded a flight from Santa Fe to Washington, D.C., on the evening of May 5, 1935. The passenger plane he was flying on ran into bad weather over Missouri. Running low on fuel, the plane crashed in an isolated field. Probably asleep when the "fasten seat belt" sign went on, Cutting was without a seat belt when the plane went down. Cutting, the copilot, and two other passengers were killed. The senator's injuries were so severe he could only be identified by documents found in his wallet. New Mexicans mourned their lost senator in newspaper editorials and in memorial services throughout the state.

It was left to Governor Tingley to appoint Bronson Cutting's replacement in the U.S. Senate. Not surprisingly, Tingley appointed his fellow Democrat, Chavez, who had barely lost to Cutting six months earlier.

Chavez went right to work. Serving on important Senate committees in Washington, D.C., he had ready access to New Deal agencies that could benefit New Mexico with federal projects, jobs, and funding. Often asked by New Mexicans to help get their proposed projects approved, Chavez used his political skills to effectively cut through government red tape; in one instance he won approval for a New Mexico project just five days after his assistance was requested in 1936.

Dennis Chavez's Political Rallies

Old-timers who attended Dennis Chavez's political rallies from the 1930s to the 1960s remember good food, good speeches, and good music, especially the senator's theme song, "Chavez for Senator," written by Luis S. Martínez. Translated into English, its lyrics included the following verses:

I will tell you about Dennis Chavez
Again for senator
Because he knows
All the rights of the worker.

In the city of Albuquerque,
Of the county of Bernalillo
Dennis Chavez was educated
Our brilliant senator.

Chavez, Chavez, Chavez,
The brilliant senator,
In November we will vote
And again we will send him
To the Senate in the election.

Knowing his duty
Chavez was never afraid.
He had to leave school
To help his father.

Looking to the future
He worked with ambition
Always trying to acquire
More education.

Chavez, Chavez, Chavez,
The brilliant senator,
In November we will vote
And again we will send him
To the Senate in the election.

Although he is senator
He has not lost his common touch.
He does not wear a larger hat
Because his head has never
swollen.

"How are you Luis, Pedro, Juan,
Jimmy, Jack, and you too, Nicanor?"
That's how he greets his friends,
Senator Dennis Chavez.

Chavez, Chavez, Chavez,
The brilliant senator,
In November we will vote
And again we will send him
To the Senate in the election.

New Deal Political Feud

At first Governor Tingley and Senator Chavez worked well together; they had been old friends and political allies in the Democratic Party. Trouble brewed, though, when these powerful leaders competed for control of the Democratic Party and New Deal programs in New Mexico. The dispute came to a head as Governor Tingley supported a state constitutional amendment allowing governors to run for a third term. (The constitution had originally limited governors to two terms.) Senator Chavez spoke out against the idea, knowing that if the amendment passed Tingley would use it to run for another term in 1938. Influenced by Chavez's opposition,

Senator Dennis Chavez

New Mexico voters defeated the proposed amendment by a considerable margin in 1937.

Largely in response to this political setback, Tingley and his political allies accused several of Chavez's friends and relatives of using New Deal programs in New Mexico for their political advantage. As many as seventy-five men and women went on trial in the largest New Deal government scandal in the United States. Fortunately for Chavez and his followers, most of the accused were acquitted; those who were found guilty faced only small fines or light sentences.

☀ New Deal Accomplishments in New Mexico

Despite their bitter differences, Tingley and Chavez were still able to bring hundreds of beneficial New Deal projects to New Mexico. As Tingley had predicted in a letter to Chavez before their political feud began, there were so many potential federal projects in New Mexico it would soon "be hard to get men in the state for all the jobs." So much federal money was eventually spent in New Mexico that Tingley declared "you would hardly know there was a depression" going on. Although Tingley exaggerated its impact, no one could dispute that New Mexico received its fair share of New Deal funds—and much more.

☀ A New Deal for Workers

New Deal programs helped Americans formerly employed in almost every kind of work, from manual labor to the fine arts. The most famous of these work programs was called the **Works Progress Administration**, or **WPA**. Almost every community in New Mexico benefited from the work and completed projects of the WPA. Hiring as many as 14,309 New Mexico workers at $18.75 per week (or $259 in today's money), the WPA constructed public facilities valued at almost $40 million (half a billion dollars in today's money), including:

The Hatch Act, 1939

In the wake of the WPA scandal and trials of 1938, New Mexico's other U.S. senator, Carl Hatch, introduced the Political Activities Act, better known as the Hatch Act, in 1939. This new law strictly limited the political activity of federal employees during election campaigns. Workers would no longer feel pressured to contribute money or otherwise assist in political campaigns to obtain or keep their government jobs.

4,214 miles of roads and highways;

1,762 bridges and viaducts;

361 new schools and 283 remodeled schools;

44 new or improved utility plants;

248 miles of sewers;

7 airport buildings;

6 airport landing fields;

426 other new or remodeled public buildings, such as city halls, post offices, libraries, courthouses, armories, hospitals, recreational buildings, community centers, and even 19,410 modern, flyproof "sanitary units," or outhouses, that were sold at low prices to families who could afford them and were given away to those who could not.

☀ A New Deal for Artists and Authors

With fewer people able to buy art during the Depression, many New Mexico artists enthusiastically worked for New Deal programs like the WPA's **Federal Art Project**. Drawn largely from the Taos and Santa Fe art colonies, more than 165 men and women shared their talents in public art projects across the state. Some of the most accomplished artists in the state, including Patricinio Barela, Gerald Cassidy, Pedro Cervántez, Eddie Delgado, Fremont Ellis, Allan Houser, Julián and María Martínez, Eliseo Rodríguez, Pablita Velarde, and five former members of the Taos Society of Artists, created hundreds of beautiful wood carvings, sculptures, etchings, murals, paintings, pots, and other pieces of art.

Specific New Deal Projects

It is almost impossible to visit a town, city, or county in New Mexico without finding at least one WPA, PWA, or other New Deal project that is still standing and, usually, still admirably serving its local community. This list provides only a small sample of the projects completed in the 1930s and 1940s and still in use today:

Alamogordo
U.S. Post Office, now a Lincoln National Forest Service Building

Albuquerque
Albuquerque Little Theater
State Fair buildings
Albuquerque Airport Terminal Building and runway
Monte Vista Fire Station
Jefferson Junior High School
Bandelier Elementary School
Lew Wallace Elementary School
Heights Community Center
Three buildings at the old Albuquerque High School
University of New Mexico's Chapel
Zimmerman Library
Student Union, now the Anthropology Building
Administration Building
Men's and women's dorms
Roosevelt Park
Tingley Field Stadium

Artesia
Artesia Municipal Hospital

Aztec
City Hall, now the Aztec Museum

Carrizozo
Lincoln County Courthouse

Clayton
Clayton High School

Clovis
Curry County Courthouse

Deming
U.S. Post Office
Public Library
Junior High School
National Guard building

El Rito
Several buildings at the Spanish-American Normal School, now Northern New Mexico Community College

Estancia
Community Center

Gallup
McKinley County Courthouse
U.S. Post Office, now a cable television office

Las Cruces
New Mexico State University's Museum
Doña Ana County Courthouse

Las Vegas
New Mexico Highlands University's administration building
San Miguel County Courthouse

Lordsburg
City Hall
Public Library
Hidalgo County Fairgrounds

Magdalena
Magdalena High School

Mountainair
Community Center

Portales
U.S. Post Office
Roosevelt County Courthouse
Eastern New Mexico University's administration building
Roosevelt County Museum
Lea and Quay Halls

Ratón
U.S. Post Office, now the Arthur Johnson Memorial Library
Colfax County Courthouse
National Guard Armory

Roswell
Roswell Museum and Art Center
Cahoon Park

Santa Fe
Public Library
State Supreme Court Building
Harvey Junior High School, now a State District Court Building
Santa Fe County Courthouse
Main buildings at the New Mexico School for the Deaf

Silver City
Western New Mexico University's Graham Gymnasium

Socorro
Socorro County Courthouse
President Hall and five other buildings on the New Mexico Tech campus

Taos
Taos High School, now part of Taos Middle School

Truth or Consequences
Sierra County Courthouse
Carrie Tingley Hospital for Crippled Children, now the New Mexico Veterans Center
U.S. Post Office

Tucumcari
National Guard Armory
Quay County Courthouse

Tularosa
Tularosa High School, now the Tularosa Schools administration building
Police station and jail

(Kathryn A Flynn, ed., *Treasures of New Mexico Trails: Discover New Deal Art and Architecture* [Santa Fe: Sunstone Press, 1995].)

Most of this work was used to decorate public buildings constructed by other New Deal programs, especially the WPA. Sixty-five large, colorful murals reflected local history, culture, the surrounding environment, or each building's public purpose. Bert Phillips, a founding member of the Taos art colony, painted "The Shadow of Crime" and two other murals at the old Taos County Courthouse. **Olive Rush** painted "The Library Reaches the People" on the walls at the entrance to the old public library in Santa Fe. **Peter Hurd** painted murals about farming and ranching for the U.S. Federal Building in Alamogordo. Manville Chapman painted eight murals about Colfax County in the lobby of Ratón's Shuler Theater, paying twenty-six local residents to pose as models for his work. Gisella Loeffler painted murals showing Indian, Hispanic, and Anglo children at play to cheer the young patients at the **Carrie Tingley Hospital for Crippled Children** in Hot Springs (now Truth or Consequences). These murals and hundreds of other works of New Deal art can still be found in

New Deal mural at the University of New Mexico

▲▲▲▲▲▲▲▲▲▲▲▲▲▲▲▲▲▲▲▲▲▲▲▲▲▲▲▲▲▲

Will Shuster's Letters to Fellow Artist John Sloan

Like many artists in New Mexico, Will Shuster of Santa Fe suffered from a lack of work and income during the worst days of the Depression. On November 11, 1933, Shuster wrote to John Sloan, a fellow artist in New York, that he had made only $75 in the last three months and local businesses were "getting tough."

> I am trying . . . to meet all my current bills and letting the old ones ride until such time as I get the cash to pay them. Yesterday I had to tell the light company to turn the . . . electricity off [if the company could not wait for my payment] . . . and that I would use kerosene lamps [if necessary].

(Letter from Will Shuster to John Sloan, November 11, 1933, Santa Fe, New Mexico, Will Shuster Collection, Fray Angélico Chávez Library, Museum of New Mexico, Santa Fe, New Mexico.)

Fortunately, Shuster never had to resort to kerosene lamps. In fact, less than a month later, Shuster wrote a much different letter to Sloan:

> The most important thing which has happened to the Shuster family is [the New Deal art program]. $42.50 a week [$576 in today's money] from the Government for painting. My God it doesn't seem real. . . . Gosh, John, I think this is a tremendous opportunity for us [and] for all organizations of artists across the country.

(Letter from Will Shuster to John Sloan, December 7, 1933, Santa Fe, New Mexico, Will Shuster Collection, Fray Angélico Chávez Library, Museum of New Mexico, Santa Fe, New Mexico.)

Shuster survived the Depression years by creating many valuable works of public art, including a series of murals about Native Americans for the inner courtyard of the Museum of Fine Arts in Santa Fe. As the creator of Zozobra, he was still able to make annual versions of Old Man Gloom, probably burning old bills he could now afford to pay.

schools, libraries, post offices, courthouses, and public buildings of every kind today.

Like many artists, most authors also suffered during the Great Depression, as few Americans could afford to buy new books or magazines. Fortunately, the WPA's **Federal Writers' Project (FWP)** offered job opportunities for as many as ten thousand authors across the United States, including New Mexico. As with every state in the country, New Mexico received federal funding for the publication of an extensive state guide, filled with information about local history, cultures, and geography.

More than half of New Mexico's 472-page volume described tour routes through the Southwest, with interesting facts about the places and people found along each of eighteen suggested routes. Researched and written by New Mexico authors, *New Mexico: A Guide to the Colorful State* encouraged tourists to explore New Mexico, appreciate its unique characteristics, and spend money to help revive local economies and the state's economy as a whole.

A New Deal for Youth

The young people of New Mexico benefited from a wide range of New Deal programs designed to help their generation survive and grow, despite the ravages of the Great Depression. Children from the earliest ages made good use of pools, parks, community centers, gyms, libraries, and similar facilities built by the WPA, the PWA, and other New Deal agencies. More schools were built or improved in the 1930s than in all previous decades of New Mexico history combined. Hundreds of students could afford to stay in school thanks to National Youth Administration (NYA) employment that allowed them to work at part-time government-sponsored jobs while also

Top: Wood carver José Dolores Lopez; middle: Pablita Velarde in her studio; and left: Photographers such as Dorothea Lange traveled the country during the Depression, capturing with their cameras the poignant scenes of a country struggling with a devastated economy

Preserving the Village: Clayton

The ranching community of Clayton, New Mexico, was one of many towns that was preserved and improved with ambitious New Deal projects during the Great Depression. Located on the western edge of the Dust Bowl, Union County had been so severely affected by adverse weather and economic conditions that at one point twenty-five hundred county residents received government relief aid in the 1930s. Discouraged, many residents either planned to move or had already left the area.

Deeply concerned, Clayton school superintendent and rancher Raymond Hull began to apply for useful New Deal projects. Starting with the WPA's building of a modern high school, other projects followed, including furniture making and curtain weaving to decorate the new school. If local workers lacked the skills necessary to complete a project, experts were brought in from other parts of the state. Soon dozens of Union County residents were at work on one New Deal project or another, improving their community and earning enough wages for them to survive the Depression without having to relocate.

Raymond Hull became known as "the superintendent who saved a county." Clayton school superintendent Jack Wiley reports that the New Deal school Hull helped build is still in use, with most rooms used for their original purposes and a large room used to display many of the New Deal artifacts Hull helped to create in the 1930s.

(Oral history interview with Jack Wiley, September 15, 2006.)

Farm Security Administration Photographers in New Mexico

Professional photographers, like most artists of the 1930s, could find few buyers for even their best work. As it did for so many professions, the Roosevelt administration created a New Deal program in the Farm Security Administration that employed the talents of photographers, while creating useful, striking photos for the nation. The often stark black-and-white photos of artists like Laura Gilpin, Russell Lee, and Arthur Rothstein captured the plight of poor, but proud, Americans as few other art forms could. Some of their most famous work depicted homeless travelers along Route 66, FSA farmers in Bosque Farms, and homesteaders in Pie Town, New Mexico.

Seeing these compelling pictures, political leaders in Washington, D.C., responded with new laws and policies that were usually helpful. Today these same photographs are among the best primary sources historians can use to document the horrible conditions Americans experienced, yet survived, during the Great Depression.

attending classes. In 1930, before the New Deal began, 144,234 students had attended school in New Mexico. By 1938, with many new WPA-built schools and the NYA, 180,680 children attended.

Many Depression-era schools taught traditional arts and crafts and, in the process, taught a new respect for native cultures. Young Hispanics learned tinsmithing, furniture making, wood carving, and other crafts that had either been forgotten or had been unjustly criticized as old, primitive, and valueless. Preserving these crafts and enhancing their value, both artistically and financially, helped preserve many small Hispanic communities whose cultures and destinies had been threatened by the Depression and changing times. Just as important, young Hispanics who learned traditional, almost forgotten skills often gained self-respect and enjoyed new confidence in themselves and their cultural heritage.

Native American arts and crafts were also highly valued by the 1920s and 1930s after a similarly long period of neglect and criticism. At the Santa Fe Indian School, where Indian culture had been suppressed for years, teachers, led by **Dorothy Dunn**, taught a new respect for Indian talents and ideas. In Dunn's words, once Indian children "realize that their native art is superior to the 'art' to which they had once aspired . . . the students develop their ideas more freely and rapidly. Out of their new freedom and confidence come . . . artistic expressions of the highest order."

Encouraged by this new attitude, students like **Harrison Begay**, **Joe Hilario Herrera**, Allan Houser, **Quincy Tahoma**, and Pablita Velarde progressed to become some of the greatest artists of their generation. Artist **Gerónima Cruz Montoya** spoke for many of her Indian classmates at the Santa Fe Indian School when she praised Dunn and her famous Studio, saying, "She made us realize how important our own Indian ways were because we had been made to feel ashamed of them. She gave us something to be proud of."

Physically handicapped children were given special attention with the construction of the Carrie Tingley Hospital for Crippled Children during Clyde Tingley's second term as governor of New Mexico. A recovered health seeker, Carrie Tingley had always been eager to help ill children, since she and her husband had never had children of their own. Using bricks made at the state penitentiary in Santa Fe, materials transported free of charge by the Santa Fe Railroad, and labor provided by local workers employed by the WPA, Governor Tingley oversaw the hospital's construction, making it his pet project. Opened to young patients in 1937, Carrie Tingley Hospital has served thousands of children, especially those struck by polio, in its location in southern New Mexico and, since 1981, in Albuquerque.

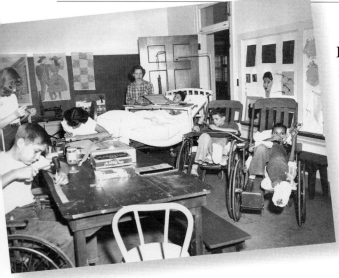

Patients at Carrie Tingley
Hospital for Crippled
Children

A nationwide program for youth was President Roosevelt's favorite New Deal project from the first days of his administration. The **Civilian Conservation Corps (CCC)** was created to provide employment opportunities for young men who seldom had the chance to finish their education, much less find anything more than temporary jobs. Facing bleak futures, more than 3 million young men, ages eighteen to twenty-five, eagerly joined the CCC as a means to help their families, themselves, their states, and their country. Fifty-four thousand of these 3 million youths served in New Mexico.

Carrie Tingley Hospital for Crippled Children

Rudolfo Anaya is one of New Mexico's most famous authors. His first, most noted novel is *Bless Me, Ultima*, but his third novel, based on his own experience as a young patient at Carrie Tingley Hospital for Crippled Children, was equally moving and memorable. Entitled *Tortuga*, meaning turtle, it is the story of a group of disabled children and their hospital lives, much of which was good, but some of which was not. Many children suffering from polio were confined to body casts or iron lungs, like turtles in their shells. Anaya described a typical day:

> After breakfast there was a lull in the ward. The kids who could make it to the dining room usually went on to therapy or swimming. Some went to arts and crafts classes, classes which were supposed to teach them to do something useful for when they were released. . . .
>
> Those of us that were bed-ridden remained in our rooms [left] to think of home, of family and of warm times eating together . . . times which seemed so distant now that the memory was inseparable from a dream. . . .
>
> Once a week the doctors visited the ward, but even they went quietly about their rounds, creating ripples in the monotony of our lives only when they announced a release or when someone was ready to get off the bed and get walking braces, crutches or a wheelchair. Those times were important, because they meant whoever could get up acquired a certain amount of freedom and they were milestones in the long process of complete freedom.

(Rudolfo A. Anaya, *Tortuga* [Berkeley, CA: Editorial Just Publications, 1979], 37, 53.)

CCC "enrollees," as participants were called, volunteered for six-month periods to work on badly needed conservation projects on both public and private lands. In New Mexico their valuable labor led to the planting of thousands of new trees, the building of miles of mountain paths and roads, the construction of a visitors center at Bandelier National Monument, and the creation of the famous bird sanctuary at Bosque del Apache, south of Socorro, to name just a few of the CCC's major projects from 1933 to 1942. A great help in emergencies, CCC enrollees came to the rescue in forest fires, floods, and searches for lost hikers and tourists.

When not hard at work, enrollees lived in two-hundred-men camps run by reserve army and navy officers. With all their room and board and uniforms provided, enrollees sent $25 ($345 in today's money) of their $30-a-month income to designated family members back home, money that often made a critical difference in family incomes and survival. In addition to learning valuable skills at work each day, enrollees also had a chance to continue their education by taking classes in camp each evening.

One of the CCC enrollees' most valuable lessons was learning how to get along with others, including fellow enrollees from states as different as Texas and Pennsylvania. Getting along with others was often a difficult life lesson to learn, but nearly every enrollee agreed it was the most important lesson of their many positive experiences in the CCC. Uneducated, poor, often-undernourished boys grew into strong, proud, healthy young men at a time in history when few "coming-of-age"

CCC boys in camp

▲▲▲▲▲▲▲▲▲▲▲▲▲▲▲▲▲▲▲▲▲▲▲▲▲▲▲▲▲▲▲▲

Si Porter and the Civilian Conservation Corps

CCC enrollees learned many important lessons, including the lesson of taking pride in their work. Si Porter of Corona, New Mexico, admitted that he had little interest, much less pride, in his work before working in the CCC:

> I had no experience with anything except dry land bean farming and trapping skunks. I couldn't catch any other kind of fur-bearing animals [other than] our family dog a few times. . . . My future didn't look very bright. . . .

Si's attitude changed considerably when he began working for the CCC. He clearly took pride in fighting forest fires, keeping a team of horses, learning surveying skills, and making a wire fence. Years later, when recalling the fence he had helped build, Si proudly reported that "some of the wire has been replaced, but I think just about all the posts are there in the same holes and it's still solid."

Si's work ethic had changed so much in the CCC that he did not even complain when he was assigned kitchen duty (KP) on his last day in camp. In fact, when Si found another enrollee not cleaning dishes well that day

> I would put [the dirty dishes] back in the wash water and tell him to clean them again. His temper started showing, and . . . he told me that we were leaving tonight and they can't put us on KP again tomorrow. We would not be eating out of these plates again, so why worry? I told him that I had a lot of good friends that were not leaving, . . . and I didn't want to leave any dirty dishes behind.

(Quoted in Richard Melzer, ed., "Leonard W. 'Si' Porter's Memories of Life in the Civilian Conservation Corps Camps in Southern New Mexico, 1936–39," *New Mexico Historical Review* 80 [Fall 2005]: 419, 426–33.)

Although never one to brag, Si admitted that "I almost developed a good reputation" in the CCC. Using what he had learned about life and work, Si left the CCC to serve admirably in World War II and pursue a productive, thirty-year career with the Santa Fe Railroad. Like most enrollees, Si saw his months working in the CCC as a major turning point in his life.

---

opportunities existed in New Mexico or anywhere in the United States. As a proud grandfather exclaimed when his grandson, Tito, and his friend returned from the CCC, "*Por Dios* (for heaven's sake), they went away *no bueno por nada* (good for nothing) and they came back big and strong."

A CCC For Women

The CCC was the most popular New Deal program in the United States, but it was not only for unemployed young men. Special branches of the CCC were created for Native Americans (with conservation and construction projects on reservations) and for economically destitute veterans of World War I.

There was even a special CCC for young women, inspired by President Roosevelt's wife, Eleanor. Jokingly referred to as the "She She She," the program was actually a part of the National Youth Administration (NYA). As with their male counterparts, young women in this program usually lived and worked in rural camps where they learned valuable work skills and earned badly needed money for themselves and their families back home.

This NYA program was never as large or as popular as the CCC, but New Mexico could boast of having probably the most successful women's camp in the nation. Camp Capitán, a former CCC camp high in the Lincoln National Forest, served more than three thousand New Mexico girls from its creation in 1933 to its closure in 1940. Under the leadership of director Lucy Shaw, girls took academic classes, learned vocational skills, created traditional arts and crafts, and studied home economics. Using their sewing skills, girls made clothes for patients at the Carrie Tingley Hospital for Crippled Children, state flags for public schools, and practical items, like kitchen aprons, that were sold to the general public in catalogs.

Camp Capitán held an annual open house to show the camp and its progress to newspaper reporters and residents of the local area. After visiting the camp's open house in April 1938, a reporter wrote that

> more than two hundred [locals visited] the camp on Sunday afternoon from 1:00 to 5:00 o'clock. . . . As visitors entered the gate, guides . . . conducted each party through the barracks, hospital, library, mess hall, and cottage, where Mrs. Shaw presided graciously as hostess. . . .
>
> All the girls seemed happy and buoyant. The Spanish girls were especially striking in their dark beauty, wearing white blouses [with] vivid colcha embroidery. . . .
>
> The climax to the afternoon's pleasure was an operetta given by the girls.
>
> The place . . . has a charm of life and manner pleasant and hospitable. . . . Above all, it has a contented group of students . . . privileged to receive this excellent training.

(*Lincoln County News*, April 15, 1938.)

A New Deal for Labor Unions

Workers in private industry also shared in the benefits of the New Deal in New Mexico. Perhaps most important, the **National Industrial Recovery Act** of 1933 granted all workers the right to organize unions and negotiate labor contracts through **collective bargaining**. After years of struggle, workers finally had the power to confront management and seek fair wages and improved working conditions.

Using this new power, coal miners in the Gallup area organized a local union of the National Miners Union (NMU) to deal with problems caused by unjust coal company policies. When Gallup coal companies refused to bargain through collective bargaining, however, the new union voted to strike. Among the main issues at stake in the strike were company recognition of the miners' union and a recent 35 percent decrease in pay. Workers and their families set up picket lines at five major coal mines in August 1933.

In response, Gallup coal companies requested that the state government provide national guard protection and establish martial (or military) law, although no violence had occurred on the picket lines. A curfew was imposed, and guardsmen escorted strike breakers, or **scabs**, to the mines to replace striking workers. Miners could not gather in groups of more than five. Several union leaders were even jailed.

Despite these and other obstacles, the walkout was finally settled after eighty-five days, making it the longest strike in New Mexico until that time. Each side claimed victory in the settlement. The coal companies claimed victory because they refused to recognize the union and rehire most of the men who had gone out on strike. The union claimed victory because it had won increased wages for most of the miners who agreed to go back to work and were rehired.

Unfortunately, trouble in Gallup did not end with the 1933 strike. In 1935, housing that had formerly belonged to Gallup's largest coal company was sold to a new owner. Most residents living in these former company houses were unemployed miners, hardly able to pay small monthly rents, much less buy their small homes at high prices, as the new owner now demanded they do. The owner resorted to evicting those who could not afford his unreasonably high prices.

Víctor Campos, an unemployed miner, was targeted for the first eviction on April 1, 1935. As deputies moved Campos's goods through the front door of his home, however, Campos and about fifty of his neighbors returned his property just as quickly through the back door. Campos and two others were arrested for breaking and entering; only Campos was jailed. Their hearing was set for April 4.

On the day of the hearing, the McKinley County sheriff, **Mack Carmichael**, and his deputies accompanied Campos from his jail cell to the courthouse. A crowd of more than a hundred gathered outside the courthouse to learn the accused men's fate. The closed hearing was brief and inconclusive, but Sheriff Carmichael thought it best to leave the courthouse with Campos through the back exit to avoid the increasingly large, hostile crowd in front. To the lawmen's surprise, about seventy-five members of the crowd now filled the back alley, demanding to know what had transpired.

Suddenly shots rang out. Within moments, Carmichael lay dead, and two of his deputies fell wounded. Two men in the crowd also died. Eight others were wounded by deputy fire. The tragic episode lasted only minutes.

With no clearly identified shooter, the police arrested 112 men and women in what became a thirty-six-hour roundup of suspected radicals, mostly NMU members, as much as a search for suspected criminals. With their rights largely ignored, many Mexican nationals among the 112 were deported, and ten men were actually charged with murder. Feelings ran so high in Gallup that the murder trial had to be moved to Aztec, New Mexico.

After a nine-day trial of questionable fairness, seven of the ten accused miners were acquitted, and three were found guilty. Those found guilty were each sentenced to forty-five to sixty years in prison. None served his full sentence; one was freed on appeal, and the remaining two were pardoned in 1939 by Gov. John E. Miles with the understanding that they must immediately leave the state.

Discredited by accusations of violence and other charges, the National Miners Union local soon disbanded in Gallup. It was not until World War II that miners in Gallup and New Mexico's other coal mines won union recognition from their companies as members of the **United Mine Workers (UMW)**. Workers' interests were finally defended but at a tragic cost in lost lives and compromised freedoms.

☼ Not Always a Good Deal

There is no doubt the New Deal provided many benefits for New Mexicans, especially workers, artists, authors, farmers, ranchers, and the young. As might be expected of a program of its scope and magnitude, however, the New Deal suffered its share of problems and criticism in New Mexico and across the country. Charges of corruption in the WPA hurt the New Deal in New Mexico, although they eventually led to some needed national reforms. Not all WPA or PWA projects were considered essential, and workers were accused of not being as productive as they might have been if they were working for private business enterprises; according to some, the letters WPA really stood for "We Putter Along."

As reflected in letters to Senator Chavez, some Hispanics complained about discrimination in programs like the WPA and the CCC. These complaints were relatively rare, though, and in most cases Hispanic citizens represented the greatest number of workers on WPA work crews and in CCC camps, rather than the fewest.

Newspaper Criticism of the New Deal

While many newspapers in New Mexico supported the New Deal, conservative Republican papers did not. Political ads, editorials, political cartoons, and news stories reflected a small, but vocal, anti-New Deal sentiment in the state.

The conservative *Belén News* made typical charges against New Deal policies and leaders. In one article, a Republican leader "lashed out vigorously" at the cost of "impractical projects" staffed by men who "lean on shovels" in jobs they were supposedly given in exchange for their Democratic votes. A political ad on October 11, 1934, accused Democrats of spending large sums of money on highways "just prior to election [as] a vote-getting stunt." An editorial even said that "goats and sheep were given away to voters before [an] election" in four New Mexico counties.

Meanwhile, according to the *News*, government workers were told "that their ballots cast at the coming election . . . would be inspected and that those that did not 'vote right' . . . would be punished [with] the loss of jobs."

Other newspapers, like the *Santa Fe New Mexican*, claimed that the New Deal encouraged and protected labor strikes and strikers, even though such "protection and encouragement resulted in the destruction of property and [the] loss of life."

The Roosevelt administration and its New Deal remained enormously popular, despite the charges that it only survived with blatant political threats and bribes in the form of jobs, sheep, goats, and roads.

 ## Sheep Reduction on the Navajo Reservation

The greatest, most legitimate complaints about New Deal programs and their impact came from Native American groups dealing with the **Bureau of Indian Affairs (BIA)**.

In 1933, President Roosevelt appointed **John Collier** as the country's new commissioner of Indian affairs to lead the BIA. Collier seemed like an excellent choice, having studied Indian cultures and problems since his arrival as a guest in Mabel Dodge Luhan's house in 1920. Collier was among the many Anglos who had allied with the All-Indian Council when it had successfully defeated the infamous Bursum Bill in 1923. Collier had long been critical of the BIA and its harmful policies.

Many were optimistic that Collier might bring New Deal benefits to Native Americans when he entered office in 1933. Collier was, in fact, largely responsible for the new respect for Indian culture taught in formerly oppressive Indian boarding schools. Even more ambitiously, Collier attempted to return much power and autonomy to Indian tribes after years of cultural and political suppression. Collier's **Indian Reorganization Act (IRA)**, which Congress passed in 1934, allowed for separate tribal constitutions and self-government. More than 170 tribes voted to accept the IRA, and it worked well for some tribes, including the Mescalero Apaches of southern New Mexico. Other tribes, including the Navajos, rejected the new plan.

After returning from their nightmare at Bosque Redondo in 1868, Navajos had rebuilt their lives based on livestock, especially sheep herding. Starting with 14,000 sheep in 1868, Navajos had increased their stock to about 800,000 sheep by the 1920s. With so many animals grazing on a limited amount of land, soil erosion followed, with terrible results for the flocks and to the ecology.

To help solve the problem of overgrazing, the **Taylor Grazing Act** of 1934 called for a reduction of livestock

Navajo sheep herder

The Stock-Reduction Plan's Impact on a Navajo Sheepherder

Charlie Yellow, a Navajo medicine man of the Many Goats Clan from Kayenta, remembers:

We were herding [our goats and sheep] some distance from here when [John] Collier's [government] men caught up with us. Right there all the goats were killed, about a hundred of them. The sheep that survived grew . . . for several years. Then along came Collier again.

I took my sheep all the way down to a place called Teel Ch'init'I', Cat Tails Come Out, and hid them. All the horses and goats and many sheep around here were killed. Their bones still lie around. We live among their bones.

When they reduced the stock, many men, women, boys, and girls died. They died of what we call ch'èèná, which is sadness for something that will never come back.

(Interview quoted in Claudeen Arthur et al., *Between Sacred Mountains: Navajo Stories and Lessons from the Land* [Tucson: University of Arizona Press, 1982], 173.)

The Stock-Reduction Plan's Impact on the Navajo Nation

In February 1940, four Navajo Council delegates wrote to their congressman to protest policies that limited the number of sheep per Navajo family as part of the federal government's controversial sheep-reduction plan. They wrote that the small number of sheep allowed per family

> is not sufficient for even the bare existence of a moderate size Navajo family without additional income, and such a policy will mean the impoverishment of the entire Navajo Tribe. . . . From a tribe [that was] self-sufficient and self-supporting, the Bureau [of Indian Affairs] is forcing us to become dependant upon charity for our subsistence.

We only desire to be financially independent and make our own way.

At the beginning of the reduction the Commissioner of Indian Affairs [John Collier] promised the Navajo people that there would be work for all sufficient to enable us to earn enough to offset our losses due to reduction. This promise of the Indian Commissioner has not been fulfilled. . . .

(Scott Preston, Julius Begay, Frank Goldtooth, Judge Many Children to John R. Murdock, February 14, 1940, quoted in Peter Iverson, ed., *For Our Navajo People: Diné Letters, Speeches and Petitions, 1900–1960* [Albuquerque: University of New Mexico Press, 2002], 23–24.)

in many parts of the country, including on the Navajo Reservation. At first, only a small number of sheep and goats were destroyed, with the approval of the Navajo Tribal Council and a promise that the federal government would provide new jobs and additional land to offset the loss of Navajo income from livestock.

Things did not go as promised. The government oversaw the killing of ever greater numbers of sheep, leading many on the reservation to distrust John Collier and whatever other reforms he proposed, including the IRA. In all, at least half of all Navajo sheep were slaughtered, with the greatest number of sheep lost to poor families who could least afford such financial losses. Many Navajo families felt betrayed, much as their ancestors had been betrayed on the Long Walk and at Bosque Redondo in the 1860s. It would take years for the Navajos to recover from the well-meaning, but tragic, stock-reduction program and the bitterness it caused.

 ## Bosque Farms

Another well-intentioned New Deal project was attempted on 2,425 acres of land in Valencia County, twenty miles south of Albuquerque. Purchased by the federal government and named **Bosque Farms**, the land was to be improved and divided among farming families from the Dust

Bowl areas of northern and eastern New Mexico. Similar Resettlement Administration projects were attempted in other parts of the United States, including smaller ones near Fort Sumner and Las Cruces.

A lottery was held in Bosque Farms on May 1, 1935, to assign forty-two plots of land among the newly arrived farmers and their families. Each family received between thirty and eighty-seven acres of land, or an average of fifty-three acres per farm. With the help of more than 450 local WPA workers, the farmers cut trees, cleared their land, and built new adobe homes.

Unfortunately, project officials soon determined that farms of fifty-three or fewer acres were not sufficient to support an average farm family. The land had to be redivided, meaning that seventeen newly arrived families were left without land and were told to leave. The remaining families supported the seventeen affected families by writing letters, signing petitions, and meeting with key political leaders, including Governor Tingley. Nothing helped, and the families had to move. Inferior soil, poor management, and overly rigid planning caused other families to move as well.

By World War II few of the original families remained in Bosque Farms. Of those who stayed, most had become dairy farmers with

Building a family home at Bosque Farms

government assistance. The community prospered as the demand for dairy goods grew in nearby Albuquerque. Later, dairy farmers sold their land to housing developers who subdivided the land and built modern homes alongside the original forty-two farmhouses. Bosque Farms became a largely suburban community, with most residents commuting to Albuquerque to work each day.

While all the original farmhouses remain, most have been remodeled, and the community's original purpose has been largely forgotten. As with the Navajo stock-reduction plan, Bosque Farms was a well-intentioned New Deal program that took unexpected, unfortunate turns, often contrary to the best interests of the very New Mexicans it was meant to assist.

The Impact of the New Deal on New Mexico

Despite some unintended, adverse results, most New Deal programs were helpful to individual workers and whole communities in New Mexico. Thanks to strong, effective leaders like Clyde Tingley and Dennis Chavez, the state received more than its share of federal support for New Deal projects, using the talents and skills of thousands of New Mexicans, from young adults to established artists and authors. Ironically, much of what was created in the midst of a prolonged economic crisis might never have been accomplished if not for the New Deal programs formed to help end the crisis. It is hard to imagine New Mexico without the schools, post offices, community centers, and libraries the WPA and other New Deal programs built. Most of these well-built structures still stand and continue to serve their communities and the fortunate people in them.

Admirably, most New Deal projects in New Mexico respected Southwest cultures and values, often after years of cultural criticism and neglect. Most buildings were built with traditional materials (such as adobe) with traditional designs (such as Pueblo Revival architecture) and decorated with traditional furniture (such as tinwork) and art forms (such as murals) with locally important themes. Hispanic and Native American arts and crafts were taught, displayed, and valued as never before. As a result, New Mexico cultures, values, and communities were often preserved, while individual New Mexicans gained or regained identity and self-respect.

Young people in particular benefited from New Deal programs. Many were able to continue their education and learn traditional skills, thanks to the NYA and new or remodeled schools from the elementary to the college level. Young men in the CCC—and young women at Camp Capitán—continued their education, learned work skills, and developed a work ethic that helped them come of age and mature, despite major obstacles the Great Depression caused.

Workers also benefited, especially with the organization and eventual recognition of unions in the coals fields of New Mexico. Unfortunately, such accomplishments often came at a high price, were seldom permanent, and were largely limited to a single industry.

Politically, many New Mexicans who had benefited from the New Deal shifted their party loyalty to the Democratic Party after years of Republican Party domination dating back to territorial days. Including Dennis Chavez, who served in the U.S. Senate until his death in 1962, six of New Mexico's nine senators elected since 1935 have been Democrats. Including Clyde Tingley, eleven of the state's seventeen elected governors have been Democrats since 1935.

Economically, the New Deal helped New Mexico and New Mexicans survive the worst days of the Great Depression. President Roosevelt is said to have thought of himself as Dr. New Deal who prescribed federal funding as the medicine the nation needed to regain its strength and enjoy good health, or prosperity. Dr. New Deal's medicine never cured his patient, but it usually reduced his pain and prepared him for a more prosperous post-Depression era. For better or worse, New Mexico's economy was more dependent on the federal government than ever before, a trend that would only increase in the decades to come.

Finally, the New Deal helped to preserve our democratic form of government. Many who had given up on capitalism in the worst years of the Depression had also given up on democracy because of its apparent inability to deal with the deepening crisis. The New Deal proved that our democracy, when ably led and equipped with new ideas, could work effectively and well in hard times as well as in good. While other countries in the world had turned to brutal forms of government in their desperate attempts to survive the Great Depression, most Americans had faith that democratically elected, strong leaders like Franklin Roosevelt, Clyde Tingley, and Dennis Chavez could rescue what was most valued and most important to the United States.

☀ Other Ways to Survive the Great Depression

The New Deal certainly helped many New Mexicans survive the Great Depression. New Mexicans survived this dismal decade in other ways as well, thanks to new technology, community unity, and basic human kindness.

▲▲▲▲▲▲▲▲▲▲▲▲▲▲▲▲▲▲▲▲▲▲▲▲▲▲

Modern Movie Ads

Movie fans eagerly combed their local newspapers for ads announcing what feature film was showing, as at the Central Theatre in Belén:

Little Women

Louisa M. Alcott's famous classic, "Little Women," with Katharine Hepburn and a great cast, including such well known players as Joan Bennett, Paul Lucas, Frances Dee Jean Parker, Edna Mae Oliver and many more.

    The world's most beloved family of girls, in the picture America has waited three quarters of a century to see. Topsy Turvy Joe, grumpy old Aunt March, sweet Beth, flirtatious Meg, fastidious Amy, . . . and Mops the dog. They are all here and they leap from the book and live. The ecstasy of moonlight, the miracle of Spring. . . . Live these golden hours with [this] beloved family of girls.

(*Belén News*, May 11, 1934.)

Billy the Kid

Wallace Beery, John Mack Brown and a good cast in "Billy the Kid." This is the story that deals with New Mexico's famous outlaw character. . . . Wallace Beery plays the character of Sheriff Garrett and John Mack Brown plays the part of Billy the Kid.

    Added: Another episode of the thrilling outdoor story, "Mystery Mountain," with Ken Marnard.

    Bargain admission prices to this program.

(*Belén News*, May 23, 1935.)

Old radio microphone

Some momentarily escaped the day-to-day problems of the Depression by enjoying modern forms of entertainment. First popular in the 1920s, radios became even more appealing as a diversion in the 1930s, at least for those who could afford them and had access to electricity. With electricity in less than 4 percent of all New Mexico farms, many radios were battery operated.

KOB, the state's first commercial radio station, broadcast from the New Mexico A&M campus from 1922 to 1932 and from Albuquerque thereafter. Families often gathered around their radio sets to listen to music, comedies, and dramas, using their imaginations to "see" what they could only hear. New Mexicans even heard their president on the radio. Franklin Roosevelt spoke to all Americans, discussing his plans for the country and its future. Known as fireside chats, it felt as if the president had personally entered American homes and was talking to families directly. In addition, farmers listened for weather reports and current market conditions. Everyone listened to radio commercials advertising new products. It was as if this remarkable new form of communication had supplied New Mexicans with a window to a broad world far beyond their small towns and farms.

Movies were as popular as radio shows for those who lived in or near towns with movie theaters. Movie tickets were inexpensive (10¢ to 50¢, or $1.38 to $6.90 in today's money); at least one theater on Central Avenue in Albuquerque even accepted IOUs if patrons were low on cash. Comedies, musicals, dramas, and especially Westerns were popular and distracting for hours at a time. Movie series, usually ending with exciting cliff-hanger scenes, kept young moviegoers coming back to theaters week after week. The introduction of movies with sound tracks, or **talkies**, in the late 1920s, as well as color and new special effects in the 1930s, made movies more entertaining and appealing for New Mexicans of all ages.

New Mexicans hardly needed movie theaters or radios to have fun and forget their economic woes. New Mexicans made their own entertainment in fondly remembered family and community activities. Celebrating their unique cultures, residents often gathered for sing-alongs, picnics, games, sporting events, and dances. Entire families (including pets) arrived at a chosen home to dance through the night (breaking for refreshments at midnight) and into the morning, while tired children slept on beds and floors in a back room. In the words of an appreciative farmer, "we made our own fun" and "had us some good times."

On a more serious level, New Mexicans survived the Depression by helping each other out on a daily basis. Old-timers recall the gratitude they felt when people aided them and, far more, the satisfaction they realized when sharing what little they had with others. As families who lived in the coal-mining camp at Madrid remembered, everyone felt needed and equal, regardless of race, ethnicity, or nationality.

The same was true in Pie Town. As poor as they usually were, Pie Town families helped their neighbors when they were sick, when food was low, when graves were dug, and even when clothes were needed to attend special events. (A farmer once lent his local preacher a

Pie Town dance

pair of dress pants to wear to Albuquerque, although the pants were "so thin at the seat you could read a newspaper through them," according to the generous farmer's wife.) Josie Caudill Endsley was a young girl on her family's farm in Pie Town, but she remembers that her parents "had a special friendship with all of the people there. They had something money cannot buy. They needed each other and were willing to share all they had. They all helped one another without expecting something in return."

Josie could have been describing nearly any community in New Mexico in the 1930s. Astonishingly, a great many New Mexicans who lived through the Great Depression recall that most troubling decade as the best years of their lives.

Conclusions

The decade of the Great Depression was the worst economic period in New Mexico history. A poor state grew even poorer during a depression that affected the entire United States and, in fact, the world.

As bad as economic conditions became, New Mexicans managed to survive with a combination of methods, including use of the federal government's New Deal programs. While some New Deal programs did not work as well as intended, most benefited New Mexicans as no other federal programs had ever benefited the state before.

As much as the New Deal helped New Mexicans survive the Great Depression, New Mexicans mostly endured the crisis by drawing on their own personal strengths and lending each other a helping hand. New Mexicans bravely faced the challenge of the Depression and prevailed, just as they had prevailed through every major crisis in their long history.

1. Describe the impact of the Great Depression on New Mexico businesses and workers, including men, women, the young, Mexican migrants, and Dust Bowl families.

2. Describe Franklin Roosevelt's New Deal and explain why it gave so many Americans new hope.

3. Which two leaders in particular brought many New Deal programs to New Mexico? How were they able to bring these valuable programs to the state?

4. How did New Deal programs like the WPA benefit New Mexico's workers, communities, community members, local economies, and the state's economy?

5. How did New Deal art and literature benefit New Mexico?

6. How did the New Deal benefit New Mexico's youth?

7. How could New Deal programs be criticized and by whom?

8. Describe the impact of the Great Depression and the New Deal on New Mexico.

9. How did modern radios and movies help New Mexicans survive the Depression?

10. How did New Mexicans help each other survive even the worst days of the Great Depression?

11. What aspects of New Mexico would you have been proud of if you had lived in the Great Depression? Why?

12. What aspects would you have been less proud of if you had lived in the Great Depression? Why?

13. What lessons can we learn from the history of New Mexico in the Great Depression?

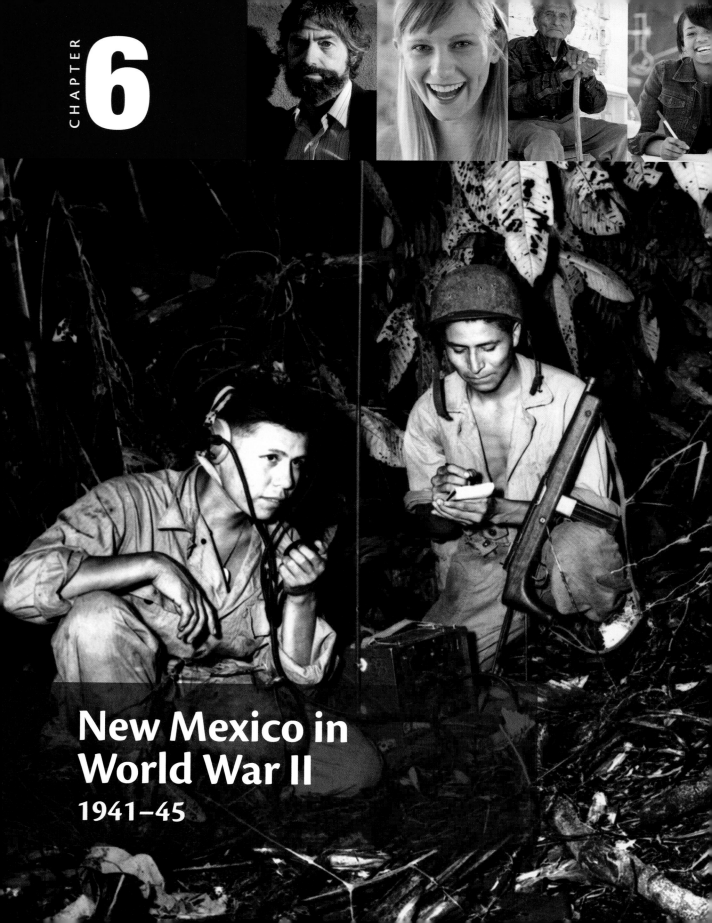

New Mexico in World War II

1941–45

TIMELINE

1939
Albert Einstein warns President Roosevelt of German experiments with an atomic weapon

1941
New Mexico's National Guard, now the 200th Coast Artillery (AA), shipped out to the Philippine Islands

December 7: Japanese surprise attack on Pearl Harbor, Hawaii, followed by attacks on the Philippines; the United States enters World War II

December 12: Rueben Elebrando García of the 200th Coast Artillery (AA) is killed in the Philippines, becoming New Mexico's first casualty of World War II

1942
April 9: American forces in the Philippines surrender to the Japanese, beginning the Bataan Death March

The Bataan Relief Organization (BRO) founded

Original twenty-nine Navajo Code Talkers recruited into the marines

Japanese-American internment camps opened in Santa Fe and Lordsburg

Bracero Program agreement signed by the United States and Mexico

German POW camps first opened in New Mexico

Rationing of essential war items begin

1943
Los Alamos opens as the key lab in the making of the atomic bomb

1944
June 6: D-Day, the turning point of the war in Europe

1945
April 12: President Roosevelt dies; Harry S Truman is sworn in as president

April 18: Ernie Pyle killed in the Pacific

May 8: V-E Day, Germans' unconditional surrender

July 16: First atomic explosion at Trinity Site

August 6: Atomic bomb dropped on Hiroshima, Japan

August 9: Atomic bomb dropped on Nagasaki, Japan

August 15: V-J Day, Japanese unconditional surrender, ending World War II

Introduction

More than 350 Japanese warplanes attacked American forces at Pearl Harbor, Hawaii, in the early morning hours of December 7, 1941. Within two hours the United States had suffered the loss of twenty-one ships, 188 planes, and 2,335 members of its armed forces, including 1,177 men on the USS *Arizona* alone. Hours later the United States declared war on Japan and, soon thereafter, on Japan's allies, Germany and Italy. The United States had entered World War II.

Every state in the Union played a major role in helping our country fight and eventually win the new world war. But no state of modest population and economy did more than New Mexico to assure victory in the largest, most costly war the world had ever seen.

The purpose of this chapter is to describe

- New Mexico's major battlefield contributions of World War II;
- New Mexico's major home front contributions of World War II;
- and the high cost of the war in lives, dollars, and lost freedoms.

The War Overseas

New Mexicans in the Philippines

Moments after attacking American forces on Pearl Harbor, the Japanese turned their guns on another U.S. possession in the Pacific Ocean, the Philippine Islands. The United States had acquired the Philippines in the

167

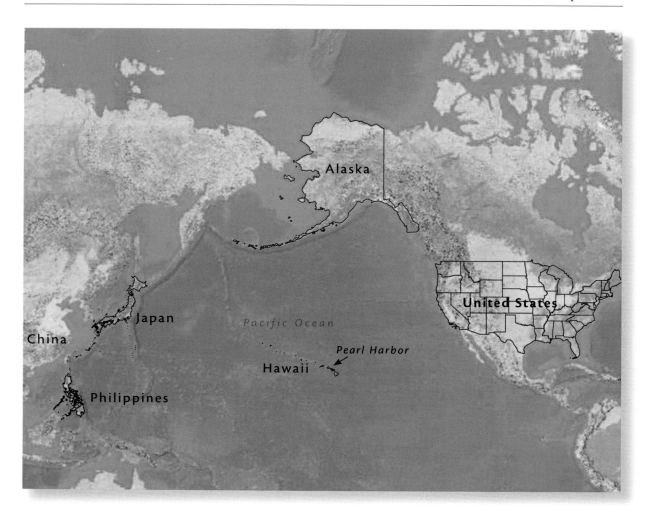

Spanish-American War of 1898; in 1941 the islands remained our largest, most valuable possession in the Far East. The Japanese were determined to capture the Philippines to force the United States from the Far East and exploit Philippine resources for themselves.

Among the Americans attacked in the Japanese invasion of the Philippines was a small, but proud, group of New Mexicans who had arrived in the islands just three months before the war began. After months of training at Fort Bliss, Texas, these 1,826 Hispanic, Anglo, and Native American members of the New Mexico National Guard had been given a heartfelt farewell as they prepared to ship out for the Pacific in August 1941. It was as if New Mexicans in towns from

▲▼▲▼▲▼▲▼▲▼▲▼▲▼▲▼▲▼

The Main Countries at War in World War II

The Allied Powers: The United States, England, France, and the Soviet Union

The Axis Powers: Germany, Japan, and Italy

Deming to Albuquerque attempted to fortify their young troops with the courage they would need to fight and, it was hoped, survive the months and years to come.

Most of the soldiers of the New Mexico National Guard had joined because they were loyal American patriots, eager to serve their state and nation. Most also joined to earn $15 a month ($195 in today's money) in extra income for themselves and their families in the last years of the Great Depression. Few imagined the sacrifice they would be asked to make for their fellow New Mexicans and the United States as a whole once the war began.

Mobilized as the **200th Coast Artillery (AA)**, which later spawned the **515th Coast Artillery**, the recently arrived New Mexicans were in the thick of the heaviest fighting from December 1941 to April 1942. Like all American troops, they experienced more and more casualties as

Wreckage of the USS *Arizona* after the attack on Pearl Harbor

The Philippines: The red area is the Bataan Peninsula, scene of many battles.

the Japanese invasion progressed. They quickly ran low on essential supplies, from food and medicine to guns and ammunition. Although the Americans searched the horizon for U.S. Navy ships that might bring new soldiers and supplies, reinforcements never came. Instead, more enemy troops and planes arrived, only increasing the odds of a Japanese victory and an American defeat. American and Filipino forces retreated down the Bataan Peninsula as they fought their hardest with no relief in sight.

Many Americans in the Philippines felt deserted by their country and its armed forces. Feeling abandoned, thousands uttered the phrase, "No Mama, no Papa, no Uncle Sam." The United States could do little to assist its soldiers in the Philippines, however, because much of the American fleet that might have carried reinforcements and supplies to the Pacific had been destroyed at Pearl Harbor, just as the Japanese had planned in their larger military strategy.

With dwindling supplies, weakened troops, and no real hope of rescue, the U.S. Army had no option but to surrender to the Japanese on April 9, 1942. Led by their commander, **Col. Charles G. Sage**, New

▲▲▲▲▲▲▲▲▲▲▲▲▲▲▲▲▲▲▲▲▲▲▲▲▲▲▲▲▲▲▲

Memories of the Bataan Death March

Pete A. Gonzales was born in Las Cruces and raised in Los Lunas, graduating from Los Lunas High School in 1940 when he was nineteen years old. Two years later, as a member of New Mexico's 200th Coast Artillery (AA), he was among the more than eighteen hundred New Mexicans who experienced the horrors of the Bataan Death March. Here, in an oral history conducted by historian Angie S. López, Gonzales described what he witnessed on the march:

> When the Death March began . . . none of us knew where we were going; we just walked. As we continued . . . , we met up with others who'd been captured and the line became longer. We were like the walking dead. The heat was unbearable. We had no food or water, although we passed some artesian wells. If anyone made a run for one of the wells he was killed. If someone was injured or ill and was about to fall, we tried to carry him, but we were weak ourselves. If someone did fall and the enemy saw him, they would bayonet or shoot that person. . . . Seemed like we walked forever.

> (Angie S. López, *Blessed Are the Soldiers* [Albuquerque: Sandia Publishing, 1990], 108–9.)

Lorenzo Banegas told a similar story, remembering his buddy from New Mexico, Adolfo Rivera:

> I was so tired I said I don't care if I live or die. [But then Adolfo] picked me up. He said, "No, Banegas! Come on, let's go out and put some water on you." He . . . threw some water on me. . . . And then when he saw that I looked up again, he said, "Come on, let's sing us a song!" And started singing this song: "Cuando se quiere deveras, como te quiero yo a ti." (When one loves truly, the way that I love you.) It was a love ballad [we] both had sung as boys in New Mexico.

> (*El Paso Times*, April 5, 1992.)

"Golly, every time I hear that song . . . ," Banegas says he bursts into tears because, with Rivera's help, Banegas survived the Death March. Tragically, Rivera later died in Japanese captivity.

Mexicans were said to be the first to have fought and the last to have surrendered to the Japanese. Twenty New Mexicans had been killed in combat from December 1941 to April 1942, but antiaircraft guns manned by New Mexican soldiers had shot down eighty-six Japanese planes in the same period, including six on a single day. By fighting as long as they did, American soldiers had achieved at least a partial victory: the Japanese were delayed by months in their timetable of expansion to other parts of the Pacific. The surviving New Mexicans, as

Medical Conditions in a POW Camp

Capt. Paul Ashton served as a medical doctor at Tayabas, a Philippine POW camp he described in his memoirs as "the worst place I ever saw." Tragically, conditions at this camp, located along a polluted river, were typical of camps throughout the islands. Here is Dr. Ashton's graphic description of what he encountered at Tayabas:

> Whether it was our [poor] diet or the [dirty drinking] water, everyone had diarrhea or dysentery and no toilet paper. Most of the men had malaria, some severely, and a few had dengue and jaundice, and they had absolutely no appetite. Some of the men in sick bay were so weak they were unable to walk or even feed themselves. They slept soundly due to their toxicity and dehydration, and we spent much time fanning away the mosquitoes that would congregate on the skin of exposed areas. We had found that the multiple bites would cause ulcerations, especially on the cheeks and foreheads. One day the river rose very quickly and higher than usual, so that one or two of the comatose patients were washed away downstream—toward home.

(Paul Ashton, *Bataan Diary* [N.p.: Privately published, 1984], 215–17.)

Prisoners on the Bataan Death March, 1942

▲▲▲▲▲▲▲▲▲▲▲▲▲▲▲▲▲▲▲▲▲▲▲▲▲

A New Mexican Captain's Last Will

Capt. William C. Porter, a graduate of New Mexico A&M's class of 1941, was being held as a prisoner in a Japanese POW prison in the Philippines when he learned that he and about a hundred other New Mexicans were about to be shipped to Japan on a hell ship, the *Oryoku Maru*, in late 1944. He quickly wrote a letter to his family, enclosing his brief last will and testament:

Bilibid Prison
Manila, Philippines
December 12, 1944

I, William C. Porter II, Captain U.S. Army, O-395518, being at present a prisoner of war and as such held by Japan, being in sound mental health do publish this as my last will and testament.

1. *I name my mother, Mrs. William Asa Porter, . . . as my sole benefactor and heiress.*
2. *I furthermore appoint my mother, Mrs. William Asa Porter, as my executrix, with full powers of attorney.*
3. *I leave to my benefactor all pay, and allowances due me from the government of the U.S., all insurances, and all property, and possessions either mine or due me through inheritance.*

Signed
William C. Porter

(Quoted in Walter Hines, *Aggies of the Pacific War: New Mexico A&M and the War with Japan* [Las Cruces: Yucca Tree Press, 1999], 151–52.)

Captain Porter was incredibly fortunate. He was one of only 430 of the 1,619 Americans on the *Oryoku Maru* who survived the nightmarish voyage. The other 1,089, or 73 percent, died from terrible conditions on board or from American air strikes at sea.

well as seventy-six thousand other American and Filipino soldiers, took small comfort in this achievement as they faced life as prisoners of war (POWs) at the mercy of the Japanese.

The POWs were forced to walk a sixty-five-mile **death march** along the east coast of the Bataan Peninsula. The highway they traveled was little more than a dirt road with no facilities and little shade to shelter them from the burning sun and hundred-degree temperatures. Captured during the islands' dry season, the men kicked dirt into the air as they struggled mile after mile, unintentionally making themselves thirstier and filthier with each step. At night they were penned in small,

A Survivor's Miracle Story

By great miracles, some New Mexicans survived the Bataan Death March, POW camps, and the hell ships of World War II. Calvin Graef of Silver City was one such survivor.

After enduring the death march and terrible disease in Japanese POW camps, Graef was aboard a Japanese ship, the *Arisan Maru*, with about eighteen hundred other American prisoners when it was hit by a torpedo launched by a U.S. Navy submarine on October 24, 1944.

With no other option, Graef jumped off the sinking vessel into the South China Sea, hundreds of miles from shore. "Looking in every direction, there was nothing but shades of darkness and walls of water. I was lost—really lost . . ."

That was when Graef's miracles began. Here is a list of just some of the miracles he experienced in his incredible journey to safety:

- In the middle of the ocean, he found an abandoned lifeboat with some food and fresh water. Four other American survivors were on board.
- When their fresh water ran out, a five-gallon wooden keg of fresh water floated by, close enough for the men to retrieve it from the waves.
- When an enemy ship came by, the five Americans pretended they were dead. The ship circled their lifeboat twice "and then, for some unknown reason, turned around and headed back in the direction it had come" without firing a shot.
- Soon, the men saw a box floating in the water. "We managed to get to it and pull it into the boat. The box contained a sail. Oh, it wasn't just a sail— it was a sail that originally had been made for the lifeboat we were in."
- Using their newly found sail, the Americans eventually landed on one of the few safe spots along the hundreds of miles of Chinese coast.

Safe at last, Calvin Graef returned to a hero's welcome. He met Pres. Harry S Truman and "arrived to a huge welcome [in Silver City]. The whole town had turned out to throw a welcoming party for me. Tables were lined with food, the high school band played . . . , and many old friends shook my hand." Countless miracles had brought Graef home to New Mexico at last.

(Melissa Masterson, *Ride the Waves to Freedom: Calvin Graef's Survival Story of the Bataan Death March and His Escape from a Sinking Hellship* [Hobbs: Southwest Freelance, 2000], 20–26, 75, 107.)

unsanitary enclosures. Those who managed to survive through the day often died of disease or starvation at night.

Conditions only worsened when the Japanese crammed survivors of the death march into railroad freight cars with no air, water, or room in which to move. Many died on trains en route to prison camps

▲▲▲▲▲▲▲▲▲▲▲▲▲▲▲▲▲▲▲▲▲▲▲▲▲▲

The Bataan Relief Organization (BRO) in New Mexico

Within days of the American surrender in the Philippines, hundreds of Albuquerque neighbors met to create the Bataan Relief Organization (BRO). A newspaper reporter described the event:

> Handkerchiefs often were raised to eyes among the group of 600 to 700 Albuquerque residents which packed the Elks Lodge ceremonial hall. But for those that wept, there were as many more who sat composed and . . . translated their feelings into action when suggestions were asked for.

(*Albuquerque Journal*, April 15, 1942.)

The group decided that the main thing they wanted was full and accurate information. As the brother of one POW put it, "Whatever the news may be, whether it's good or bad, give us the truth." Those present also hoped to collect money to fund a mercy ship with medicines and supplies for the POWs. The BRO collected $300 on that first night alone. Their pledge became "We will not let them down."

True to their word, the BRO and its members worked tirelessly to stay in contact with their friends and relatives held captive in Japanese POW camps over the next three years. After much effort, they successfully shipped eighteen hundred tons of food, medicine, and other supplies to the camps aboard two vessels, although the enemy confiscated much of what was sent and little reached the hands of the POWs.

Despite such setbacks, devoted members of the BRO continued to work in every way possible, sometimes even after they had learned that their loved ones had already perished in captivity.

throughout the Philippines. Thousands more died in the terrible POW camps, "dropping like flies," according to those fortunate enough to survive.

Later, the Japanese forced thousands of POWs onto Japanese ships for transport as badly needed workers to factories and mines elsewhere in the Far East. Out at sea, American planes often attacked these enemy ships, never knowing that thousands of their fellow countrymen were held as prisoners below deck. POWs who had not perished in the airless, filthy holds of the **hell ships** usually died in air attacks by American planes; 117 New Mexicans were killed in a single American attack on such a vessel.

Some American POWs in the Philippines were able to escape from POW camps, frequently with the help of local Filipino civilians. Those who escaped often died in the mountains and jungles of the Philippines

Las Cruces's Bataan monument

Bataan Remembered

Grateful to the brave men who survived or perished on the Bataan Death March, in POW camps, and on hell ships, New Mexicans have honored their memory by creating several monuments and an annual event. Bataan Memorial Park in northeast Albuquerque, with monuments that name every member of the 200th and 515th Coast Artillery (AA), was dedicated in 1960 and just recently remodeled. A nine-foot-high bronze statue of two New Mexico soldiers helping a fellow soldier on the death march was dedicated in Las Cruces's Veterans Park on the sixtieth anniversary of the march in 2002. Other impressive Bataan monuments stand in Jarales and outside the Deming Luna Mimbres History Museum in Deming. Albuquerque's Lovelace Regional Medical Center was once known as the Lovelace-Bataan Memorial Hospital. The Bataan Memorial Military Museum and Library, with more than thirty thousand military artifacts, is open to the public in Santa Fe. Finally, New Mexico's former state capitol building is now called the Bataan Memorial Building in downtown Santa Fe.

Since 1988, thousands of walkers and runners have remembered death march victims by participating in an annual twenty-six-mile walk and marathon along desert paths and roads on the White Sands Missile Range. Young and old, men and women, civilians and soldiers participate, often stopping to thank the death march survivors who still attend the event.

The survivors do not think of themselves as heroes, though. According to Winston Shillito, who grew up near Las Cruces and lived through the death march, "We were caught in a situation that we couldn't help. We did what we had to do."

(Quoted in the *Albuquerque Journal*, April 15, 2002.)

or were soon recaptured to face horrible forms of punishment. Most POWs did not escape because they never found a chance, were physically unable, or were deterred by the Japanese rule that if one American in each group of ten POWs escaped, the other nine would be automatically executed.

Only about half the New Mexico soldiers who were forced to surrender in 1942 lived to see the end of the war. Those who lived often survived because they helped their New Mexico friends and relatives whenever they could; eighty-one were brothers and seventy-nine were cousins. Others had grown up in the same New Mexico towns or villages. A number had even served in the Civilian Conservation Corps together. All had become friends in the national guard before they had gone to the Philippines.

Liberated by U.S. troops in 1945, Bataan survivors were thrilled to return to New Mexico at last. Sadly, a good many died from their ongoing medical problems within a few years of their return home. Others suffered from physical and emotional trauma the rest of their lives. Later, some were willing to write or talk about their memories. For many years, those who were able attended reunions, forever bonded by the nightmarish wartime experience of their youth.

 ## The Navajo Code Talkers

A select group of Navajo men made a unique and significant contribution to the United States' victory in World War II. In 1942, twenty-nine young Navajos were recruited into the marines not only to be trained as combat troops but also to send and receive radio messages in a new, top-secret code they themselves helped to devise.

Suggested by Philip Johnston, who had grown up as the son of a missionary on the Navajo Reservation, the Navajo military code was actually a code on a code. When a message was to be sent, a word in the message was "translated" into a basic code consisting of 411 of the most frequently used military terms. Code words often related to nature and Navajo culture. For example, naval

The original twenty-nine Navajo Code Talkers swearing into the U.S. Marines

Some Examples of the Navajo Code

Military Term	Code Name	Navajo Word(s)
commanding officer	war chief	hash-kay-gi-na-tah
plane	bird	tsidi
bomb	egg	a-ye-shi
observation plane	owl	ne-as-jah
patrol plane	crow	ga-gih
fighter plane	hummingbird	da-he-tin-hi
bomber	buzzard	jay-sho
submarine	iron fish	besh-lo
battleship	whale	lo-tso
destroyer	shark	ca-lo
aircraft carrier	bird carrier	tsidi-moffa-ye-hi
tank	tortoise	chay-da-gahi
grenade	potato	ni-ma-si

Letter of the Alphabet	Code Name(s)	Navajo Word(s)
A	ant or apple or axe	wol-la-chee or be-la-sana or tse-nihl
B	badger or bear or barrel	na-hash-chid or shush or toish-jeh
C	cat or coal or cow	moasi or tla-gin or ba-goshi
D	deer or devil or dog	be or chindi or lha-cha-eh
E	elk or eye or ear	dzeh or ah-nah or ah-jah

and so on, with three possible code words for almost every letter of the alphabet.

For example, "World War Two" would be spelled: Weasel-owl-rabbit-lamb-dog Weasel-ant-rabbit Turkey-weasel-owl, which would be translated into Navajo as Gloe-ih ne-ahs-jah gah dibeh-yassie lha-cha-eh Gloe-ih wol-la-chee gah Than-zie gloe-ih ne-ahs-jah.

ships were different kinds of fish, airplanes were different kinds of birds, and bombs were referred to as eggs. Words not in the basic code had to be spelled out, with three different code words for most letters of the alphabet.

Next, Navajo messengers spoke each code word in their native language. The Navajo language is very difficult to learn or understand, with some words having entirely different meanings, depending on how they are said and in what context. The enemy would have a difficult time learning or understanding the language, much less the code and the messages it concealed.

This was not the first time the American armed forces had used Native American languages to send messages in combat; it had been done in World War I and was done elsewhere in World War II. This was the first time the Navajo language had been used for this purpose, though, and the first time a code on a code had been devised.

The new code worked extremely well. In addition to the "Original 29," 421 other Navajo youths were recruited, 70 percent of whom had attended Indian boarding schools where they had learned to speak English well. Called the **Navajo Code Talkers**, the young marines were trained in eight-week periods to become fast and accurate in sending and receiving important military messages. Everything had to

Code Talkers in action

Navajo Soldiers: Why Did They Fight?

The Navajo Code Talkers must be admired for their brave, loyal service in World War II, especially given the U.S. government's treatment of their tribe in the Long Walk, at Bosque Redondo, in many Indian boarding schools, and during the livestock-reduction program of the 1930s. Those who lived on the Navajo Reservation could not even vote in New Mexico, according to the state constitution of 1910.

Nevertheless, the Code Talkers and many other Navajos proudly served their country in World War II. In the words of Code Talker Albert Smith, "Being second-class citizens didn't bother us [when we enlisted in the marines]. Our main concern was our mother earth. A foreign nation was ready to take what little we had on the reservation. That is why we went into the military [and were so] willing to fight."

Once enlisted in the marines, the Code Talkers' Navajo language skills were prized and respected. Often for the first time in their young lives, the Code Talkers proudly understood the value of their language to the military, their fellow marines, their country, and, for those who had been punished for speaking Navajo in school, themselves.

▲▲▲▲▲▲▲▲▲▲▲▲▲▲▲▲▲▲▲▲▲▲▲▲▲▲▲▲▲▲▲

Honoring the Navajo Code Talkers

Much like the survivors of the Bataan Death March, surviving Navajo Code Talkers have been honored in many ways in the years since the U.S. government finally revealed their secret code in 1968. Here are just some of their many honors:

- Pres. Ronald Reagan honored them by declaring August 14, 1982, National Navajo Code Talkers Day. The president gave each Code Talker a certificate of appreciation at a ceremony conducted in Washington, D.C. National Navajo Code Talkers Day has been celebrated annually in the United States ever since.
- The Code Talkers have been honored at Navajo gatherings and parades, especially at powwows and the Gallup Inter-Tribal Ceremonial.
- In 1971, the Code Talkers organized a Navajo Code Talkers Association.
- In 1982, New Mexico Gov. Bruce King proclaimed April 10 as New Mexico Code Talkers Day.
- A nine-foot-high, nine-hundred-pound bronze statue of a Code Talker, created by Navajo artist Oreland Joe of Kirtland, New Mexico, has been dedicated outside the Gallup Cultural Center, along old Route 66. A similar statue was dedicated at the visitors center in Window Rock, Arizona, the capital of the Navajo Nation.
- Several Code Talkers have become cultural and political leaders, including the Indian artist Carl Gorman and former Navajo Nation president Peter McDonald.
- A movie about the Code Talkers, entitled *Windtalkers*, was released, although its accuracy has been questioned by some Code Talkers.
- Pres. George W. Bush honored surviving Code Talkers in a special ceremony held in Washington, D.C., in July 2001.

be memorized; all but 30 of the 450 recruited Navajos met the high standards required of them to be combat ready.

Sent to the Pacific, the Code Talkers snapped into action each time the words "New Mexico" or "Arizona" were broadcast on a field radio, meaning that the message that followed would be relayed in the Navajo code. Responding quickly and accurately, the Code Talkers flawlessly sent or received as many as eight hundred messages in a single forty-eight-hour period. The Navajos' success in relaying messages helped the United States win victories in every major battle in the Pacific, including at Guadalcanal in 1942, Iwo Jima in 1945, and Okinawa in the same year. Bewildered by the unusual sounds they heard on American field radios, the Japanese were continually frustrated in their efforts to crack the code. Expert American cryptologists, or code breakers, had no greater success. After centuries as fierce Southwest warriors, the Navajos discovered that their language had become their greatest weapon in modern warfare.

The Code Talkers faced dangerous assignments in the Pacific, however. To many American soldiers, especially those who had not been raised in the Southwest, Navajo Code Talkers sometimes looked like the Japanese enemy; some Navajos were captured by their fellow marines before they could prove their true identity as U.S. servicemen. Code Talkers had to be guarded by Anglo marines to avoid such hazardous confusion. Also, it was feared that the Japanese might resort to any means, including torture, to force Code Talkers to reveal their code if captured. Fortunately, no Code Talkers were captured, although eight lost their lives in combat, and the enemy captured and tortured a Navajo Army sergeant untrained in the code.

☀ Other New Mexicans in the U.S. Armed Forces

As in World War I, thousands of New Mexicans enlisted or were drafted to serve their country in World War II. Many, like the Navajo Code Talkers, were Native American; 1,065 Pueblo Indians served on either the European or Pacific fronts. Hispanics served in large numbers as well; 28 percent of New Mexico's 1,826 soldiers on Bataan were of Spanish descent. Hundreds of students and much of the faculty at the University of New Mexico enlisted, including Coach Roy Johnson, who reported for duty as a major in the army even before the Japanese attack on Pearl Harbor. By January 1942, 150 graduates of New Mexico A&M's Reserve Officer Training (ROTC) program were listed as army officers, and even the college's president, an officer in the reserves, had been called into active service in 1941; thirty-two former Aggies were among the New Mexicans who were forced to surrender on Bataan. More than 2,800 graduates of the New Mexico Military Institute served in the war, mostly as officers. Of the graduates of the Los Alamos Ranch School, forty-two had enlisted by the spring of 1943. A total of 49,549 New Mexicans served in the army, navy, marines, and coast guard, the highest per capita ratio of any state in the country. New Mexicans served on all fronts and in every capacity.

Hispanic Soldiers: Why Did They Fight?

Sabine R. Ulibarrí of Tierra Amarilla was a twenty-two-year-old college student from northern New Mexico when he volunteered to serve in the Army Air Force during World War II. Years later, he wrote about his memories of the war, recalling why many Hispanic youths eagerly enlisted to fight in the war:

> [On the day after Pearl Harbor] there were long lines of young men at the Tierra Amarilla draft board. The Hispanos came out of the mountains, out of the valleys, from all the surrounding villages to volunteer for combat duty for their country. . . . We heard the roll of distant drums, and we answered the call.
>
> We wanted to fight for our country, for our way of life, our native land. . . . That was America to us. . . .

Trained as a B-17 gunner, Ulibarrí described one of the most frightening moments of his life in the war in Europe. On one of his thirty-five bombing raids over German targets, his plane was hit by enemy fire when

> I felt the blow on my side. A piece of shrapnel, the size of my fist, hit . . . my left side with such force that it knocked me out. I thought I had been killed. . . . When I didn't answer the intercom, my companions came down and pulled me out. I woke up inside the plane. Bewildered. Confused. I felt my entire body, expecting to be mortally wounded. Nothing. Nothing was wrong with me. The powerful blow had knocked the wind out of me and deprived me of my senses. I went back to my position.

(Sabine R. Ulibarrí, *Mayhem Was Our Business: Memorias de un Veterano* [Tempe, AZ: Bilingual Press, 1997], 27–29, 69.)

Gold Star Mothers

New Mexicans were proud to have their sons and daughters serve in the American armed forces during World War II. Families hung small banners in their front windows to show how many of their sons and daughters were serving in the military. Each star on the banner represented a soldier, sailor, or marine away at war. Mrs. Senalda V. Nunez could proudly display four stars, representing her four sons in the armed forces by May 1942. Stars were used much as yellow ribbons are used by the anxiously waiting families of American troops today.

If a son or daughter was killed in World War II, a gold star was sown over the first one; mothers with gold stars in their windows were known as Gold Star Mothers. Mrs. Arturo García of Albuquerque became New Mexico's first Gold Star Mother when her son, Rueben Elebrando García of the 200th Coast Artillery (AA), was killed defending the Philippines on December 12, 1941.

WACs and WAVES from New Mexico

More than 265,000 women joined special units of the U.S. military during World War II. Almost 180,000 joined the Women's Army Corps (WACs), while 86,000 joined the Women Accepted for Volunteer Emergency Service (WAVES), a part of the U.S. Navy. Members of the WACs and WAVES did mostly clerical work and served as nurses, freeing males for combat duties. Many women from New Mexico served in these valuable roles.

A woman historian has interviewed twenty former WAVES and sent questionnaires to eighty others in New Mexico. When asked why they volunteered to be WAVES, most cited patriotism and a desire to "help out" in the war. To join, women had to be between twenty and thirty-six years of age, stand at least five feet tall, and weigh at least ninety-five pounds. When asked about the rules they had to obey, the women described a strict dress code, with hair cut so short it could not touch their shoulders. They were not allowed to smoke or even chew gum while in uniform. Few said they experienced discrimination or sexual harassment in the military. All believe women should still be able to contribute their special skills in the military today, although most are opposed to women in combat roles. They remain proud of their work in World War II and have mostly fond memories of their years as WAVES.

(Donna Eichstaedt, "WAVES in World War II: New Mexico Women Remember Their Service," *Southern New Mexico Historical Review* 8 [January 2001]: 27–31.)

A New Mexico WAC

Two New Mexicans served in especially unusual, but very important, capacities during the war. **Bill Mauldin** was born and grew up in southern New Mexico. Raised in a poor family during the Great Depression, Mauldin had volunteered to join the national guard in 1939 when he was only eighteen. Fortunately for Mauldin, his unit was sent to Europe rather than the Philippines. Mauldin, who had always enjoyed drawing, soon began drawing cartoons depicting the life of average soldiers on the front lines.

Mauldin's main cartoon characters, scruffy, unshaven Willie and Joe, became instant favorites among the many GIs, or soldiers, who identified with the pair's humorous trials and tribulations. "Willie and Joe" became a popular feature in the army's *Stars and Stripes* newspaper and, eventually, in daily newspapers across the United States. In 1945, Mauldin won the Pulitzer Prize for his work, although, in his typically humble manner, he confessed that when he first heard the news, "I wasn't even sure exactly what a Pulitzer Prize was." Mauldin was less interested in winning prestigious awards than in improving the average

Ernie Pyle with soldiers
....

GI's morale with pointedly honest cartoons that often angered the brass, or officers, but consistently humored the troops.

Ernie Pyle played a similarly unique role in the war. Born in Indiana, Pyle moved to southeast Albuquerque in 1940 after many years of travel writing for newspaper columns about interesting Americans he met along the way. When the war began, Pyle left his wife, Jerry, in their new home in Albuquerque to write similar columns about the soldiers, sailors, and marines he met overseas in North Africa

Ernie Pyle Wrote About New Mexican GIs

Ernie Pyle never served in the U.S. military, but he knew about life in the army because he lived among the troops or interviewed them whenever he could. He wrote so many newspaper columns during World War II that they were later compiled and published as popular books, including *Brave Men* and *This Is Your War*. Like his friend Bill Mauldin, Pyle won a Pulitzer Prize for journalism in 1944. His columns, which often featured New Mexicans, regularly appeared in New Mexico newspapers, including the *Albuquerque Tribune* and the *Portales Daily News*. A typical Pyle column appeared in early 1944:

> There was an Army hospital where . . .
> I got acquainted with . . . Walter Jentzen
> of Carlsbad, New Mexico. . . . Back in

Carlsbad he had a two-month-old baby whom he had never seen.

> It was the second time Jentzen had been wounded. In Sicily he got shot in his behind when a German tank let loose on him. And then . . . he got a shell fragment in his chest. A notebook which he always carried in his left shirt pocket was all that saved him. . . .
>
> Having [visited] Albuquerque recently, I tortured him by telling him what the New Mexico sun felt like, how the air smelled, and how beautiful the Sandias were at sunset.
>
> The only trouble with torturing a guy that way was that I tortured myself at the same time.

(*Albuquerque Tribune*, January 11, 1944.)

The War in Europe, Especially D-Day

While thousands of New Mexicans fought the Japanese in the Pacific Ocean during World War II, other New Mexicans fought Germany and its Axis allies in Africa and Europe. Many New Mexicans took part in the massive invasions of North Africa (November 1942), Sicily (July 1943), and Italy (September 1943). Many more took part in the largest air and sea invasion in all of history, known simply as D-Day, on June 6, 1944.

The invasion of northern France, across the English Channel, was so enormous and complex that the operation took years to plan. When D-Day finally arrived, nearly 175,000 men from twelve Allied nations assembled in England and landed on the beaches of Normandy, France, along with tons of supplies and fifty thousand vehicles (from motorcycles to tanks), aboard 5,333 ships. Almost eleven thousand planes provided air support against German defenses. American Gen. Dwight D. Eisenhower and his staff of officers planned and coordinated the enormous operation.

General Eisenhower was the first to agree that the Allies' success on D-Day would have been impossible without the work and sacrifice of the fighting men who landed on Normandy, including Staff Sergeant Tony J. Ortega of Tucumcari, New Mexico. Only twenty-five years old in 1944, Ortega remembers landing on Omaha Beach, the bloodiest landing point along the entire Normandy coast.

Ortega recalls that "it took almost all day to get [our] heavy equipment [on shore]" as the Germans fired their weapons down on the beach from the high cliffs above. "Our buddies were dying around us, [but] the only way we could go was forward; we couldn't go back. [Our leaders] told us we were going to be facing death all the time, and it was true. I think about it now, and it just seems like a dream" (*Clovis News-Journal*, September 8, 2005).

Although not a soldier, Ernie Pyle was among only twenty-eight reporters chosen to accompany American troops and report their story. Like the Navajo Code Talkers who fought in the Pacific, thirteen Comanche Code Talkers, using a similar code in their own language, played a critical role in Allied communications on D-Day.

Fortunately, Sergeant Ortega, Ernie Pyle, and the Comanche Code Talkers survived to tell of the battle. Nearly five thousand Allied soldiers, sailors, and marines did not. While the Allies made their share of mistakes, the Germans made many more, and the Allies finally won this key battle.

Having invaded northern Europe on D-Day, the Allies went on to liberate Paris (August 1944) and finally invade and defeat Germany by May 8, 1945. V-E Day (meaning Victory in Europe) was only possible because of D-Day, the true turning point of World War II in Europe.

and Europe. While other reporters wrote articles about generals and admirals, Pyle remained focused on stories about the "Willies and Joes" of the war. Although he was never a soldier, Pyle was described by one New Mexican GI as "one great fellow. They don't make them more regular [than Pyle]."

Other GIs and their families agreed. For many, reading Pyle's columns about average men and women was much like getting a letter from a loved one in the war: friendly, reassuring, and usually good for morale. Sadly, Pyle was killed by a sniper on a small island in the Pacific shortly after he had gone to cover the war on that front in 1945.

The Home Front

Victory Bonds and Rationing

Like most Americans, New Mexicans were ready to make whatever sacrifices were needed to help win the war and bring their soldiers home safely. As in World War I, this sacrifice included the purchase of government bonds to help finance the enormous cost of the conflict. New Mexicans consistently purchased war bonds far beyond whatever quotas were set for their state. In 1943, for example, the federal government promised to name a new bomber whatever New Mexicans preferred if they could sell $30,000 in war bonds. Accepting the challenge, New Mexicans, led by the Bataan Relief Organization (BRO), sold twice as many bonds as requested and proudly named the new plane the *Spirit of Bataan* in honor of the hundreds of New Mexicans who had fought so bravely on Bataan.

That same year a patriotic parade down Albuquerque's Central Avenue featured a two-man Japanese submarine captured after the Japanese attack on Pearl Harbor. The huge crowd that came for the parade and to see the enemy sub bought $175,000 in war bonds. On another occasion, Ernie Pyle offered an autographed copy of his book *Brave Men* to whoever bid

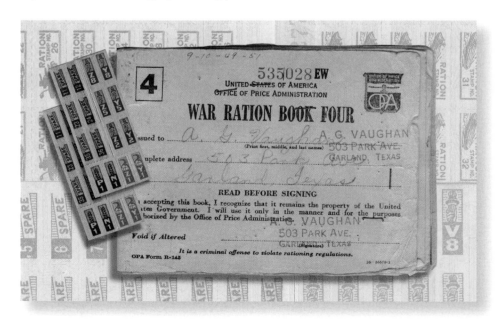

A ration book
and stamps

New Mexico Recipients of the Medal of Honor in World War II

Of the 433 recipients of the Medal of Honor during World War II, eight were either native New Mexicans or young men who had spent much of their lives in the state before entering the armed forces. Of the eight, five died in combat while performing their heroic deeds, usually involving the saving of American lives from heavy enemy attack. New Mexico's eight Medal of Honor winners were

Medal of Honor

- Army Brig. Gen. Kenneth N. Walker, in the Pacific, 1943
- Marine Lt. Alexander Bonnyman, Jr., in the Pacific, 1943
- Army Lt. John C. "Red" Morgan, a 1934 graduate of NMMI, in Europe, 1943
- Army Lt. Robert S. Scott, in the Pacific, 1943
- Army Pvt. Joseph P. Martínez, in the Pacific, 1943; the first Hispanic Medal of Honor winner of World War II; among minorities in the United States, Hispanics won the highest percentage of Medals of Honor in the war
- Army Pvt. Harold Herman Moon, Jr., in the Pacific, 1944
- Army Pvt. José F. Valdez, in Europe, 1945
- Army Pvt. Alejandro "Machine Gun Al" Ruiz, in the Pacific, 1945.

the highest amount in war-bond purchases. An Albuquerque businessman bid $15,000. Now the mayor of Albuquerque, former governor Clyde Tingley was especially active in war-bond sales, as were New Mexico's two wartime governors, John E. Miles and Jack Dempsey.

As in World War I, the country also faced severe shortages of certain materials needed for the war effort. Unlike the First World War, the United States resorted to **rationing** these essential items to ensure there would be enough for dire military needs. Gasoline, rubber, silk, shoes, meat, sugar, coffee, cheese, and canned goods were just some of the many goods rationed to families and businesses in New Mexico and all parts of the United States.

Most Americans accepted rationing willingly, hoping their sacrifices would help end the war sooner. Many large New Mexican families, who received rationing coupons based on the number of people in their families, hardly noticed a difference, especially if they were poor and could not have afforded to buy much sugar or other items anyway. Other New Mexicans used clever food substitutes or even traveled to Mexico to purchase goods beyond their rationed limits. Unfortunately, some resorted to hoarding goods or acquiring them illegally on the black market.

▲▲▲▲▲▲▲▲▲▲▲▲▲▲▲▲▲▲▲▲▲▲▲▲▲▲▲▲▲▲▲▲▲▲▲

Cooking with Rationed Foods

With sugar as one of the first foods to be rationed during World War II, resourceful housewives had to find good sugar substitutes for their meals and desserts. In a typical recipe of the 1940s, cooks used molasses as the key ingredient in a dessert appropriately known as Victory Pudding:

2 cups milk	1 teaspoon ginger
⅔ cup cooked rolled wheat flakes	⅛ teaspoon salt
⅓ cup molasses	1 large egg, lightly beaten

✓ Preheat oven to 350 degrees Fahrenheit.

✓ Bring milk just to a boil in a heavy saucepan over low heat, stirring occasionally.

✓ Meanwhile, lightly grease a 1-quart casserole or baking dish.

✓ Combine cooked rolled wheat, molasses, egg, ginger, and salt in a heatproof bowl.

✓ Gradually beat hot milk into wheat mixture.

✓ Transfer to the casserole.

✓ Bake until center is set, 35 to 40 minutes. Cool 20 to 30 minutes, then serve warm.

4 servings

(Joanne Lamb Hayes, *Grandma's Wartime Kitchen: World War II and the Way We Cooked* [New York: St. Martin's Press, 2000], 89.)

Most families cooperated with government regulations. Thousands helped in the crisis by growing victory gardens, as their parents had done in World War I; even Albuquerque firemen grew a victory garden next to their fire station so they could weed and cultivate their crop between fires in 1943. New Mexicans were especially active in national scrap-metal drives. Eager to help supply the materials needed to build new ships and planes, New Mexicans donated everything metal they could spare, including two Civil War cannons (from a park in Albuquerque), old pot-iron stoves, metal bars from an old jail, and, most appropriately, a German machine gun and helmet from World War I. New Mexicans found and contributed more than twelve thousand tons of scrap metal in a single three-month drive in 1942.

Businesses expanded and profited as never before. Farmers gladly grew more crops, especially cotton in southern New Mexico. Ranchers increased the total size of their herds to 1.4 million cattle by 1944. Crude oil produced from thirty-eight hundred active wells equaled $32 million in value by 1942. Coal-mining companies set new production records, and thousands of trains carried cargo, civilians, and military personnel through New Mexico to distant destinations. Though the Great Depression had clearly ended, people now had more money to spend but less to spend it on because of wartime cutbacks and emergency rationing.

A New Labor Shortage in New Mexico

As in World War I, labor was the main problem in producing great quantities of crops and other essential war goods. Many New Mexicans volunteered to help deal with the emergency; businessmen from Deming's Lions Club helped local farmers harvest their bean crop, and high school students helped save crops in several counties. Volunteers could not do it all, though, especially as more and more

Newspapers Advertised for War Jobs on the West Coast

Thousands of New Mexicans were drawn to the West Coast by the magnet of high-paying war jobs, as advertised in ads in the *Albuquerque Journal* and other New Mexico newspapers:

```
              KAISER SHIPYARDS
  PORTLAND, OREGON, AND VANCOUVER, WASHINGTON
             URGENTLY NEED MEN

Chippers, sheet metal workers, shipwrights,
painters, electricians, welders, pipe fitters,
machinists, welders trainees, general helpers.
Work week 48 hours. Time and half over 40 hours.
Housing guaranteed. Transportation advanced.
See representative at U.S. Employment Office,
105 S. 6th St., Albuquerque (Albuquerque Journal,
August 7, 1945).
```

Many New Mexico women also responded to the call for labor on the West Coast. Women who worked in heavy industrial jobs were even given a nickname: Rosie the Riveter, or, in the case of Hispanic women, Rosita the Riveter. Susie Parks, the heroic telephone operator during Pancho Villa's 1916 raid on Columbus, served as a Rosie the Riveter in a war factory in Washington State, thus playing another important role in another national crisis.

New Mexicans left to take high-paying factory jobs in the booming war industry on the West Coast. As many as thirty thousand Hispanics were drawn by employment in California. An equally high number of Native Americans followed a similar path to new opportunities for themselves and their families.

Many New Mexico employers looked south across the border to solve their dire labor problem. Thousands of Mexican nationals were interested in work in the Southwest, but many remembered the often-harsh treatment and deportation their countrymen had experienced in the United States during the Great Depression. To deal with these issues, the U.S. and Mexican governments signed an agreement that specified not only the number of Mexican workers who could work in the United States but also protections workers could expect to receive once they were here. Known as the **Bracero Program**, the international agreement was signed in 1942. By the end of the war almost 169,000 Mexican workers labored as braceros, providing important assistance in New Mexico and other states, particularly California and Texas.

A Bracero Speaks

In 1969, María Herrera-Sobek traveled to Mexico to interview sixteen men who had previously worked in the Bracero Program. A typical Mexican worker described the problems he faced in the United States:

> I went to work early [each day] because my job was fumigating the tomatoes [but I could not work for long] because the temperature would start going up [and when it did] the powder gets in your eyes and . . . ohhhh, your eyes sting very badly. . . .
>
> The food was just awful. . . . When we Mexicans came to eat, we had to be there at exactly the right time because if we were a tiny bit late [we were told], "There is no more left. . . ." [The cook] would send us our lunch, a couple of sandwiches with only some bologna. . . . Not a single taco did she send us. . . . Sometimes we would go to a restaurant to eat what we wanted.
>
> The medical treatment [was also bad] there; the doctors did not care about us. For any [ailment] we had we were prescribed pills, that is all . . . and they were the same kind too. . . . "What effect did it have on you?," we asked each other. "Nothing, I feel the same," we would answer.

(María Herrera-Sobek, *The Bracero Experience* [Los Angeles: UCLA Latin American Center Publications, 1979], 70–71.)

▲▲▲▲▲▲▲▲▲▲▲▲▲▲▲▲▲▲▲▲▲▲▲▲▲▲▲

The Corrido of the Uprooted

Si alguno lo toma a mal	If someone doesn't like what I say
Es ques no lo ha conocido.	It's because he wasn't there.
Que se vaya a contratar	Let him go as a bracero
A los Estados Unidos.	To the United States.
Y verá que va trabajar	He will see that he will work
Como un esclavo vendido,	Like a sold slave.
Antes éramos honrados,	Before we were honorable men,
Y de eso nada ha quedado.	Now we have lost it all.
Con eso del pasaporte	With our passport
Nos creemos americanos.	We think we are Americans.
Pero tememos el nombre	But we are called
De ser desarraigados.	The uprooted.

(María Herrera-Sobek, *Northward Bound: The Mexican Immigrant Experience in Ballad and Song* [Bloomington: Indiana University Press, 1993], 165.)

Unfortunately, all did not go well with the Bracero Program. While 169,000 workers came into the United States legally in the program, more than 112,000, or 40 percent of all those who crossed the border, did so illegally. To make matters worse, Mexican workers enjoyed few of the protections guaranteed in the 1942 agreement, especially regarding fair wages, good housing, adequate food, and racial discrimination.

Hispanic New Mexicans, led by Senator Chavez, also expressed misgivings about the Bracero Program, opposing any source of manual labor that could take jobs away from American workers and otherwise drive down wages. Despite hardships for Mexicans and objections by New Mexicans, the Bracero Program worked so well for large American employers that it was continued long after the war, until 1964.

☀ Prisoner of War Camps

New Mexico still lacked enough labor for its farms, ranches, railroads, and mines, however. In another attempt to solve this problem, the U.S. government opened German and Italian prisoner of war camps in various parts of New Mexico. New Mexico was an ideal location for the camps. Kept far from the coast and isolated, prisoners could not escape without being easily found and either returned to camp or killed, as

▲▲▲▲▲▲▲▲▲▲▲▲▲▲▲▲▲▲▲▲▲▲▲▲▲▲▲▲

The Geneva Conventions

War is always horrible. It is especially horrible when warring nations do not respect the basic human rights of their prisoners of war. In the past, when captured, POWs were often tortured, publicly insulted, experimented on, used as hostages, and executed for their roles as combat soldiers.

Starting in 1864, nations from around the world sent representatives to Geneva, Switzerland, to write civilized rules, or conventions, of war. Over the years (and especially in 1929 and 1949) additional Geneva Conventions have been agreed on, stating that

- POWs must be treated humanely. They must never be tortured or be used for scientific experiments;
- when questioned, POWs are only required to give their names, ranks, birth dates, and serial numbers;
- POWs must never be punished for their acts as soldiers in combat;
- POWs must be housed in clean facilities, receive medical attention, and be fed enough food to maintain their weight and prevent malnutrition;
- and POWs may be required to work but only at jobs that are not dangerous, unhealthy, or humiliating.

It is essential that the United States and all nations that have agreed to the Geneva Conventions respect these important rules of war. If the United States does not abide by these agreements when dealing with enemy POWs, we cannot expect our enemies to treat American POWs fairly in times of war. The United States must obey the Geneva Conventions because

- we have promised to do so;
- they are fair and humane;
- and our soldiers will suffer retaliation if they are ever captured by our nation's enemies during war.

happened in two tragic shootings in southeast New Mexico. As many as twelve thousand POWs were detained in former CCC camps in Roswell and Lordsburg and, in smaller camps, in Albuquerque, Las Cruces, and elsewhere in the state. Unlike Japan, the United States adhered to the **Geneva Conventions**, or international agreements specifying the humane treatment warring nations should grant all POWs.

Adhering to the Geneva Conventions, POWs were used to work in several kinds of needed labor but especially on cotton farms in southern New Mexico. Often working side-by-side with New Mexicans and Mexican immigrants from the Bracero Program, the POWs were seldom

A German POW in New Mexico

Walter Schmid was a German soldier, captured in North Africa in 1943. After a year in various POW camps, he was transferred by train to southern New Mexico, where he and his fellow POWs lived at a former CCC camp and worked on cotton farms for about two years. Later, home in Germany, he wrote his memoirs, recalling his first impressions of the Southwest:

> All 400 [POWs] got out in Las Cruces. . . . After a short march, we entered a camp [that] was much different than all the others [we'd been in]. There was no fence; everything was open, and right on the edge of town! There were five big, long barracks in the middle of a green lawn, with silvery poplars all over the area. . . . We were greeted by Captain [Ivan] Williams, our new camp commandant, but his first order was to prohibit us from leaving the camp and going into town. Some of us didn't follow that order, so a nine-foot barbed-wire fence was erected around the whole camp with a high wooden watchtower at each corner; now it was a regular POW camp.

Despite the changes at his camp and problems with Captain Williams and one guard in particular, Schmid received humane treatment, in accordance with the Geneva Conventions, and had generally good memories of New Mexico. He especially enjoyed the Hispanic people he met, describing them in a poem he wrote in 1945:

German POWs at work in New Mexico

> Loyal and industriously committed
>   to their work,
> In low houses, drafty and crooked
> They live and lead a happy life,
> Mexicans, called by the cotton.

(Walter Schmid, *A German POW in New Mexico*, trans. Richard Rundell [Albuquerque: University of New Mexico Press, 2005], 45, 147.)

overworked. In fact, most preferred outdoor labor—and at least some wages—to inactive lives in their camps. Farmers appreciated the POWs' hard work, befriended some, and acknowledged their contribution to crop production in these crucial years.

The SS *Columbus* Crew at Fort Stanton

New Mexico served as the location of several different kinds of military facilities during World War II. None of these facilities was as unusual as the German internment camp on the site of a former CCC camp outside Fort Stanton.

Crew members of the German passenger ship, the SS *Columbus*, were interned at Fort Stanton even before the United States entered the war. Having sunk their ship rather than surrender it to their English enemies, these 410 German seamen were rescued by the U.S. Navy and held at Fort Stanton for the balance of the war.

The German crew made the most of their circumstances by keeping busy, making an attractive camp, building a large swimming pool, and even competing in what they called the Fort Stanton Olympics of July 1941. The men got along so well with the nearby residents of Capitán that the Germans presented a large engraved stone as a gift to the town.

Few Germans attempted to escape, and although some insisted on celebrating Adolf Hitler's birthday each year, acts of violence were rare in the generally peaceful camp outside Fort Stanton.

(James J. McBride, *Interned: Internment of the S.S.* Columbus *Crew at Fort Stanton, New Mexico, 1941–1945* [Santa Fe: privately printed, 2003].)

 ## Japanese-American Internment Camps

POW camps in New Mexico and in other parts of the United States must not be confused with another type of prisoner camp the federal government operated. Made nervous by Japan's surprise attack on Pearl Harbor in 1941, the government feared similar attacks along the West Coast aided by Japanese residents of California, Oregon, and Washington. As a result of this alarm, the U.S. government rounded up more than 120,000 Japanese men, women, and children and forced them to spend most of the war in **relocation camps** far inland from the coast. In addition to usually losing their homes, farms, businesses, and other possessions, the Japanese lost what we value most: their freedom.

Even more unfairly, the U.S. government identified Japanese males who were considered to be the greatest threat to American safety if Japan launched another invasion of the United States. Some of these "dangerous enemy aliens" had had military experience in the Japanese military

Yoshiaki Fukuda at the Japanese-American Internment Camps in Lordsburg and Santa Fe

Yoshiaki Fukuda was born in Japan in 1898. Trained as a minister in the Konko religion, he and his wife immigrated to the United States in 1930. When World War II began, he was one of the hundreds of Japanese residents of the West Coast who were rounded up and classified as "dangerous enemy aliens," perhaps because he had served in the Japanese army in the First World War.

Separated from his family, Fukuda was kept in the Lordsburg internment camp from May 1942 to July 1943, when he was transferred to the internment camp in Santa Fe, where he was imprisoned until February 1944. Based on his memory of these twenty-one months, Fukuda later wrote his memoirs, recalling many incidents in his role as a religious leader in the Santa Fe camp:

> On July 23, 1943, I was moved to Santa Fe. . . . Here . . . I conducted services at 5:30 each morning for members of the Konko faith. . . .
>
> Camp life created a psychologically stressful environment toward which internees showed various patterns of behavior. Some became servile and very much afraid of the federal government, while others . . . resisted the camp authorities. There were very few who took a middle road. . . .
>
> Confinement in the internment camp led to . . . confusion regarding what was right or wrong. . . . Fights and disputes occurred among internees almost every day. . . .
>
> [Just as I was ready to leave the Santa Fe camp at last, an opponent of mine] burst into our barracks . . . and demanded that we fight a duel [to resolve an earlier personal dispute]. This man was not only an amateur sumo grand champion, but also a second degree in kendo (Japanese fencing).
>
> I prayed . . . for a resolution to this situation [especially because my transfer to a camp to be with my family might be canceled if I fought.]

Fukuda resolved this dispute by refusing to fight. Instead, he apologized for the dispute (but not for his position in the conflict) because he was a minister and because his opponent was an older man, who should always be treated with respect in Japanese culture. "I bowed to him and shook his hand. . . . The onlookers cheered; peace had been restored."

Although reunited with his family in another camp in 1944, Fukuda was not released from custody until September 29, 1947, meaning he had spent a total of six years in confinement, including two (1945 to 1947) after the war was over. He died ten years later in San Francisco.

(Yoshiaki Fukuda, *My Six Years of Internment: An Issei's Struggle for Justice* [San Francisco: Konko Church, 1990], 14–22.)

Guards inspect a Japanese American's possessions as he enters the Santa Fe internment camp

An Internee's Tanka

A Japanese internee in Santa Fe wrote a tanka, or poem, to express his deep feelings about the impact of imprisonment on his and his fellow internees' lives.

Many a friend
Who is incarcerated
Ages visibly.
Summer is passing by.

(Jiro Nakano and Kay Nakano, eds., *Poets Behind Barbed Wire* [Honolulu: Bamboo Ridge Press, 1983], 52.)

before coming to the United States, but most were either quite elderly, were suspected because they had certain skills, such as ancient martial arts, or possessed certain items, such as a carved ceremonial bow. These so-called dangerous individuals were separated from their families and brought to former CCC camps, known as **internment camps**, in Santa Fe and, when it was not used as a POW camp, in Lordsburg.

In all, more than five thousand Japanese males were detained in New Mexico from 1942 to 1946. These internees were used to help solve the state's labor shortage until many New Mexicans began to learn of the Bataan Death March and of the treatment of Americans in Japanese POW camps. Confusing the Japanese held in New Mexico's internment camps with POWs from the Japanese military,

The Treatment of Japanese New Mexicans

Only about 150 Japanese-Americans lived and worked in New Mexico at the beginning of World War II. Some became early victims of the war; ten families who worked for the Santa Fe Railway in Clovis were forced to remain at a small camp near Fort Stanton in 1942 until they were sent to relocation camps in Utah and Arizona. Former governor Clyde Tingley suggested that all Japanese be banned from Albuquerque, and thousands of New Mexicans expressed their strong opposition to rumors that West Coast Japanese Americans were about to come to New Mexico to form agricultural colonies. Other Japanese New Mexicans faced discrimination at schools, including the University of New Mexico and New Mexico A&M. **Roy Nakayama**, a New Mexico A&M student who had enlisted in the army and had been held in a German POW camp for a year, was refused readmission to A&M when he finally returned home to New Mexico.

Most Japanese New Mexicans were treated kindly by their friends and neighbors, though, especially if they were known as trusted residents of their communities before the war started. Members of the Gallup town council went so far as to ask the federal government not to place local Japanese residents in relocation camps. In the case of Roy Nakayama, his professors at New Mexico A&M remembered him as such a good, trustworthy student before the war that they interfered in his behalf so he could continue his studies. He completed his degree in horticulture, earned advanced degrees in the field, and made so many contributions to the development of chile as a major crop in New Mexico that he became known as Mr. Chile.

New Mexicans objected to even seeing the internees on work crews outside their camps. Resentment was so great that the American officer in charge of the Santa Fe camp said he need not have locked the camp's front gate each night because the internees knew their fate if they were found anywhere in town. As a result, only one man attempted to escape in Santa Fe, and two older men, who were supposedly attempting to escape, were shot and killed in Lordsburg.

Despite such treatment, most internees and their families remained loyal Americans, somehow tolerating the injustice they suffered in relocation and internment camps. As proof of their families' loyalty to the United States, many of the internees' son and grandsons served in the U.S. Army's **442nd Regimental Combat Team/100th Infantry Battalion**, one of the most highly decorated combat units in the war in Europe. Sadly, some of these Japanese-American soldiers visited their relatives at the Santa Fe camp, often wearing their army uniforms as they talked with the internees through barbed-wire fences. As in World War I, Americans identified with the enemy suffered the unfair loss of the very freedoms the country as a whole was fighting for.

 ## New Planes and Weapons

New Mexico Air Bases

New Mexico therefore contributed to winning World War II much as it had contributed to victory in World War I: with troops, much sacrifice, and important products. The state also contributed in new ways during the Second World War, especially with the development of new planes and modern weapons.

Charles Walsh had flown the first airplane flight in New Mexico at the territorial fair held in Albuquerque in October 1911. New Mexico's **Art Goebel** flew the first plane from California to Hawaii in 1927, and Albuquerque's first airport opened in 1928. Transcontinental Air Transport (later Trans World Airlines, or TWA) had established a coast-to-coast commercial air route through

Charles Walsh in Albuquerque

Charles Lindbergh
in Santa Fe

Army air bases and
bombing ranges in
New Mexico during
World War II

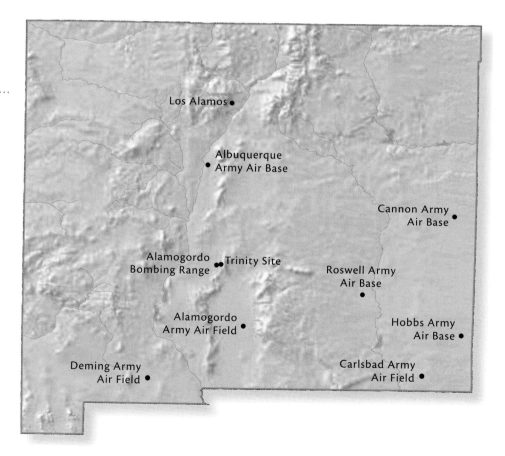

The Wartime Growth of Albuquerque

The building of Kirtland Army Air Base and other wartime activities caused a great boost in population in Albuquerque. Housing construction could not keep up with the needs of new families moving into the expanding community. A record 442 new residents, from thirty-two states and Washington, D.C., arrived in 1943. So many arrived that the city council, which normally advertised in national magazines to urge people to move to town, now urged them to "stay at home." By 1944, the Albuquerque Chamber of Commerce was receiving twenty calls a day from families desperately searching for housing. Real estate companies took waiting lists until the lists grew so long the companies announced that they could add no more names.

House building continued but could never keep up with the demand because the demand kept growing and because, with so much military and industrial growth, building materials were scarce everywhere in the country. The situation got so bad in Albuquerque that families who would not normally pay as high as $35 a month for housing ($374 in today's money) were willing to pay as high as $60 a month ($640 today) to find a place to live.

What was true of Albuquerque was also true, on a smaller scale, in every New Mexico town with new, modern air bases during the war.

(*Albuquerque Tribune*, October 6, 1943, and July 26, 1944.)

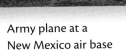

Army plane at a New Mexico air base

the state by 1929. **Charles Lindbergh**, the most famous pilot of the twentieth century, flew to various parts of New Mexico to help promote airline travel in the 1920s and 1930s. These were all important achievements in aviation history, but only small steps in comparison to what occurred in New Mexico during World War II.

Attracted by the open spaces and usually ideal flying conditions of New Mexico, the Army Air Corps built four major air bases in the state in 1941 and 1942: Kirtland in Albuquerque, Cannon near Clovis, Holloman near Alamogordo, and Walker south of Roswell. Smaller air bases were built in Carlsbad, Deming, Hobbs, and Fort Sumner. The army used these bases to test new planes and train thousands of rookie pilots, crewmen, and flight-maintenance personnel.

Bombing ranges covering many thousands of square miles were used for day and night practice flights, with simulated cities, ships, and other military targets scattered over New Mexico's vast landscape. Army planes became a common site in the skies over New Mexico, and most test flights were successful, although some bombers crashed and accidental explosions took a toll on the New Mexico terrain. In one case, a bomb was accidentally dropped into an inactive volcano in the Malpais south of Grants.

☼ The Manhattan Project and the Atomic Bomb

New Mexico played a central role in developing and testing the first atomic bomb, the most powerful weapon of World War II and in all of history. Top physicists from universities and scientific labs across the United States were recruited to live and work in Los Alamos as part of a national program, code named the **Manhattan Project**.

The Manhattan Project's military leader, **Gen. Leslie Groves**, chose Los Alamos for the site of this secret program because he hoped its remote location would make it easy to guard against enemy spies and saboteurs. **J. Robert Oppenheimer**, the lead scientist at Los Alamos, had visited the area when he had vacationed in New Mexico as a teenager. Knowing the land, he recommended it as an ideal location for the Manhattan Project. As a result, the government closed the Los Alamos Ranch School in early 1943 so that the campus and its buildings could be used for the scientists' work space and living quarters. The project's needs quickly surpassed the school's small size; five thousand men, women, and children lived on the mesa by 1945.

Security was strict at Los Alamos. No one could enter the site without a government pass checked by military policemen posted at gates at the main entrances to town. Travel from the site was mostly limited to Santa Fe, with FBI agents often shadowing scientists who visited the capital city during rare leisure times. All mail to Los Alamos was addressed to a single mailbox, number 1663, at the U.S. Post Office in Santa Fe. Army agents stationed at the post office censored outgoing letters to make sure enemy agents could not discover what the scientists and the U.S. Army were doing in northern New Mexico. With all these rules, the scientists' families felt so isolated and restricted that they claimed Los Alamos should have been renamed "Lost Almost."

Led by J. Robert Oppenheimer, famous scientists like Enrico Fermi, Edward Teller, and William "Deak" Parsons (of Fort Sumner) worked hard to develop the atomic bomb so that it could be used to help end World War II. Despite several major setbacks, the scientists' work

Albert Einstein's 1939 Letter to President Roosevelt

The urgent need for the United States to develop an atomic weapon was first conveyed to President Roosevelt in a letter from Albert Einstein, the famous creator of the scientific theory of relativity. Einstein's letter warned that the Germans were already developing such a weapon, implying that the United States must act soon or experience a great disadvantage in dealing with the increasingly powerful German nation. Einstein's 1939 letter is considered the inspiration for the eventual creation of the Manhattan Project, with its most important site in Los Alamos.

Albert Einstein
Old Grove Road
Nassau Point
Peconic, Long Island [New York]

August 2, 1939

F. D. Roosevelt
President of the United States
White House
Washington, D.C.

Sir:

Some recent work [in physics] leads me to expect that the element uranium may be turned into a new and important source of energy in the immediate future. . . . This new phenomenon [could] also lead to the construction of . . . extremely powerful bombs. . . . In view of this situation you may think it desirable to have some permanent contact maintained between [your] Administration and the . . . physicists working on [nuclear] chain reaction in America . . . [It would also be wise to give] particular attention to the problem of securing a supply of uranium ore for the United States. . . .

[Such a course of action is especially desirable because] I understand that Germany has stopped [the] sale of uranium [so that this scarce resource can be used in German experiments similar to current] American work on uranium. . . .

Yours very truly,

Albert Einstein

(Quoted in Michael B. Stoff, Jonathan F. Fanton, and R. Hal Williams, eds., *The Manhattan Project: A Documentary Introduction to the Atomic Age* [New York: McGraw-Hill, 1991], 18–19.)

Location of Los Alamos
and Trinity sites in New
Mexico
....

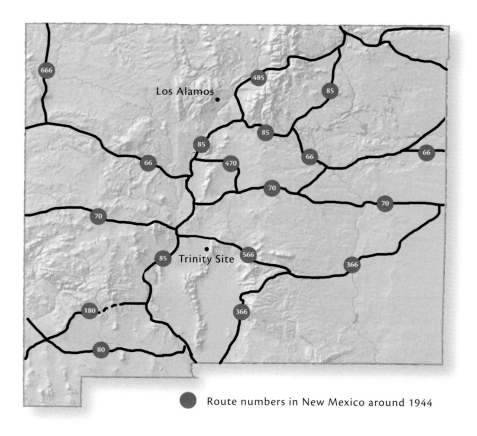

Route numbers in New Mexico around 1944

progressed until they were finally ready to test their new weapon in the summer of 1945. Although several sites for the test were considered, a location in southern New Mexico was chosen because it was well isolated, yet relatively close to Los Alamos for easy transport.

The bomb's parts were carefully carried to **Trinity Site**, the test site's secret code name Oppenheimer had selected. The bomb was assembled at a nearby ranch, owned by the David McDonald family. The armed weapon was then lifted to the top of a hundred-foot-high metal tower. At 5:29:45 on the misty morning of July 16, 1945, Oppenheimer, Groves, and other Manhattan Project leaders watched from a safe distance as the first atomic bomb in history exploded over the desert floor of New Mexico. The explosion was so great that the bomb's metal tower was completely destroyed.

Most physicists at Los Alamos were relieved their experiment had been a success, in scientific terms. Some men and women at Los Alamos, however, were overwhelmed by what they had helped to create. Emotions varied. Amazed by the power he had helped unleash, one scientist at Trinity Site had

J. Robert Oppenheimer
....

Daily Life at Los Alamos

Life at Los Alamos was difficult for everyone, from scientists and their families to soldiers and their officers. Eleanor Jette, the wife of scientist Eric Jette, described many of these difficulties in her memoirs, entitled *Inside Box 1663*. In addition to the problems caused by tight security, Eleanor wrote that housing was scarce and

- "the apartment buildings looked like hell. The green barracks-type structures sat . . . in a sea of mud";
- most homes had showers rather than whole bathtubs. In fact, most of the houses with tubs were left from the Los Alamos Ranch School era and were enviously referred to as Bathtub Row;
- water was so scarce that fire was a constant danger at home and in the technical labs where the atomic bomb was being made. According to Eleanor, "Fire sirens wailed constantly";
- the wind was so bad that "great icy blasts parched the earth and swirled dust into the houses."

Still, Eleanor Jette and most of her neighbors in the scientific community found much to do and enjoy in and around Los Alamos during the war. "Los Alamos was like a giant ant hill," wrote Eleanor. "The atomic bomb was its queen and the Tech Area was her nest. The queen's demands . . . were unceasing, but on Sundays she dozed and the workers fanned out to [enjoy the countryside]." Many workers and their families

- hiked, explored, rode horses, skied, ice skated, or simply enjoyed New Mexico's incredible natural scenery;
- befriended Pueblo Indians (many of whom worked in Los Alamos), attending public dances and learning about Native American art and culture;
- befriended Hispanic New Mexicans (many of whom also worked in Los Alamos), often attending fiestas, especially the Santa Fe Fiesta each summer;
- staged amateur plays, relieving tension by poking fun at security rules and other wartime hardships;
- hosted parties with dancing and many interesting guests, some of whom were nearly as talented in music as they were in science;
- and visited with some of the most brilliant, creative men and women of the twentieth century.

(Eleanor Jette, *Inside Box 1663* [Los Alamos: Los Alamos Historical Society, 1977], 15, 35, 42, 62, 63, 69, 70, 71, 74, 81.)

gasped, "What have we done?" Another at the July 16 blast exclaimed, "It's beautiful," to which a fellow witness replied, "No, it's terrible."

Fearing the destructive power of their invention, some scientists petitioned **Pres. Harry S Truman** not to use the new bomb in combat.

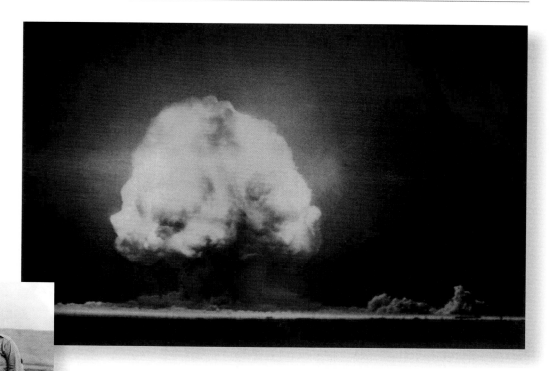

Top: Atomic bomb exploding at Trinity Site; above: Groves and Oppenheimer at what's left of the metal tower, 1945

As an alternative, these scientists suggested the United States might invite the Japanese to witness another detonation of the weapon, hoping that such a demonstration would convince the enemy to surrender rather than see the bomb used against Japan and its civilian population.

President Truman weighed the scientists' advice but made the difficult decision to drop the atomic bomb on real targets in Japan. The president and his top military advisors were convinced that if the United States did not end the war quickly by using the bomb, American troops would have to invade Japan with an estimated loss of a million American lives and an even larger loss of Japanese civilian and military lives. The Japanese were, after all, committed to defending their homeland to the last man, woman, and child.

Two atomic bombs made in Los Alamos were transported to the Pacific in late July 1945. Assembled on a small Pacific island, the first bomb, nicknamed **Little Boy**, was dropped from a U.S. Army B-29 over **Hiroshima**, Japan, at 8:16 a.m. on August 6. When the Japanese did not surrender immediately, a second bomb, nicknamed **Fat Man**, was dropped over **Nagasaki**, Japan, at 11:01 a.m. three days later. Combined, 214,000 Japanese lives were lost at Hiroshima and Nagasaki. Thousands of survivors were so badly injured that they died within days or suffered for years before dying from complications caused by radiation from the atomic blasts.

Replicas of the Little Boy and Fat Man bombs at the National Museum of Nuclear Science and History, Albuquerque.

Yet the atomic bomb was a success. In an ironic way, the bombs saved millions of American and Japanese lives because an American invasion would have been so much more costly. Militarily, the bombs were a success because they caused the Japanese to finally surrender unconditionally on August 15, 1945. With all that New Mexicans had done to help win the war, it was fitting that the USS *New Mexico* was present in Tokyo Bay when Japanese leaders signed their surrender papers aboard the USS *Missouri*, a ship named after President Truman's home state.

Hiroshima after the bomb, 1945

☀ The End of World War II

New Mexico's Contributions and the High Cost of War

August 15 became known as **V-J Day**, for victory over Japan, just as V-E Day had meant victory in Europe three months earlier. The long war had ended. New Mexicans joined all Americans in celebrating their victory in the deadliest, most destructive war in history.

New Mexico contributed to the United States' victory in World War II in valuable ways, from the Navajo Code to the Manhattan Project.

Descriptions by Witnesses near Trinity Site, July 16, 1945

When the atomic bomb was first tested at Trinity Site

- "the explosion was seen in three states [Texas, Arizona, and Colorado]";
- "the heat at the center of the blast approximated that at the center of the sun, and the light created equaled almost twenty suns";
- "every living thing within the radius of a mile was annihilated— plants, snakes, ground squirrels, lizards, even the ants. The stench of the death lingered about the area for about three weeks";
- "Ranger Ray Smith, on duty near Lookout Mountain tower north- west of Silver City, felt certain he had experienced an earthquake, as did several people in Carrizozo";
  - "eight-year-old Thomas Treat of Deming was sleeping on his front porch when the light [from the bomb] awak- ened him and the roosters began crowing. He ran for his Methodist parents, and they solemnly considered if this might be the end of the world";
  - "Mrs. H. E. Wieselman had just crossed the Arizona-New Mexico line en route [east] when she saw [the blast]. She remembered, ... 'The surrounding countryside was illuminated like daylight for about three seconds. Then it was dark again. The experience scared me. It was just like the sun had come up and suddenly gone down again'";
  - "[UNM student] Georgia Green of Socorro . . . was being driven up to Albuquerque for her nine o'clock class by her brother-in-law. 'What was that?' she asked. This might not be unusual except that Georgia Green was blind";
  - the army tried to keep news of the blast out of the news- papers, although one officer said, "You might as well try to hide the Mississippi River." The army finally announced, "A remotely located ammunition magazine containing a considerable amount of high explosives and pyrotecnic exploded." In short, the army claimed that the great explosion was nothing more than an accident involving powerful conventional weapons. Few who witnessed the actual explosion were fooled by this official explanation. They knew that they had seen something far worse.

(Ferenc Morton Szasz, *The Day the Sun Rose Twice: The Story of the Trinity Site Nuclear Explosion, July 16, 1945* [Albuquerque: University of New Mexico Press, 1984], 83–85.)

Trinity Site monument today

New Mexican POWs Witnessed the Atomic Bombs in Japan

The U.S. Army did not realize that American POWs were in or near Hiroshima or Nagasaki when atomic bombs were dropped on those cities in early August 1945. Capt. John W. Farley, a dentist from Ratón, was in a POW camp in Nagasaki when he recalled seeing

> a terrific flash. The light was projected upward as well as downward and quivered for thirty seconds. I hit the ground. . . . I heard breaking glass. . . . I saw a tall white cloud-like pillar four to five thousand feet high. Inside, it was brown and churning.

Captain Farley spent the next week caring for the sick and dying. Forty-eight American POWs were among the thousands who died of terrible burns and radiation poisoning in Japan in the days and weeks after the bomb.

(Walter Hines, *Aggies of the Pacific War: New Mexico A&M and the War with Japan* [Las Cruces: Yucca Tree Press, 1999], 140.)

Japanese Victims of the Bomb

Shortly after the dropping of the atomic bomb on Hiroshima, American author John Hersey interviewed several victims of the bombing. His famous book, *Hiroshima*, remains the most accurate account of the misery and pain felt by the men, women, and children who experienced that fateful day in August 1945. A young medical doctor 1,650 yards from the center of the blast recorded the following memories:

> [Twenty-five-year-old Dr. Terufumi Sasaki walked along the main hall of Hiroshima's large, modern Red Cross Hospital.] He was one step beyond an open window when the light of the bomb was reflected, like a gigantic photographic flash, in the corridor. He ducked down on one knee and said to himself, . . . "Sasaki, gambare! Be brave!" Just then . . . the blast ripped through the hospital. The glasses he was wearing flew off his face; the bottle of blood [he carried] crashed against one wall; his Japanese slippers zipped out from under his feet—but otherwise, thanks to where he [had] stood, he was untouched. . . .
>
> The hospital was in horrible confusion: heavy partitions and ceilings had fallen on patients, beds had overturned, windows had blown in and cut people, blood was spattered on the walls and floors, instruments were everywhere, many of the patients were running about screaming, many more lay dead. . . . Dr. Sasaki found himself the only doctor in the hospital who was unhurt. . . . [O]utside, all over Hiroshima, maimed and dying citizens turned their unsteady steps toward the Red Cross Hospital to begin an invasion that [soon overwhelmed Dr. Sasaki and the few nurses well enough to assist him].

(John Hersey, *Hiroshima* [New York: Alfred A. Knopf, 1946], 8–9, 14–15, 25–26, 88.)

▲▲▲▲▲▲▲▲▲▲▲▲▲▲▲▲▲▲▲▲▲▲▲▲▲▲▲▲▲▲▲▲

U.S. Naval Ships Named after New Mexico Communities

In addition to the USS *New Mexico*, at least a dozen other naval vessels were named after communities in New Mexico, including:

An attack submarine: *Ratón*, launched January 24, 1943; six Battle Stars for service in the Atlantic and Pacific Oceans in World War II; decommissioned on June 29, 1969, to become a target ship for gunnery exercises;

A cruiser: *Santa Fe*;

An attack cargo ship: *Torrence*;

Four tankers: *Caliente*, *Pecos*, *Rio Grande*, and *Tularosa*;

Seven other vessels: *Albuquerque*, *Catron*, *Gallup*, *Hidalgo*, *Sandoval*, *Union*, *Valencia*.

(*Farmington Times-Hustler*, May 17, 1946.)

As in every violent conflict, however, the cost of war was high in lost lives, money, and freedoms.

In lives, 2,263 of the 49,549 New Mexicans who served on the European and Pacific fronts were killed; 40 percent of them perished in the Bataan Death March, in Japanese POW camps, and aboard enemy hell ships. Thousands returned home to New Mexico only to suffer from physical and psychological problems for many years or, in some cases, for the rest of their lives.

In money, the war cost the United States $288 billion (in today's money) or more than $15,000 for every American alive in 1945. New Mexicans helped finance this enormous amount by purchasing war bonds far beyond the sums the federal government requested. New Mexicans also gave their time and money to other worthwhile organizations, especially the BRO and the International Red Cross. New Mexicans increased the production of needed war materials and, in most cases, helped conserve scarce resources through rationing.

The cost in lost freedoms was especially high. People identified with the enemy often suffered unfair discrimination. This was especially true for the more than five thousand men of Japanese descent detained in internment camps where they were denied their freedoms, lost most of their property, and suffered separation from their families for months, if not years. To New Mexico's credit, several towns in the state protected their Japanese residents, asking the U.S. government not to imprison them in relocation or internment camps simply because of their race and national origin. ✢

Santa Fe Welcomes Bataan Survivors Home

26 Make Hike to Chimayo
500 Journey to Santuario For Mass
Santa Fe New Mexican, April 29, 1945

More than five hundred, probably the largest congregation ever to attend services in El Santuario, Chimayo's famed chapel, were present at 10:00 a.m. High Mass yesterday. . . . The crowd was so large in the tiny edifice that it was difficult to kneel. . . .

Twenty-three veterans—all but two members of New Mexico's 200th Coast Artillery (AA) . . . made the twenty-six mile march, the last eleven miles of which was over open, mountainous terrain, [as a way to express their gratitude for returning home safely at last. In addition,] three women, two of them wives of the participating veterans, and Fuzzy, a little, shaggy, white-and-yellow-haired terrier, owned by S/Sgt. Gavino Rivera [of Santa Fe] completed the hike.

Santa Fe Pays Record Tribute To Bataan Men
Santa Fe New Mexican, September 13, 1945

The 200th Coast Artillery (AA) found out how the hometown felt about it yesterday when thousands of Santa Feans marched in cheering tribute past the Plaza reviewing stand packed with survivors of Bataan.

Young and old, many defying a nipping wind to wear Fiesta costumes, joined in the procession which oldtimers declared the most impressive patriotic ceremony in memory. . . .

Three trucks, [occupying a space] ninety feet long, furnished a reviewing stand that was jammed with returnees who . . . ribbed and greeted friends in the line of march. . . .

[In addition to the march, Santa Fe's] welcome home celebration . . . included religious services of prayer for the dead and thanksgiving for the nation, a supper dance at the Elks Club, and a football game, won by Santa Fe High against their rivals from Las Vegas High School.

Controversy Surrounds World War II Monuments

Public monuments sometimes provoke outrage, especially when people have much different memories of the past. This was clearly true some fifty years after World War II when two monuments, in Los Alamos and Santa Fe, caused public outcries not heard in New Mexico for decades.

The Children's Peace Statue

The origin of the first monument can be traced to postwar Japan. Two-year-old Sadako Sasaki had been one of the thousands of Japanese exposed to the "black rain" of radioactive poison that fell on Hiroshima on August 6, 1945. Ten years later, when Sadako became ill, doctors diagnosed her disease as leukemia, or what many Japanese called the atomic bomb disease.

When Sadako was hospitalized, a friend told her about the legend of a white crane with mystical powers. The crane would grant a wish to whoever folded a thousand origami cranes, or paper birds. Sadako began making the paper cranes, drawing pictures on some and writing poems on others. On one bird she wrote, "I shall write peace upon your wings, and you will fly around the world so that children will no longer have to die this way."

Sadako made 645 origami cranes before she died, one of seven thousand Japanese children who died of the atomic bomb disease. Her classmates made the remaining 355 birds and collected enough money to have a statue in Sadako's memory made in Hiroshima's Peace Park. The statue's inscription reads: "This is my cry: This is our prayer; peace in the world."

Inspired by Sadako's story, children at Arroyo del Oso Elementary School in Albuquerque created another peace statue, decorated with plant and animal origami students from more than a hundred countries had made. When nearly completed, the children went to Los Alamos to propose that their statue, symbolizing peace, be placed in the town where the first atomic bomb had been made.

The proposal met considerable opposition at a meeting of the Los Alamos county council in November 1994. Although a handful of local residents supported having the peace statue in their community, many others objected. One councilman called the statue a "simple and innocent . . . desire for future peace" but worried, "How will it be used against us?" He feared that peace advocates would use the statue to demonstrate against atomic research. Others claimed that the statue disputed the need to use the atomic bomb as a means to end World War II. In short, they worried the statue would belittle the valuable work done at Los Alamos to shorten the war.

With such opposition, the statue was not placed in Los Alamos but in Albuquerque and, since 1995, in Santa Fe. Many still hope that it will someday find a place in Los Alamos.

A Japanese-American Internment Camp Monument

A second, even more controversial monument was proposed to remember the Japanese-American men who were interned in Santa Fe during World War II. A meeting of the Santa Fe city council almost ended in a fight when many local citizens objected to such a marker, saying that it would be a "kick in the teeth" to the New Mexicans who served at Bataan and elsewhere in the war against Japan. Some opponents were confused, thinking that the men held in the camp were Japanese POWs; others believed that most of the Japanese-Americans held in the camp needed to be interned because they really were a threat to the country's security.

The city council finally approved the marker, officially unveiling it near the location of the old internment camp overlooking Santa Fe in April 2002. To acknowledge the service and sacrifice of Santa Fe veterans, the council later passed a proposal to create a monument to honor all men and women who served the United States during World War II.

1. Why did many New Mexicans join the national guard in the 1930s and early 1940s? Where was the 200th Coast Artillery (AA) sent in mid-1941?

2. What happened to the 200th Coast Artillery, the 515th Coast Artillery, and all American forces in the Philippines from December 1941 to April 1942? Why did they finally have to surrender?

3. Describe conditions that American POWs faced on the Bataan Death March, in POW camps, and on Japanese hell ships.

4. What made the Navajo Code so different and so hard to decipher? Why was being a Navajo Code Talker so dangerous?

5. How successful were the Navajo Code Talkers?

6. What made Bill Mauldin's cartoon, "Willie and Joe," so popular among soldiers and civilians during World War II?

7. What made Ernie Pyle's newspaper column so popular among soldiers and civilians during World War II?

8. Why was rationing necessary during World War II? What were some of the main items that had to be rationed? How successful was the program? Why?

9. What caused a new labor shortage in New Mexico during World War II?

10. Was the Bracero Program a success or failure? Why?

11. Why was New Mexico chosen as the site of two major and several smaller POW camps?

12. How were German and Italian POWs treated in these camps? Why was this treatment so important to the fate of American POWs held in Europe?

13. Why were hundreds of Japanese males forced to spend much of the war in internment camps in Santa Fe and Lordsburg? Was it fair to imprison them? Why?

14. Why was Los Alamos chosen as a major site for the development of the atomic bomb?

15. Describe the hardships of life at Los Alamos during the war. What were some of the joys of life at Los Alamos?

16. What did some scientists urge President Truman to do after they had witnessed the atomic bomb experiment at Trinity Site? What did the president finally decide to do with the atomic bomb? Why?

17. Describe the destruction the atomic bomb caused at Hiroshima and Nagasaki.

18. Describe at least five major contributions that New Mexico made to the United States' victory in World War II.

19. Describe the cost of World War II in lives, property, and freedoms.

20. How do we remember and honor our World War II veterans today? Have we done enough?

21. What has made some of the ways that we remember World War II controversial today?

22. What aspects of New Mexico would you have been proud of if you had lived during World War II? Why?

23. What aspects would you have been less proud of if you had lived during World War II? Why?

24. What lessons can we learn from the history of New Mexico in World War II?

New Mexico in the Early Cold War

1946–65

☀ Introduction

Like all Americans, New Mexicans looked forward to leading lives of peace and prosperity after World War II. Many adjusted to the postwar years well, making good use of new educational, housing, and employment opportunities, especially available to veterans and their young families.

Just as World War II ended, however, the United States found itself confronted by a new international enemy, the Soviet Union. The United States and its western allies struggled to prevent the spread of Soviet communism in all parts of the world. This new challenge to contain communism while promoting democracy in Europe, Asia, Africa, and Latin America became known as the **Cold War**.

New Mexico played a major role in the Cold War, from its start shortly after World War II to its end in the early 1990s. As in every modern war, patriotic New Mexicans readily offered their resources, energy, and, when called on to fight, even their lives. Modern forces released in the Cold War era would challenge and forever change New Mexico.

The purpose of this chapter is to teach you

- how New Mexicans adjusted to the postwar era;
- what role New Mexico played in the Cold War;
- and what impact the Cold War had on New Mexico.

TIMELINE

1944
Pres. Franklin D. Roosevelt signs the GI Bill of Rights

1945
White Sands Proving Grounds are established

Senator Dennis Chavez proposes the Fair Employment Rights Bill, but it is defeated in the U.S. Senate

1947
Rancher William "Mack" Brazel discovers what many believe to be the site of a UFO crash near Corona

1948
Pres. Harry S Truman integrates the U.S. armed forces with Executive Order 9981

A special three-judge court rules in favor of Isleta resident Miguel Trujillo, guaranteeing Indian voting rights in New Mexico

1949
State Senator Tibo J. Chavez takes the lead in the passage of New Mexico's Fair Employment Practices Act

1950
The Dixon school case, involving the separation of church and state, is resolved

Patricio "Paddy" Martínez discovers uranium near Grants

Manzano Base, a top-secret nuclear weapons storage facility, is opened near Kirtland Air Force Base

An air force B-29 with an unarmed nuclear weapon on board crashes near Manzano Base

The United States enters the Korean Conflict

Members of the International Union of Mine, Mill, and Smelter Workers strike against the Empire Zinc Corporation in the longest strike in New Mexico history

1951
Corporal Hiroshi Miyamura wins the Medal of Honor for his bravery in the Korean Conflict

The United States tests its first H-bomb in the South Pacific

1953
The Korean Conflict ends

Julius and Ethel Rosenberg are executed for their alleged roles in a communist spy ring during World War II

1954
McGregor Missile Range opens

The Salt of the Earth movie opens

CONTINUED TOP OF NEXT PAGE

Postwar Adjustments

Many New Mexicans never returned home after World War II. More than 2,260 New Mexicans had been killed. Thousands of others had taken high-paying out-of-state jobs, especially on the West Coast. Small towns and villages lost large percentages of their populations, especially among young adults.

Thousands of men and women did return to New Mexico after the war, eager to restart their lives after years far from home. To help young veterans train for new careers in the civilian world, the federal government created the Servicemen's Readjustment Act, or GI Bill of Rights, or simply the GI Bill, in 1944. The GI Bill offered many benefits, including government loans to help veterans start small businesses or purchase first homes. Most valuably, the government agreed to pay the veterans' full tuition at technical schools and colleges across the United States.

Thousands of New Mexico veterans used their GI benefits to attend in-state colleges and universities. Enrollment at the University of New Mexico skyrocketed from about a thousand students in the fall of 1946 to almost five thousand students in the fall of 1949. Of the seventeen hundred students enrolled at New Mexico A&M in the fall of 1947, a thousand were World War II vets, with male students outnumbering females four to one. Not expecting such high enrollments, colleges ran short on everything, from classrooms and teachers to student housing and books. Temporary buildings were brought from former CCC camps, air bases, and, in the case of the New Mexico State Teachers College in Silver City, a nearby mining community. Despite crowded conditions, veterans learned the skills they needed to become some of the most successful businessmen, community leaders, and professionals of their generation.

 ## Civil Rights

Native American Voting Rights

Miguel Trujillo of Isleta Pueblo was one of the many veterans who used the GI Bill to complete his education in New Mexico. He had already earned his college degree at the University of New Mexico in 1940,

A Zuni Soldier Returns Home

Virgil Wyaco was just a teenager when he entered the U.S. Army to serve his country in Europe during World War II. With V-E Day in May 1945, this Zuni Pueblo native and thousands of other American soldiers like him began their long-awaited journeys home:

> We knew we were home [in the United States] when we saw the Statue of Liberty in New York Harbor waiting for us. Everyone was shouting and waving, much different than when we'd left. We'd been pretty quiet then....
> [After traveling across country] when I arrived in Gallup, my uncle was waiting for me in his pickup truck. He had a medicine man with him. . . . Before we crossed the Zuni River, my uncle stopped the truck and the medicine man blessed me with corn meal, brushing me down with an eagle wing fan, taking all the evil I might have brought with me from where I'd been. . . . They wrapped up whatever they found [on me] in corn husk and had me throw it into the river.

(Virgil Wyaco, *A Zuni Life: A Pueblo Indian in Two Worlds* [Albuquerque: University of New Mexico Press, 1998], 41–43.)

Hispanic Soldiers Return Home

Sabine R. Ulibarrí was one of the thousands of Hispanic soldiers who returned home after World War II. Most Hispanic veterans would agree with him that

> the Second World War . . . was the greatest thing that ever happened to the Hispanic population of New Mexico. It opened our eyes. We saw vistas and horizons we didn't even know existed. The new panorama provided an expansion of the spirit. Now we wanted more. We had become accustomed to something more.

(Sabine R. Ulibarrí, *Mayhem Was Our Business: Memorias de un Veterano* [Tempe, Arizona: Bilingual Press, 1997], 27–29, 69.)

Like many other Hispanics, Ulibarrí had gone off to war to defend what he had known but returned eager to create something new. In Ulibarrí's case, he finished his education and went on to become a highly respected professor of Spanish at the University of New Mexico, where he received many awards for his books about Hispanic culture.

becoming the university's first Native American graduate. In 1942, he had volunteered for the marines, although he was already forty-two and, with a wife and family, could not be drafted. Trujillo did his patriotic duty, though, and served an important role, helping to recruit young

Veterans Suffered Even After World War II

Many New Mexico veterans suffered physical injuries and psychological damage from the war. After army veteran Virgil Wyaco returned to his home in Zuni, he began to have nightmares, especially about the liberation of Jewish prisoners at the Dachau concentration camp, "the worst experience of war, of my life. . . . There were dead people piled everywhere. . . . Those that were still alive looked like they ought to be dead." In order to help their son recover from these memories, Virgil's

> parents asked my grandfather to help me. He belonged to the Newekwe clown society, and they knew how to cure problems like mine. He started me on a four-day cure that began each morning when he'd come to the house and mix herbs for me to drink. I'd vomit four times before noon. At the end of the fourth day, he told me I'd get over it. He was right. . . . I no longer had nightmares and [I] had started treating [my parents] with respect, not showing temper like I had before.

(Virgil Wyaco, *A Zuni Life: A Pueblo Indian in Two Worlds* [Albuquerque: University of New Mexico Press, 1998], 36–37, 49.)

Sabine R. Ulibarrí, the decorated B-17 gunner from Tierra Amarilla, also suffered recurring nightmares after returning home. He described his dreams as

> a whirlpool of blood, something like a tornado, that started in the distance, moving ever closer. When it came upon me and threatened to suck me in, I'd wake up screaming and bathed in sweat. . . .
>
> A physical and psychological examination determined that I was suffering from severe combat fatigue. I was sent to a convalescent hospital [but that didn't help]. . . .
>
> Forty-five years later . . . the results of combat fatigue are still with me. Any time I'm under pressure I break out in a rash. On my hands, on the back of my neck, behind my ears, on my elbows or knees. The itching is just as fierce as it used to be.

(Sabine R. Ulibarrí, *Mayhem Was Our Business: Memorias de un Veterano* [Tempe, Arizona: Bilingual Press, 1997], 107, 113.)

Native Americans for military service. Returning home after the war, he resumed his civilian career—teaching—and earned a master's degree at UNM in 1946.

As a good American citizen, Trujillo went to the Valencia County courthouse in Los Lunas to register to vote but was turned away. According to the state constitution of 1910, Trujillo could not vote because he lived at Isleta Pueblo and paid no state property taxes. Upset by this injustice,

Native Americans Still Could Not Vote in New Mexico

Miguel Trujillo of Isleta was not the first or the only Native American to be turned away when he tried to register to vote in New Mexico. Julia Denetclaw of Shiprock documented her experience in a certified statement:

Shiprock, New Mexico

May 6, 1946

I, Mrs. Julia Denetclaw C#22698, hereby certify that on May 6, 1946, I appeared at the Shiprock Public School, Shiprock, New Mexico, for the purpose of registering to vote in the coming elections. I was there refused permission to register. I have been a resident of the State of New Mexico [for] forty-eight years; the County of San Juan [for] forty-eight years; the voting precinct #13 [for] forty-eight years.

Signed: Mrs. Julia Denetclaw

Witnesses: E. G. Jones and Alison S. Dodge

(Peter Iverson, ed., *For Our Navajo People: Diné Letters, Speeches, and Petitions, 1900–1960* [Albuquerque: University of New Mexico Press, 2002], 148.)

A Navajo Code Talker expressed his frustration in moving terms a month after Julia Denetclaw's experience in Shiprock:

We went to Hell and back for what? For the people back here in America to tell us we can't vote . . . because you don't pay taxes and are not citizens! They did not say we were not citizens when we volunteered for service against the ruthless and treacherous enemies, the [Japanese] and the Germans!

(Quoted in Doris A. Paul, *The Navajo Code Talkers* [Bryn Mawr, PA: Dorrance and Company, 1973], 111.)

Miguel Trujillo

Trujillo enlisted legal assistance and brought his case to the U.S. District Court in Albuquerque. On August 3, 1948, a special three-judge panel ruled in Trujillo's favor, stating that no American citizen could be denied the right to vote simply because he did not pay a certain tax. The ruling gave Miguel Trujillo and all New Mexico Indians the right to vote at last. A courageous citizen, Trujillo led the way as a college student, a teacher, a marine recruiter, and, finally, as a civil rights leader in the postwar readjustment era.

Minority Rights

Other progress was made in the early years of the American civil rights movement. Nationally, Jackie Robinson became the first Black baseball player in the major leagues when he joined the Brooklyn Dodgers in 1947. Issuing Executive Order 9981, Pres. Harry S Truman ended segregation in the U.S. armed forces in 1948. In 1954, the U.S. Supreme Court ruled that a third-grade Black student named Linda Brown had the right to attend a white school in Topeka, Kansas. The famous *Brown v. Topeka Board of Education* case ended segregation not only in Kansas but also in public schools across the nation, including New Mexico.

Based on laws passed in New Mexico in the 1920s, several towns in the state still practiced segregation in the 1950s. As with other segregated schools in the United States, Black schools in New Mexico were usually inferior to white schools, with secondhand furniture, old books, and small, inadequate facilities. A 1949 report found Black schools in New Mexico to be in a "shameful condition." As an example, the report noted that at the Carver School for Black students in Roswell water for a science lab had to be brought into the lab through a hose that ran through an outside window.

The end of unjust segregation came peacefully and quietly in most New Mexico towns where it still existed. This was especially true in towns where Black leaders and educators like Lawrence Pigford of Alamogordo and Wendell P. Sweatt of Roswell were well respected by

Graduates from Las
Cruces's Booker T.
Washington School

▲▲▲▲▲▲▲▲▲▲▲▲▲▲▲▲▲▲▲▲▲▲▲▲▲▲▲▲

Sammie J. Kent at Tucumcari High School

Integrating white schools was a difficult experience for Black children in much of the United States, including New Mexico. Sammie J. Kent recalled his first days at Tucumcari High School:

> Even after integration began, a lot of white teachers in the Tucumcari schools were very prejudiced. My Algebra teacher was so prejudiced that he would actually use the word "nigger" in the classroom....
>
> Some of the coaches were very prejudiced. I remember one coach in particular who was so prejudiced that he would instruct the white football players, "Don't block for Sammie. We don't want him to score more touchdowns than our white stars." [The coach] said that at a state championship game in my senior year, and we lost the game....
>
> I sometimes experienced prejudice in towns in which we played.... The prejudice was not so much with the players as with their parents sitting in the stands. They'd yell, "Don't let that nigger do that!" When I heard things like that it would really anger me, but I tried to hold my anger inside. The more I held it inside, the better athlete I became. I'd push myself harder and play much better. I'm sure such incidents affected the other black athletes as well.

(Quoted in Richard Melzer, ed., *When We Were Young in the West* [Santa Fe: Sunstone Press, 2003], 238–40.)

men, women, and children of all races. Only Hobbs experienced a threat of violence before the opening of the 1954 school year. Fortunately, cool heads prevailed, and school segregation in Hobbs ended without incident. The academic record of excellent Black students and the performance of exceptional Black athletes undoubtedly helped improve race relations and allowed for a relatively smooth integration of New Mexico schools in the 1950s.

This did not mean the end of racism in New Mexico, however. Blacks, Hispanics, and Native Americans often experienced direct or indirect discrimination in businesses, employment, and housing.

Blacks were still made to sit in separate sections of theaters and restaurants, especially in eastern New Mexico, but elsewhere as well. In Albuquerque, a Black university student was refused service at Oklahoma Joe's, a popular student hangout near the UNM campus. A committee studying race relations in Albuquerque discovered that while Blacks did not experience discrimination at every restaurant, hotel,

Separation of Church and State: The Dixon School Case, 1950

Another important change in New Mexico education occurred in 1950. For more than a hundred years the Roman Catholic Church had played a major role in New Mexico schools. A large percentage of children attended parochial schools, like St. Michael's in Santa Fe and St. Mary's in Albuquerque, where they were taught by Roman Catholic priests and nuns. Many priests and nuns also taught in public schools because New Mexico suffered from a shortage of qualified teachers, especially in small towns and villages. Few parents objected because most New Mexicans were members of the Roman Catholic Church.

After World War II some New Mexicans protested that hiring priests and nuns to teach children in public schools was a violation of the principle of separating church and state. Separating church, or religious matters, from state, or public matters, is an important principle in a democracy because it helps to guarantee our freedom, or choice, of religion without fear that one religion will dominate or exclude all others.

Presbyterian families in the small northern New Mexico town of Dixon were especially concerned about Roman Catholic nuns teaching their children in public school. In the famous Dixon case, officially known as *Zeller v. Huff*, Protestants filed a civil suit to ban the hiring of nuns to teach in the local public school. Before a final court decision was made, Archbishop Edwin O. Byrne announced that the Roman Catholic Church intended to withdraw its teaching nuns from all public schools in New Mexico. Although resolved, the Dixon case had caused friction and hard feelings in Dixon and many towns across the state.

Wounds have since healed. Dixon was, in fact, chosen as the site of a reconciliation ceremony between the Roman Catholic and Presbyterian churches in 1999. In the words of Archbishop Michael Sheehan, "I'm very excited about [the 1999 event]." The archbishop was confident that Roman Catholics and Protestants would now focus "on things we have in common and not just the things that separate us."

barber shop, and swimming pool in Albuquerque, they faced discrimination at most of these public facilities. A city ordinance banning such unfair practices was passed before a cheering audience on Lincoln's birthday, February 12, 1952.

Isolated acts of racism continued in Albuquerque and other parts of the state, though. Six years after Albuquerque's city ordinance was passed, a Black resident was refused service at five of the nine barbershops he visited in Santa Fe. In 1962, members of the world famous Harlem Globetrotters basketball team were denied service at a local Roswell restaurant moments after they had played before a sold-out crowd at Roswell High School.

Housing was similarly segregated. A study in 1958 showed that of thirty thousand new houses built in Albuquerque since 1950, only twenty-four had been made available to Black residents for purchase. Many deeds specifically banned Blacks, "Orientals," and lungers from

▲▲▲▲▲▲▲▲▲▲▲▲▲▲▲▲▲▲▲▲▲▲▲▲▲▲▲▲▲▲▲▲▲▲▲▲▲▲

Housing Discrimination

African Americans often faced unfair discrimination when they searched for housing for their families. When housing was available, it was usually confined to certain sections of town. As one example of this discrimination, an advertisement in the *Albuquerque Journal* of June 17, 1932, read:

> Colored Folks
> Here is your chance to buy a
>   furnished double house at
> 704–6 South High St.
> Live in one side and rent the other.
> ALSO 711 E. MANUEL
> Good three-room house. Cash or terms.
> Phone 41–43, 206 West Gold Ave.

Conditions in Albuquerque had not changed twenty-two years later. In 1954, Fred M. Strait, the president of the Albuquerque branch of the National Association for the Advancement of Colored People, wrote to Senator Dennis Chavez:

> Thousands of homes are being built in Albuquerque for sale at reasonable cost, but the builders will not sell to Negroes. How long must this discrimination continue, backed by federally insured loans?

(Fred M. Strait to Senator Dennis Chavez, Albuquerque, June 22, 1954, Box 33, File 2, Dennis Chavez Papers, Center for Southwest Research, Zimmerman Library, University of New Mexico, Albuquerque, New Mexico.)

ownership. Black families often lived in overcrowded, segregated neighborhoods where they were sold substandard housing at high prices. Rented properties were often little more than converted garages. A 1960 report found equally difficult housing conditions for Black families in Alamogordo, Farmington, Hobbs, and Tucumcari.

☀ Fair Employment Rights

Senator Dennis Chavez fought for the rights of New Mexico veterans and all American workers in the postwar era. During World War II a law had been passed making it illegal for the federal government to discriminate in hiring workers based on their race, color, religion, national origin, or ancestry. After the war, Senator Chavez sought to make this law permanent by introducing the **Fair Employment Rights Bill**. Chavez was especially interested in protecting the rights of Hispanic workers. In his pointed words, "If [Hispanics] go to war, they are called Americans. If they run for office, they are Spanish-Americans. But if they are looking for jobs they are referred to as damn Mexicans."

Southern senators, unwilling to guarantee fair employment rights to southern Blacks, blocked Chavez's bill in early 1945. It would take another nineteen years before southern opposition was overcome and the

Civil Rights Act of 1964 accomplished what Dennis Chavez had hoped to achieve for all minorities. Fortunately, a state senator, Tibo J. Chavez, was more successful in the New Mexico State Senate than Dennis Chavez had been in the U.S. Senate. Led by Tibo Chavez, the New Mexico state legislature enacted the Fair Employment Practices Act, which banned discrimination in the employment and promotion of workers. Gov. Thomas J. Mabry signed the important bill into law in 1949.

Despite the Fair Employment Practices Act of 1949, Blacks were still often refused jobs and opportunities. In many school districts, for example, Black teachers were not hired even after Black students had integrated local public schools. In Albuquerque, of a hundred Black applicants for full-time classroom teachers, none were hired in 1955. When employed, Black workers labored for below average wages and seldom received raises or promotions, much less supervisory positions. Unemployment among Blacks was two and a half times higher than unemployment for whites.

Women in *Salt of the Earth* movie

What was true of Black New Mexicans was often true for Hispanics and Native Americans as well. For many years Hispanics were denied higher-level, responsible jobs on New Mexico railroads; all were strictly prohibited from speaking Spanish while at work. Hispanic workers in the zinc mines of southwestern New Mexico faced discrimination in wages, benefits, and sanitary conditions, compared to Anglo workers employed in similar labor. Organized as Local 890 of the International Union of Mine, Mill, and Smelter Workers, miners struck the Empire Zinc Corporation in October 1950. Known as the Salt of the Earth strike, the bitter conflict lasted fifteen months, making it the longest strike in New Mexico history. As in the Gallup coal strike of 1933, women played an important role, replacing their husbands on picket lines when a court order forbade the men from picketing. Women faced insults, jail, and acts of violence but remained steadfast in their protest. The conflict was finally resolved to both sides' satisfaction in early 1952, thanks to the brave, unified action of the miners, their wives, and their union leaders.

Native Americans faced similar problems at work and in their daily lives. When able to find employment, most were given low-paying manual jobs, even in normally high-paying industries. After years of discrimination, Native Americans often asked white friends to negotiate the price of goods, like new cars or trucks, because white businessmen usually charged Indians higher prices when they went to purchase items on their own. While shopping, one Native American mother told of a white cosmetics saleswoman who refused to apply makeup on her Indian daughter's dark skin. Native American males often faced beatings and robberies when they ventured into towns located near their reservations. The list of indignities went on and on.

Mexican immigrant workers faced these and other problems, despite the supposed guarantees spelled out in the Bracero agreement of 1942. Their labor was exploited while their human needs and rights were routinely ignored. Some businesses went so far as to post rude, degrading signs that read, "Dogs and Mexicans not allowed."

☼ New Mexico's Contributions to the Cold War

New Mexico's role in the Cold War was nearly as important as its role had been in World War II. As in World War II, the state was used as the site for scientific weapons labs, weapons' testing, and four major air bases. It also served as the source of thousands of loyal soldiers, airmen, sailors, and marines sent to fight on far-off Cold War battlegrounds.

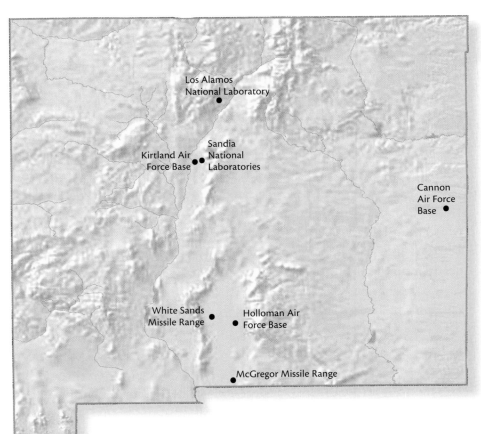

Location of air force bases, labs, and missile ranges

☀ Scientific Labs

Having successfully developed the first atomic bomb in 1945, there was serious talk about the scientific lab at Los Alamos closing down after World War II. Most of the scientists, starting with J. Robert Oppenheimer, had left the site to return home when the war ended. The new Atomic Energy Commission (AEC), created to oversee all atomic energy issues, decided, however, that Los Alamos still had a vital role to play in the nation's defense system. Many more atomic weapons were needed to fight the Cold War, and Los Alamos, with its supposedly secure location and already established facilities, seemed the best place for the job.

Led by a new director, **Norris Bradbury**, and staffed with many new scientists, Los Alamos National Laboratory continued its work in conjunction with other national labs, including the Livermore Laboratory in California. Scientists developed newer, more destructive bombs, including, by 1952, a **hydrogen bomb**, or **H-bomb**, said to be five hundred to a thousand times more powerful than the atomic bombs, or **A-bombs**, dropped on Japan. Scientists and technicians from Los Alamos helped test nuclear weapons in isolated parts of Nevada and the South Pacific from 1946 to 1958. As a highly secretive operation, Los Alamos was closed to anyone without a security pass until 1957, when most of the town, though not the lab, was finally opened to the public.

More atomic weapons were needed by 1949 when the Soviet Union detonated its first atomic bomb. Greatly concerned, the United States became engaged in an extensive arms race to defend itself against Soviet military aggression. To help keep pace in the frantic new competition, a second research lab was opened in New Mexico. Sandia National Laboratories, in southeast Albuquerque, were originally known as Z Division, an important branch of the Manhattan Project during World War II. By 1949, the labs' work was so important they became a separate operation, which the Western Electric Company managed. The labs grew quickly. By 1951, Sandia was the state's largest employer. By 1962, Sandia employed nearly a hundred PhDs. With so many highly educated scientists at Los Alamos and Sandia, the state boasted the highest number of PhDs per capita in the United States.

☀ Air Force Bases

Also as in World War II, New Mexico served as the site of several valuable air bases during the Cold War. In fact, all four of the state's Cold War air force bases had originally been built as army air bases during the Second

World War. (The air force became a separate branch of the U.S. armed forces in 1947.) Ideal weather conditions, open spaces, and isolation were the main reasons for keeping, and expanding, these facilities in New Mexico.

Albuquerque's **Kirtland Air Force Base**, named for military aviation pioneer Col. Roy G. Kirtland, played an essential role in aviation support and weapons' testing for the Sandia and Los Alamos labs. In 1949, it became the Air Force Special Weapons Center, in charge of the nation's nuclear weapons arsenal. By 1950, it was the site of a top-secret missile storage operation made up of concrete and steel vaults built in tunnels within the Manzano Mountains southeast of Albuquerque. With hundreds of nuclear warheads, **Manzano Base** became the main nuclear warhead storage facility in the United States during most of the Cold War.

Walker Air Force Base, south of Roswell, was named for Brig. Gen. Kenneth N. Walker, a New Mexico native who was killed in an air battle during World War II and won the Medal of Honor for his bravery in 1943. From 1947 to 1958, the base served as a key part of the nation's Strategic Air Command (SAC), responsible for delivering atomic bombs in the event of nuclear war. Walker also served as the home base for many other important weapons programs, especially powerful Atlas nuclear missiles. Atlas missiles, stored in thirteen silos, were ready for use at a moment's notice at the height of the Cold War.

Cannon Air Force Base, west of Clovis, was named for Gen. John K. Cannon, a top-ranking army air force commander in Europe during World War II. Cannon served as the main base of operations and training for the F-100 Super Sabre fighter plane from 1953 to 1972. Able to fly faster than a thousand miles an hour, Super Sabre jets were deployed in several Cold War crises, especially in Asia in the 1950s and 1960s.

Holloman Air Force Base, southwest of Alamogordo, was named for Col. George V. Holloman, a pioneer in guided missile research. The base became an early center for space travel research and testing, especially after the Soviet Union launched **Sputnik I**, the first man-made space satellite, in 1957. The base also became the home of an aeromedical lab where primates were trained for early American space travel. Ham, a small chimpanzee whose name stood for Holloman Aero Med, was chosen to be the first U.S. primate launched into space after months of training at Holloman. Later, human astronauts were trained at Holloman's Aeromedical Lab in preparation for many successful manned space flights of the 1960s and 1970s.

Estimated Number of Bombs in the U.S. Nuclear Arsenal, 1945–55	
1945	3
1947	13
1948	56
1950	298
1952	832
1955	2,280

(http://www.globalsecret.org)

Ham, the Astrochimp

Ham was one of sixty-five chimpanzees trained in the Mercury space program at the Holloman Aeromedical Lab. Considered the brightest—and most mischievous—of his group, Ham was only four years old when he was selected to become the first higher primate to be launched into space as part of the American space program.

Ham's famous launch occurred on January 31, 1961. Prelaunch problems caused a four-hour delay before Ham was finally lifted into space in a capsule atop an eighty-three-foot-high rocket. Launched from Cape Canaveral, Florida, Ham reached a speed of 5,857 miles per hour and an altitude of 155 miles before he was rescued 420 miles out at sea in the Atlantic Ocean. Ham's capsule almost sank before it could be recovered, but the chimp performed well throughout his trying ordeal. He eagerly accepted an apple and half an orange as his much-deserved reward.

Following his flight, the famous "astrochimp" retired to a zoo in North Carolina where he lived the rest of his life. Ham is buried near the entrance to the New Mexico Museum of Space History in Alamogordo, having helped to prove that higher primates—and eventually man—could live and work in space. Reassured by this proof, the United States launched its first human astronaut, Alan B. Shepard, in a suborbital flight just four months after Ham's safe return to earth in 1961.

Ham, the Astrochimp

☀ Missile Ranges

With so much weapons' research conducted in New Mexico and elsewhere in the United States during the Cold War, it was important to find an isolated, but convenient, location for weapons' testing. Days before testing the first atomic bomb at Trinity Site in 1945, the U.S. Army had established the White Sands Proving Grounds on largely desolate land in southern New Mexico. The Trinity Site explosion was the first test conducted on the new proving grounds, but many others followed, starting just two months after Trinity. Observers predicted that the area would become "the world's largest shooting gallery."

The United States had become increasingly interested in rocket weaponry during World War II after the German military launched its first successful rocket, the Vengeance Weapon, or V-2, in 1942. When Germany surrendered in May 1945, a team of several hundred top-level German

▲▲▲▲▲▲▲▲▲▲▲▲▲▲▲▲▲▲▲▲▲▲▲▲▲▲▲▲

Robert H. Goddard and Early Rocket Research in New Mexico

J. Robert Oppenheimer and his fellow scientists at Los Alamos were not the first to experiment with new, modern weapons in New Mexico. From 1930 to 1932 and from 1934 to 1942, Robert H. Goddard, a Massachusetts college professor, lived and worked on the Mescalero Ranch three miles northwest of Roswell, creating a lab to develop, and a launch tower to test, liquid-fueled rockets. With the support of scientific leaders and aviators like Charles Lindbergh, Goddard launched a total of fifty-six experimental rockets.

Goddard and his assistants faced their share of natural as well as technical problems in conducting their experiments in eastern New Mexico. Goddard's diary of June 1938 reports:

> Went out to tower, arriving at 4:30 [a.m.]. At 3:15 [p.m.] a twister had hit the tower and made it a pile of rods and bent angles. . . . Charles [an assistant] was putting cover around lower part of rocket, and was therefore able to run from the tower [when the twister hit]. . . . He killed a small rattlesnake that was under the trailer. . . . The men [later] . . . killed a tarantula [that had made] a hole near the base of the tower.

(Esther C. Goddard, ed., *The Papers of Robert H. Goddard, vol. 3, 1938–1945* [New York: McGraw-Hill, 1970], 1169.)

Robert H. Goddard in Roswell

Despite these obstacles, Goddard's early research became the basis for rocket research during World War II as well as space travel much later. In fact, when the Apollo XI astronauts prepared for the first manned landing on the moon in 1969, the *New York Times* printed a formal apology for an earlier editorial that had ridiculed Goddard for his firm belief that rockets would someday fly to the moon.

To honor his work in New Mexico, Robert H. Goddard High School (with its Rockets teams) and the Goddard Planetarium at the Roswell Museum and Arts Center were named in his memory.

scientists and technicians, led by Werner Von Braun, surrendered to the United States and agreed to continue their rocket research at Fort Bliss, Texas, and the White Sands Proving Grounds in a program known as Operation Paperclip. German and American scientists worked quickly, launching Tiny Tim, the first American V-2 rocket, in 1946. More than sixty V-2 tests followed, helping to make the United States the world's leader in rocket development in the early years of the Cold War.

Witnessing a V-2 Rocket Test at the White Sands Proving Grounds, 1949

Albuquerque Journal reporter Rick Raphael had the rare opportunity to witness an early V-2 rocket test conducted at the White Sands Proving Grounds in 1949. His report appeared on the front page of the next day's Journal:

Atop the twenty-seven foot thick concrete blockhouse beside the huge rocket a loud-speaker blared over the desert sands:

"Two minutes to firing time.

"One minute. . . . Ten seconds. . . . Five, four, three, two, FIRE."

With an earth-shaking roar, flaming liquid oxygen began pouring out of the tail of the sky-pointed missile.

The rocket shuddered, then like some fantastic visitor from another planet, rose slowly. . . . [G]aining speed, [it] thundered toward outer space. In a second it was gone from sight in the heavens, leaving only a trail of white fuel smoke to curl like a snake across the sky.

Around the outside of the fenced area dozens of soldiers, civilian technicians, and observers began chattering excitedly. . . .

The shot was over. The forty-eighth experimental V-2 had attained a height of seventy-nine miles, traveling nearly 4,500 feet per second at top velocity.

Recovery parties started immediately to the site of the fallen rocket, thirty-seven miles north of the launching site. . . .

The results of the experiments [will be important]. But in the minds of nearly every man and woman who witnessed Thursday's firing was the thought expressed by one of the open-mouthed observers:

"Imagine being hit by that thing loaded with two thousand pounds of high explosives."

(*Albuquerque Journal*, February 18, 1949.)

Rocket Testing at the White Sands Missile Range, 1945–60

The U.S. Army, Navy, and Air Force tested thousands of missiles during the early Cold War, including weapon systems with names like Nike, Falcon, Dart, Little John, and Honest John.

Missiles Tested	
1945–50	255
1951–55	2,565
1956–60	10,339
Total	**13,159**

(http://www.wsmr.army.mil)

The Missile Dogs of White Sands Missile Range

Dingo, a Weimaraner, and Count, a German [shorthaired pointer], were the famous Missile Dogs of White Sands. . . . Small missile parts needed to be recovered after firing in order to analyze [the] success or failure [of each test flight]. Before . . . 1961, ground-recovery crews spent countless hours searching the desert for a rocket part, which had often [been] buried . . . in the sand upon impact.

[The search became much easier with Dingo and Count on the trail.] [B]efore firing, important [parts] of a missile were sprayed with squalene, a shark-liver oil that the dogs could smell from hundreds of feet away. . . . Dingo and Count were trained to search out the scented object . . . without being distracted by desert wildlife.

[The dogs worked] every day, in all types of weather: intense heat, snow, or wind. . . . With a ninety-six percent recovery rate, the program was so successful that other military and scientific agencies requested their services. . . . The program was discontinued in 1965. There had been eight dogs in the program, but Dingo and Count were the first and the best of the Missile Dogs at White Sands Missile Range.

(http://www.wsmr-history.org/Dogs.htm)

Two World Records Set at White Sands

Many records were set in the testing of men, bombs, and equipment at White Sands. Of all these records, none surpass the achievements of Col. John Paul Stapp and Capt. Joseph W. Kittinger, Jr.

Army Col. John Paul Stapp broke the world record for ground speed when his rocket-propelled sled, known as Sonic Wind No. 1, reached a speed of 632 miles per hour on December 10, 1954. After surviving this and twenty-eight other high-speed test rides, the "fastest man in the world" was asked what he thought about while waiting for each dangerous test to begin. Stapp replied, "First I look around at the mountains and at the bright skies and I don't think about anything. Then I say to myself, 'Paul, it's been a good life.' " Asked why he insisted on being the human guinea pig in the experiments he conducted, Stapp said, "If there was a fatality, I didn't want it to be anybody but me."

Capt. Joseph W. Kittinger, Jr., set a far different record at White Sands in 1960. Jumping from a helium balloon called the Excelsior III, the air force officer set a world-record descent of 102,800 feet (about twenty miles), reaching a speed of 714 miles per hour and landing after a jump lasting just four minutes and thirty-six seconds. He was the first human to exceed the speed of sound outside an aircraft. Captain Kittinger described each moment of his famous jump in his book, *The Long, Lonely Leap*:

Capt. Joseph W. Kittinger, Jr.

I stood in the open door of the gondola perhaps for forty-five seconds. . . . I placed my hands on the gondola. . . . I looked up, and the words rang sharp and clear as I said: "Lord, take care of me now." I stepped out—102,800 feet above the earth. . . .

Sixteen seconds after leaving the gondola, I feel the timer fire, then the jolt in my back as the timer yanks the cable to release [my parachute]. . . . I suck in deeply, grateful for the air. It is my first breath since stepping away from the gondola. . . .

Suddenly I feel as if I were being strangled by some invisible force! . . . I fight desperately for air. Gray clouds swirl through my brain; I fear I will lose consciousness. . . . The choking sensation lasts for some fifty seconds total. Then the pressure vanishes. I breathe normally, am grateful. . . .

Each second as I fall I race back into air closer to earth, air dense and rich and warm. . . .

Everything is going beautifully! I am almost wild with elation!

Now the clouds—so remote a short time ago— rush rapidly toward me. . . . I reassure myself that they are vapor and not the unyielding earth. . . .

[I'm] through the clouds—and the landing area [is] directly in sight beneath me! . . .

I'm down! It was a wonderful thought to contemplate as I sprawled on the ground, surrounded by clumps of desert sand, sage, and salt grass. . . . The clean desert air washed over me with a delicious feel and taste. . . .

Thank you, God, thank you.

(Joseph W. Kittinger, Jr., with Martin Caidin, *The Long, Lonely Leap* [New York: E. P. Dutton and Company, 1961], 212–24.)

Other military testing followed at White Sands, with weather balloons and advanced missiles launched from the southern end of the proving grounds at targets in the far northeastern sector. Renamed the White Sands Missile Range in 1958, the forty-by-one-hundred-mile area also served as the target for long-range missiles launched from more distant sites in New Mexico, Utah, and Idaho. The McGregor Missile Range, measuring more than twice the size of White Sands, provided even more space for weapons' testing and research when it opened south of the Sacramento Mountains in 1954.

Cold War Industries

Uranium is the key element used in the making of atomic weapons. This rare element was discovered in limited amounts in various parts of the United States, including New Mexico, before 1950. In mid-1950, a Navajo sheepherder named **Patricio "Paddy" Martínez**, discovered a

Patricio "Paddy" Martínez Discovers Uranium Near Grants, 1950

In the early 1950s, Patricio "Paddy" Martínez told a newspaper reporter the story of how he had discovered uranium near Grants:

Early one morning in June of 1950 my wife told me that she was out of baking powder, so saddling up my horse I set off for a trading post at Bluewater. After buying a carton of Luckies and a can of baking powder, I headed [back to our sheep camp].

As I rode along on my fourteen-mile return trip to the sheep camp the sun got hotter. . . . [B]y the time I reached the mesa at the foot of Haystack Mountain it was after noon. I was tired and hot, so I got off the horse, found a big flat rock, and went to sleep.

It was late in the afternoon when I woke up. Laying on the warm limestone rock I was thinking about getting back to camp when I rolled over and saw a streak of yellow running through the stone beside my head. I reached over and touched it, but finding it tough to break with my fingers I got a big loose rock and used it for a hammer. The yellow ran all through the gray limestone.

I pried some other rocks up and found that they had the same color in them, so picking up a piece I put it in my back pocket and headed to camp to tell my wife. . . .

This yellow rock looked just like some rock a couple of Colorado prospectors had shown me at the Yucca Hotel in Grants several months before. They said it was worth a lot of money, but I didn't know where to find any of it [until that day].

(Quoted in Wayne Winters, *Blood and Gold in the Land of Enchantment* [Prescott, AZ: privately published, 1953], 51–52.)

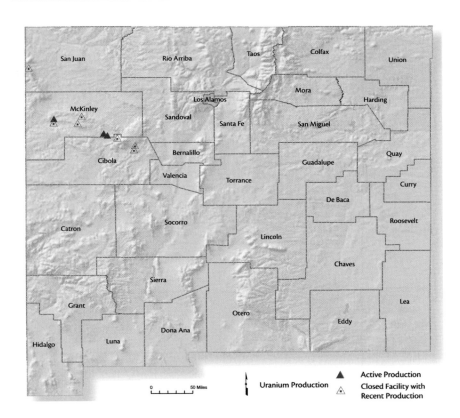

deposit of uranium oxide, nicknamed yellow cake, at the base of Haystack Mountain near Grants. Encouraged by Martínez's find, dozens of men searched western Valencia County (now Cíbola County), finding deposits and filing claims, much like hardy miners had done in gold rush days.

Larger companies, like the Kerr-McGee Corporation, soon entered the field, buying out early claims and opening both underground and open-pit mines. The Grants field was said to be the largest single source of uranium in the United States, with as much as 72 percent of all uranium reserves in the country. Five uranium refining mills built near Grants produced eighty-five hundred tons of yellow cake per year, or 46 percent of all U.S. production from 1956 to 1983. Grants justifiably called itself the Uranium Capital of the United States.

Oil and natural gas production also boomed in the first twenty years after World War II. As the Cold War continued and the nation's economy flourished, the demand for oil and gas rose to record highs. Oil and gas companies in New Mexico shared in the industry's rapid growth, especially when rich new fields were discovered in both San Juan County to the northwest and in Lea County to the southwest. The total value of crude oil drilled in New Mexico jumped from about $113 million in 1950 to nearly $312 million a decade later. Active oil

Oil and Natural Gas Production in New Mexico, 1945–65

Year	Barrels of Oil	Cubic Feet of Natural Gas
1945	37,351,000	124,480,000,000
1950	47,351,000	225,212,000,000
1955	82,426,000	520,209,000,000
1960	107,388,000	792,541,000,000
1965	119,141,000	901,522,000,000

(Jerry L. Williams, ed., *New Mexico in Maps* [Albuquerque: University of New Mexico Press, 1986], 281.)

Making an Oil Deal

Oilman Al Greer of Farmington told how he and other local oilmen did business in the early days of the oil and gas industry in northwestern New Mexico. Greer recalled a typical transaction with his good friend, Tom Bolack, a future governor of New Mexico:

> Tom and I were out examining an oil lease that he was considering selling. After I thoroughly inspected the well, I decided I wanted to buy it. We discussed the details of the transaction out in the field while leaning against my car. When we finally agreed on the terms of the deal, we decided [to] put them in writing so that they would be clear in our memories. Tom pulled out a lunch sack and, right there on the hood of my car, wrote out our deal on one side of that paper bag. On the other side, I wrote Tom a check for the purchase price.
>
> We concluded many other deals on scrap paper . . . and you know we never had any problems. In those days, we didn't consult attorneys— we respected and trusted each other.

(Quoted in Jerri Antunes, *Two Fists Full: The Story of Tom Bolack* [Farmington: privately published, 1999], 99.)

and gas wells dotted the landscape. New pipelines carried oil and gas to distant markets.

In 1925, an oil geologist accidentally discovered potash deposits in Eddy County near Carlsbad. Mining companies began to extract potash, used in the production of commercial fertilizers, creating jobs for local residents and newcomers alike. By 1957, the value of potash production

▲▲▲▲▲▲▲▲▲▲▲▲▲▲▲▲▲▲▲▲▲▲▲▲▲

Coal Camp for Sale: Madrid, 1954

Like all other coal camps in New Mexico, Madrid closed when trains, homes, and factories began to use more modern fuels. The coal company that owned Madrid ran an ad in the *Wall Street Journal*, asking $250,000 for the entire company town:

```
ENTIRE TOWN
200 houses, grade and high school, power house,
general store, tavern, machine shop, mineral rights,
9,000 acres, excellent climate, fine industrial
location. (Wall Street Journal, June 17, 1954.)
```

Although several potential buyers expressed an interest, no one bought Madrid as a whole town. The houses and other buildings were finally sold to individual buyers in the 1970s. Today it is a thriving town with tourist shops, restaurants, and a museum on its main street. Most recently, it was used to stage a popular movie, *Wild Hog*.

in New Mexico reached more than $73 million. With 85 percent of the nation's total production in Eddy County, it appeared that potash would remain an essential part of the local economy for years to come.

Other extractive industries were not as fortunate. With the use of more modern forms of energy like oil, gas, and diesel fuel, coal production plummeted after World War II. One after another of New Mexico's coal camps closed, including the state's largest camp at Dawson in April 1950. Owned by the Phelps Dodge Corporation, Dawson's mines had produced as much as 1.4 million tons of coal a year during World War I, but by 1949 production had dropped to a record low of 280,323 tons. As also happened in the Gallup fields and in the small mining community of Madrid, the few remaining miners packed their possessions and left Dawson for Ratón and other towns in search of new employment for themselves and new homes for families.

Copper and zinc mining in southwestern New Mexico fared better than the coal industry, largely because copper and zinc were essential materials used in most modern weapons. Increased production helped breathe new life into company towns like Santa Rita. Cold War military demands increased the demand for copper and zinc, especially at the height of a major new military confrontation known as the **Korean Conflict**.

▲▲▲▲▲▲▲▲▲▲▲▲▲▲

Coal Production in New Mexico, 1900–1960

Year	Tons
1900	1,299,000
1910	NA
1920	3,683,000
1940	1,111,000
1950	727,000
1960	295,000

(Jerry L. Williams, ed., *New Mexico in Maps* [Albuquerque: University of New Mexico Press, 1986], 283.)

The Korean Conflict

Japan had captured and occupied Korea before World War II. With Japan's defeat in 1945, the Soviet Union occupied Korea north of the 38th parallel, while the United States occupied the peninsula south of the 38th. The original goal was to reunite the country as soon as possible, but the Soviets installed a communist regime in their portion of Korea, while the United States and the United Nations supported a democratically elected government in the south.

In June 1950, North Korean troops crossed the 38th parallel, invading South Korea with the goal of reuniting the country's two parts under a single communist government. Communist forces controlled nearly the entire Korean peninsula before the United States and its allies in the United Nations finally pushed the North Koreans back in a bitter, hard-fought

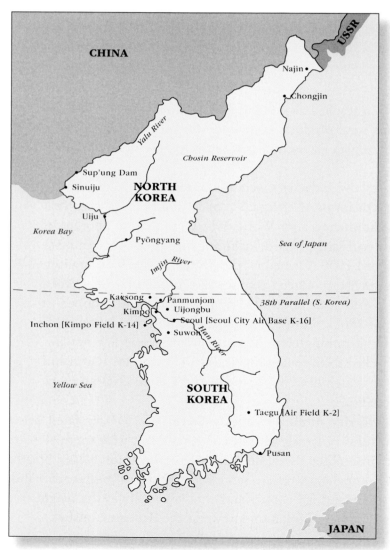

North and South Korea

▲▲▲▲▲▲▲▲▲▲▲▲▲▲▲▲▲▲▲▲▲▲▲▲▲▲▲▲▲▲▲▲

Corporal Hiroshi H. Miyamura and the Medal of Honor in the Korean Conflict

On the night of April 24, [1951,] the enemy fanatically attacked [Cpl. Hiroshi Miyamura's unit]. Miyamura, a machine-gun squad leader, ... unhesitatingly jumped from his shelter, wielding his bayonet in close hand-to-hand combat, killing approximately ten of the enemy. Returning to his position, he administered first aid to the wounded and directed their evacuation. As [the enemy launched] another savage assault . . . , he manned his machine gun and delivered withering fire until his ammunition was expended. He ordered his squad to withdraw while he stayed behind to [cover them]. He then bayoneted his way through infiltrated enemy soldiers to a second gun, [which he used to kill] more than fifty of the enemy before his ammunition was depleted, . . . he was severely wounded, and . . . his position was overrun.

(Medal of Honor Citation for Hiroshi Miyamura, November 4, 1953; http://www.medalofhonor.com/HiroshiMiyamura.com.html.)

Captured, Corporal Miyamura spent twenty-eight months as a prisoner of war before he was released in August 1953. Miyamura had won the Medal of Honor for his extreme bravery in 1951, but news of the award was kept a top secret while he remained a POW for fear that the enemy might retaliate against him.

Three months after his release, Miyamura finally received our nation's highest military honor from Pres. Dwight D. Eisenhower in a public ceremony held at the White House. The whole world now knew Miyamura's story and his remarkable courage.

Corporal Hiroshi H. Miyamura, recipient of the Medal of Honor in the Korean Conflict, shakes hands with Pres. Dwight D. Eisenhower

war to contain communism. Although both the Soviet Union and communist China supported North Korea's invasion, a direct confrontation between the United States and these two superpowers was averted. An armistice was signed in July 1953, but relations between North and South Korea remained tense throughout the Cold War.

The Korean Conflict has been called America's forgotten war, perhaps because the United States never officially declared war on North Korea and because the conflict was fought largely to a draw. With the loss of more than fifty-four thousand American lives and with more than eight thousand Americans reported **missing in action** (**MIA**), the conflict should not be forgotten. Of the 189 New Mexicans who died in the violence, thirty were listed as MIAs, and ten died while being held as prisoners of war. Most New Mexicans fought willingly and well; several received medals for their brave service, including army **Corporal Hiroshi "Hershey" Miyamura**, a descendent of one of the original Japanese families to settle in Gallup.

Social Changes

The Cold War and modern changes made a deep impact on life in New Mexico.

With new or enlarged science labs, air force bases, missile ranges, oil and gas fields, and mining operations, new jobs became available at all levels of employment. Many of these jobs were filled by increasingly well-trained New Mexicans. While some New Mexicans still left for high-paying jobs in other states, the labor drain of World War II had slowed considerably by the 1950s.

New economic activities brought highly skilled workers to New Mexico. Scientists moved to Los Alamos and Albuquerque. Air force personnel moved to towns near air bases and missile ranges. Mining engineers moved to Grants.

As a result of this new migration, New Mexico's cities and large towns grew as never before. In the center of New Mexico's uranium boom, Grants's population jumped from 2,251 residents in 1950 to 10,274 in 1960. Roswell, near Walker Air Force Base, grew to nearly 40,000

Large Town and City Populations

Large Towns and Cities with U.S. Air Force Bases

Large Town or City	Base	1940	1960
Albuquerque	Kirtland	35,449	262,199
Roswell	Walker	13,482	39,593
Clovis	Cannon	10,065	23,713
Alamogordo	Holloman	3,950	21,723

Large Towns and Cities with Major Research Labs

Large Town or City	Lab	1940	1960
Albuquerque	Sandia	35,449	262,199
Los Alamos	Los Alamos	*	13,037

Large Towns and Cities with Oil, Gas, and Mining Industries

Large Town or City	Industry	1940	1960
Carlsbad	Potash	7,116	25,541
Hobbs	Oil	10,619	26,275
Farmington	Oil & Gas	2,161	23,786
Grants	Uranium	2,251	10,274

* less than 6,500

(Jerry L. Williams, ed., *New Mexico in Maps* [Albuquerque: University of New Mexico Press, 1986], 230.)

residents in the same decade. Farmington, near the northwest oil and gas fields, experienced such a burst in population that its city limits had tripled by 1960.

In the greatest urban growth in the state, Albuquerque's population climbed 171 percent, from 96,815 citizens in 1950 to 262,199 in 1960. The city expanded with new housing, especially to the west, southeast, and northeast. With only slight exaggeration, a national magazine asserted that in Albuquerque "new houses go up in batches of fifty to three hundred and transform barren mesas [into housing developments] before you get back from lunch." By 1954, Dale Bellamah's construction company had built two shopping centers and sixteen hundred new homes in northeast Albuquerque; in 1961, Bellamah's was honored as one of the top twelve construction companies in the country. With similar growth in other large towns and cities, most (51 percent) of New Mexico's population lived in urban settings for the first time in New Mexico history.

Public Service Company of New Mexico Electric Customers, 1930–2000	
1930	8,400
1940	28,800
1950	60,000
1960	102,000
1970	166,000
1980	213,000
1990	291,000
2000	368,000

(Larry Smith, Public Service Company of New Mexico, to the author, March 27, 2007.)

Urbanization, or the growth in the size and number of cities, brought modern conveniences that few New Mexicans had previously enjoyed. In 1932, for example, Hobbs had had only 240 telephones, but by 1951, with a new oil boom and a sudden increase of population, the growing town had close to 4,000 phones in its homes and businesses. In 1950, the new Public Service Company of New Mexico had 60,000 electric customers. In 1960, the company had 102,000 mostly urban customers as more and more New Mexicans used electricity in their daily lives and businesses. Modern roads were built, including I-25, I-40, and Albuquerque's Big-I interchange by the mid-1960s. New shopping centers followed, with the opening of Albuquerque's Nob Hill in 1949, Winrock Center in 1961, and Coronado Center in 1965. The number of schools increased as well. In 1945, Albuquerque had only one public high school. By 1966, there were eight. Albuquerque boasted five major medical centers, three of which had begun as TB sanatoriums. Albuquerque's new International Sunport was completed in 1965, replacing the Municipal Airport built with WPA funds and labor in 1939.

☀ Cold War Dangers

While many New Mexicans benefited socially and economically from their state's important role in the Cold War, other New Mexicans did not fare as well in the post–World War II era. In time, a growing number

Albuquerque Public High Schools, 1891–2010

High School	Year Founded
Albuquerque	1891
Highland	1949
Valley	1954
Sandia	1958
Rio Grande	1959
Manzano	1962
Del Norte	1963
West Mesa	1966
Eldorado	1970
Cíbola	1976
La Cueva	1986
Volcano Vista	2007
Atrisco Heritage Academy	2008

Some Albuquerque Street Names

Many drivers have wondered about the name origin of large streets and boulevards in cities like Albuquerque. Here are the name origins of six of Albuquerque's busiest thoroughfares:

- Menaul Boulevard was named after a minister, James A. Menaul, who organized the First Presbyterian Church soon after his arrival in Albuquerque in 1881. The road led to the Menaul School for boys, which was named for James Menaul in 1897.
- Eubank Boulevard was named to honor Gen. Eugene L. Eubank, who was an early commander of the Albuquerque Army Air Base, later Kirtland Air Force Base, during World War II.
- Gibson Boulevard was named for Edward J. Gibson, an early superintendent of the Santa Fe Railway in Albuquerque.
- Montgomery Boulevard was named for Eugene Montgomery, whose family farmed a homestead near what is now Montgomery and Carlisle boulevards in the early 1900s.
- Unser Boulevard was named for Bobby Unser, whose family home was located on this street when it was just a narrow dirt road. The Unser family had run a car wrecking service on nearby Central Avenue for many years. Bobby Unser won three Indianapolis 500 races, including in 1981 when the boulevard was named in his honor. Other Unser family members have won car races of all kinds since the 1950s.
- Juan Tabo Boulevard's name origin is a mystery. Although no one knows for sure, some say that Juan Tabo was a sheepherder who grazed his sheep in nearby Tijeras Canyon.

Other urban streets have been named for famous men and women in U.S. and New Mexico history, including César Chávez, Martin Luther King, Jr., Georgia O'Keeffe, and Clyde Tingley in Albuquerque and Kit Carson, Mabel Dodge Luhan, and Padre Martínez in Taos.

(Donald Gill, *Stories Behind the Street Names of Albuquerque, Santa Fe and Taos* [Chicago: Bonus Books, 1994], 55, 66, 78, 99, 102–3, 144.)

of state residents feared the potentially dangerous consequences of the Cold War and modern changes in the Southwest.

 ## Growing Pains

Rapid urban growth and modernization brought problems as well as benefits. With so many new residents arriving daily in cities like Albuquerque, housing shortages became an even greater problem than they had

Urban Housing Shortages

City Home Construction Boom Sets New Mexico Pace

By Henry Mathews

Roswell is setting the pace in house construction in New Mexico and last week topped existing records with 83 residential permits for a total [cost] of $768,400, more than double the number and amount for all of January....

[W]e are way ahead of any city in the Southwest.... And [city building inspector Henry C.] Sorrells pointed out, "This is the [normally] slow season [of the year for new house construction]...."

During the past three months the city council has annexed more than 500 acres in the southwest and northeast sections [of town. With all the new building going on,] Sorrells commented, "It's quite a long trip to get through town."

(*Roswell Daily Record*, February 18, 1962.)

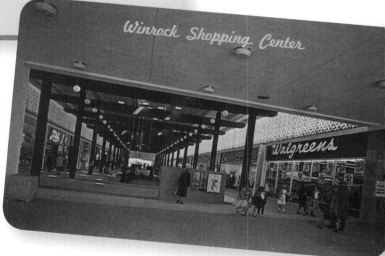

Winrock Shopping Center in the 1960s

been during World War II. Public utilities could hardly keep up with the demand; it often took months to have phone service installed. Schools were overcrowded until new ones could be built. Water pollution grew worse, especially for rural communities on the Rio Grande south of urban centers like Albuquerque. Crime and vice increased. In fact, when Los Alamos was opened to the public in 1957, many of its thirteen thousand residents voiced concern that "meddlers" and "peddlers" would soon invade their privacy. In 1954, the state penitentiary in Santa Fe experienced a deadly riot, in part because it had grown so overcrowded; a new, larger prison was opened south of the city in 1956. Cities across the United States suffered similar growing pains, but they were particularly difficult for New Mexicans to bear after centuries of much slower, peaceful growth.

☼ Rural Decline

Urban growth often spelled rural decline. More than four thousand New Mexico farms and ranches closed in the 1950s as many rural residents left the countryside for urban centers that offered higher incomes and modern

John Prather Resists the U.S. Army

Not all New Mexicans were pleased with the development and testing of modern weapons in the Cold War era. The U.S. Army forced settlers on the White Sands and McGregor missile ranges to leave their homes and ranches in exchange for minimal compensation. Many local ranchers, miners, and wool growers objected in heated arguments but lost out to the Department of Defense, which soon expanded its missile ranges beyond their original boundaries.

One eighty-two-year-old rancher refused to leave when the army ordered him off his land on the new McGregor in 1955. Cradling a rifle in his arm, John Prather declared, "You can bury me, but you can't move me."

Army officials faced a real dilemma. If they forced an elderly man off a ranch his family had occupied since 1883, the army would appear to be an "oppressive monster," according to the press. If the army allowed Prather to remain, then it would have to allow all recently removed ranchers to return to their homes as well.

John Prather

With reporters and photographers on the scene, Prather and twenty-five of his relatives armed themselves for a showdown with the army. When the army offered Prather $200,000 for his land and warned him that exploding test missiles might kill him if he stayed, Prather refused the money and replied, "I'm not afraid of missiles. I've raised mules all my life."

The army finally gave in. It allowed Prather to remain in his home and its fifteen surrounding acres for the rest of his life. Prather only left when he was in need of additional health care in Alamogordo. He died in Alamogordo in 1965 at the age of ninety-one. He is buried beside his ranch house with cacti and a cinder-block wall guarding his remains. John Prather's story became the basis of a 1962 novel by Edward Abbey entitled *Fire on the Mountain*.

Other ranchers protested the loss of their family's property. Dave McDonald and his niece, Mary, occupied their former ranch house on the White Sands Missile Range in 1982. Their adobe house had been used for the final assembly of the atomic bomb at Trinity Site but had never been returned to the McDonalds after 1945. Although promises were made to the McDonalds, the family received no additional pay for the loss of their ranch. In fact, the federal government has spent more money restoring the family's former home to make it into a museum than it ever paid the McDonalds.

(C. L. Sonnichsen, *Tularosa: Last of the Frontier West* [Albuquerque: University of New Mexico Press, 1980], 280–91.)

lifestyles. Some small farms and ranches were absorbed by larger farms and ranches, while others became part of the state's new missile ranges and air force bases. Farm and ranch land near large cities was often used to build new housing developments, as happened on Albuquerque's west mesa. Although fewer New Mexicans now left the state for employment, rural counties continued to experience a labor drain, if not to California and other states, then to Albuquerque and other New Mexico cities that benefited from the Cold War economy. A typically poor rural county, Mora County's population dropped from about eleven thousand in 1940 to about six thousand in 1960.

☀ Military Accidents

New Mexicans who still lived in rural areas often feared their proximity to busy military bases and missile ranges. With hundreds of nuclear warheads stored at Manzano Base outside Albuquerque, New Mexico's largest city was considered a primary potential target, had a nuclear war broken out with the Soviet Union. The death and destruction to Albuquerque and surrounding rural areas would have been devastating.

Nuclear accidents were also possible, especially as planes transported atomic weapons to and from Manzano Base. The U.S. government confirmed that thirteen nuclear accidents, known as broken arrows, had occurred between 1950 and 1968. Two of these incidents had occurred in New Mexico. On August 11, 1950, a B-29 bomber carrying a nuclear weapon in its cargo bed took off from Kirtland Air Force Base, heading east. Three minutes after takeoff the B-29 crashed into the Manzano Mountains, dangerously near the nuclear storage facility, causing a large fire that could be seen fifteen miles away. All thirteen crewmen aboard were killed. A far worse disaster was averted because the atomic bomb on board had not been armed with its nuclear device.

Seven years later, on May 22, 1957, a B-36 was transporting a nuclear weapon to Kirtland Air Force Base from a base in Texas when the bomber experienced turbulence and its crew accidentally dropped their Mark 17 hydrogen bomb from an altitude of seventeen hundred feet. Landing about five miles south of Kirtland, the bomb exploded on impact, creating a crater twenty-five feet wide and twelve feet deep. Debris from the blast was found as far as a mile from the crash site. Fortunately, as in 1950, the bomb was not armed with its nuclear device, and no greater damage was done.

Unidentified Flying Objects in New Mexico

On June 14, 1947, rancher "Mack" Brazel was mending fences when he discovered a strange crash site about thirty miles southeast of Corona and seventy-five miles northwest of Roswell. Brazel took some of the unusual material he had discovered to the Lea County sheriff, who then notified Roswell Army Air Field (later Walker Air Force Base). An information officer at the air field announced to the press that Brazel had stumbled on a "flying disc" from another planet in outer space.

UFO headline in the *Roswell Daily Record*

Soon after the *Roswell Daily Record* reported the startling news with front-page banner headlines, the air force changed its story and said the found object was actually part of a weather balloon that had been launched from the nearby White Sands Proving Grounds in a top-secret experiment called Project Mogul. Many doubted this official version of the incident, charging the government with a high-level cover-up. After all, several local residents, including two nuns sitting on their porch in Roswell, had reported seeing a strange craft in the night sky about the time of

Brazel's discovery. The testimony of air force personnel, including a major who handled the strange "alien" debris, added credence to these claims.

The debate over what Mack Brazel did or did not discover in 1947 has raged for more than half a century. True or false, it ranks as the most famous incident of its kind in the world. Many other sightings of unidentified flying objects, or UFOs, have been made in New Mexico, including at a site northeast of Aztec in 1948, at Kirtland Air Force Base in 1950, and at a location south of Socorro in 1964. While a large number of New Mexicans—and millions of men and women around the world—believe in UFOs, others say the unusually high number of UFO sightings in New Mexico may well result from

- New Mexicans coming to expect invasions after a fictional invasion of Earth from Mars in the controversial radio broadcast, *The War of the Worlds*, in 1938 and the very real Japanese surprise attack on the Pearl Harbor navel base in 1941;
- top-secret military tests at White Sands. White Sands's first experimental balloon was launched on June 4, 1947, less than a month before the UFO sighting near Corona;
- New Mexicans' belief that the U.S. government does not always tell the public the whole truth about important events, especially after the government reported that the atomic explosion at Trinity Site was nothing more than an accidental explosion of conventional explosives;
- New Mexico's vast, largely unobstructed day and night sky where people can see —or imagine—much more than in most other states or countries in the world.

Watching the Universe and Beyond from New Mexico

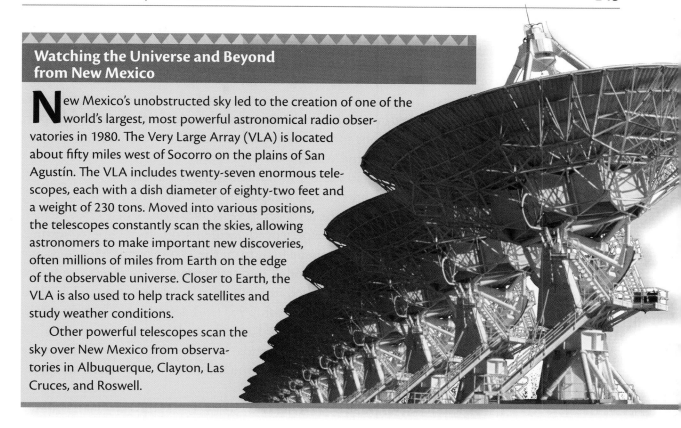

New Mexico's unobstructed sky led to the creation of one of the world's largest, most powerful astronomical radio observatories in 1980. The Very Large Array (VLA) is located about fifty miles west of Socorro on the plains of San Agustín. The VLA includes twenty-seven enormous telescopes, each with a dish diameter of eighty-two feet and a weight of 230 tons. Moved into various positions, the telescopes constantly scan the skies, allowing astronomers to make important new discoveries, often millions of miles from Earth on the edge of the observable universe. Closer to Earth, the VLA is also used to help track satellites and study weather conditions.

Other powerful telescopes scan the sky over New Mexico from observatories in Albuquerque, Clayton, Las Cruces, and Roswell.

The Very Large Array

Three accidental explosions occurred at Atlas missile sites near Walker Air Force Base in 1963 and 1964. As in 1950 and 1957, these weapons were not armed with nuclear devices, and only one man was reported as injured in these potentially devastating incidents.

Nuclear bombs developed in New Mexico and experimentally exploded in Nevada and on Pacific islands did great damage to the surrounding environment, killing plant and animal life and spreading radiation for many miles. American soldiers and workers near the blasts were exposed to large doses of radiation; some claimed the government had never warned them of the danger, allowing them to unknowingly serve as human guinea pigs for studies on the effect of radiation on human health. Many suffered from cancer and other fatal illnesses.

Two atomic bombs were tested in New Mexico for peaceful purposes. Part of a national program known as Project Plowshare, the first of these underground tests took place near Carlsbad in 1961. Scientists hoped that the blast, known as Project Gnome, would create an underground heat reservoir that might be used as a new source of power. In 1967, an atomic bomb (equal in strength to the bombs dropped on Hiroshima and Nagasaki combined) was detonated underground near Farmington.

Known as Project Gasbuggy, the blast was meant to improve gas flow from low-producing natural gas fields. Despite high expectations, the words of a scientist regarding Project Gasbuggy applied to both experiments: "It didn't work." The best that could be said about the underground experiments is that after years of monitoring, scientists report that the explosions spread only small amounts of radiation into the surrounding subsoil and water.

The United States tested its last aboveground nuclear bomb in 1962. It tested its last underground weapon in 1992. The country tested nearly a thousand bombs in the forty-seven years after Trinity in 1945.

Missile ranges also experienced accidents during weapons' testing. In 1964, a long-range missile fired from the White Sands Missile Range overshot its target and exploded in a small town in southwestern Colorado. Later, missiles launched in Utah missed White Sands and crashed over the Mexican border in both 1967 and 1970; it took three weeks to find and recover the wayward missile and its radiated material in 1970. Officials at the White Sands National Monument frequently complained about test flights over the monument's restricted air space.

A Pueblo Bomb Shelter

In 1956, young Teresa Pijoan lived with her parents at San Juan Pueblo. Well aware of the Cold War and its dangers, Teresa's father, a respected doctor, decided to build a fallout shelter to protect his family if an atomic bomb were dropped nearby. Surprised, Teresa's mother shouted, "An atomic bomb? What makes you think that the Russians are going to drop an atomic bomb on an Indian reservation miles from anywhere?" Mrs. Pijoan especially objected because her husband planned to build the tunnel to their proposed shelter under the cows' stalls in their barn. Teresa's mother could foresee the problem of cow manure falling on her family in their emergency quarters.

Dr. Pijoan's bomb shelter was soon the talk of the pueblo. Teresa's adopted uncle burst out laughing when he heard people talking about the danger. "What will people do when they run out of food and water in their shelters?" he asked. "Radiation doesn't go away. It stays around forever."

Later, when the danger of a nuclear war had passed, Dr. Pijoan turned his underground shelter into a cold cellar to store fruits and vegetables. Even Teresa's mother eventually recognized its value and readily used it for years.

(Interview with Teresa Pijoan, January 30, 2007.)

▲▲▲▲▲▲▲▲▲▲▲▲▲▲▲▲▲▲▲▲▲▲▲▲▲▲▲▲▲▲▲▲▲▲▲▲▲

Evacuating Los Alamos, 1954

As a main nuclear weapons research center, Los Alamos was considered a potential target if nuclear war broke out with the Soviet Union. Residents of the Atomic City prepared for such an emergency by organizing a practice evacuation of their town in 1954. A reporter from the *Santa Fe New Mexican* described the evacuation in the following words:

> The terrifying threat of atomic warfare came to the Atomic City yesterday [as more than] eight thousand residents and almost three thousand cars evacuated the city through the three main exits.
>
> [T]he town was almost completely evacuated in something less than one hour. . . . Downtown, simulated looting and panic tested [the] plans of police and auxiliary police units. Teams for bomb reconnaissance, panic control, and identification of [the] dead and injured spun into action. . . .

Los Alamos Civil Defense Director James R. Maddy . . . said he was "extremely well satisfied with the results" of his town's practice evacuation.

(*Santa Fe New Mexican*, June 15, 1954.)

Shortly after the evacuation, several scientists in Los Alamos realized that their families would have needed certain essential supplies if a real nuclear attack had occurred and they were really forced to leave their homes. The scientists created well-stocked survival kits, each with matches, a flashlight, a whetstone, candles, a hunting knife, a rifle, ammunition, an ax, first-aid equipment, sunglasses, a pair of scissors, a needle and thread, cord, a fishing hook and line, soap, a police whistle, blankets, canned food, water, water purification tablets, and a Boy Scout handbook.

(*Santa Fe New Mexican*, August 1, 1954.)

None of these mishaps of the 1960s and 1970s caused major damage, and fortunately no lives were lost.

Fire was a danger to the Los Alamos National Laboratory. Although large earthquakes have been rare, Los Alamos is located in an active fault zone. Some fear that an earthquake could start fires at the lab where nuclear material is worked on and stored. Forest fires, like the catastrophe that destroyed 250 homes but not the lab in 2000, are also a major cause for concern in Los Alamos and its surrounding area.

☀ Civil Defense

Fearful of nuclear war or accidents, New Mexicans willingly participated in a national **civil defense** system. Civil defense signs directed the public to safe areas if a nuclear attack occurred. Many communities held civil defense drills. Thousands of families in the United States built **fallout shelters** in their backyards in hope of surviving a nuclear blast.

American families were especially eager to build fallout shelters in 1962 during the Cuban Missile Crisis when the Soviet Union placed nuclear weapons in communist Cuba, with many of these missiles aimed directly at American cities. The worst crisis of the Cold War was finally resolved but not before the United States and the Soviet Union had gone to the brink of nuclear war. On the eve of this crisis, the residents of Artesia, south of Roswell's Walker Air Force Base, went so far as to build a new elementary school completely underground so it could serve as a fallout shelter for as many as 2,160 local men, women, and children. Built eighteen feet belowground, Abo Elementary School had twenty-one-inch reinforced concrete

President John F. Kennedy in New Mexico, 1962–63

Shortly after the Cuban Missile Crisis, Pres. John F. Kennedy demonstrated his commitment to a strong national defense system by inspecting weapons' development programs at both the Los Alamos and Sandia national labs on December 7, 1962.

Visiting Los Alamos National Laboratory first, the president, accompanied by the vice president, Lyndon B. Johnson, and New Mexico's two U.S. senators, Joseph Montoya and Clinton P. Anderson, was greeted by an estimated ten thousand people. In a brief speech, Kennedy thanked New Mexicans for their "contribution in the cause of freedom in the world." After touring the lab in Los Alamos, Kennedy flew by helicopter to Albuquerque, where as many as forty thousand New Mexicans came to see him as he entered Sandia National Laboratory.

Kennedy was the first U.S. president to ever visit the labs.

Kennedy was also the first and only U.S. president to visit White Sands Missile Range. On June 5, 1963, the president witnessed the launching of seven missiles in less than two and a half hours.

While President Kennedy helped prepare the United States for possible nuclear attacks, he also worked to create peace and prosperity in the world. His Peace Corps, established in 1961, provided American volunteers to help develop some of the poorest nations of Asia, Africa, and Latin America. Peace Corps volunteers were trained in special programs on several college campuses, including at the University of New Mexico from 1962 to 1967. If they were to serve in Latin American countries, many volunteers practiced their Spanish by staying with New Mexico families as part of their training at UNM. The eighteen hundred volunteers who trained at UNM worked in valuable fields like education, public health, and agriculture.

President Kennedy never visited New Mexico again. New Mexicans watched in horror as the president was assassinated in Dallas less than a year after his short, but memorable, stay in their state.

President Kennedy watching a missile launch at White Sands Missile Range, 1963

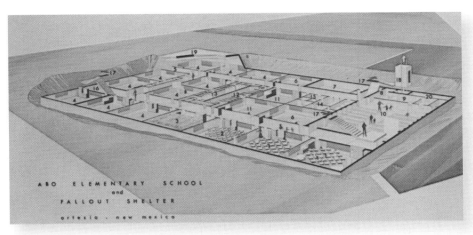

walls, uncontaminated water sources, an emergency power generator, air filters, survival kits, abundant food, and heavy steel doors. Appropriately, the school's sports teams were known as the Gophers.

In Roswell, school officials designed the city's new high school, named after rocket scientist Robert H. Goddard, aboveground but without windows. When first opened, the school's principal suggested that all students wear dog tags for identification in case there was a nuclear attack on their town, so close to Walker. While no other schools in the country went to these lengths for protection, every school practiced nuclear drills, with students ducking under their desks and covering their heads with their arms for at least some protection.

 ## Uranium Mining

Uranium mining in western Valencia County created other Cold War dangers. Unaware and not warned of the safety hazards they faced, uranium miners were regularly exposed to radioactive materials throughout their workdays. Miners were exposed to steady doses of radiation from the uranium they handled, the air they breathed (few mines had ventilation systems), and the water they sometimes drank that dripped off mine walls. As a result, many miners suffered from serious illnesses, especially cancer, leading to slow, painful deaths. Native American miners were particularly vulnerable. The government and uranium companies did little in response to expressions of concern because the price of uranium was so high and uranium was so important to the making of atomic weapons. Uranium that had sold for 77¢ a pound in 1944 reached $7.14 a pound in 1948 and $12.51 a pound in 1955. For years, national security and handsome profits were given higher priorities than human lives.

Communist Spies in New Mexico

Americans became increasingly fearful of communists in their country when communist spies were accused of stealing the secret of the atomic bomb from Los Alamos. Twenty-three-year-old David Greenglass, an army technician at Los Alamos during World War II, confessed that he had handed over all he knew about the bomb to a Soviet agent in 1945. The information was given to the agent at Greenglass's

Spy house on High Street in Albuquerque

apartment on High Street SE in Albuquerque. To prove he was dealing with the right person, Greenglass showed the agent half a Jell-O box, which he matched to the Soviet agent's half in a simple test of identity.

Arrested by the FBI in 1950, Greenglass confessed his guilt and identified his sister and brother-in-law as leaders of a communist spy ring. Julius and Ethel Rosenberg were arrested and tried for treason in the most famous case of espionage in American history. The couple was found guilty and, in a highly controversial punishment, executed for their crime in 1953. Leaving two young sons, the Rosenbergs were the only convicted spies ever executed for treason in the United States during peacetime. David Greenglass served a ten-year sentence in federal prison.

In another famous case, British authorities arrested Klaus Fuchs, a high-level physicist at Los Alamos, who had turned over far more detailed information about the bomb to a Soviet agent he met in Santa Fe on several occasions in 1945. Tried in England, Fuchs was found guilty of espionage and served nine years in English prisons.

A third spy, Ted Hall, was never arrested, although late in his life he admitted he had handed top-secret information about the bomb to a female Soviet agent in Albuquerque. A young genius, Hall was only nineteen years old when he worked as a physicist and stole the secret of the atomic bomb from Los Alamos.

Using information from Greenglass, Fuchs, Hall, and perhaps other spies, the Soviet Union built its first atomic bomb and tested it in 1949. Despite great efforts to make Los Alamos as secure as possible, even amateur communist spies had stolen key information and helped the Soviets develop a bomb much sooner than they would have been able to do on their own in the Cold War.

(Richard Melzer, *Breakdown: How the Secret of the Atomic Bomb Was Stolen during World War II* [Santa Fe: Sunstone Press, 2000].)

 ## McCarthyism

As in all wars, people who were fairly or unfairly identified with the enemy were often considered the enemy and were often denied their rights as American citizens. In World War I it had been German Americans. In World War II it had been Japanese Americans. During the Cold War, it was anyone who was suspected of being a member of the Communist Party or a supporter of the Soviet Union.

Many Americans feared the spread of communism, not only in distant places like Europe, Asia, and Latin America but also in the United States itself. Beginning in 1950, Senator Joseph McCarthy of Wisconsin led a highly publicized search for communists everywhere in the country, including among high-ranking officials in the federal government. **McCarthyism**, or the unfair identification of communists in the United States, led to the tragic destruction of individual reputations, personal lives, and professional careers.

Many people applauded Joe McCarthy for his efforts to combat communism. In the words of one woman who wrote to Senator Dennis Chavez, "As an American, I am eternally grateful to Senator McCarthy for alerting the American people to the dangers of Communism." Leaders of New Mexico's civil defense system were told to be on the lookout for communists, especially in towns like Carlsbad, Taos, and Silver City. Most citizens were simply intimidated by the Wisconsin senator and his hearings in Washington. In fact, most were afraid to object to McCarthy and his extreme intolerance for fear of being labeled communists themselves.

Fortunately, some Americans recognized that McCarthyism was destroying the very freedoms the United States was fighting to defend against the Soviet Union in the Cold War. Some, like Dennis Chavez, were brave enough to speak out against Joe McCarthy and his brutal methods. In a famous speech on the senate floor on May 12, 1950, Senator Chavez declared:

> I should like to be remembered as the man who raised a voice
> . . . at a time in the history of [the Senate] when we seem bent upon
> placing limitations on the freedom of the individual. I [refuse] to sit
> idly by, silent, during a period which may go down in history as an
> era when we permitted the [limitation] of our freedoms, a period
> when we quietly shackled the growth of men's minds.

Dennis Chavez was the first senator brave enough to defy McCarthyism in the U.S. Senate.

It would take four more years before enough senators had the courage to finally join Senator Chavez and end Joe McCarthy's grip on power in Congress. During those years many Americans were unjustly exposed to accusations and charges regarding their political beliefs and loyalty to the United States. Even J. Robert Oppenheimer, the lead scientist at Los Alamos during World War II, lost his top security clearance in 1954 when he was accused of having associated with communists in the 1930s.

The Hollywood motion picture industry suffered particular scrutiny. As a result, more than two hundred actors, directors, producers, and other movie-making personnel were accused of being communists and blacklisted, or denied work in their industry for most, if not all, of their careers. Angered by such treatment, a small group of these blacklisted men and women came to New Mexico to make a movie on their own. *Salt of the Earth* portrayed the famous 1950–52 zinc-mining strike against the Empire Zinc Corporation near Silver City. The film focused on racial discrimination, women's rights, and the generally poor living conditions of miners in the Southwest. Those who appeared in the movie were either blacklisted actors or local miners and their families who had been active in the real strike, including Juan Chacón, who starred in the leading role.

Poster advertising
Salt of the Earth

The filming of *Salt of the Earth* went well in early 1953 until a congressman from California charged that communists were making a communist movie near Silver City, New Mexico. Local residents reacted by disrupting the movie's production with threats and acts of violence. The leading female actor in the film was even deported to Mexico. Despite this opposition, the movie crew finished its work, and *Salt of the Earth* opened in movie theaters in 1954. Although banned in Silver City's main theater, the movie was shown to record crowds in the local drive-in theater. A product—and victim—of McCarthyism, *Salt of the Earth* remains a classic drama that is often ranked among the best American-made movies of the twentieth century.

New Mexico State Governors, 1943–67

New Mexico's seven governors from 1943 to 1967 were

- John J. Dempsey, Democrat, 1943–47
- Thomas J. Mabry, Democrat, 1947–51
- Edwin L. Mechem, Republican, 1951–55, 1957–59, 1961–62
- John F. Simms, Jr., Democrat, 1955–57
- John Burroughs, Democrat, 1959–61
- Tom Bolack, Republican, 1962
- Jack Campbell, Democrat, 1963–67

1. How did World War II change many of the veterans who returned home to New Mexico after 1945? How did the GI Bill help veterans adjust to civilian life?

2. How were Native Americans finally able to win their right to vote in New Mexico?

3. How were Blacks finally able to end segregation in New Mexico's public schools?

4. What other forms of discrimination did Blacks, Hispanics, and Native Americans often face?

5. Describe important rural and urban changes that took place in the period from 1945 to 1965.

6. Describe Cold War dangers involving
   - military accidents,
   - uranium mining,
   - McCarthyism.

7. How did New Mexicans plan to protect themselves in case of an atomic war?

8. Explain possible reasons many people have claimed to have seen UFOs in New Mexico.

9. What aspects of New Mexico would you have been proud of if you had lived in these first years of the Cold War? Why?

10. What aspects would you have been less proud of if you had lived in these first years of the Cold War? Why?

11. What lessons can we learn from the history of New Mexico in the early Cold War?

Years of Conflict and Growth
1965–95

☼ Introduction

New Mexico had experienced dramatic changes in the first decades of the Cold War. The state—and the nation—faced even greater challenges in the next three decades, 1965 to 1995. The civil rights movement and the Cold War continued to dominate state and national headlines as events took new, often dangerous turns. Most issues were resolved peacefully for the common good. Others were not.

The purpose of this chapter is to teach you

- how New Mexico participated in the civil rights movement of the 1960s and 1970s;
- how the state contributed to the Cold War in both new ways and old;
- and what political, social, and economic changes occurred, for better or worse.

☼ Civil Rights

The Black civil rights movement that began in the United States in the 1940s and 1950s grew in size and strength in the 1960s and 1970s. Led by **Dr. Martin Luther King, Jr.**, activists used peaceful **civil disobedience** to focus national attention on unjust segregation in public facilities, from city buses and restaurants to bathrooms and even drinking fountains. Racist opponents to integration resorted to vile insults and harsh violence. Black men, women, and children faced high-pressure fire hoses, attack dogs, and police nightsticks when they attempted to protest nonviolently. White extremists went so far as to bomb southern Black churches, leading,

1950
The Phelps Dodge Corporation closes Dawson, the largest coal-mining camp in New Mexico

1962
César Chávez and Dolores Huerta organize the National Farm Workers Association, later known as the United Farm Workers

UNM Pres. Tom Popejoy defends the right of free speech in an address to the American Legion in Carlsbad

1963
Reies López Tijerina organizes La Alianza Federal de Mercedes

1964
Congress passes the Civil Rights Act

Escalation of U.S. involvement in Vietnam

1966
Robert J. Nordhaus and Ben Abruzzo complete construction of the Sandía Peak Tramway, the longest tram of its kind in the world

UNM's new basketball arena, the Pit, is opened

Reies López Tijerina leads 330 Alianza Federal de Mercedes members on a protest march from Albuquerque to Santa Fe

Reies López Tijerina leads an invasion of the Carson National Forest, creating the Republic of San Joaquín on the former San Joaquín land grant

1967
Reies López Tijerina leads the Tierra Amarilla courthouse raid

Walker Air Force Base near Roswell is closed

1968
Enriqueta Vasquez publishes the first edition of *El Grito del Norte*, an influential newspaper of the Chicano rights movement

1969
A controversial poem read in a freshman English class leads to conflict over the issue of free speech at UNM

Albuquerque's new Sports Stadium is opened

1970
A Black rights protest disrupts a UNM-BYU basketball game

Pres. Richard Nixon signs legislation that finally gives control of Blue Lake to Taos Pueblo

National Guard troops confront anti–Vietnam War protesters on the UNM campus

1971
Dr. Frank Ángel is hired as the new president of New Mexico Highlands University, becoming the first native-born Hispanic president of an American university

CONTINUED TOP OF NEXT PAGE

CONTINUED TOP OF NEXT PAGE

in one case, to the deaths of four Black girls. Dr. King's own home was bombed. Black and white civil rights activists were often arrested, jailed, brutally beaten, and, in some cases, killed.

Dr. King and his followers refused to abandon their ideals and peaceful methods. Despite many setbacks, they achieved major victories, including passage of the **Civil Rights Act** of 1964, a crucial measure New Mexico Senator Dennis Chavez had proposed as early as 1945.

Some Black leaders grew impatient with the scope and slow pace of change. Organizations like the Black Panthers resorted to violent protests and crimes. Urban riots broke out in several cities. In one of the greatest tragedies of the era, Dr. King fell victim to this violence when he was assassinated by a white extremist in Memphis, Tennessee, in 1968.

Other minorities also fought for their civil rights, first using Dr. King's peaceful means but tragically turning to acts of violence as well. This mixture of nonviolent and violent protests occurred in many parts of the United States, including New Mexico.

☀ Hispanic Rights

Hispanics defended their rights as American citizens and workers by employing admirable nonviolent methods. In California, **César Chávez** and **Dolores Huerta** organized mostly Hispanic and Filipino migrant laborers by creating the National Farm Workers Association, later renamed the **United Farm Workers** (**UFW**), in 1962. The UFW struggled hard to improve working conditions, wages, and housing for migrants and their families. In its greatest triumph, the UFW organized a five-year national grape boycott against large grape growers until the growers recognized the UFW and signed contracts that helped improve workers' lives and labor. The UFW used marches, strikes, and other boycotts to secure additional workers' rights and benefits.

New Mexicans hoped to make similar progress, mainly by reclaiming the land grants their ancestors had often lost, despite U.S. guarantees offered in the Treaty of Guadalupe Hidalgo. Though not a native New Mexican, a young Hispanic leader named **Reies López Tijerina** listened to New Mexicans describe the loss of their land grants and vowed to help them. As López Tijerina later wrote in his autobiography, "I felt in my heart a stab: these ancient humble people had a just and sacred cause. I felt in my body and my soul and my spirit that these people were worthy of justice."

López Tijerina was also concerned that young Hispanics "were losing our culture and adopting Anglo [ways], as if they were Anglos. The youth were at the point of losing the last roots and fibers of their culture. . . ." In López Tijerina's opinion, the

1992
The KUMSC underground nuclear-warhead storage facility is opened at Kirtland Air Force Base

1997
Nadine and Patsy Córdova are fired by the Vaughn Public School district for teaching "radical" Chicano history

1999
The Waste Isolation Pilot Plant (WIPP) opens near Carlsbad

Civil Disobedience

Civil disobedience is a form of illegal, nonviolent public protest staged against unjust government laws or policies. Protesters who use civil disobedience are willing to go to jail to help publicize their cause. In an early act of civil disobedience, author Henry David Thoreau refused to pay taxes that helped support the Mexican-American War and Black slavery, both of which Thoreau opposed in the 1840s. Thoreau spent two days in jail as his punishment.

In the twentieth century, Mahatma Gandhi used acts of civil disobedience to protest British rule and social injustice in India. Gandhi fasted, led a 240-mile march to the sea, spent two years in jail, and rallied the support of his admiring countrymen. Expressing his firm commitment to nonviolence, Gandhi once declared, "An eye for an eye makes the whole world blind." Gandhi's tireless efforts led to Indian independence from Great Britain in 1947.

Dr. Martin Luther King, Jr., admired both Thoreau and Gandhi, going so far as to visit India in 1959 to learn more about Gandhi and his effective use of civil disobedience. King applied many of Gandhi's ideas and methods in the civil rights movement in the United States, protesting and facing time in jail at least seven times to help expose the social injustice that a majority of African Americans still experienced in the 1950s and 1960s. In his most famous speech, given on August 28, 1963, before an estimated 250,000 people gathered at the Lincoln Memorial in Washington, D.C., King declared:

> I have a dream that one day this nation will rise up and live out the true meaning of its creed: "We hold these truths to be self-evident, that all men are created equal. . . ."
> I have a dream that my four little children will one day live in a nation where they will not be judged by the color of their skin but by the content of their character.
> *I have a dream today!*

(Clayborne Carson, ed., *The Autobiography of Martin Luther King, Jr.* [New York: Warner Books, 1998], 226.)

Martin Luther King, Jr., using peaceful resistance

only way to reclaim Hispanic pride was to reclaim the land grants that had been the basis of Hispanic culture until outsiders had acquired them by legal and illegal means.

At first López Tijerina used peaceful methods to rally his followers and gain public support. On February 2, 1963, he organized **La Alianza Federal de Mercedes** (Federated Alliance of Land Grants) on the 115th anniversary of the signing of the Treaty of Guadalupe Hidalgo. Claiming as many as thirty thousand members, Alianza leaders gathered petitions, broadcast radio and television shows, and wrote letters to national figures in both the United States and Mexico. In 1966, López Tijerina led 330 Alianza members on a famous Fourth of July march from Albuquerque to Santa Fe, where they met with Gov. Jack Campbell to voice their concerns about the fate of Hispanic land grants and culture.

Dolores Huerta

Dolores Huerta and the United Farm Workers

Dolores Huerta was born in Dawson, New Mexico, in 1930. Moving with her mother to California, Dolores began to work for community-action groups in the 1950s. By the late 1950s, she had become increasingly concerned about migrant farm workers who were often exposed to dangerous pesticides at work, received little pay, enjoyed few benefits, and lived in shacks or tents in crowded migrant camps.

Reacting to these conditions, Huerta and César Chávez organized the National Farm Workers Association, later known as the United Farm Workers. Huerta and Chávez committed themselves to nonviolent tactics in the tradition of Mahatma Gandhi and Dr. Martin Luther King, Jr.

Dolores led picket lines during strikes, helped direct the national grape boycott, negotiated hundreds of contracts with employers, and made thousands of speeches to rally support for the workers' cause. Regularly working eighteen-hour days, she is often referred to as *la pasionaria*, or the passionate one. In César Chávez's words, "Dolores Huerta is physically and spiritually fearless."

Despite her nonviolent practices, Huerta was arrested at least twenty times and suffered life-threatening injuries when attacked by police at a peaceful protest in San Francisco. She survived the attack and continues to strive for social justice for all workers. Her work is celebrated in a corrido by Carmen Moreno:

El Corrido de Dolores Huerta

En Dawson, Nuevo México,
El diez de abril,
Nació Dolores Huerta.
Nadie se lo imaginaba
Que ella iría encabezar
Parte del gran movimiento.

In Dawson, New Mexico,
on the tenth of April,
Dolores Huerta was born.
Nobody imagined
That she would someday lead
Part of a great movement.

Unfortunately, López Tijerina and La Alianza soon turned to more drastic, violent methods of protest. In October 1966, they invaded the Carson National Forest, claiming the national forest had been unfairly created from parts of the old San Joaquín land grant. With supporters arriving in more than a hundred cars and trucks, López Tijerina declared the creation of the independent Republic of San Joaquín and arrested two forest rangers for trespassing. Newspapers and television stations covered the unusual event closely. La Alianza invaders soon retreated from the forest, having accomplished their main goal of drawing national attention to their cause.

To their dismay, public reaction to López Tijerina and La Alianza was largely critical. While some New Mexicans watched events unfold at the Carson National Forest with interest, most denounced the movement as too radical. Leaders like New Mexico's Senator Joseph Montoya went so

En Stockton, California,	In Stockton, California,
Donde ella se crió	Where she grew up
Empezó a ver la injusticia	She began to see the injustice
Que el campesino ha sufrido	That the migrant workers have suffered
Sin la representación	Without the representation
Que una unión le daría. . . .	That a union would give. . . .
El sesenta y dos	In 1962
Se asoció con César Chávez	She worked with César Chávez
Y entre él y la Dolores	And between him and Dolores
Formularon una unión	Created a union
Que llegó a cambiar las leyes. . . .	Dedicated to changing the laws. . . .
Después que organizaron	After they organized
La gente en la unión	The members of the union
Imponieron una huelga	Threatened to strike
Para hablar de los contratos	To obtain labor contracts
También para negociar	And to negotiate for them
Apuntaron a la Huerta.	They appointed Huerta.
Y un día . . . la gente decía,	And one day the people said,
"Ay, Dolores, ¡no se puede!"	"Oh, Dolores, it cannot be done!"
La Dolores les contesta,	To which Dolores answered,
"Esto será nuestro grito:	"This will be our cry:
¡Sí se puede! ¡Sí se puede!"	It can be done! It can be done!"

(http://www.lyricsdir.com/los-lobos-corrido-de-dolores-huerta-39-lyrics.html)

▲▲▲▲▲▲▲▲▲▲▲▲▲▲▲▲▲▲▲▲▲▲▲▲▲▲▲▲▲▲▲▲▲▲▲▲▲▲

What Had Happened to New Mexico Land Grants?

Historians estimate that Hispanic New Mexicans had lost 80 percent of their land grants by the end of the nineteenth century, despite guarantees of protection in the 1848 Treaty of Guadalupe Hidalgo. Additional land grants were reduced or lost in the course of the twentieth century.

What had happened to so many of New Mexico's valuable land grants in so short a time? Here are a few of the many explanations:

- New Mexicans were required to prove ownership of their land grants before the American Court of Private Land Claims. In all, the court ruled on 282 grants, totaling more than 34 million acres. The court rejected most of the claims.
- Many land-grant heirs could not prove their land ownership because they could not produce required land-grant documents. As valuable as these papers were, they were often lost or destroyed over time. After all, no one had ever challenged Hispanic land ownership while New Mexico remained part of the Spanish empire or the Republic of Mexico.

Reies López Tijerina

- Understandably, land-grant heirs frequently hired American lawyers to assist in presenting their cases before the Court of Private Land Claims. Often lacking cash to pay these expensive lawyers, land-grant heirs often compensated their lawyers with the main resource they owned: their land. Attorney Thomas Catron acquired so much land in this manner that he was said to be the largest landowner in the United States by the early twentieth century.
- Many land-grant heirs could not prove the size of their grants because the grants had been given in earlier times when their ancestors had no access to modern surveying techniques.
- Some land grants were lost because their owners were unable to pay property taxes under American rule.
- Some had sold their land when they were unable to pay their water fees. Farmers could no longer farm and earn a living if they could not afford to pay for water.
- Other individuals lost their land because they had to use it to pay off debts to local merchants.
- Community grants were sometimes lost when they were sold to land-development companies at what seemed like good prices—but seldom were.

far as to declare that the event had been nothing less than a communist-inspired plot.

La Alianza resorted to its most tragic use of violence less than a year later. On June 5, 1967, López Tijerina and nineteen armed followers attacked the courthouse in Tierra Amarilla to search for the Rio Arriba County district attorney, Alfonso Sánchez, and make a citizen's arrest. La Alianza accused Sánchez of harassing its members with burdensome legal procedures and unconstitutional arrests. Confusion reigned as López Tijerina and his men entered the courthouse. Shots rang out. Two law officers soon lay wounded. Two others were taken hostage. Moments later, López Tijerina and his cohorts fled the scene without District Attorney Sánchez, who was never found in the courthouse building.

In the largest manhunt in New Mexico history, more than five hundred members of the New Mexico National Guard, state police, New Mexico Mounted Police, and U.S. Forest Service searched for López Tijerina and his fellow courthouse raiders, using every weapon at their command, from army helicopters to heavily armed tanks. Authorities searched vehicles and buildings throughout northern New Mexico to no avail. Moving quickly, López Tijerina and his men had hidden in the mountains, finding refuge in the home of an elderly Alianza sympathizer. Finally, on June 10, the police arrested López Tijerina in a car that had stopped at a service station near Bernalillo. Claiming he was en route to Albuquerque to turn himself in, López Tijerina was arrested without incident.

López Tijerina now faced several trials. Found guilty in federal court for assaulting federal officers in the 1966 Carson National Forest invasion, López Tijerina was sentenced to two years in federal prison. In his second trial, for his part in the Tierra Amarilla courthouse raid, López Tijerina surprised the court by announcing he intended to defend himself. After a month-long trial and four and a half hours of deliberation, a jury, consisting of seven Hispanics, a Black woman, and four Anglos, returned a highly controversial verdict. To the cheers of his supporters, López Tijerina was acquitted of all charges.

Chilili land grant sign: not for sale

López Tijerina was not a free man, though. La Alianza's leader spent two years in federal prison, finally gaining his release in 1971. Found guilty on other state charges, he served additional prison time in 1974. Considering himself a political prisoner, López Tijerina claimed that he and his family had been subjected to government violence and harassment for years.

With its impassioned leader in prison, La Alianza lost much of its popular support. Despite the hopes of thousands, La Alianza had not reclaimed a single acre of land for a single land grant community or heir. On the other hand, López Tijerina's fiery determination may well have inspired land grant heirs to take action in their efforts to win back lost grants or better defend what remains of their property.

Caught up in the rising tide of radicalism in the late 1960s and early 1970s, many Hispanic youths sought additional change, starting

They Called Me *King Tiger*

In the most famous nonviolent protest in its history, La Alianza staged a march from Albuquerque to Santa Fe. Reies López Tijerina described this event in his memoirs, entitled *They Called Me "King Tiger"*:

> On July 2, 1966, 320 persons began that march of sixty-six miles. This was a significant day for me, as it was for all of us. Young and old, men and women began that historic journey with great enthusiasm and expectation. Some of the Anglos who passed us by in their cars would yell at us, "Wetback, go back to Mexico." These epithets revealed the mentality of the North American. The first night that we stopped, a car full of Anglos came by and fired gunshots at us. But other than that incident and the epithets, everything went well. We took three days to arrive in Santa Fe. . . . Upon our arrival in Santa Fe, [Gov. Jack Campbell] gave us a brief audience out of courtesy, and we . . . asked that he convene a task force to investigate the theft of our land. This is well documented, and no one can say that we did not ask for justice in a peaceful way.

(Reies López Tijerina, *They Called Me "King Tiger"* [Houston: Arte Público Press, 2000], 63.)

Unfortunately, Reies López Tijerina and La Alianza did not always rely on peaceful methods in their attempts to help recover Hispanic land grants. As their protests grew more violent in the late 1960s, their cause became better known, but they lost the support of disillusioned followers. Songwriter Roberto Martínez expressed his opinion of La Alianza's most violent act in a corrido sung by Martínez and his band, Los Reyes de Albuquerque:

on their own college campuses in New Mexico. Activists demanded that their schools recruit Hispanic faculty, hire Hispanic administrators, and offer classes on Hispanic history and culture. Calling themselves **Chicanos**, protesters were especially active at New Mexico Highlands University and the University of New Mexico. At Highlands, students went so far as to occupy the university's administration building for five days to protest the hiring of a new Anglo president in 1970. Partly as a result of this protest, **Dr. Frank Ángel** was hired to lead the university in 1971, becoming the first native-born Hispanic to serve as a

El Corrido de Río Arriba

Año de '67	In the year of '67
Cinco de Junio fue el día	The fifth of June was the day
Hubo una revolución	There was a revolution
Allá por Tierra Amarilla.	Up there in Tierra Amarilla.
Allá en la casa de corte	There at the courthouse
Pueblo de Tierra Amarilla	Town of Tierra Amarilla
Nuevo México del Estado	New Mexico the state
Condado de Río Arriba.	Río Arriba the county.
Un grupo de nuestra raza	A group of our people
Muy descontentos vajaron	Came down very discontented.
Y en oficial del Estado	And on a state official
Su venganza los tomaron.	They took vengeance.
Las mujeres y los niños	The women and children
Iban corriendo y llorando	Went running and crying
En ese instante pensamos	At that moment we thought
Que el mundo se iba acabando.	That the world was ending.
Fueron treinta que lograron	There were thirty who managed
Para la sierra escapar	To escape to the mountains
Y el Gobernador llamó	And the governor called out
A la Guardia Nacional.	The national guard.
Cuando fueron capturados	When they were captured
A la prisión los llevaron	They took them to prison
Para que fueran juzgados	So they could be judged
Del crimen de que se acusaron.	For the crime of which they were accused.
Este corrido termina	This ballad shall end
Cuando se haga la justicia	When justice is done
Para que no se repita	So never again will be repeated
Lo de allá en Tierra Amarilla.	What happened in Tierra Amarilla.

(Quoted in Enrique R. Lamadrid, "Los Corridos de Río Arriba," *Aztlan* 17 [Fall 1988]: 32–33.)

university president in the United States. Other changes followed. At UNM, a Chicano Studies program was established in 1971 and additional Hispanic faculty were hired, including the famous Hispanic novelist **Rudolfo Anaya** in 1974.

Politically, some Hispanics were drawn to new political leaders, including Rodolfo "Corky" Gonzales, and new political parties, such as La Raza Unida, organized to protect and assert Hispanic rights. Many more Hispanics hoped to defend their rights by supporting well-established organizations like the **League of United Latin American**

Enriqueta Vasquez and *El Grito del Norte*

Hispanic civil rights leaders of the 1960s and 1970s fought for social justice with many tools. While some resorted to violent methods, others employed nonviolent acts of civil disobedience. **Enriqueta Vasquez** wielded the power of her pen to inspire her readers to take action.

Based in northern New Mexico, Vasquez published one of the most effective newspapers of the Chicano movement. From 1968 to 1972, *El Grito del Norte* reported on events of *la causa* and, as in the following editorial, encouraged Chicanos to reclaim their rights and proud culture:

> [H]istory books are all slanted to glorify the Anglo and to make him look like a superior. Right in the schools, our children are taught a history they can't identify with. They . . . don't even know that they belong in this land. Their ancestors are not given credit . . . for the many things they did. . . .
>
> Let's speak up. . . . Let's discuss our language and our history and our culture and way of life. Let's look at ourselves and see who we are and let's take pride in what we are. . . . Don't take a back seat for anyone. Don't let the schools un-educate you into thinking that you are a second-class citizen. . . . When we start to do this we will find peace and pride in ourselves once again. We must come forward and make ourselves heard, NOW.

(*El Grito del Norte*, October 31, 1968, as quoted in Lorena Oropeza and Dionne Espinoza, eds., *Enriqueta Vasquez and the Chicano Movement: Writings from El Grito del Norte* [Houston: Arte Público Press, 2006], 33–34.)

Teachers who responded to Enriqueta Vasquez's plea to teach Chicano children to be proud of their heritage often suffered criticism and sometimes even lost their jobs. In 1997, two teachers at Vaughn Junior-Senior High School attempted to teach their students about leaders like César Chávez, while organizing a school chapter of the Movimiento Estudantil Chicano de Aztlán, or MEChA. School superintendent Arthur Martínez and the local school board charged **Nadine and Patsy Córdova** with helping to cause ethnic friction in the community. The sisters, with a combined total of thirty-five years of teaching experience, were fired.

Nadine and Patsy Córdova sued the Vaughn public school system for violating their freedom of speech. Their case was settled out of court for more than half a million dollars. The Córdovas remain outspoken champions of free speech, especially for public schoolteachers in New Mexico. They have been honored with many awards for their courageous efforts.

(*Córdova v. Vaughn Municipal School District Papers*, 1997–2000, Center for Southwest Research, University of New Mexico, Albuquerque, New Mexico.)

Citizens (LULAC) and the GI Forum and by helping to elect **Jerry Apodaca** in 1975 as the first Hispanic governor of New Mexico since 1924. In Congress, **Joseph Montoya** represented New Mexico in the U.S. House of Representatives from 1961 to 1965 and in the U.S. Senate from 1965 to 1977, while Rep. **Manuel Luján, Jr.**, served in the House for twenty years (1968–88) and Rep. Bill Richardson served for another fourteen (1983–97).

Author Rudolfo Anaya

Native American Rights

The national civil rights movement also helped stir interest in Native American rights. Sadly, violent acts marred the movement in towns closest to the Navajo Reservation where discrimination had created tension and poor relations for decades.

Tension was especially great in Gallup where Navajos often faced discrimination by local businesses and residents. They felt particularly exploited by bars and liquor stores that sold them liquor, adding to the tragic problem of alcoholism in the tribe. In particular, Native Americans criticized the Gallup city government for police brutality and for maintaining a filthy jail where intoxicated prisoners were kept in unsafe conditions. Native American activists focused their wrath on the mayor, Emmett García, who sold liquor to Navajos at his Gallup Inn yet offered no effective treatment for alcoholism in his role as the city's leader.

Navajo students at the University of New Mexico were especially upset when Mayor García was appointed to serve on the UNM Board of Regents. Led by nineteen-year-old **Larry Casuse**, Native American students at UNM voiced their opposition to García's selection at a highly charged board of regents meeting. Frustrated that García's nomination was not withdrawn, Casuse and a fellow Navajo kidnapped García from Gallup's city hall on March 1, 1973.

Marching García through town at gunpoint, Casuse and his friend forced the mayor into a local sporting goods store. Gallup police soon surrounded the store, and a shoot-out ensued. In the moments that followed, García escaped, and Casuse's companion surrendered, but Casuse was shot and killed. Three thousand people attended the young leader's funeral, and as many as eight thousand participated in protest marches and rallies in both Gallup and Albuquerque. Speakers demanded reforms and García's resignation, but little changed as a result of Larry Casuse's misguided act of protest.

Toney Anaya's Clemency Act, 1986

In the most controversial act of clemency in New Mexico history, Gov. Toney Anaya converted the death sentences of six death-row inmates on the eve of Thanksgiving in 1986. The governor's decision, based on his firm Roman Catholic beliefs, drew national attention, reopening the national debate over capital punishment. Hundreds of letters, telegrams, and cards poured into the governor's office, many from residents of New Mexico, others from people around the world.

In a favorable letter, Ian M. Haldane wrote:

December 1, 1986

Governor Tony [sic] Anaya:

Congratulations on your stand on capital punishment. This took a lot of moral courage. . . . I am so opposed to capital punishment [that in my will I] have asked my wife to be a witness in the event I am murdered. I want her to testify that if I were on a jury I would never vote for capital punishment. Actually, serving twenty-five years without a chance for parole is much more severe punishment. . . .

Sincerely,

Ian M. Haldane

In sharp contrast, Kurt Brink of Albuquerque wrote:

November 26, 1986

Honorable Governor Anaya:

This day, November 26th, when you announced the commutation of the sentences of . . . death row inmates of the State Penitentiary at Santa Fe, will go down in history as one of infamy. I herewith register to you my most deep-hearted opposition to your action for the following reasons:

1. *It is a violation of the oath you took upon becoming governor to uphold the laws of the State of New Mexico.*
2. *It placed your private opinion above the will of the vast majority of the citizens of our great State.*

Even greater violence occurred north of Gallup, in Farmington. Within weeks of Casuse's death, the mutilated bodies of Navajo men began appearing on the outskirts of town. In what are now known as **hate crimes**, each of five victims had been robbed and tortured before being brutally murdered. Only three of the five murders were ever solved, and

3. It made a total mockery of the justice that lawful courts and juries had meted out to the guilty.

4. It was a kick in the teeth to all of the families, eight in number, whose loved ones were wiped out without a shred of concern being shown by the killers.

5. It makes human life (yours, too, governor) still cheaper [in all of New Mexico,] from Raton to Lordsburg.

6. It showed no sensitivity for the survivors of the murdered, whose awesome trauma you unearthed, forcing them to re-live it.

7. It will lead to a still greater breakdown of respect for law and for those charged with keeping the peace and protecting the law-abiding citizens.

8. It will make our fine state the laughing stock of the other forty-nine [states].

9. It blatantly ignored the experience of all recorded history — that in whatever land . . . when the death penalty is swiftly carried out, it is the greatest deterrent to murder any society has ever utilized.

10. It was as inhumane as it possibly could be because it placed a higher value upon the life of the murderers who have no respect for human life than upon the lives of law abiding citizens who work for a living, pay taxes, and respect law.

11. It was totally out of accord with what the Holy Scriptures teach and with what the church of which you are a member officially teaches. Jesus said: "All they that take the sword shall perish with the sword." Matt. 26:52. . . . Capital punishment is the clear teaching of God's holy Word, regardless of how men may twist it.

Sincerely,

Kurt Brink

(Gov. Toney Anaya Papers, Box 6/6, New Mexico State Records Center and Archives, Santa Fe, New Mexico.)

Modern DNA testing and other techniques have proven that many men and women facing the death penalty were innocent. As a result, in 2009 New Mexico became one of fifteen states that have finally eliminated capital punishment.

the teenage boys found guilty of the three crimes received short sentences at the juvenile correctional facility in Springer. Outraged that the teenagers had received such light sentences for their heinous crimes and that the other two murders went unsolved, Native Americans staged protest marches, rallies, and boycotts in the spring of 1974. As in Gallup, they demanded the end of police brutality, the fair treatment of Navajos by local merchants, and the closing of notorious bars and liquor stores. As in Gallup, their demands went unanswered by most white leaders, who refused to admit the serious nature of these many problems.

Other tribes enjoyed greater success in resolving important issues peacefully. This was especially true at Taos Pueblo. The northern pueblo's rights to sacred Blue Lake had not been adequately protected, despite government promises of the early twentieth century. The situation had grown increasingly worse by the 1960s with the construction of new campgrounds, water contamination, and the building of new roads near Blue Lake.

Taos Pueblo leaders reacted with a wide range of nonviolent political strategies. For example, thousands of tourists who visited the pueblo were given flyers explaining the issue and requesting that they write letters to their senators in support of Taos Pueblo's claim to Blue Lake. Many complied. In 1965, pueblo leaders published a small pamphlet called *The Blue Lake Appeal* that was mailed to hundreds of newspapers, politicians, churches, and other organizations to seek support for the Indians' cause. A public-relations success, the pamphlet generated support from across the country, including from the influential *New York Times*. A television documentary entitled *The Water Is So Clear That a Blind Man Could See* had a similar result. Respected pueblo leaders like Paul Bernal and ninety-year-old Juan de Jesús Romero traveled to Washington, D.C., to appear before congressional committees. In Romero's stirring words, "If our land [and Blue Lake are] not returned to us . . . it is the end of [Taos] Indian life. . . . It is our religion [centered at Blue Lake] that holds us together."

Hate Crimes

Hate crimes are violent crimes, speech, or acts of vandalism motivated by feelings of hatred against a specific social group.

Of about eight thousand hate crimes committed in the United States in 1995, about 60 percent were crimes committed against minorities (especially Blacks, Hispanics, and Native Americans), 16 percent were crimes against religious groups, and the rest were largely crimes against homosexuals.

In 2003, New Mexico joined forty-four other states in passing a hate-crimes bill. The law defines what hate crimes are and what stiff penalties a person must face if convicted of committing such cruel, harmful acts.

Taos Flyer, 1967

Visitors to Taos Pueblo were given this flyer when they arrived for tours of the pueblo in the mid-1960s:

WELCOME TO TAOS PUEBLO

Our people have lived in this same village and on these lands since 1300 A.D. We hope you enjoy yourself while you are here learning of our Indian ways.

WE NEED YOUR HELP!

The people of Taos Pueblo have been engaged in a struggle for sixty years to regain possession of our sacred Blue Lake Area, which lies in the mountains that you see to the east. This Blue Lake Area has always been and is today the religious sanctuary and the source of sustenance and water to our people. Here in the Pueblo you can see the stream, the Rio Pueblo de Taos, that flows down from Blue Lake.

These holy lands were confiscated from the Pueblo by the Federal Government in 1906 and placed in the National Forests.

Legislation to correct this injustice has been pending in the United States Senate . . . after unanimous passage by the House of Representatives. This bill . . . would end forever the desecration of our sacred shrines by placing the Blue Lake Area in trust for the Pueblo and protecting its sanctity as a wilderness. Unless the Senate acts soon, however, the bill will die.

You can help our people to obtain justice by sending a letter or wire urging the United States Senators . . . to support passage of H.R. 3306 before Congress adjourns. . . .

We appeal to you to add your voice to this historical struggle for justice and religious freedom.

The Governor and Council
of Taos Pueblo

(R. C. Gordon-McCutchan, *The Taos Indians and the Battle for Blue Lake* [Santa Fe: Red Crane Books, 1995], 123.)

President Nixon signing the Taos Blue Lake bill, 1970

Through these and other efforts, the tribe finally convinced Congress to pass legislation giving Taos Pueblo sole possession of Blue Lake. With Juan de Jesús Romero and other tribal leaders present, **Pres. Richard M. Nixon** signed the bill into law in a special ceremony held in the White House on December 15, 1970. A struggle that had lasted more than half a century was resolved at last, thanks to the nonviolent efforts of patient, persistent Taos leaders.

The Equal Rights Amendment (ERA)

Women played important roles in the national civil rights movement of the 1960s. By the early 1970s, many women began to organize to secure additional rights for themselves, some fifty years after the Nineteenth Amendment guaranteed their right to vote. Women were particularly concerned about equal rights in the workplace, from hiring and promotions to equal pay.

"Help Wanted" ads in newspapers across New Mexico reflect the strong bias against women in many careers. A typical ad of this kind appeared in the *Albuquerque Journal*, three years before the first space flight to the moon in 1969:

> **Help Wanted: Male**
> **NASA**
>
> The NASA Manned Spacecraft Center, Houston, has a number of positions available immediately. These career opportunities in the nation's manned spaced flight program are in the flight operations and flight crew operations areas.
>
> At least a B.S. in Engineering, Mathematics or Physical Science is needed to qualify.
>
> Local interviews at Albuquerque.
>
> (*Albuquerque Journal*, May 26, 1966.)

Women were limited in career choices based on unfair assumptions about their interests, education, and skills. The following ads appeared shortly before and after NASA's ad in the *Journal*:

> **Help Wanted: Women**
>
> PENNEY'S has an opening for 2 saleswomen in our drapery department. Must have knowledge of drapery measuring and home decorating. 30 hrs. per week ...
>
> **J.C. PENNEY CO., 39 WINROCK CENTER**
>
> (*Albuquerque Journal*, May 19, 1966.)
>
> **Help Wanted: Women**
>
> Waitresses, sizes 8–12.
>
> Excellent tips and working conditions. Apply in person. Mary Butters, between 6–7 p.m.
>
> (*Albuquerque Journal*, May 28, 1966.)

In 1972, an **Equal Rights Amendment (ERA)** was passed by Congress (with affirmative votes cast by all New Mexico congressmen) and sent to the states for acceptance or rejection. The ERA simply stated that "equality of rights under the law shall not be denied or abridged by the United States or by any state on account of sex." If passed, the amendment would guarantee equal legal treatment for women in every

The Later Cold War, 1965–95

The Cold War between the United States and its western allies and the Soviet Union and its communist bloc continued in the era from 1965 to 1995 but changed in scope and battlefields. The most dramatic change in this tension-filled conflict occurred in Southeast Asia, in the narrow coastal nation of Vietnam.

aspect of their lives. If thirty-eight states voted to accept the ERA within seven years, it would be added as the twenty-seventh amendment to the U.S. Constitution.

New Mexico joined thirty-five states in approving the ERA. **Feminists,** or activist women, worked to have the ERA approved by using peaceful methods, many of which they had learned earlier while participating in acts of civil disobedience during the civil rights and antiwar movements.

The women's rights proposal soon ran into trouble. Conservative men and women argued against the amendment, saying that it would lead to the elimination of existing laws that specifically protected women. Scare tactics were also used; some claimed that passage of the ERA would lead to women being drafted into the army and being made to fight in combat. Some even believed that the ERA would force men and women to use unisex restrooms.

Facing this opposition, the ERA was defeated in many states and lacked the required thirty-eight states needed to approve within seven years. Although its deadline date was extended until 1982, the ERA was still defeated. Seven states rejected the amendment and five states even reversed their earlier votes of support.

Although never passed on the national level, the ERA has become law in twenty states, including New Mexico, prohibiting discrimination based solely on a person's gender.

The Vietnam Conflict, 1956–73

As in Korea, Vietnam had been split in two, with the country's northern region controlled by a communist government and its southern region, below the 17th parallel, controlled by a government the United States and its allies, particularly France, supported. As in Korea, the plan to reunite Vietnam's two sections had stalled, especially after communist forces mounted ever-greater attacks against French military positions in the south. Exhausted, the French withdrew from Vietnam in the mid-1950s, leaving the South Vietnamese government to defend itself against the north. To halt communist expansion into South Vietnam, the United States sent military advisors to help train the Vietnamese army. Using a domino theory, the U.S. government justified its involvement in Vietnam by contending that if Vietnam fell to the communists, all of Southeast Asia would eventually fall as well.

The war in Vietnam grew much larger by the mid-1960s. Unable to resist communist aggression on its own, the South Vietnamese government appealed to the United States for additional aid in money, soldiers, and matériel. Led by **Pres. Lyndon B. Johnson**, the United

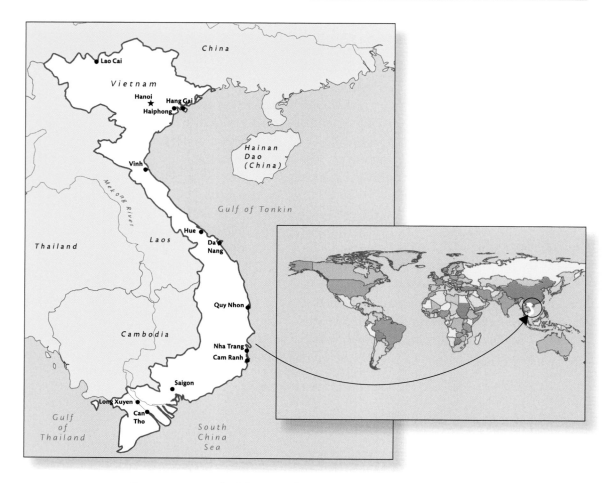

Vietnam

States responded by sending the requested support, including more than half a million troops in a single year, 1969. To keep up with the demand for so many ground troops, Congress passed a new conscription law; in all, the army drafted nearly 2 million young men, ages nineteen to twenty-five, from 1965 to 1973.

The fighting grew far worse by 1968. Aided by the Soviet Union and Communist China, the North Vietnamese Army had stepped up its attacks using not only its own soldiers but also South Vietnamese civilian fighters, known as the National Liberation Front, or simply the Viet Cong. The Viet Cong included men, women, and children of all ages. U.S. troops could never be sure who the enemy was when even innocent-looking civilians could attack them at any moment.

The war became increasingly unpopular in the United States as newsmen reported the deaths of more than 12,500 American servicemen and servicewomen in the worst two years of the war, 1968 and 1969; 542 were killed in the worst single month, January 1969. To make matters worse, the South Vietnamese government was exposed as brutal and corrupt, hardly the democracy that Americans had hoped to defend at the cost of so many American lives.

Many Americans willingly volunteered to fight or were drafted to stop communist aggression in Vietnam and Southeast Asia. New Mexicans, like eighteen-year-old **Daniel Fernández** of Los Lunas, volunteered in numbers far beyond expectations. More than sixty thousand New Mexicans served in the conflict, winning many medals for bravery, including five Medals of Honor from 1966 to 1970.

As time went on, winning the war appeared less and less possible and far too expensive, given its uncertain results and growing cost in human lives. An increasing number of Americans

U.S. Troop Levels and Deaths in Vietnam, 1959–73

	Troop Level	Men Drafted	Killed In Action
1959	760	96,153	
1960	900	86,602	
1961	3,205	118,586	
1962	11,300	82,060	
1963	16,300	119,265	
1964	23,300	112,386	
1965	184,300	230,991	636
1966	385,300	382,010	6,053
1967	485,600	228,263	11,058
1968	536,100	296,406	16,511
1969	475,200	283,586	11,527
1970	334,600	162,746	6,065
1971	156,800	94,092	2,348
1972	24,200	49,514	561
1973	50	646	0
			Total 58,156*

*Based on final counts taken after the war. (http://www.wsmr.army.mil; for troop levels; http://cybersarges. tripod.com/casualties.html; *Congressional Quarterlies*: for draftees, www.landscaper.net/draft70–72.htm.)

A Hispanic Marine's Combat Experience in Vietnam

Lupe (not his real name) was a young U.S. Marine when he arrived for combat duty in Vietnam in January 1969. Years later, he described his wartime experiences, including the day he was almost killed:

The next thing I know, there was all kinds of machine gun fire going on and I don't remember really being hit. I think I was so busy firing that . . . I didn't realize how bad I was wounded. I thought it was sweat, but it was blood. I had blood all over me and within a split second there was another explosion.

I don't remember nothing until the next day, when somebody was trying to put me in a body bag. I guess . . . I was in such bad shape that they . . . thought I was dead. . . .

I saw what the Viet Cong did and so from then on I didn't think whether there was some legal rights to it or whether they were right or wrong. It didn't matter. I saw a real young, I would say five-year-old, kid blow up my best friend. [The boy] was wrapped with a sack of charge explosives around his body. When he got up to [my friend, the boy] pulled the pin, blew himself up, and blew my buddy up. . . . There was nobody that was safe. . . . I mean, to me they were all the same.

(Quoted in Lea Ybarra, *Vietnam Veteranos: Chicanos Recall the War* [Austin: University of Texas Press, 2004], 132–33.)

Daniel Fernández and New Mexico's Medal of Honor Recipients of the Vietnam Era

Daniel Fernández was born in Albuquerque and moved to Los Lunas with his family when he was eleven years old. He ran track and field, belonged to the 4-H Club, and loved to ride horses. In 1963, while a junior in high school, Fernández volunteered to serve in the U.S. Army, finishing his high school education in the military. After basic training, Private Fernández was sent into combat in Vietnam.

Fernández served bravely and was wounded twice. After four tours of duty, he asked to return for a fifth, although few soldiers lived through as much time in combat.

In the early morning of February 18, 1966, twenty-one-year-old Daniel and his army patrol experienced heavy enemy fire. When one of their fellow soldiers was wounded, Daniel and three of his men went to the fallen soldier's aid. While they administered aid, an enemy hand grenade landed nearby. Realizing the weapon could kill them all, Daniel threw himself on the grenade as it exploded, sacrificing his own life to save four others.

Daniel Fernández was awarded the Medal of Honor posthumously, or after his death, on April 6, 1967. His parents received the nation's highest honor on his behalf in a special ceremony held at the White House in Washington, D.C. His incredible act of bravery is still remembered and honored. In Los Lunas, a school, a park, and a Veterans of Foreign Wars post are named in his memory, as is a building at Kirtland Air Force Base in Albuquerque.

Of the 239 recipients of the Medal of Honor during the Vietnam conflict, five were either native New Mexicans or young men who had spent much of their lives in the state before entering the armed forces. In addition to Daniel Fernández, New Mexico's Medal of Honor recipients were

- Army Sgt. Delbert Owen Jennings for his heroic action in 1966;
- Army Staff Sgt. Franklin D. Miller for his heroic action in 1970;
- Army Warrant Off. Louis Richard Rocco for his heroic action in 1970;
- Marine Lance Cpl. Kenneth L. Worley for his heroic action (similar to Daniel Fernández's) in 1968.

New Mexico's Vietnam veterans are honored in places across the state. At Eagle Nest, Victor Westphall led the construction of the Vietnam Veterans Memorial State Park to honor those who died in Vietnam, including his son, First Lt. Victor David Westphall III, who had been killed in Vietnam in 1968. The memorial is now a New Mexico State Park. In Farmington, a monument honors Vietnam veterans from the state's Four Corners region. Touring replicas of the Vietnam Memorial Wall in Washington, D.C., have traveled to towns across the nation, including several communities in New Mexico. In 2003, Truth or Consequences acquired one of these replicas. Known as the "Wall that Heals," it was installed and dedicated on a knoll just west of the town's veterans' hospital. Veterans of all American wars, including Vietnam, are honored at the New Mexico Veterans Memorial near the entrance to Kirtland Air Force Base in Albuquerque and at the Veterans Memorial Park in Las Cruces.

began to protest the war and specifically the draft, which forced young men to fight in a conflict that many now recognized as hopeless. Antiwar protests swept the nation, especially on college campuses. Some expressed their opposition to the war by burning their draft cards; a great many left for Canada to avoid the draft. Thousands were classified as conscientious objectors based on their opposition to war of any kind. In New Mexico, increasing numbers of students became active in the national peace movement, especially at UNM.

Protests were not new on the UNM campus. Students and faculty had boycotted a local business to protest segregation in the early 1950s. Protests to defend free speech at UNM had become increasingly frequent in the 1960s. Strongly supporting free speech, UNM **Pres. Tom Popejoy** had addressed an American Legion convention in 1962, declaring:

> The free play of ideas in the classroom, free and easy access to books . . . in the library, freedom to search out the truth in the laboratory are the best guarantees of a free society. . . . It is the one way that our democratic way of life will survive in the world, a large portion of which is trying to tear down and erode the dignity of man as an individual.

Senator Pete V. Domenici

Pete Domenici was the dominant Republican Party leader in New Mexico for more than thirty years. First elected to the U.S. Senate in 1972, he was reelected five times, giving him thirty-six years in the Senate, a record for New Mexico senators. Domenici was able to bring many important defense and energy projects to New Mexico, especially to the state's air force bases and national labs. He proved equally able in saving programs when they were threatened by federal budget cutbacks. A newspaper reporter gave him the nickname "Saint Pete" because of his many miracles in bringing projects to New Mexico and saving them if they were about to be lost.

Governor Bruce King

Bruce and Alice King

Bruce King was the dominant Democratic Party leader of New Mexico for more than thirty-five years. King was elected governor three times, serving from 1971 to 1975, from 1979 to 1983, and from 1991 to 1995, for a record twelve years in office. King wrote of his accomplishments, including the creation a new Department of Children, Youth, and Families, in his autobiography, *Cowboy in the Roundhouse*. His equally popular wife, Alice King, supported anything that benefited children and their education.

Lobogate

The University of New Mexico's basketball teams enjoyed great success in the 1960s and early 1970s, thanks to the leadership of the school's head basketball coach, Bob King, and the excellent play of athletes like Ira Harge and Petie Gibson. In 1972, Norm Ellenberger became UNM's new head coach. A flamboyant, ambitious coach, Ellenberger recruited many good players and won two Western Athletic Conference championships, making the Lobo squad one of the best teams in the country.

Trouble brewed in 1979 when it was discovered that Coach Ellenberger had become more focused on his players' winning record than on their academic success. The coach and members of his staff were accused of tampering with academic records to ensure that their players would to be eligible to play ball. The resulting scandal, known in the national press as Lobogate, rocked the basketball world and led to Ellenberger's resignation and later conviction in state court. It would be years before new coaches, like Gary Colson, and new players, like Royce Olney of Truth or Consequences and Rob Robbins of Farmington, made the Lobos' basketball program respectable again, both on and off the court.

Coach Norm Ellenberger

Despite Tom Popejoy's advice regarding free speech, some campus leaders debated the right of guest speakers to express their often-controversial views on campus. In the most heated debate over free speech at UNM in the 1960s, factions clashed when a teaching assistant had his students read an erotic poem in a freshman English class during the spring of 1969. While many professors and students defended the teaching assistant's right to free speech, **Gov. David F. Cargo** received as many as fifteen thousand letters and telegrams denouncing the poem, the teacher, and the university; the New Mexico state legislature went so far as to cut more than $100,000 in UNM funding to express its displeasure with the sensational poem. The teaching assistant lost his job, but the protests continued.

As important as these controversies were at UNM, they dimmed in comparison to the anti–Vietnam War protests that began in Albuquerque in 1965 and only ended when American involvement in the war ended in 1973. The height of antiwar protests at UNM and across the United States occurred in 1970, when the United States expanded the conflict from Vietnam to its neighbor, Cambodia. The crisis began on May 4, 1970, when four students at Kent State University in Ohio were killed by national guardsmen sent to the campus to break up antiwar demonstrations following the U.S. invasion of Cambodia. On the same day the shootings occurred at Kent State, actress Jane Fonda appeared at a large rally at UNM and urged students to step up their protests against the war's expansion.

That night antiwar protesters replaced an American flag on the campus flagpole with a flag featuring a raised fist, symbolizing protest. Prowar students objected, leading to shouting and fighting among the two hundred students who gathered at the site on the following day. University officials attempted to resolve the conflict by taking all flags down while tempers cooled.

Antiwar marches and rallies continued at UNM and schools across the country in the following week. More than two hundred colleges and universities ended their spring semesters early in an effort to calm the unrest. At UNM about four hundred protesters occupied the Student Union Building (SUB). By Friday, May 8, the sit-in had largely ended when many students joined a march off campus and Albuquerque police officers arrested most of those who remained in the SUB.

Despite these developments, a battery of national guardsmen arrived on campus about six that evening. Events unfolded quickly as the guardsmen swept across the courtyard east of the SUB with gas masks on and bayonets drawn. Eleven students and bystanders were wounded. Fortunately, no one was gravely injured, and no one was killed. In the aftermath of this crisis, many argued that the national guard should never have been called onto campus and that they had used excessive force while there. Six of the eleven people injured outside the SUB sued five officers of the national guard and Gov. David Cargo for $260,000 in damages. After a dramatic seven-day trial, the guardsmen were acquitted of all charges in 1971.

Other antiwar protests followed, creating additional unease between pro- and antiwar groups. Prowar students from Albuquerque High School clashed with antiwar protesters when the latter group marched down

Central Avenue. In 1972, city police clashed with protesters when activists set up barricades to disrupt traffic on I-25. That same year hundreds of protesters locked arms to form a human barricade at the entrance to Kirtland Air Force Base. The police used tear gas and arrested 435 protestors to break up the demonstration.

Different Views of What Happened Outside the SUB

Observers and participants have widely different memories of what happened when the national guard arrived on the University of New Mexico campus on May 8, 1970.

Capt. Félix Torres, who commanded the national guard troops sent to UNM, recalls:

We unloaded the men [from our national guard trucks] and they all formed and never have I seen a faster formation conducted. . . . [A]s we got closer you could hear the crowd, a big crowd. . . . We stopped and of course [we] were at fixed bayonets to show them [we] were serious about the line [we formed]. . . . Everybody was in position and I got my bull horn after . . . the noise seemed to have calmed down and I made my announcement that my orders were to clear the [area]. . . .

[Next, we put on our gas masks as] standard procedure . . . ; in the event that something flares up . . . you have to be ready. [As we moved forward with our bayonets at forty-five degree angles, most of the crowd] moved out with very little problems. [A few] really put us on guard . . . because they would . . . go forward and then back. [The one closest to me] was on crutches [and one of my men said,] "Buddy, you better move or you're going to get hurt." And [the one on crutches] cussed him out and said, "You blank blank, you're going to have to move me." As he got closer he started to wave that crutch . . . and I think that's when he [was hurt].

[We moved forward in formation, as we had practiced many times in drills.] Our men were under orders that they would not allow anybody through the line and they would have to handle [anyone in the way] in the best way they know how. [If anyone was hurt] I don't think that the decision was made by [my men] to do so intentionally. It was the circumstances.

(Félix Torres interview, May 11, 1991, Socorro, New Mexico, tape #16, University of New Mexico Archives, Oral History Collection, University of New Mexico, Albuquerque, New Mexico.)

Bill Norlander, a television photographer, attempted to photograph the scene as the guardsmen moved forward in formation:

When I approached the Guardsmen I held my camera in front of me with camera side to them. There is large lettering on the side [of the camera] saying KOB-TV 4; I also shouted, "Press!" I was walking backward and to the side. . . . The Guard approached and I saw . . . the three on the end of the line coming toward me. . . . The three men, all wearing gas masks, were holding their rifles in front of them, parrying the bayonets. All three [soldiers] put the bayonets in the upper area of my body and pushed. I received a wound, about one inch long and two and half inches deep in the upper left arm. I received another wound in the chest. I thought, "I'd better get out of here—these guys are going to kill me!"

(Quoted in the *Albuquerque Journal*, June 21, 1970.)

Hippies and Their Communes in New Mexico

Young men and women of the late 1960s and early 1970s often defied the establishment, consisting of the government and all other institutions that, in their minds, threatened world peace, free thought, and social justice. Many protested against the Vietnam conflict. All opposed mainstream American culture and its materialistic values. Commonly called **hippies**, these youths were known for their long hair, informal dress, hallucinatory drugs, modern art, and rock music.

Many hippies chose to live in small, largely self-reliant, idealistic communities known as **communes**. By 1970, counterculture communes dotted the New Mexico landscape, especially in or near Taos. According to one estimate, more than three thousand hippies lived in the Taos area in the summer of 1970. Even Mabel Dodge Luhan's former house was used as a commune, led by Dennis Hopper, the star (with Peter Fonda) of *Easy Rider*, a 1969 movie that first drew national attention to Taos as a hippie mecca.

Many hippies were attracted to the beautiful scenery, mild climate, and varied cultures of the Southwest. Nonconformist in every way, their communes were known by such names as Morningstar, the Reality Construction Company, Hog Farm, the Lama Foundation, and, perhaps the most famous, New Buffalo.

Arthur Kopecky and his friends struggled to create an ideal commune at New Buffalo, northwest of Taos. From 1971 to 1979, Kopecky kept a personal journal in which he described the successes and failures of communal life and labor. In mid-1972, he wrote:

Thursday:

I feel very good.... Reggy, Gerard, and I ... worked hard all day. Donald, who arrived yesterday on his Harley, gave us some help. We work because it is a commune job, and we work for the commune—great trust, faith, and spirit. Gerard, Reggy, and Ian are all strong, experienced men. This is what I like, working with these people....

Saturday:

At the boogie [dance in town] there was a rumble. A group of local kids jumped the [commune's van, called the] Mind Machine. Sandy, Ron, John, and Rebel got roughed up, and Pepe got stitches. Came home with bullet holes in the top of the van. Terrible.

More trouble surfaced later that year:

Tuesday:

What can you believe? This morning Ron says the silver concho belt [our most valuable possession is] missing! We had it too long. Still, where is it? A mystery....

I feel a little uneasy.... Ismael has gone back to city life and Pepe, my closest brother, [is] not getting it on so well in this revolution....

It takes a long time and many tests to find our brothers. "Brothers, find your brothers" is a call of our time. Any movement worth its salt has its disappointments, its betrayals, and its opportunists....

The "revolution" is a thing on our minds. ... Sometimes I have Kemal describe to me all the kinds of food he can remember [when we had more to eat]. Sometimes we talk about why we work, what we see in the future.

The wind is blowing very loudly tonight.

After years of hard work and focused effort, Arthur Kopecky finally left New Buffalo; internal disputes and family needs caused his departure. Like most other communities of its kind in New Mexico and the rest of the country, New Buffalo eventually closed. It was later reopened as a bed and breakfast resort, and it is now an educational center.

(Arthur Kopecky, *New Buffalo: Journals from a Taos Commune* [Albuquerque: University of New Mexico Press, 2004], 64, 165, 182–83; and *Leaving New Buffalo Commune* [Albuquerque: University of New Mexico Press, 2006], 180–83.)

Vietnam Veterans Return Home

Lupe, the same young marine who told of his combat experiences in Vietnam, recalled how hard it was for him to return home to the United States in February 1970:

> By the time I returned from Vietnam, . . . I was not the same person at all. When I came back, I was just one angry person. If somebody looked at me, . . . I would just blow up. It was just like an explosive inside me. When I came back, my family didn't understand me. . . . I couldn't be around people. I couldn't stand loud noises. I couldn't sleep in the house. I lived out in the country and I slept in the grape orchards, in the almond orchards, on the back lawn, and I always had a weapon. . . .
>
> When I [finally] saw a psychiatrist . . . he told me, "You're not crazy. What you're suffering is real. [The war] happened to you at such a young age. You had responsibilities that were beyond what a normal human can take. . . ." [T]hat was good to know.
>
> Group therapy was really helpful, dealing with all the vets who had similar problems. [And later I had a family of my own and a need to be close to them.] Vietnam took that [need for closeness] away, but those feelings are coming back.
>
> (Quoted in Lea Ybarra, *Vietnam Veteranos: Chicanos Recall the War* [Austin: University of Texas Press, 2004], 133–35.)

Although Lupe suffered terribly in the war and afterward, he was fortunate compared to many of his fellow veterans. He had a supportive family, received therapy, and eventually had his own family he could feel close to. Tragically, thousands of other veterans never received such care and still suffered after many years. Some wounds never healed.

The Vietnam conflict finally ended when the United States withdrew its last troops from the Southeast Asian country in March 1973. The longest war in U.S. history was over. In all, 58,249 Americans, including 399 New Mexicans, had lost their lives. Among the fifty states, only Hawaii suffered a higher percentage of servicemen and servicewomen killed in the war. Sadly, about a third of all American fatalities were draftees, most of whom were members of minority groups and the poor. In New Mexico, Hispanic residents represented 30 percent of the state's population but 39 percent of all New Mexicans killed in Vietnam.

Returning veterans felt unfairly discriminated against for the conduct of the war. Cheering crowds seldom welcomed veterans home,

▲▲▲▲▲▲▲▲▲▲▲▲▲▲▲▲▲▲▲▲▲▲▲▲▲▲▲▲

Vietnam's Boat People in New Mexico

Shortly after the last American soldiers left South Vietnam in 1973, the country and its government fell to communist forces. Many South Vietnamese had fled earlier, but, with a communist government in power, thousands more sought escape, especially if they could be accused of helping the United States during the war. Refugees tried to escape any way they could, including on the last American helicopters to leave Saigon, the country's capital city, in 1975. Later, many attempted to sail away on small, leaky, often overcrowded crafts. Known as boat people, some men, women, and children on these crafts drowned. In all, 150,000 survivors sought refuge in the United States.

More than three thousand Vietnamese refugees eventually settled in Albuquerque, creating yet another ethnic and cultural group in New Mexico. Albuquerque's Vietnamese residents have worked to maintain their culture with a radio station, a newspaper, mutual aid societies, and an annual holiday held each April 30 to honor their fellow countrymen who died in the war or in their desperate efforts to flee to safety and freedom.

as they had after all previous American wars. Once home, many vets suffered terrible physical ailments and psychological disorders based on their combat experience and, for 766 Americans, life in captivity as often-tortured POWs. Remembering the horrors of what they had witnessed in Vietnam, many vets suffered from **posttraumatic stress disorder** (**PTSD**), a psychiatric condition that often occurs after a person experiences or witnesses life-threatening events, especially during combat. Some 75,000 vets also suffered terrible physical consequences, including cancer, as a result of exposure to **Agent Orange**, a powerful herbicide the U.S. military used to destroy native plant growth and reveal enemy positions from 1963 to 1971. Finally, twelve New Mexicans are among hundreds of men still listed as missing in action (MIAs). For all these American veterans, the tragedy of Vietnam continues more than thirty years after the last American left Southeast Asia.

 ## Cold War Changes in New Mexico

New Mexico played an increasingly large role in the Cold War beyond Vietnam. The state's scientific labs, missile ranges, and air bases were essential parts of the American response to Cold War events around the world. According to experts, New Mexico contained "the most extensive nuclear weapons research, management, training, and testing facilities in the United States."

Los Alamos and Sandia National Labs helped to develop important new weapons for the nation's defense. Nuclear weapons' research was conducted in only ten major laboratories in the world, three of which were in the United States and two of which were in New Mexico. As a result, New Mexico could claim to have more scientists and technical workers in proportion to its population than any other state in the country.

Military bases played similarly key roles in the Cold War era. In 1992, for example, Holloman Air Force Base became the home base for the

Below from the top:
Harrison "Jack" Schmitt,
Sidney "Sid" Gutierrez,
and Dr. Laurel Blair Clark

New Mexican Astronauts

New Mexico has played a major role in space exploration, with experiments, training, and, in 1982, the landing of the space shuttle *Columbia* at White Sands Missile Range. Several New Mexicans have also served as astronauts, brave men and women who have risked their safety and, in some cases, sacrificed their lives in the interest of scientific knowledge and space travel.

Harrison "Jack" Schmitt was born and raised in Grant County, New Mexico. Educated as a geologist at Harvard University, he served as an American astronaut from 1965 to 1975. As the lunar module's pilot on the 1972 *Apollo 17* mission, he became the first and only civilian to ever walk on the moon. Schmitt and his fellow crewmen collected about 250 pounds of moon rock and soil samples to be transported back to Earth for study. Once safely home in New Mexico, Schmitt entered politics, was elected to the U.S. Senate in 1976 and represented his state in Washington, D.C., until 1983.

Sidney "Sid" Gutierrez, a 1969 graduate of Albuquerque's Valley High School and a graduate of the U.S. Air Force Academy, became the country's first Hispanic astronaut when the National Aeronautics and Space Administration (NASA) selected him for this coveted role in 1985. After extensive training, Gutierrez flew on two space missions, in 1991 and 1994, during which he orbited Earth 329 times while spending more than twenty days in flight.

Dr. Laurel Blair Clark spent two years of her childhood in Albuquerque before growing up to become a U.S. Naval medical doctor and a member of the space shuttle *Columbia*'s crew. After a seventeen-day mission in space, Dr. Clark and her six fellow crewmates were reentering the earth's atmosphere over Texas when the *Columbia* exploded in midair on February 1, 2003. Fragments of the spacecraft were discovered not only in Texas but as far away as New Mexico. The Astronaut Memorial Garden at the New Mexico Museum of Space History in Alamogordo is a monument built, in part, in memory of Dr. Clark and all those who perished in that horrific disaster.

F-117 Nighthawk, an advanced jet bomber better known as the Stealth Fighter. Unlike other planes, the Nighthawk could fly without detection by enemy radar, making it possible to strike deep into enemy territory on strategic bombing missions. With a range of more than eleven hundred miles and a speed exceeding six hundred miles per hour, the Nighthawk can hit targets as small as one square yard in size. The air force spent $100 million to build the hangars and support buildings needed to house and operate the F-117s based at Holloman.

At Kirtland Air Force Base the air force closed its Manzano Base operations and opened a new, even more secure nuclear storage facility known as the **Kirtland Underground Munitions Storage Complex**, or **KUMSC**, in 1994. The air force built KUMSC under a main runway so weapons could be delivered and transported more safely and securely. Nearly nineteen hundred nuclear warheads are stored at KUMSC, making it the largest of ten nuclear weapons' storage facilities in the United States.

Meanwhile, the United States continued to test new weapons at the White Sands Missile Range, the largest military installation in the entire country. According to one estimate, more than twenty thousand missiles had been launched from the range from 1960 to 1980, for an average of 1,045 missiles per year. American military allies like Germany and South Korea used the range for testing weapons. Privately produced explosive devices were also tested on the range, starting in 1989.

By the 1970s, the United States faced a major problem in the use of atomic energy: nuclear waste. The development of nuclear weapons (after 1943) and nuclear power plants (after 1957) had produced tons of materials exposed to low to high levels of radiation. For years this dangerous waste had been piling up at sites near research labs and power plants. By the late 1970s, an estimated 75 million gallons of nuclear waste had accumulated in the United States. At Los Alamos so much contaminated waste had accumulated in one canyon that it was known as Acid Canyon. Great efforts were made to clear the canyon of this waste, but many feared the effect of so much contaminated waste on the health of those who lived or hiked nearby. What was true at Los Alamos was also true, to one degree or another, at every site where waste had been stored over the years.

What could the United States do with this dangerous waste material? Few appropriate, long-term storage facilities existed in the United States, and of those that did, few local residents wanted such potentially lethal material anywhere close to their homes and communities.

The exception was found in Carlsbad, New Mexico. There, miles of stable salt beds, submerged 2,150 feet below ground, were identified as

Estimated Sizes of U.S. and Soviet Nuclear Stockpiles, 1955–85		
	United States	Soviet Union
1955	2,760	280
1960	18,900	3,430
1970	28,200	17,700
1975	28,400	24,300
1980	25,600	30,800
1985	24,898	22,709–32,823

(Tomas B. Cochran, William M. Arkin, Robert S. Norris, and Jeffrey I. Sands, *Nuclear Weapons Databook* [New York: Harper and Row, 1998], 4:25; William M. Arkin and Richard W. Fieldhouse, *Nuclear Battlefields: Global Links in the Arms Race* [Cambridge, MA: Ballinger Publishing Company, 1985], 38.)

Estimated World Nuclear Stockpiles, 1985	
United States	24,898*
Soviet Union	22,709–32,823
Great Britain	686
France	514
China	251–331
Total	**49,058–59,252**

* 410 of these 24,898 nuclear weapons were stored at Manzano Base, Kirtland Air Force Base, Albuquerque, New Mexico

(William M. Arkin and Richard W. Fieldhouse, *Nuclear Battlefields: Global Links in the Arms Race* [Cambridge, MA: Ballinger Publishing Company, 1985], 38, 200.)

an ideal storage location for nuclear waste. Furthermore, polls showed that most of the people in Carlsbad did not object to the proposed project. Many men and women in southeastern New Mexico actually saw the project not only as a lucrative new industry but also as a patriotic contribution to American energy and Cold War problems. They were assured the storage facility, which scientists and engineers at Sandia Labs designed, would be safe not only for their generation but for centuries to come.

Later Cold War Dangers

If the Cold War provided opportunities for New Mexico to serve the nation and share in at least some of its economic prosperity, it also exposed the state to many dangers. The cost of Vietnam in internal dissent and deaths can never be measured; the war's deep wounds have yet to heal. As in the early Cold War era, nuclear accidents and misguided test missiles were still possible, although greater safeguards were established to help prevent such potentially disastrous mishaps. The dangers of uranium mining remained high not only for miners but also for anyone directly or indirectly exposed to radioactive waste from mining operations. New Mexico also remained a probable target if a nuclear war broke out. With nuclear research labs, major testing ranges, and nuclear missiles stored within its borders, seven of the nation's highest-risk targets were located in New Mexico.

The Waste Isolation Pilot Plan (WIPP)

Many New Mexicans had particular concerns about the proposed nuclear waste storage facility near Carlsbad. A 1979 statewide opinion poll showed that 53 percent of New Mexicans expressed concern that the potential costs of such a storage facility might well outweigh its potential benefits. Many questioned:

- the transport of even low-level nuclear waste on busy roadways, like I-25, as well as on more isolated roads leading to Carlsbad via large towns and cities like Santa Fe and Roswell;
- the strength of specially designed canisters that would hold the transported waste materials, especially in the event of accidents or acts of sabotage;

Nuclear Winter

In 1983, famed scientist Carl Sagan calculated the possible destruction caused by an all-out nuclear war between the United States and the Soviet Union. Sagan wrote that the explosive power of a single American or Soviet nuclear bomb would be equal to all the bombs dropped in World War II. According to Sagan's **nuclear-winter theory,** a war using many such powerful weapons would not only kill millions of humans but also "blot out the sun, plunge the earth into a deep freeze and cause mass starvation, wiping out ninety percent of the earth's population, or billions of people." Sagan concluded that "except for fools and madmen, everyone knows that nuclear war would be an unprecedented catastrophe."

(Carl Sagan, *The Nuclear Winter* [Boston: Council for a Livable World Education Fund, 1983], 1–10.)

- the skills of emergency teams trained to deal with possible medical and environmental disasters;
- the impact of nuclear waste on the clean air, soil, and water of southeastern New Mexico;
- and the impact of the facility on the safety and general health of those who would work at the site, their families, and the larger community in Carlsbad.

The Department of Energy had to respond to numerous concerns...

Many New Mexicans question the effectiveness of WIPP to safely isolate radioactive waste

The U.S. government attempted to address these and other concerns as it developed what became known as the **Waste Isolation Pilot Plant**, or simply **WIPP**. The government promised to store only low-level waste, kept in well-tested canisters, and transported along safe, much-improved roadways; a twelve-mile, four-lane bypass, known as the Veterans Memorial Highway, was built, for example, around Santa Fe to avoid transport through the city's congested streets. First-response emergency teams were trained in communities along all routes. The project was designated as a pilot plant, meaning that its impact would be studied for many years before a decision would be made on whether the storage site was to be made permanent.

Could the government be trusted to do all it promised? Some expressed their doubts by staging nonviolent protests, much like protesters had done during the civil rights and antiwar protests of the 1960s and 1970s. In one instance, protestors occupied Congressman Steve Schiff's offices in Albuquerque, although Schiff shared their concern that New Mexico was about to become a dumping ground for the rest of the country's nuclear waste.

After years of debate, postponements, and promises, the state of New Mexico and the federal government finally agreed to open WIPP. WIPP became the first licensed underground nuclear waste storage area in the world when the first shipment of low-level radioactive materials arrived at the site on March 26, 1999. A total of one thousand canisters of waste arrived over the next three years. By 2006, two dozen shipments arrived each week.

☀ Dependency and Boom-Bust Economies

Since the beginning of World War II, New Mexico had become increasingly dependent on the federal government and large corporations to make most major decisions regarding the economic health of individual New Mexico communities and the state as a whole. This dependency meant New Mexico prospered during good economic times but remained vulnerable to sudden changes in national or international economic conditions. Decisions regarding the expansion or reduction—or even closing—of major operations were left in the hands of individuals and forces far beyond New Mexico's borders and control.

New Mexico towns were especially vulnerable to outside control if they relied on one major product or employer for their economic well-being. Like a house of cards, the whole economic structure of a town could tumble if the "house" depended on one "card" (business) in particular and the crucial card was gradually weakened or, worse yet, suddenly removed. Even the rumor of such a catastrophe could prove disastrous for an economically vulnerable community.

Mining towns were among the earliest victims of this dependency and vulnerability. With the use of more modern fuels, the Phelps Dodge Corporation closed Dawson, the largest coal-mining town in New Mexico, in 1950. By the mid-1950s, all other coal camps in the state had closed, with dire consequences not only for miners and their families but also for residents and businesses in nearby towns like Ratón in Colfax County and Gallup in McKinley County. Federal government policies favoring the importation of foreign potash led to a similar decline in potash mining near Carlsbad, with a similarly ruinous impact on Eddy County's economy by the mid-1960s.

The federal government's decision to cut military spending at home, given increased spending in Vietnam, led to dismal consequences for Roswell in Chaves County. In 1967, the air force announced that it planned to close Walker Air Force Base, the largest employer and contractor in Chaves County. Although local business leaders optimistically asserted they could survive the shutdown without major losses, it was soon clear that Roswell's economic boom had ended in a bust once Walker closed. Without military families, hundreds of houses and apartments stood empty. With a shrinking economy, many stores and businesses locked their doors for good. The *Roswell City Directory*, which had expanded to 510 pages in 1964, shrank to 390 the year after Walker closed.

Roswell took years to retrain its workforce, attract new employers, and gradually recover. The community's economic health only improved significantly when it began to profit from the famous UFO incident of 1947. UFO enthusiasts flocked to Roswell to visit the town's new UFO museums and tourist shops, especially during the town's annual UFO festival, held early each July. About twelve thousand travelers visited Roswell's main UFO museum in 1993, the museum's first full year of operation. By 2007, more than 2 million people from thirty-five countries and all fifty states had visited the museum. Even this tourist boom is vulnerable, though; when gasoline prices rise, fewer tourists can afford to visit Roswell and help pump money into the local economy.

Roswell's UFO Walmart sign

Grants suffered from another boom-bust economy. After an early boom based on high uranium prices in the 1950s, the uranium market suddenly collapsed in the 1960s, causing considerable unemployment and economic decline in Grants's uranium industry. Then, just as suddenly, the market improved, largely because of an international energy crisis in the 1970s. Many Americans hoped that nuclear power plants were the energy source of the future; the world's total nuclear power-plant capacity rose from just 16 gigawatts in 1970 to 135 gigawatts a decade later. Uranium mining in western Valencia County climbed to its highest levels ever, with more than seventy-five hundred workers employed in forty-five mines by the late 1970s. Optimists compared the Grants area uranium boom to the California gold rush of 1849.

As a result of this new boom, Grants's population mushroomed to 11,439 residents in 1980. Town leaders were so confident about their economic future that they supported a movement to separate from Valencia County and form a county of their own. Cíbola County was created with much fanfare in 1981.

The new boom went bust again by 1982. A reduction in the number of nuclear weapons and the occurrence of tragic accidents at nuclear power plants in the United States and the Soviet Union severely affected the uranium market. These larger, outside economic forces caused the closing of all but twelve mines and the firing of some three thousand miners in Cíbola County; unemployment rocketed to 20 percent of the workforce in the new county. Grants's population dropped by 25 percent from 1980 to 1990. Many residents attempted to sell their homes. Businesses went bankrupt or moved away. Like Roswell after the closing of Walker Air Force Base, Grants slowly recovered with new employers, including a new state prison, but it has never matched the prosperity of its former economic boom. Understandably, recent talk of opening new uranium mines has been received with mixed reactions as some local residents recall the opportunities, but others remember the great risks of living in a boom-bust, often unhealthy mining economy.

New Mexico's oil and gas industries have been equally vulnerable to boom-bust economics, depending on national and international energy demands. Hobbs, Artesia, Farmington, and other towns near New Mexico's oil and gas fields have experienced spurts of prosperity followed by sharp economic declines. With more than half of the New Mexico state government's income based on oil and gas taxes, the entire state suffered when the oil and gas market was weak, leaving few oil and gas revenues to spend on essential state programs like education and health care. It is as if the state government's income were on a roller coaster, with outside economic forces driving the speed, direction, and duration of New Mexico's fortunes.

Not even the state's national labs were immune to economic decisions made far from the Southwest. The labs' mission began to change by the mid-1970s with the end of the Vietnam War and improved U.S.-Soviet relations. Starting with the Strategic Arms Limitation Talks (or SALT) agreements of 1972 and 1979, the United States and the Soviet Union agreed to gradually reduce their nuclear capabilities. The labs' scientists

Little Toxic Cleanup

Despite promises from the federal government and large mining companies, little was done to clean up the toxic waste left when the uranium industry collapsed in western New Mexico. Few efforts were made to seal the abandoned mine shafts, fence the polluted sites, or remove the piles of radioactive tailings or waste, especially on parts of the Navajo Reservation.

A newspaper article in the *Albuquerque Journal* told the story of a Navajo family who lived near a uranium mine when it was in operation during the uranium boom from 1968 to 1982:

> Before long, [the family] got used to the rumble of pickup trucks dropping low-grade [radioactive] ore off a ridge [by their home]. In time, the [polluted] waste pile reached the top of the cliff and stretched along its breadth.
>
> Teddy Nez, his wife, and their children lived about five hundred feet from the heap. When [the] United Nuclear [Corporation] closed the mine in 1982, Nez assumed the company would haul away the waste. He was wrong. He watched with concern as sheep, goats, and cattle climbed up the [polluted] pile and . . . people [ironically] searched the property for sacred herbs for healing ceremonies.

(Judy Pasternak, "On Dangerous Ground," *Albuquerque Journal*, December 17, 2006.)

Little has been done about this toxic waste. Many families now fear a similar fate if the uranium mines are reopened with little concern for the environment and human health.

Fortunately, with Senator Jeff Bingaman's help, Congress passed the Radiation Exposure Compensation Act of 1990 to at least compensate former uranium miners and their families for illnesses caused by working in the mines.

(*Gallup Independent*, July 6, 2001.)

New Mexico's Oil and Gas Industry

As of 2007:

- the San Juan Basin in northwestern New Mexico is the largest field of natural-gas reserves in the United States. It produces 10 percent of the natural gas used in the country each day;
- the Permian Basin in southeastern New Mexico has three of the nation's hundred leading oil fields;
- New Mexico has about fifty-six thousand oil and gas wells, of which fifty thousand are currently producing;
- New Mexico's oil and gas industry employs twenty-three thousand workers;
- among the states in the United States, New Mexico is the fifth largest producer of oil and gas;
- the oil and gas industry pays more than $2 billion in state taxes each year, amounting to more than half the state government's annual income.

(*Albuquerque Journal*, February 18, 2007.)

began to focus less on the creation of new nuclear weapons and more on the invention of nonnuclear weapons, methods of arms-control inspection, and the dismantling of hundreds of existing atomic bombs.

End of the Cold War

New Mexico's dependent economy became even more vulnerable with the end of the Cold War in the early 1990s. The rise of democratic movements in various communist countries led to the collapse of the Soviet empire and, eventually, the Soviet Union itself. Russia, the main country of the former Soviet Union, became an American friend, if not quite an American ally, in international relations.

The threat of nuclear war between the world's superpowers declined with these startling events. Nuclear weapons still existed in countries besides the United States and Russia, however; many of these armed nations were American allies, but many were not. New Mexico's role in the storage and maintenance of hundreds of American nuclear weapons therefore remained important, but the danger of base closings, lab cutbacks, and boom-bust economies loomed ever larger. As before, the federal government and large corporations far beyond New Mexico's control often made decisions regarding such crucial developments.

Valuable Peacetime Spin-Off Products from New Mexico's National Labs

Los Alamos National Laboratory, managed by the University of California, and Sandia National Laboratories, operated by the Lockheed Martin Corporation, are best known for their research and development of nuclear weapons, especially during the Cold War. It is important to remember, though, that while researching and developing nuclear weapons, the labs' scientists have discovered thousands of valuable peacetime products, including many that have greatly changed our modern world. Some of these spin-off products include:

- the clean room to remove dust and bacteria from the air. This major discovery has made the microelectronics industry possible for Intel and other computer corporations;
- working with Intel, new super computers, which set computer speed records;
- working with the University of New Mexico's School of Medicine, a miniature insulin pump that could be implanted in diabetic patients to replace insulin shots;
- strong, well-tested canisters for the transport and storage of nuclear waste for the Waste Isolation Pilot Plant (WIPP);
- alternative, renewable clean-energy sources, such as solar, wave, and wind energy;
- model water usage plans;
- improved security systems for airports and schools;
- improved fingerprint detection methods;
- trained bees (with their extraordinary sense of smell) to find dangerous land mines and other explosives;
- airbags to cushion NASA's Pathfinder space probe landing on Mars;
- new printed circuit boards developed for space science.

(*Albuquerque Journal*, November 26, 2006.)

Scientists at LANL and SNL have won more than a hundred research and development awards for important peacetime products that benefit society as well as major businesses in the American economy.

(Leland Johnson, *Sandia National Laboratories: A History of Exceptional Service in the National Interest* [Albuquerque: Sandia National Laboratories, 1997]; http://www.llanl.gov/orgs/tt/awards/rd100/06.shtml.)

Urban Growth

While much of New Mexico became increasingly vulnerable to national and international events, other parts of the state grew in size and wealth. This was especially true for urban centers whose economies were less

Early construction
in Rio Rancho
....

dependent on a single major product or employer. Albuquerque, the state's largest city, was relatively the least dependent and, consequently, the most successful in consistent modern growth and prosperity. New Mexico's urban growth from 1965 to 1995 can be measured in several ways:

- Albuquerque's population soared from 244,501 in 1970 to 386,988 in 1990, making it one of the fastest-growing cities in the American Southwest. Other cities grew as well. Las Cruces grew so quickly that by 1990 it was second in size to Albuquerque, passing Santa Fe as the state's second largest city.
- A whole new city grew from practically nothing into the state's sixth largest community by 1990. Originally planned as a suburban community mainly populated by newcomers from the East Coast, Rio Rancho grew so fast that it incorporated as a city in 1981, created its own chamber of commerce, opened its own high school in 1997, and even built its own modern sports arena.
- Based largely on urban population growth, New Mexico gained a third representative in the U.S. House of Representatives in 1980.
- Albuquerque's business sector grew so quickly that its *Yellow Pages* telephone book expanded from 421 pages in its 1965 edition to 1,661 pages in its 1990 edition.

Urban Populations, 1970–90

	1970	Rank in Size	1990	Rank in Size
Alamogordo	23,035	6	27,986	8
Albuquerque	244,501	1	386,988	1
Carlsbad	21,297	8	25,320	9
Farmington	21,979	7	34,588	5
Gallup	14,596	9	19,340	10
Hobbs	26,025	5	29,445	7
Las Cruces	37,857	3	62,648	2
Las Vegas	13,835	10	14,565	11
Ratón	6,962	12	7,282	13
Rio Rancho	*	14	32,551	6
Roswell	33,908	4	44,480	4
Santa Fe	41,167	2	57,605	3
Silver City	8,557	11	10,984	12
Taos	2,475	13	4,401	14

* less than 1,000
(Mark C. Resta and Lee B. Zink, *The New Mexico Economy: Change in the 1970s* [Albuquerque: University of New Mexico Press, 1978], 15; http://www.unm.edu/~bber/demo/cityhist.htm.)

- Once small, two-lane roads like Juan Tabo Boulevard to the east, Coors Boulevard to the west, Gibson Boulevard to the south, and Montgomery Boulevard to the north became major thoroughfares. With major renovations, the Big-I interchange, originally designed for up to sixty thousand vehicles per day, can now handle up to four hundred thousand vehicles each day.

- In another sign of urban progress, Albuquerque's buildings were built higher and higher. In 1922, the First National Bank's downtown building stood nine stories high. In 1963, the same bank's new building at San Mateo Boulevard and Central Avenue stood seventeen stories high. As of 1988, the twenty-two-story Bank of Albuquerque office building could claim the title as the state's tallest structure.

- On December 1, 1966, the University of New Mexico opened a new, modern University Arena, better known as the Pit. By 1996, 8 million fans had watched basketball games played in the Pit. It was remodeled in 2010.

- Located southwest of the Pit, Albuquerque's modern Sports Stadium opened on March 31, 1969. Home of the Albuquerque Dodgers (later the Dukes and now the Isotopes), an opening day standing-room-only crowd of 13,767 watched Willie Mays become the park's first hitter in an exhibition game played between the San Francisco Giants and the Cleveland Indians.

Old and new economic activity helped stimulate this remarkable urban growth in New Mexico. Despite their vulnerability, air force bases, scientific labs, and testing ranges still employed thousands of men and women. Tourism still flourished as travelers continued to visit popular places, like Carlsbad Caverns, and attend famous events, like the Santa Fe Fiesta. Now, thousands of travelers arrived to see new places and events, including a tram to the top of Sandia Peak, opened in 1966, and the Albuquerque International Balloon Fiesta, begun as a small balloon rally in 1972. Many came to ski in the winter or enjoy New Mexico's art and native cultures in all seasons of the year. Gamblers enjoyed horse races at New Mexico's racetracks or games of chance at casinos, opened on many Indian reservations by the 1990s. Tourism provided seasonal and permanent jobs of all kinds, from security guards to golf-course professionals. Many tourists admired the Southwest so much they decided to stay, bringing new talents and new business to the region.

New Mexico's fine weather and health industry continued to attract newcomers long after tuberculosis was largely conquered with the use of new methods of cure and prevention after World War II. Former sans, like St. Joseph's and Presbyterian in Albuquerque, became modern general

First balloon flight in New Mexico, 1882

The Sandia Peak Tram

Skiing had become an increasingly popular sport in New Mexico when Robert J. Nordhaus and Ben Abruzzo had what they called a "crazy idea." Avid skiers, the two friends hoped to build a tram up the west slope of the Sandia Mountains, giving people in Albuquerque access not only to the ski basin on the east slope but also to the spectacular view from the mountain's peak, 10,378 feet above sea level.

Although many said it could never be done, Nordhaus and Abruzzo realized their dream with a great deal of hard work and determination. After two years of difficult, often dangerous construction, the Sandia Peak Tram was opened with great fanfare on May 7, 1966. A cable car carried Nordhaus, Abruzzo, Gov. Jack Campbell, and other dignitaries to the top of the mountain on the tram's maiden trip.

The completed tram traveled 14,850 feet in a vertical rise of 4,000 feet over breathtaking scenes, full of sharp cliffs, beautiful forestland, and wildlife. The tram's two cable cars each carry fifty passengers in seven-minute trips up the mountain, or seven seconds straight down, as cable-car pilots kiddingly tell nervous first-time passengers. Only high winds and bad weather prevent the tram's daily operation. The longest passenger tram of its kind in the world, the tram carried about a hundred thousand visitors to the peak in its first year of operation alone.

hospitals. Retirees from the cold, generally more expensive Northeast, or **Rust Belt**, arrived in growing numbers to the mild climate and less expensive South, or **Sun Belt**, which includes the Southwest. Retirement communities and new health-care facilities opened in response to the retirees' needs as aging citizens.

While manufacturing has never been a strong sector of New Mexico's economy, some major new manufacturers began operations in several urban centers. Corporations like GTE Lenkurt, Honeywell, Motorola, Singer, General Foods, and Levi Strauss opened factories in Albuquerque. In the best—and largest—example of this kind, computer giant Intel opened a plant in Rio Rancho with fewer than twenty-five employees in 1980. Attracted to New Mexico by tax breaks and other economic incentives, Intel rapidly expanded its operations and workforce; by 1995, its huge plant covered 465,000 square feet, and its workforce equaled fifty-two hundred men and women. Manufacturing flash memory chips and Pentium processors, the plant became New Mexico's largest single industrial employer.

Early balloon festival in Albuquerque

The Albuquerque International Balloon Fiesta

More than twenty thousand people gathered in the parking lot at Coronado Center (now Coronado Mall) to witness thirteen hot-air balloons rise over northeast Albuquerque in April 1972. This first balloon rally was certainly exciting, but it was not the first balloon ascension in the city's history. On July 4, 1882, Prof. Park A. Van Tassel amazed a crowd of several thousand spectators by rising in a gas balloon from a vacant lot on Gold Avenue between Second and Third streets. It had taken two days to inflate the professor's balloon with enough gas to launch his airborne voyage. Van Tassel waved an American flag as he rose to an altitude of at least ten thousand feet.

In the years that followed Professor Van Tassel's ascent, Albuquerque became known for its nearly ideal flying conditions in an area called the Albuquerque Box. In 1972, the balloon rally near Coronado Center featured a race between a balloon, designated as a roadrunner, and twelve others, designated as coyotes. The winning "coyote" balloon was the one that landed closest to the "roadrunner" target.

Other balloon rallies followed, with balloons taking off from various Albuquerque sites, including the infield of the racetrack at the New Mexico State Fair Grounds. By 1978, there were 273 entries in what had become a much-anticipated annual event. More and more balloonists came from across the United States and around the world, making it a truly international festival. Soon known as the Albuquerque International Balloon Fiesta, a record 1,019 balloons ascended from a new Balloon Fiesta Park in 2000. Thousands of tourists attended the fiesta to watch the ascensions, purchase souvenirs, and photograph the balloons' unusual shapes and colorful designs. In fact, the fiesta has become the single most photographed event in the world. Although several other New Mexico towns have their own, smaller versions of the fiesta, Albuquerque justifiably calls itself the Balloon Capital of the World. New Mexicans are so proud of their balloon rallies that a balloon, with a New Mexico Zia design, was long featured on the state's license plates.

The Double Eagle II's Record Flight to Paris, 1978

Departing from Maine on August 11, 1978, three Albuquerque balloonists flew their eleven-story-high helium balloon, the Double Eagle II, to a wheat field sixty miles west of Paris, France. In the process of becoming the first crew to fly a balloon across the Atlantic Ocean, **Maxie Anderson**, **Ben Abruzzo** (who had earlier helped build the Sandia Peak Tramway), and **Larry Newman** set many world records, including marks for the longest balloon flight (3,233 miles) and the longest time afloat (137 hours, 18 minutes). The trio faced many dangerous moments, especially when they experienced radio trouble, when they feared that their balloon was leaking, and when the temperature dropped so low that their balloon iced and almost crashed.

Once in France,

[the] Double Eagle II . . . came sweeping over the village of Miserey, toward a barley field golden and ripe for the harvest. For the first time they saw that the highway was choked with cars. Max, looking down, saw hundreds of people leaping from their cars and running toward the field. . . .

Men and women and an army of children swarmed over the [balloon when it was deflated]; they clawed at it, seeking to take a piece of it as a souvenir. Some fell to their knees and tried to rip the tough nylon with their teeth. . . .

[Max stood at a distance surrounded by thousands of] laughing, excited people. [Watching it all, Ben] felt two things—sadness that [their adventure] was over, and something nearly like regret that the Atlantic had at last been conquered by men in a balloon.

(Charles McCarry with Ben Abruzzo, Maxie Anderson, and Larry Newman, *Double Eagle* [Boston: Little, Brown and Company, 1979], 268, 270.)

An equally enthusiastic, but far calmer, crowd welcomed Anderson, Abruzzo, and Newman home in a special parade down Central Avenue in Albuquerque.

The history of ballooning, including the flight of the Double Eagle II, is now documented in exhibits at the Anderson-Abruzzo Albuquerque International Balloon Museum built just south of the Albuquerque International Balloon Fiesta grounds.

 ## Growing Pains

Urban growth brought its share of positive benefits but more than its share of urban problems. To make way for wide roads and modern buildings, many architectural treasures were demolished in the name

Bill Gates and the Personal Computer in Albuquerque, 1975–79

The U.S. Army developed the world's first, rather primitive computers during World War II. By the early 1950s, engineers had created more advanced mainframe computers, but they were large, complicated, expensive, and unavailable to most people. It was not until the mid-1970s that a personal computer was designed by a former air force engineer, Ed Roberts, and his small Albuquerque company, Micro Instrumentation and Telemetry Systems, or MITS. Roberts's Altair was so small and so affordable ($397 for a kit) that MITS could hardly keep up with the three hundred orders it received each day.

When two young men in Massachusetts read about the Altair 8800 in an edition of *Popular Mechanics* magazine, they realized that the new computer could be even more valuable and successful if it included a software program. **Bill Gates** and **Paul Allen** developed such a program and flew to Albuquerque to show it to Ed Roberts in early 1975. Roberts was so impressed that he offered Allen and Gates important new roles in his small company.

Based on this early success, Gates and Allen founded their own company, called Micro Soft (now Microsoft) in Albuquerque in April 1975. Employing just thirteen men and women by 1978,

the company supplied software programs not only to MITS but also to other, larger companies in the growing personal computer business.

Working day and night, Gates and Allen built Microsoft into such a success by 1979 that the partners moved their operations to Seattle, Washington, where both men had been born and raised. They had liked and appreciated New Mexico but had decided to go home to further expand their business and live their lives.

Microsoft became one of the most successful companies in the world, with more than fifty-six hundred employees and sales worth more than a billion dollars in 1990 alone. Now among the richest men in the world, Gates and Allen contribute much of their wealth to important causes, especially education and health.

Microsoft's Business Growth		
Year	Number of Employees	Sales
1975	3	$16,500
1980	40	$7,520,720
1985	910	$140,417,000
1990	5,635	$1,183,446,000

(http://www.thocp.net/companies/microsoft/microsoft_company.htm.)

Microsoft and other computer companies have made computers accessible and affordable to people everywhere, revolutionizing the flow of information and the ability to do work of all kinds. A calculation that would have taken the Altair 8800 about a day to complete in the 1970s can be done in a single minute using a typical personal computer today.

(*Startup: Albuquerque and the Personal Computer Revolution*, exhibit, New Mexico Museum of Natural History and Science, Albuquerque, New Mexico.)

Bill Gates and the Albuquerque Group

GTE Lenkurt

The opening of Albuquerque's **GTE Lenkurt** plant in 1971 was heralded as a wonderful opportunity for hundreds of New Mexicans interested in assembly jobs in the modern semiconductor industry. A large percentage of those hired by the company were minority women who were glad to have jobs to help support themselves and their families. With fourteen hundred workers, GTE Lenkurt had become the largest manufacturing employer in New Mexico by 1982.

In 1984, a thirty-seven-year-old former GTE Lenkurt employee became so seriously ill with cancer that she went to see an attorney to seek legal advice in dealing with her increasingly large medical bills. Amy Cordova Romero believed that her illness had been caused by her work at GTE Lenkurt.

She was not alone. Dozens of her female co-workers from two of the plant's most dangerous departments suffered from major medical illnesses, from brain cancer to frequent miscarriages. Most believed their serious health problems were caused by working with extremely hazardous chemicals over several years. Many of the women had breathed toxic acids without masks for protection. Others had put their hands in a dangerous chemical called Freon, causing their hands to turn white like chalk. None of the women had been told what kind of chemicals they were working with, much less how bad the chemicals could be for their health.

More than a hundred plant workers eventually sued GTE Lenkurt in the largest occupational disease and disability trial in New Mexico history. After extensive investigations and much turmoil, 115 workers finally reached a settlement of between $2 and $3 million with the company. The money helped pay for the workers' expensive medical treatment but nothing could compensate them for their pain and suffering. The court settlement came too late for Amy Cordova Romero, who died of cancer before the final agreement was reached.

Meanwhile, GTE Lenkurt moved much of its Albuquerque operation to Mexico, where workers earned far less than they did in New Mexico and where health and safety regulations were far less strict than in the United States.

of urban renewal, a movement that changed the landscape of towns and cities across the country. In Albuquerque, famous homes like the Huning Castle in 1955 and businesses like the Alvarado Hotel in 1970 were destroyed rather than remodeled. With the Huning Castle and the Alvarado Hotel gone, both their properties were used as nothing more than parking lots until the recent past.

Manufacturers brought other problems to urban centers. Some companies paid their employees well and provided good, safe working conditions. Other companies built their plants in New Mexico largely because most workers in the state were not well organized or represented in labor unions. Without unions, many workers were poorly paid and faced unsafe working conditions on the job.

LANL and Its Neighbors

Largely based on income earned at the Los Alamos National Laboratory (LANL), the town of Los Alamos has enjoyed considerable wealth, making it one of the richest communities in the United States. The percentage of Los Alamos children living in poverty is low, few students drop out of school, most students attend college, and most families enjoy good health care. The crime rate is low, as is drug use.

Critics of LANL point out that these enviable conditions exist in stark contrast to conditions found in the largely Hispanic and Native American communities located within miles of Los Alamos. In towns like Española and pueblos like San Ildefonso, unemployment is high, many children live in poverty, the high school dropout rate is high, few students attend college, and few families have adequate health care. The crime rate is high, and drug problems abound.

Critics acknowledge that there are many reasons for these problems but contend that LANL employment practices have been largely to blame for the great contrast between Los Alamos and its neighboring communities. The lab was accused of unfair hiring practices that discriminated against native New Mexicans. In 1995, LANL was also accused of discriminating against native New Mexican employees when budget cuts forced the lab to lay off 256 workers, most of whom were Hispanic men and women. One of the laid-off workers expressed her feelings about working at the lab and leaving LANL after many years:

> I am a native of Santa Fe and I am Hispanic. I worked at the Lab for twenty-one years and I was one of the people who was laid off in November [1995]. [For most of my twenty-one years there] I thought

Some companies moved to New Mexico, built large plants, and hired hundreds of employees, only to reduce their operations or close down completely when economic conditions suddenly changed in the nation or the world. As before, major decisions regarding New Mexico's economy were made far away with little input from New Mexico leaders, much less from workers.

In 1970, for example, the Singer Company opened a plant to manufacture business machines in Albuquerque. The plant closed six years later, leaving thirteen hundred workers unemployed. Digital and GTE Lenkurt followed suit, with terrible consequences for thousands of former employees. In 1975, the Fairchild Corporation closed its Shiprock electronics plant, laying off 140 mostly Navajo workers. Although protesters from

that Los Alamos . . . was a wonderful institution. [But then about 1990]
I had an opportunity to work in management. [I soon found that]
as a Hispanic female my input was ignored. When I was able to say
something, it was dismissed as not relevant. Basically it was a total lack
of understanding of certain cultural values and a certain view of the
world that I represented. . . .

I think the science at the Laboratory is commendable but unfortunately it has come at the sacrifice of people. And I think that if people
are sacrificed, then the product is useless.

(Theresa Connoughton, quoted in "Impact Los Alamos Symposium," *New Mexico
Historical Review* 72 [January 1997]: 78.)

Many of the laid-off workers helped organize Citizens for LANL Employee
Rights; 102 of them also sued the lab for the illegal loss of their jobs. Their case
was settled when LANL agreed to pay the former workers almost $3 million
and rehire about half of them.

Other lab employees defend LANL, arguing that the lab has created jobs
and opportunities in a region where few jobs and opportunities otherwise
exist. Poverty and social problems may have been far worse without LANL as
a major regional employer. Hiring opportunities for high-level jobs at the lab
have been limited because many local New Mexicans lacked the advanced
education required for these best positions. Finally, LANL's defenders point
out that income earned at the lab has often been used to help preserve local
cultures, rather than endanger them.

the American Indian Movement (AIM) occupied the plant building for
eight days, the decision to close the operation never changed.

Urban growth often caused major problems for New Mexico's environment. Nonrenewable fossil fuels used in homes, vehicles, and businesses
caused air pollution; a dark haze settled over Albuquerque for much of
each day. Urban waste was released not only into the air but also into water
sources, like the Rio Grande, causing problems for smaller communities,
like Isleta Pueblo, located downriver from cities, especially Albuquerque.
Noise pollution from increased air and ground traffic disturbed the peace.
Intel's residential neighbors in the village of Corrales complained about
offensive odors emanating from the huge plant. New laws were passed
to help control air, water, and noise pollution, but they were sometimes

The Santa Fe Prison Riot, 1980

New Mexico's high crime rate in the 1970s led to many criminal convictions and, eventually, overcrowding in the state's penitentiary in Santa Fe. The prison, built in 1956 in the aftermath of a riot in 1954, was designed to house a maximum of 974 prisoners; it held 1,157 men in 1980. Inmates also complained that services were inadequate, with poor food, little access to legal resources, and few educational opportunities. Conditions had become so dismal by the mid-1970s that a group of inmates, led by Dwight Durán, had sued the governor of New Mexico and his secretary of corrections in an effort to force extensive changes. Handing down the more than hundred-page **Durán Consent Decree** in 1979, a U.S. district court ordered that improvements in conditions at the prison begin immediately. Little had happened by early 1980, though, adding to frustration and friction within the prison's walls.

Poorly paid, inadequately trained guards made the situation far worse. With low starting salaries, four out of every five guards quit within the first year of their service. New guards were so urgently needed that most rookies were put on duty before they received much, if any, training. Of those who remained, several were known as brutal and abusive, according to complaints prisoners filed.

With few guards, prison authorities had to rely on informants, known as snitches, in the prisoner population to know what was happening in the prison from day to day. Other prisoners so hated the snitches that most were housed in a specially guarded area, the prison's notorious Cellblock 4.

All these conditions contributed to the outbreak of the prison riot that began at 1:45 a.m. on Saturday, February 2, 1980, when prisoners jumped a poorly trained rookie guard. Within twenty-five minutes rioters had taken control of the entire institution. Twelve of the fifteen guards on duty were taken hostage and, in eight cases, tortured. Thirty-three inmates (including a dozen in Cellblock 4) were brutally murdered. Another hundred inmates were beaten or raped. While horror reigned within, many inmates fled to safety in the prison's exterior exercise yard. Friends and relatives parked on the road outside the prison, anxiously awaiting news of their loved ones among the inmates and captured guards.

Prisoner Mike Rolland recalls the first moments of the bloody nightmare:

> I had been kicked-back reading in bed for about twenty minutes when I noticed the lights blink on in the cellblock through the small window in my cell door. I didn't pay it any particular attention [until] someone ran by my cell door. I dropped the magazine and got up to see what was happening. . . . Then I heard the lock box open that controls the cell doors on the bottom floor. . . . [D]oors were pushed open and convicts streamed out of their cells. . . . I couldn't fathom what was going on. Nothing like this had ever occurred at

ignored or not enforced sufficiently to be effective. Much had been done, but much more demanded attention.

High crime rates were yet another problem typically caused by rapid urban growth, among other reasons. Conditions at the state penitentiary in Santa Fe had grown so crowded, corrupt, and miserable by 1980

this time of night. Then I heard the lock box again and felt my cell door tremble [and open when I pushed against it]. It dawned on me then and I said out loud, "This is the riot, the takeover that everyone's been talking about." We stood there and watched as the riot got in full swing.

(Mike Rolland, *Descent into Madness: An Inmate's Experience of the New Mexico State Prison Riot* [Cincinnati: Anderson Publishing, 1997], 21.)

Burned out cell after the Santa Fe prison riot, 1980

In the course of the thirty-six-hour riot, Rolland witnessed scenes of brutal horror and destruction such as he had never seen before. Rolland described how the inmates used fire, picks, knives, pipes, blowtorches, and any other weapon they could find to commit murders and leave most of the prison in ruins. Somehow Rolland survived to tell his dreadful story.

Gov. Bruce King responded to this crisis by calling in the state police and the New Mexico National Guard. Finally, on Sunday, February 3, national guardsmen stormed the facility and regained control of the devastated prison.

The Santa Fe prison riot, second in death toll only to New York's Attica prison riot of 1971, led to changes in the New Mexico prison system. New prisons in Los Lunas and Grants reduced overcrowding in Santa Fe, where a new, more secure facility replaced the old, largely destroyed prison. Prisoners were classified and separated based on the nature of their crimes and their threat to security. New guards received higher pay and better training.

Much remained to be done, though, especially as the crime rate in New Mexico continued to rise. The Durán Consent Decree was not always enforced well, and the decree had expired by 1999. Many New Mexicans expressed their concern that not enough had been done and that the potential for new trouble in the state's prisons remained high.

that inmates rioted in what became the second worst prison riot in U.S. history. The riot ended, but crime continued to rise in New Mexico. Of seven southwestern cities of a similar size, Albuquerque ranked second only to Tucson in crime rate by 1987. That same year, New Mexico ranked eleventh among the states in violent crime rates and seventh in

New Mexico State Governors, 1967–2010

- David F. Cargo, Republican, 1967–70
- Bruce King, Democrat, 1971–74
- Jerry Apodaca, Democrat, 1975–78
- Bruce King, Democrat, 1979–82
- Toney Anaya, Democrat, 1983–86
- Garrey Carruthers, Republican, 1987–90
- Bruce King, Democrat, 1991–94
- Gary E. Johnson, Republican, 1995–2002
- Bill Richardson, Democrat, 2003–10
- Susana Martinez, Republican, 2011–

In addition to its state governor, New Mexico has nineteen Indian tribal governors, leading nineteen Pueblos, and three tribal presidents, leading the Navajo, Jicarilla Apache, and Mescalero Apache reservations. In 1986, **Verna Williamson-Teller** made Indian and state history by becoming the first woman elected as the governor of a New Mexico Pueblo.

crime overall. While there were 5,550 crimes committed for every ten thousand people in the United States, there were 6,547 crimes committed for every ten thousand residents of New Mexico.

Central Avenue, once Albuquerque's main street and entryway for travelers on Route 66, symbolized these deteriorating conditions. By the 1970s, this once proud route had become better known for its dangerous vice and criminal activity than for its modern motels and stores. ❖

1. What is meant by civil disobedience? How did Dr. Martin Luther King, Jr., use civil disobedience to lead peaceful opposition to racism in the United States?

2. How did César Chávez, Dolores Huerta, and their fellow members of the United Farm Workers use civil disobedience to win migrant workers' rights?

3. What were Reies López Tijerina's goals in organizing La Alianza Federal de Mercedes in New Mexico?

4. What protest methods did López Tijerina first use? How did his methods change over time? What impact did this change have on his movement, its support, and its chances of success?

5. Should teachers teach cultural appreciation and pride to their students? Why or why not?

6. How did Hispanic activists assert their rights on New Mexico campuses? In politics?

7. Do you agree or disagree with Gov. Toney Anaya's conversion of death-row convictions in 1986? Why?

8. Do you agree or disagree with the elimination of capital punishment? Why?

9. How did Native Americans attempt to assert their rights in Gallup? In Farmington? In Taos Pueblo? Were they successful?

10. Can bullying be considered a hate crime? Why?

11. What was the original goal of U.S. involvement in Vietnam? Why did this goal become so controversial by the late 1960s and early 1970s?

12. What issues caused protests at the University of New Mexico? What methods of protest did UNM activists use?

13. What caused the tragic events of May 8, 1970, on the UNM campus? What could the protestors, political leaders, and national guardsmen have done differently to avoid such a confrontation?

14. Describe the tragic impact of the Vietnam conflict on many Vietnam veterans and their families.

15. How did New Mexico's role in the Cold War change or remain the same in the later years of that worldwide conflict?

16. Describe several main dangers of New Mexico's role in the later years of the Cold War.

17. What made New Mexico's economy so vulnerable to national and international changes from 1965 to 1995? How did this vulnerability affect communities like Roswell, Grants, Hobbs, Farmington and Los Alamos?

18. How did the Cold War end? How did the end of the Cold War affect New Mexico?

19. What indicators can be used to measure urban growth in cities like Albuquerque?

20. What existing economic activities stimulated urban growth? What new economic activities further stimulated growth?

21. What bold actions did people like Ben Abruzzo, Maxie Anderson, Bill Gates, and Paul Allen take when many dismissed their dreams as "crazy ideas"?

22. What problems accompanied modern growth?

23. What problems caused the Santa Fe prison riot of 1980? How might these problems have been prevented?

24. What can be done to help prevent crime in New Mexico?

25. What aspects of New Mexico would you have been proud of if you had lived in the last thirty years of the Cold War? Why?

26. What aspects would you have been less proud of if you had lived in the last thirty years of the Cold War? Why?

27. What lessons can we learn from the history of this period of conflict and growth?

Current Issues
1995–Present

1950

Artist William Longley creates a female figure, representing fertility, on a wall of the new state capitol building; the figure is later removed

1972

Someone chiseled out the word "savage," which described Native Americans, on the Monument to the Veterans in the Santa Fe plaza

1973

The U.S. government establishes the Endangered Species Act

1974

John Nichols writes *The Milagro Beanfield War,* warning against rapid modernization in New Mexico

1982

375 New Mexicans killed in DWI accidents

1983

The Isleta Bingo Palace opens, becoming the first Indian gaming business in New Mexico

1992

Melanie Cravens and her three daughters are killed by a drunken driver driving the wrong way on I-40

1994

The New Mexico state lottery is established

1995

Robert R. Chavez is killed in a motorcycle accident while driving with more than twice the legal blood-alcohol limit

1997

Gov. Gary Johnson signs gaming compacts with New Mexico's Indian tribes

1998

Someone cuts off the right foot from a statue of Don Juan de Oñate on the four-hundredth anniversary of the Spanish conquest of New Mexico

The U.S. Fish and Wildlife Service reintroduces Mexican gray wolves into the New Mexico and Arizona wilderness

1999

New Mexico ranks eighteenth among the states in the trade of high-tech products

2002

346 Mexican immigrants die from exposure while trying to cross the U.S.-Mexican border into the United States

2006

Five members of the Paul Gonzales family are killed by a drunken driver driving the wrong way on I-25

2007

Archeological evidence of an ancient culture is destroyed during construction of a new Albuquerque high school

☀ Introduction

We have learned a great deal about major controversies, attempted solutions, and, in many cases, continued debate in New Mexico history. Twelve of these famous controversies involved:

- women's rights, as won with the Nineteenth Amendment and New Mexico's Equal Rights Amendment;
- civil rights, as with integration, voting rights, and fair employment and housing practices;
- workers' rights, as fought for in the Gallup coal strike of 1933 and in the Salt of the Earth copper strike from 1950 to 1952;
- teaching evolution in public schools, as contested in Fort Sumner in 1924;
- prohibition, as attempted from 1920 to 1933;
- separation of church and state, as in the Dixon public school case;
- religious rights, as with Taos Pueblo's struggle for Blue Lake;
- land grants, as with La Alianza Federal de Mercedes movement of the 1960s;
- freedom of speech, as with McCarthyism in the late 1940s and 1950s;
- capital punishment, as with Gov. Toney Anaya's clemency act of 1986;
- economic dependency, as with boom-bust cycles in towns like Roswell and Grants;
- and environmental issues, as in uranium mining, WIPP, dangerous factories, and urban pollution.

Deaths Caused by Drunken Driving in New Mexico	
1996	235
1997	213
1998	188
1999	193
2000	195
2001	201
2002	219
2003	198
2004	213
2005	184
Total	**2,039**

(*Albuquerque Journal*, May 5, 2002; Mothers Against Drunk Driving, New Mexico Chapter.)

Impatient with the slow progress and limited results of many reforms, some men and women have attempted to resolve these controversies with violent means, including raids, kidnappings, and even murder. In every case, violence failed to solve existing problems and, without exception, only made matters worse.

Fortunately, many men and women tried to solve controversies with more peaceful methods through civil disobedience, negotiations, lawsuits, and the passage of important new laws. Not every issue was resolved peacefully, but the odds of solution were far better than if people resorted to violence instead. This is a valuable lesson to be learned from history: no matter how difficult the problem, it can be solved, especially if New Mexicans rely on peaceful methods, rather than violent, destructive, and harmful acts.

The purpose of this chapter is to

- identify eight of the most important issues still facing New Mexico today;
- consider different points of view regarding each of these controversies;
- and think about how we, as responsible New Mexico citizens, can help solve these difficult issues in the best interest of the state and its people.

Issue #1

Driving While Intoxicated (DWI)

The Issue

There are no two sides regarding the issue of driving while intoxicated, or DWI. This crime has caused endless misery, especially when it has led to so many senseless deaths: the intoxicated drivers', their passengers', and their victims' in other vehicles. An average of more than two hundred New Mexico men, women, and children were killed in DWI accidents each year from 1996 to 2005.

Many ideas have been suggested or attempted to try to stop DWI tragedies in New Mexico, including:

- teaching children at an early age so that they will learn about the tragic consequences caused by alcohol and drugs;
- having family members and friends insist that loved ones with drinking or drug problems get immediate help with counseling and treatment;

Victims of DWI: Melanie Cravens and Her Daughters, 1992

On Christmas Eve in 1992, Melanie Cravens, her husband, and her three young daughters were driving on I-40 when their car was hit in a head-on collision with a truck traveling more than ninety miles an hour in the wrong direction. Melanie, age thirty-one, and her daughters, Kandyce, age nine; Erin, age eight; and Kacee, age five; were killed in the tragic accident. Only Melanie's husband, Paul Cravens, survived. The driver of the other vehicle was driving while intoxicated. Gordon House served a long prison term for a crime for which he is deeply sorry and that has damaged both the Cravens family's and his family's lives forever. The *Albuquerque Journal* reports that "Drunken driving is the leading cause of injury and death for New Mexicans between the ages of one and forty-four." The problem is especially serious among teenagers. About five hundred teenagers a year were arrested for DWI in New Mexico in the 1990s. And according to the *Journal*, "A person who begins drinking at age sixteen or seventeen has a four to five times greater chance of becoming involved in an alcohol-related crash as an adult."

Descansos, or roadside crosses, often mark the place where a death caused by drunken driving occurred

Victims of DWI: The Paul Gonzales Family, 2006

Paul Gonzales and his wife, Renee, were driving to their home in Las Vegas, New Mexico, after attending a soccer tournament in Bernalillo when Dana Papst drove his pickup truck head-on into the Gonzaleses' van. Papst, who had been drinking on his airplane flight from Phoenix, bought even more alcohol at a convenience store after landing. By the time of the crash, Papst's blood-alcohol level was four times the legal limit. He was so drunk that he was driving the wrong way on I-25 when he crashed into the Gonzales family near Santa Fe.

The crash was so terrible that Paul and Renee Gonzales and three of their daughters, Selena, age ten; Jacqueline, age eleven; and Alicia, age seventeen; were killed. Only their fifteen-year-old daughter, Arissa, and the family's puppy, Amor, survived. Dana Papst died within hours.

The shocked community of Las Vegas mourned the highly respected Gonzales family with a memorial created in their front yard and with special ceremonies held at the schools the girls attended.

Victims of DWI: Robert R. Chavez, 1995

Robert R. Chavez was first arrested for DWI ...at age seventeen. His blood-alcohol content was a staggering .19—more than twice the current legal limit.

[In court Chavez was sent to an alcohol treatment program and given] probation for six months in exchange for the charge being dismissed.

He completed the probation, but apparently didn't get the message about drinking and driving.

Chavez was arrested for drunken driving [five years later]...as an adult.... [He] drove drunk for the last time on the evening of February 3, 1995.

He was heading south on Tramway Boulevard on a motorcycle shortly before 10:00 p.m. He was speeding, estimated between 85 and 122 miles per hour.

A teenage girl heading north on Tramway turned west onto Academy Road...[The two vehicles collided.]

Chavez was dead in an instant. His body was torn apart. A severed leg struck the traffic light some eighteen feet above the intersection.

(*Albuquerque Journal*, May 5, 2002.)

- never letting friends or relatives drive when they are under the influence of alcohol or drugs;
- staging larger public campaigns on television and on the Internet to teach New Mexicans of all ages about the dangers of DWI;
- requiring alcohol treatment for all men and women who are arrested for DWI;
- taking away the driving licenses of men and women who are arrested for DWI;
- taking away the vehicles of men and women who are arrested for DWI;
- installing ignition interlocks to prevent those convicted of DWI from driving while under the influence;
- calling #DWI when we see someone we suspect of DWI driving anywhere in New Mexico;
- using newspapers to publish the names and photographs of the men and women who are arrested for DWI;
- hiring more policemen to patrol the streets and staff sobriety checkpoints during frequent DWI superblitzes;
- taking away the liquor licenses of stores or restaurants that sell alcohol to customers who are intoxicated and are later arrested for DWI;

- giving jail terms to bartenders or store employees who sell alcohol to customers who are intoxicated and are later arrested for DWI;
- lowering the legal blood-alcohol limit in New Mexico;
- giving long prison terms to men and women who are arrested for DWI, especially if they are repeat offenders.

 ## Issue #2

Endangered Species

The Issue

The **Endangered Species Act** of 1973 provides protection for fish, wildlife, and plants whose survival as a species is gravely threatened in the United States. These plants and animals must be protected not only for their own survival but also because they play key roles in maintaining an ecological balance in nature.

When included on the endangered species list, a plant or animal is protected with a plan of action drafted and carried out by the U.S. Fish and Wildlife Service in cooperation with local residents and communities. It is against the law to violate the Endangered Species Act, punishable by a fine of up to $5,000 or six months in prison, or both, for a first offense.

Many endangered species have been cared for and released back into the wild in New Mexico, including aplomado falcons and river otters. While the release of falcons and otters stirred no controversy, the release of Mexican spotted owls and silvery minnows sparked bitter debates, although each conflict was eventually resolved through patient negotiations. The main wildlife issue today involves the reintroduction of the **Mexican gray wolf** into New Mexico's southern wilderness.

The Case for Reintroducing the Mexican Gray Wolf

Mexican gray wolves roamed the Southwest for many years before people who feared them resorted to trapping, poisoning, and hunting these animals, often with the encouragement of the federal government. By the early 1940s, gray wolves were on the brink of extinction in the United States. By 1990, only thirty-seven wolves remained alive. None lived in the wilderness; all resided in zoos across the country. Clearly an endangered species, gray wolves have been protected by the Endangered Species Act since 1976.

Mexican gray wolves cartoon

In 1982, the U.S. Fish and Wildlife Service developed a plan to breed the wolves in captivity and release them into their natural habitat. Where, though, could they be released with the least impact on humans, livestock, and domestic animals?

In 1998, the U.S. Fish and Wildlife Service began releasing the wolves back into their historic range in the national forests of southwestern New Mexico and southeastern Arizona. By 2007, there were about fifty-nine wolves in New Mexico and Arizona, including twenty-two living in five packs in New Mexico.

The Case Against Reintroducing the Mexican Gray Wolf

- Saving endangered animals like the gray wolf can lead to the loss of businesses—especially ranches—essential to the well-being of individual families, and, sometimes, whole communities.
- Groups like the New Mexico Cattle Growers Association and the Catron County Commission argue that gray wolves are

Wolves Not Dangerous to Humans

To the Editor:

There has never been a record of a wolf attack on a big or little human being in North America, with the possible exception of [a wolf with] rabies. . . . Wolves have been proven to be beneficial members of a wilderness ecology, in that they largely kill only the old and sick animals, and help keep their numbers down. . . .

I love wolves and have all my long life (I'm eighty-seven)! . . . I give money to rescue them from being euthanized and keep them alive until they die of old age. . . . They won't hurt you unless you attack them. Just watch them and enjoy them in their wild freedom. . . .

Charles H. Rundles
Belén

(Valencia County News-Bulletin, March 31, 2007.)

dangerous to other animals, especially livestock on ranch-
land. Several alpha male wolves have had to be shot for
killing horses and cattle.

- Some also fear that gray wolves may be dangerous to
humans, especially small children in rural areas.

 ## Issue #3

Indian Gaming

The Issue

Native American tribes have long faced the problem of attracting acceptable enterprises to operate businesses on their reservations. Unsafe uranium mines and the firing of employees at the Fairchild plant in Shiprock are
just two examples of unacceptable operations on the Navajo Reservation.

Beginning in 1983 with the opening of the Isleta Bingo Palace, Native
American tribes opened gaming casinos as sources of needed income and
new jobs in New Mexico. Based on the success of these early bingo halls,
many tribes sought to expand their casinos to include other forms of gaming, from slot machines to poker. After many years of political activity
and negotiation, tribal leaders finally secured gaming compacts with New
Mexico Gov. Gary Johnson.

The 1997 compacts opened new economic opportunities for the
tribes, while committing a percentage of all Indian gaming profits to the
state. Although disputed, the compacts still exist, and, as of 2004, there
were fifteen large and small Indian casinos operating in various parts of
New Mexico.

The Case for Indian Gaming

- Indian casinos provide jobs for more than sixteen
thousand Indian and non-Indian employees, helping to
reduce high rates of unemployment on reservations and
in nearby communities.
- With jobs at casinos, young tribal members are less likely to
move from their reservations in search of employment. With
more young people remaining on their home reservations,
Native culture is more likely to be preserved.
- Profits from Indian casinos are used to help tribes build
valuable new facilities, including new housing, health clinics,
schools, senior centers, police stations, and roads.

- Casino profits also help finance important social programs, especially in health care and education.
- Indian casinos attract tourists from outside New Mexico who pay for other, nongambling goods and services that, in turn, profit many off-reservation private businesses.
- Indian casinos often include attractive resorts that offer other forms of recreation, such as golf and concerts, attracting nongaming customers and additional income for the tribes.
- A percent of casino profits is paid to the state. Averaging more than $54 million per year, these funds can be used for programs that benefit all citizens of New Mexico.

Anti-gaming cartoon

- Gambling is permitted at many nonreservation locations, including racetracks, and in the state lottery, approved by New Mexico voters in 1994. If gambling is permitted elsewhere, why should it not be permitted on reservations?
- Programs are in place to help compulsive gamblers. Television ads warn about the problem, a help hotline has been created, and therapy is available for those who suffer from this addiction.

The Case Against Indian Gaming

- As many as 108,000 New Mexicans may be compulsive gamblers, if not addicts. Most gambling addicts do not realize they are addicted and do not seek help to deal with their problem until their addiction causes major crises in their lives. A 1996 study by the New Mexico State Department of Health concluded that one out of every twenty New Mexicans who gamble become seriously addicted. The New Mexico Council on Problem Gambling answered fifty-six hundred calls on its gambling addicts' hotline in 2004 alone.
- People use their money to gamble rather than pay essential bills, including bills for housing, food, and health care for themselves and their families. According to an Albuquerque therapist, "I have five single mothers who are losing their

homes, who have gambled away their children's college funds. Two others are [now] living in their cars with their children."

- While Indian-gaming supporters claim that as much as 30 percent of all casino gamblers are tourists from out of state, those who oppose gaming contend that the number is closer to only about 5 percent.
- Casino jobs are usually low-paying service jobs that offer little opportunity for higher wages or promotions.
- Gambling draws money from true community economic development. In the words of Guy Clark of the New Mexico Coalition Against Gambling, "Gambling is not economic development. It does not add to the economy. It drains the economy."

 ## Issue #4

Mexican Immigration Restriction

The Issue

Mexico is a generally poor nation, where millions of men, women, and children lack employment and enough income to survive, much less improve their social and economic lives. Since the early twentieth century the United States has been seen as a land of opportunity for many Mexicans eager to make better lives for themselves and their families. Most immigrants are men who cross into the United States in search of jobs that can pay enough for them to send most of their money home to support their families in Mexico. Others save for the day when they can have their families join them in the United States.

Mexican immigrants have been welcomed in New Mexico, and much of the rest of the United States, during periods of great labor shortages, as during World War I and World War II. Mexican immigrants have been less welcomed during periods of history when other issues, like economic depressions and international security, have created concerns. Rather than being welcomed, as during the world wars, illegal immigrants and their families are often criticized, mistreated, banned, and even deported.

Although New Mexico offers fewer job opportunities compared to states like California and Texas, the state still draws many illegal immigrants whose presence causes considerable debate, especially along the state's 180-mile border with Mexico. As of 2005, the state's population of illegal immigrants equaled between 50,000 and 65,000, as compared to the estimated 12 million illegal immigrants in the United States as a whole.

The Case for Mexican Immigration Restriction

- The United States needs to secure its borders to help prevent terrorists from entering the country. Although the U.S. Border Patrol caught more than 1.2 million illegal immigrants entering the United States in 2005, it is estimated that four times as many immigrants elude border patrolmen. To secure our borders, we must use one or more of the following strategies:

  - build a formidable fence or wall along much of the U.S.-Mexican border;
  - employ more border patrol officers to watch the border and capture illegal immigrants;
  - deploy national guardsmen to assist the border patrol;
  - use American volunteers, including the Minuteman Defense Corps, to watch the border and assist the Border Patrol;
  - round up all illegal aliens in the United States and force them to return to Mexico;
  - allow Mexican immigrants to apply for worker permits if they want to legally enter or reenter the United States, with each permit costing $3,500.

Immigrant border crossing dangers cartoon

Increased illegal traffic across New Mexico's southern border sometimes led to tragedy as immigrants perished in the desert or in highway crashes.

- Illegal immigrants are often used as human "mules" to smuggle illegal drugs into the United States by car, horseback, or on foot. The U.S. Border Patrol seized a record $122 million worth of drugs from immigrants crossing the border in 2004.
- The number of cases involving illegal immigrants is overwhelming our federal court system. In 1997, New Mexico detained an average of five hundred immigrants per day. The state's average equaled twenty-four hundred a day by 2005.
- Illegal immigrants use schools and public health services without paying taxes that support these

Stopping the Immigration Flood

To the Editor:

What can [we] do about the illegal immigrants that are flooding into this country?

U.S. borders must be sealed, and all persons in the country illegally [must be] deported back to their native countries. Change our laws to deny citizenship to children born in the U.S. to illegal immigrant women. Deny foreign aid to countries that allow their citizens to immigrate to the U.S. illegally.

By stopping the flow of monies from this country sent by illegals to Mexico and other countries, perhaps we would . . . force [these countries] to help their own citizens.

Leroy Lozier
Las Cruces

(*Albuquerque Journal*, December 27, 2005.)

expensive social programs. Some illegal immigrants intentionally give birth to their babies in the United States so that these children are native-born American citizens, with legal rights to all the benefits available to U.S. citizens.

- Illegal immigrants send much of their earnings home to their families in Mexico, sending millions of American dollars out of the country where they cannot benefit American businesses and the U.S. economy as a whole.

- With 5,868 students from illegal immigrant families in the Albuquerque public school system alone, schools have a difficult time teaching students whose education has suffered from frequent moves and general poverty. These students can affect the quality of education provided to other students and can prevent schools from meeting the educational standards set by the federal government for continued funding.

- Offering amnesty and an easy path to U.S. citizenship will only encourage more immigrants to enter the United States.

- Illegal immigrants accept low wages, driving down wages for nonimmigrant American laborers.

The Case Against Mexican Immigration Restriction

- The cost of building a fence or wall along the entire U.S.-Mexican border would equal between $851 million (for a standard ten-foot-high prison chain link fence topped by razor wire) and $2 billion (for a twelve-foot-high, two-foot-thick concrete wall). It would only be a matter of time before immigrants could climb over or dig under even the most expensive fence or wall. This money would be far better spent on other, more efficient, solutions to the immigration problem.
- If illegal immigrants are rounded up in raids on their homes and workplaces, force may be used, and people may get killed or injured.
- If illegal immigrants are rounded up and are forced to leave the United States, what will happen to their children who are often U.S. citizens and will not be made to leave?
- The United States needs immigrants to work in low-paying jobs that must be done, but most American citizens refuse to do, in agriculture, construction, landscaping, maintenance, food service, health care, and many other service industries.
- Most immigrants are healthy young people who come to the United States for work and not for special treatment in health care, education, and other public services. A 2005 *Albuquerque Journal* survey found that 72 percent of New Mexicans favor providing emergency medical care for illegal immigrants and their children. Of those surveyed, 54 percent agreed that public school education should be available for family members of illegal immigrants.
- Since illegal immigrants live in fear of being identified and deported, many do not apply for government services other than emergency health care and schooling for their children.
- Illegal immigrants pay income taxes and sales taxes that benefit our state, local, and national governments. They also pay into the social security system, although they are not allowed to collect social security benefits.
- Citizen volunteers, like the Minutemen, are not well trained and may resort to violence or other illegal measures in confronting immigrants crossing the border.
- The U.S. border with Canada is far longer and less secure, meaning that immigrants who are true security risks are far more likely to enter the United States from the north via Canada than from the south via Mexico. Using security

issues to oppose Mexican immigration is simply a way to mask racist prejudice against Mexican immigrants.

- Crossing the U.S.-Mexican border is expensive and often dangerous, leaving illegal immigrants penniless and, in 346 cases in 2002, dead from exposure to extreme desert conditions, where temperatures can soar to as high as 130 degrees in the summer months. In especially tragic cases, coyotes, or human smugglers, charge thousands of dollars only to take the immigrants' money and then abandon helpless men and women in the border wilderness.

- The cost of proposed worker permits is higher than the price usually charged by coyotes, meaning that Mexican immigrants will likely continue to cross into the U.S. illegally because the cost of paying a coyote is often lower than the cost of taking a legal route into the United States.

- Immigrants who have an opportunity to become American citizens are among our nation's best, most loyal citizens. Many have worked hard and opened their own businesses. Others have put their lives at risk and have died for the United States while serving in the U.S. armed forces during periods of war. A Mexican immigrant, Octaviano Ambrosio Larrazolo, Sr., served as New Mexico's fourth state governor (1919–21) and as the first Hispanic senator in the U.S. Senate (1928–29).

 Issue #5

English Only

The Issue

English has been the main language taught, spoken, and read in the United States. Many Americans firmly believe that everyone in this country should speak only English. Others contend that this is unnecessary and is, in fact, harmful. The issue is especially important in New Mexico, where not only many immigrants but also many native residents speak Spanish, Indian languages, or other languages besides English.

The Case for English Only

- If immigrants to the United States want to make their new homes in this country, they must learn the country's main language, even if they speak their native languages privately at home.

- Everyone in the United States needs to know English in order to get good jobs and succeed in the nation's economy.
- If immigrants want to become American citizens someday, they must learn the nation's language to fully participate in our political process.
- Bilingual education only prevents non-English speakers from learning English as quickly and as well as possible.
- Having everyone speak one language is beneficial, especially during emergencies when everyone must be able to communicate quickly and accurately.

The Case Against English Only

- According to the First Amendment, Americans have the right to free speech. The U.S. constitution does not specify which language they are required to speak.

Disaster in the Desert

In June 2003, an inexperienced sixteen-year-old coyote named Diez led a group of illegal immigrants into the northern Mexican desert and across the U.S.-Mexican border:

Diez never knew the names of anyone on the trip. He preferred not to ask. It was business. He didn't want to know their personal lives. Each person would pay him . . . thirteen hundred dollars to have him cross the border. . . .

On the way [to where they would begin their trip], Diez . . . told them not to wear bright clothing that would stand out to a [Border Patrol] helicopter. . . .

[As] they settled into the trip [north to the border by bus], the new acquaintances talked. The conversation naturally drifted to what each hoped from the United States. . . . Visions of ten-dollars-an-hour wages danced before them.

One of the women was . . . determined . . . to work really hard and hoped to earn a lot of money. . . . Her husband had beat [sic] her and left her penniless [with] two children.

She left the kids with her mother [in Mexico]; one day she would send for them. . . .

Before dawn the next morning, they . . . began walking north [across the border].

Together, [Diez's] group carried six limes, cans of corn and sardines, a sheet, a blanket, and twenty-two five-liter bottles of water. . . . No one had sunglasses, and, other than Diez, no one had a hat. . . . [Most] wore the cheap formal shoes that serve as all-purpose footwear for Mexico's poor. The group had eaten very little . . . , conserving their money for what lay ahead.

During the first few hours, the trek proceeded as planned. The group walked single file behind Diez. . . . Within a few hours, though, the sun was high in the sky, and its intensity unnerved the tenderfoots. . . . Each walker quickly learned to concentrate on what was before him. The rocks could twist an ankle. Cactus spines pierced shoe soles. . . . Talking ceased. All their mental energy focused on avoiding the dangers the desert presented with every step.

- The New Mexico state constitution states that Spanish speakers cannot be discriminated against in voting or receiving an education.
- Individuals should speak their native languages to help preserve their cultures, their self-respect, and their self-identity.
- Some of New Mexico's best literature, including poems, fiction, and essays, have been written in Spanish, especially in Spanish-language newspapers.
- Based on oral tradition, much of New Mexico's history and culture has been preserved in Spanish and Native American languages.
- Bilingual education helps preserve native cultures while helping non-English speakers learn English.
- Bilingual education helps English speakers learn other languages and, in the process, understand and respect other cultures.

Four hours into the walk, . . . things began to fall apart. The [woman whose husband had beaten her] couldn't keep up. . . . [Diez] tried to encourage her, but she had to stop. [After resting a few moments] they began walking with her, pulling her along at times. As she walked, she grew delirious. She hallucinated . . . and finally she foamed at the mouth. She collapsed. . . . The woman lurched her head to the side, threw up, and died. . . .

The others gathered around. Looking down at her, the sun above, their shadows fell over her corpse. . . . She'd been talking, hoping. Now she lay dead.

[Some of the immigrants agreed to stay with the woman's body and wait for the border patrol to come by and pick them up. The others continued on with Diez, but they were soon out of water.] Diez's skin burned and was stuck with cactus spines. His face was lacerated from the brush. It was so hot, he felt, that if you had put a plate of beans on his head, it would have cooked.

[O]nly one source of water remained. To survive, Diez told them, they would now have to drink their own urine. . . . Diez was so dehydrated that his body could produce no urine at all. He drank the urine of one of the men from Tijan, [Mexico. Diez was too weak to go on, but told the others how to get to safety.]

The six men . . . stumbled on. . . . Their skin boiled. . . . Their lips were torn and no one could talk. No one cared anymore about the dollars he was going to make.

Finally the small group came to a house where a family sold them water, a few sodas, and some bread for a hundred dollars. The men returned to rescue Diez. Later, most of the survivors got jobs installing carpets at low wages in the United States. They slept on a garage floor. Not knowing English and without legal protection, "they were more or less captive workers of Mr. Quiñónez and his carpet business."

(Sam Quinones, *Antonio's Gun and Delfino's Dream: True Stories of Mexican Immigration* [Albuquerque: University of New Mexico Press, 2007], 150–61.)

▲▲▲▲▲▲▲▲▲▲▲▲▲▲▲▲▲▲▲▲▲▲▲▲▲▲▲▲

You're in America Now

To the Editor:

This last Saturday, while standing in line at [a] McDonald's Restaurant, I noticed that the two young teenage boys standing in front of me were speaking in Spanish. Leaning towards them, I told them softly, "You're in America." They were shocked. . . .

They responded indignantly, in heavy Spanish accents, that this is America and they were free to speak whatever language they wanted. . . .

[But these boys] are doing themselves a disservice by not learning how to speak proper English without an accent. In a few years, when they have graduated from high school, they will be interviewed by people of authority, in a position to make important decisions that will affect their future lives. It could be a prospective employer or the father of the young lady they hope to marry or a recruiter for a university or a recruiting officer for the military services. . . .

Be it fair or not fair is not the question. They will be judged. . . . This is America. English is the official language here.

Martha R. Thomas
Belén

(*Valencia County News-Bulletin*, August 9, 2006.)

- The ability to speak more than one language gives a person a great business and political advantage, especially when dealing with business leaders and citizens of foreign countries.
- Cultural diversity is one of New Mexico's major strengths. Enforcing English Only would only weaken the state's diversity and strength.

 Issue #6

Public Art and Monuments

The Issue

Since the 1930s, state, federal, and local governments have sponsored the creation of public art to decorate public buildings and other public space in New Mexico. Sculptures, murals, and paintings have been

"Miss Fertility" Divided Santa Fe, 1950

Artist William Longley included a nude female figure, representing fertility, on the exterior of the new capitol building under construction in Santa Fe in 1950. A Baptist minister, Robert Brown, objected, arguing, "As a minister of God I feel that this thing is repugnant on a public building."

Many Santa Feans, especially members of the local art colony, disagreed with Reverend Brown, defending the statue, commonly known as "Miss Fertility," and Longley's right to express himself through his art. The editor of the *Santa Fe New Mexican* entered the debate by writing an editorial in which he stated:

> Whether [Miss Fertility] is on the [capitol building's] wall or not won't make much of a difference.... It does make a difference, though, that all public statuary ... must be tailored to fit within the pattern of the most extreme [censure], even in Santa Fe which likes to kid itself about being cultured and cosmopolitan.

(*Santa Fe New Mexican*, October 4, 1950.)

Gov. Thomas J. Mabry resolved this dispute by having the offending image of Miss Fertility removed. Many applauded the governor's action, although other residents of Santa Fe still criticize his decision and oppose similar attempts to censor public art.

placed in schools, libraries, post offices, courthouses, and parks. Artists have been hired to create this art, often leaving the artists to decide about the subject and the meaning of their public work. Many citizens approve of this form of government spending, while others take a dim view of this use of taxpayer money.

The Case for Public Funding of the Arts Without Censure

- Public art enhances the beauty of our public spaces.
- Public art helps preserve our native cultures.
- Based on their First Amendment freedom of speech (expression), artists have the right to express their creative ideas in any way they please. They must not be censored by critics who disagree with their values or goals.

The Case Against Public Funding of the Arts Without Censure

- Tax money should be spent on government services of greater importance, such as health and education, in a poor state like New Mexico.

Albuquerque's so-called "Chevy on a Stick," an example of controversial public art

Statue of Don Juan de Oñate and his fellow Spanish colonists of 1598

Tax money should not be spent on art that may offend the moral standards of tax-paying New Mexico citizens.

In the process of honoring some native cultures, public art or monuments can insult other cultures and their history.

 Issue #7

Modernization and Development

he Issue

Many citizens of New Mexico are eager to develop the state with new industries, new facilities, and modern communities. This growth, or **modernization**, is less welcomed by other New Mexicans who see such rapid change as dangerous, with far more costs than benefits for the state and its citizens.

Santa Fe's Monument to the Soldiers

In 1866, shortly after the Civil War, patriotic New Mexicans erected an obelisk in the center of Santa Fe's town plaza. Each side of the monument honored the memory of U.S. soldiers who had fought in New Mexico. Three of the four sides honored men who had fought in Civil War battles. The fourth side, focusing on the Indian wars, read, "To the heroes who have fallen in the various battles with the savage Indians in the territory of New Mexico."

Many New Mexicans, particularly Native Americans, objected to the word "savage" on the monument. All sides in a battle can be accused of being savage in one way or another. Is it not racist, some asked, to claim that only Native Americans were savage in the Indian wars?

In 1996, historian Tom Chávez was interviewed on a local Santa Fe radio show and was asked to describe what became of the word "savage" on the obelisk. Standing at the controversial north side of the monument, Chávez said:

> Back in the 1960s that word became a source of great questioning why it was there and insisting that it should be taken out. Others argued that it's a historical document, in effect, and it should stay there because it reflects the attitudes of the people of [1866]. . . .
>
> And then one day a guy dressed as a construction worker, who was not an Indian, . . . came in and chiseled [the word "savage"] out. So what you have there where the "savage" was [inscribed is now] just a chiseled . . . empty spot. . . .

(Tom Chávez radio interview, December 1996, as quoted in Ardeth and William Baxter, eds., *The Best of From the Plaza: Interviews and Opinions from the Plaza of Santa Fe* [Santa Fe: Lone Butte Press, 1998]: 13.)

Santa Fe's Monument to the Soldiers

"Land and Water Inseparable" sign

The Case for Rapid Modernization and Development

- Modernization brings new public facilities into a community. These facilities include new parks, sewer systems, sidewalks, streetlights, and roads that benefit all residents of growing cities and towns.
- Modernization brings new public services into a community. These services include

Don Juan de Oñate's Foot, 1998

In 1998, New Mexico celebrated the four hundredth anniversary of Don Juan de Oñate's conquest of 1598—or at least most Hispanics celebrated Oñate's anniversary. Many Native Americans did not, remembering the Spanish leader's treatment of Indian men, women, and children following the Acoma Revolt of 1598. In particular, many Native Americans opposed the creation of a public statue, built with public funds, to honor a man they considered to be their enemy.

> Gordon Church
> Public Arts Program
> City of Albuquerque
> P.O. Box 1293
> Albuquerque, New Mexico 87103
>
> Dear Mr. Church:
>
> This letter is written to protest the use of tax dollars to fund a memorial project "honoring" Don Juan de Oñate and [his] Spanish colonizers. . . .
>
> [Oñate is] remembered for committing one of the greatest atrocities in New Mexico recorded history by sentencing Acoma captives to a cruel and inhumane punishment. He ordered all men over twenty-five years old to have their right foot cut off. He also had women and children enslaved. Many were sent to live and die in Mexico.
>
> For the city of Albuquerque to use public money to honor such a controversial figure is outrageous. Would the city for one second consider such a monument for a historic figure like Hitler?
>
> Sincerely,
> Conroy Chino

(*Albuquerque Journal*, February 1, 1998.)

Oñate's Hispanic defenders replied to these charges and proposed a statue for the conqueror, arguing that "the sentence imposed [by Oñate] was intended to punish the Indians who had rebelled [against the Spanish] and to serve as a warning to other pueblos. From Oñate's perspective, it was important to send a message because unified pueblo opposition . . . would, most likely, have been successful in driving the Spanish settlers out of New Mexico."

(John P. Salazar, "There's More to Oñate Than Event at Acoma," *Albuquerque Journal*, February 19, 1998.)

With all this controversy, even an existing statue of Oñate was "attacked" early in his anniversary year. Symbolically, the right foot of Oñate's bronze statue in Alcalde, New Mexico, was removed and never returned—although a replacement was welded on soon after.

The statue that was finally built in Old Town Albuquerque in 1998 was carefully designed to honor the Spanish settlers and their families who arrived with Oñate, if not Oñate himself.

new or improved education, emergency medical care, police protection, fire protection, and public transportation that benefit all residents of growing cities and towns.

- Modernization often brings modern stores and businesses that offer easy access and affordable prices for needed goods and services.
- When carefully selected and monitored, "clean" modern industry can bring new jobs and promote local economic development without the hazards of air, water, soil, and noise pollution. High-tech companies are particularly clean and attractive. Successful in attracting many of these companies, New Mexico ranked eighteenth among the fifty states as an exporter of high-tech products by 1999, up from twenty-eighth among the states the previous year.
- Modern industry often contributes funds to important community projects. Intel, for example, has contributed millions of dollars for road improvements, a new library, and, most of all, a large new high school in Rio Rancho. The Louisiana Energy Services Company, which owns a new uranium-enrichment plant in southeastern New Mexico, contributed funds to improve the local water system, renovate the local swimming pool, and hire additional local policemen for the town of Eunice, even before the plant began operations.
- Modernization attracts new industries and businesses that employ New Mexicans in jobs at all levels.
- Modernization will help New Mexico become a center of important high-tech projects of the future. In southern New Mexico, for example, a new spaceport, known as **Spaceport America**, is being planned on twenty-eight acres north of Las Cruces. The spaceport will launch commercial satellites as well as private passenger vehicles (at $200,000 per passenger ticket) into space.

The Case Against Rapid Modernization and Development

- Modernization brings urban development, which threatens small town and rural lifestyles and land uses.
- Traditional cultures are swept away by the speed and sameness of mainstream modern American culture.
- Although laws exist that require that new building sites must be studied for their archeological value, sites are not always studied thoroughly enough to avoid major, irreversible damage to ancient evidence of previous cultures.
- Even when carefully selected, so-called "clean industries" can cause air, water, soil, or noise pollution. In Clovis, for example, many applauded the planned building of an ethanol plant three miles from the center of town. The plant, which would use corn to produce 110 million gallons of ethanol fuel each year, was said to be "clean" because it met all state and federal air-quality standards. Residents living closest to the site disagreed, arguing that while pollutants from the plant would not affect most of Clovis's thirty-three thousand residents, they would affect residents living in neighborhoods nearest the plant most directly. Even if low-level pollutants were not immediately harmful, no one knows their long-term effects on the health of nearby residents, most of whom are of Hispanic and African American descent. Similar concerns have been expressed on the Navajo Reservation where a coal-fired electric power plant is planned at a site south of Farmington. Opponents of the Desert Rock Power Plant are

Evidence of Ancient Culture Destroyed at Volcano Vista High School Construction Site, 2007

Construction of a waterline for the new Northwest [Albuquerque] high school has ruined part of a prehistoric site that an archeologist says is the first proof of Folsom culture presence in the Albuquerque basin.

Although Albuquerque Public Schools designed the school to avoid the Boca Negra Wash Folsom Site and hired archeologists to help plan around it, engineering plans for the water line failed to mark the archeologically sensitive area. . . . Because the Folsom site is shallow [about a foot below the surface], damage started when crews were clearing the area before digging [even] began.

(*Albuquerque Journal*, January 29, 2007.)

▲▲▲▲▲▲▲▲▲▲▲▲▲▲▲▲▲▲▲▲▲▲▲▲▲▲▲▲

Warnings from John Nichols's *The Milagro Beanfield War*

In 1974, John Nichols wrote one of the most famous novels in twentieth-century New Mexico literature. *The Milagro Beanfield War* is about a traditional, largely Hispanic town called Milagro that faces rapid modern change with the building of a major resort, complete with summer homes and a golf course. The resort threatens local water rights, natural landscape, and traditional culture enjoyed by the people of Milagro.

In one of the novel's most memorable scenes, Charley Bloom, a sympathetic lawyer, speaks at a town meeting and warns local residents that

> when middle-class or wealthy people from other states [buy] expensive vacation homes up in the canyon or around the golf course . . . , they [will] want a school for their children, sewer systems, a cleaner water supply, and for that all the people of Milagro would have to pay.

Bloom also argued that it was a

> myth that this development would bring wealth to every inhabitant, and jobs and security for all. . . . Skilled construction workers and technicians were always brought from the outside. For the poor and the rural people [little would change], except that in taking service jobs for low wages, they [would] no longer have the time to work their land, and so [would wind up] selling it, only to discover themselves poorer than before, with not even the security of their own land and a home on it to take the sting out of [their lives] of poverty.

(John Nichols, *The Milagro Beanfield War* [New York: Ballantine Books, 1974], 208–9.)

Many New Mexicans believed that what Charley Bloom warned about for Milagro in fiction could be applied to dozens of rural communities in reality.

deeply concerned about air pollution from the plant, pointing out that coal-fired power plants are the largest single source of global warming pollution in the world.

- Modernization often brings increased road traffic, which adds to air pollution, noise pollution, and the cost of new or expanded road construction.
- Modern highways, like I-10, I-25, and I-40, often bypass small towns, causing great harm to local businesses that depend on money spent by travelers.
- Large, modern stores often charge lower prices, causing smaller stores to lose business and close down. Knowing this, residents of several communities, including Albuquerque and Santa Fe, have filed lawsuits to prevent the construction of superstores

▲▲▲▲▲▲▲▲▲▲▲▲▲▲▲▲▲▲▲▲▲▲▲▲▲▲▲▲▲▲▲▲

It's Time to Put an End to Growth in Albuquerque

To the Editor:

It is time to put an end to growth [in Albuquerque]. Consider the consequences of all this growth. It has meant an inevitable growth in taxes. These taxes are used . . . to build more schools, more sewers, more water lines, more public transportation, more roads, more hospital rooms.

[As a result,] we use more and more [water] because of the growth in population. . . . Population growth has jammed our roadways with resultant injuries and death from accidents. Our air is increasingly polluted, which means additional taxing of the resources for health care. . . .

Crime is at an all-time high and many of us who have been victimized by burglaries see these same people back on the street because we don't have facilities to house them [all in prison].

The price of land and homes [continues to rise], increasing the cost of living.

More taxes, more pollution, more traffic, more consumption of non-renewable resources, more crime, more shortages of health care, [and] more prisons are but a few of the reasons we need to put a stop to growth.

Let us build a comfortable oasis in the desert for our present populace and let others have their growth [elsewhere].

Rev. Jim Anderson
Albuquerque

(*Albuquerque Journal,* August 22, 2006.)

---

in their neighborhoods. Residents are also concerned about the increased traffic and accidents that usually accompany the building of "big-box" stores in a neighborhood.

- Modernization will mar New Mexico's remarkable natural beauty.
- New housing developments are often built without plans for **wildlife corridors**, where plants and animals can continue to survive in their native habitat.
- Modernization causes such high taxes and such a high cost of living that many families can no longer afford to live in growing cities and towns like Albuquerque, Santa Fe, and Taos, although many had lived in these communities for generations.

A Bridge in Tomé?

Tomé is a small, rural community, founded in 1739 when a Spanish governor granted the land to a small group of colonial settlers. After heated debate, the settlers' heirs voted to sell the land grant to a land-development company in the 1960s. By the 1990s, several modern, new housing developments had been built on the old land grant, increasing traffic and leading to a new debate regarding a proposed new bridge across the Rio Grande, connecting Tomé, on the east side of the river, to I-25, on the west side. The debate pitted those who wanted modern development, including the bridge, and those who hoped to preserve as much as they could of their peaceful rural heritage.

For the Bridge:
The *Albuquerque Journal* ran a three-part series about the bridge dispute, quoting a resident of one of the new subdivisions built on the old Tomé land grant. This new resident commuted to his job in Albuquerque and argued that "with all the growth [near Tomé], a bridge is eventually going to have to be built, either now or later, and it's probably better to do it now."

Against the Bridge:
Tomé residents who opposed the construction of a bridge expressed their strong feelings at public meetings, in letters to newspaper editors, with street signs, with a new community organization, and even with an antibridge float in the Fourth of July parade held in neighboring Los Lunas in 2000.

Men and women on the parade float tossed flyers to the crowd. The flyer, entitled, "Why We're Against a New Bridge in Valencia County," argued that the bridge would hurt local wildlife, the environment, agricultural lifestyles, and spiritual traditions. The flyer focused on **urban sprawl**, or unplanned urban development, in particular:

Developers and promoters want a new bridge . . . to sell their uncontrolled, high density, single family housing developments. This is sprawl, which rarely pays for its required road, school, police, fire, water, and sewage infrastructure. Everyone's taxes increase. Sprawl generates more traffic, [major] air pollution, [and] demands for additional roads.

Antibridge activists cele-brated when they learned that the state highway department had finally abandoned its plans to build a new river crossing in Tomé. But not all communities have been as successful in their opposition to new roads and bridges. Residents in Albuquerque's North Valley could not stop the construction of a new two-lane bridge (which soon expanded to four lanes) on Montaño Boulevard. Native Americans, despite their considerable opposition, could not stop the building of a major new road near ancient petroglyphs, considered sacred to the Pueblo Indians, on Albuquerque's west mesa.

- The cost of modern enterprises is often passed on to tax-payers who may or may not benefit from these projects. For example, $115 million in state taxes have been committed to the construction of Spaceport America in southern New Mexico. Additional tax money for the project is being raised through a tax increase in three southern counties. These funds would be better spent in helping the thousands of poor families who will seldom benefit from a spaceport any-where near their homes and communities. In the words of one Spaceport opponent, "Don't tax me to send somebody to space so that my daughter can go to make beds in the hotels [the rich space travelers] will sleep in."
- The best jobs in modern, high-tech industries often go to out-of-state applicants and not to native New Mexicans. According to the U.S. Census of 2000, 890,000 of New Mexico's 1.8 million residents, or 49 percent, are not native to the state. Almost 1.6 million native New Mexicans now live in other states. Only about 2 percent of these natives ever return to New Mexico to live and work.
- Modern, high-tech industries often eliminate jobs through automation.
- Modern industries can suddenly reduce production (leading to a loss of jobs) or completely move to other, often foreign, sites where safety standards, environmental controls, and pay scales are lower.
- Modern industries with headquarters located outside New Mexico only increase the state's dependence on distant centers of control.
- Modernization requires far more water than a desert state like New Mexico can provide.

 ## Issue #8

Water Rights and Usage

The Issue

"La agua es la vida" ("water is life") has long been a popular saying in New Mexico. There is a limited amount of water, though, and many years the state suffers extreme droughts, making the normal amount of usable water even less available. Most water in the state is already

Waiting for Rain on the Llano

Fabiola Cabeza de Baca was born and raised on a ranch on the llano, or plains, of eastern New Mexico. Recalling her childhood days, Fabiola wrote that

> From the time I was three years old . . . I began to understand that without rain our subsistence would be endangered. I never went to bed without praying for rain. . . . My friends in the city would be upset when rain spoiled a day's outing, but I always was glad to see it come. In the years of drought, Papa's blue eyes were sad, but when the rains poured down, his eyes danced like the stars in the heavens. . . .
>
> Rain for us made history. It brought to our minds days of plenty, of happiness and security. . . . The droughts were as impressed on our souls as the rains. . . . We knew that the east wind brought rain, but if the winds persisted from other directions we knew we were doomed.
>
> (Fabiola Cabeza de Baca, *We Fed Them Cactus* [Albuquerque: University of New Mexico Press, 1954], 11–12.)

Fabiola's ranch was typical of thousands of farms and ranches in New Mexico, long ago and now.

appropriated, or assigned, so existing water rights are often lost in order to meet new demands.

The conflict focuses on which existing water rights will be kept and which will be sacrificed for new uses. Small farmers and traditional acequia communities usually suffer the most in the redistribution of water resources. Large businesses and urban consumers usually benefit the most. Intel, in Rio Rancho, used 2 to 3 million gallons of water per day *prior to* its enormous plant expansion in the 1990s. In Albuquerque, each urban family uses about 100 gallons of water per day; the city as a whole uses more than 300 million gallons of water each day. In another popular expression, it is said that "water flows uphill to money."

Many argue that New Mexico's aquifers, or underground water caverns, hold enough water to serve current needs as well as meet water demands well into the future. Others say that these natural reservoirs are being used up quickly by overly optimistic developers, with little thought to wise planning in rapidly growing cities like Albuquerque, Rio Rancho, Santa Fe, and Las Cruces.

Water problems affect small towns as well. In Truth or Consequences, for example, spa water has long been used for its therapeutic value. Small

2-13-02

Some nearby residents complained the plant was emitting toxins, but tests were inconclusive.

Concerns about Intel cartoon

businessmen who own spa resorts are concerned that new users, including new residential neighborhoods and the planned Spaceport south of their community, will draw off water the spa owners need to stay in business and serve their guests.

New Mexicans cannot rely on their rivers as consistent sources of needed water. Droughts limit the amount of water in our rivers, especially after mild winters when there has been little snowfall, meaning that there is little snow that can melt and run off as water in the spring and summer. River water is limited even during good snow years because New Mexico must share

Water Haulers on the Navajo Reservation

In many parts of New Mexico people have little or no access to water. On the Navajo Reservation an estimated seventy thousand tribal members are without running water. As a result, water must be hauled to homes and ranches on trucks; many people resort to collecting water from their roofs when and if it rains. Families have to use their water carefully for drinking, cooking, and bathing as well as to water their crops and livestock. Sanitation is a problem, as are illnesses that often result from poor sanitation.

The federal government has promised new water pipelines for thirty years. In the words of a seventy-seven-year-old Navajo, "I believe the government has forgotten us down here." Not optimistic about his chances of having access to water in his lifetime, this man only wishes that his grandchildren will someday be able to take showers in their own homes. Ironically, most of the water from the San Juan Basin on or near the Navajo Reservation is sent for use in Santa Fe and Albuquerque, where the average modern household uses more than a hundred gallons of water per day.

A new water-rights settlement has been made with the Navajo tribe, although many tribal members are understandably leery of the agreement and wonder if and when it will finally be enforced.

Cutting Back on Water Usage

With so little water in New Mexico, we must all think about how we can reduce the amount of water we use each day. Large users must cut back, but so should individuals and families if we are to have enough water in the future.

Here are just a few of the many ways in which we can reduce our daily use of this most valuable resource:

- Report water breaks.
- Fix leaky faucets, toilets, and water sprinklers. A small leak from a worn faucet washer can waste as much as twenty gallons of water per day.
- Take shorter showers. A four-minute shower uses between twenty and forty gallons of water.
- Close the tap while brushing your teeth; only use water to rinse your mouth.
- Only run washing machines and dishwashers when they have full loads.
- Turn off the hose while you are soaping your car during a car wash; only use the hose for rinsing. As much as 150 gallons of water can be saved in this way.
- Water plants and lawns in the morning hours rather than in the afternoon when it is hotter and water will evaporate more quickly.
- Avoid watering plants and lawns when it is windy. The wind blows the water away from plants and lawns and only speeds evaporation.
- Xeriscape yards, using mostly drought-resistant native plants, little water, and Southwest landscaping.
- Become active in community planning, questioning new businesses and developments that may consume large amounts of scarce water.

(http://eartheasy.com/live_water_saving.htm)

this valuable resource with its neighbors, especially Colorado, Texas, and Mexico, where our main river, the Rio Grande, originates and drains off into the Gulf of Mexico. New Mexico has faced many lawsuits regarding its river resources; regrettably, it has lost many of these suits to its neighbors, making what water remains even more scarce and valuable.

Scientists predict that **global warming** will make our Southwest climate even more arid, creating many more and much longer droughts.

Only a reduction in greenhouse gas emissions and other environmentally responsible reforms will slow global warming and help prevent droughts and similarly devastating natural disasters in the future.

It is no wonder that water remains New Mexico's number-one issue. Many contend that it is the main issue facing the entire West. ✦

☀ A Final Thought about New Mexico's Past and Future

History is like a long river, along which each generation travels on its own small craft. The river's course is constantly changing; some sections are smooth and easy, while others are full of rapids, snags, and other dangerous obstacles.

No part of the journey is exactly alike, but each generation can navigate its present course much better if it learns about and remembers how previous generations in history navigated similar sections of the river.

We will confront many snags, or issues, in our part of the river journey, but we will be better equipped to deal with them and avoid new obstacles if we remember what lessons we have learned from New Mexico's past. The more history we know, the more skills and equipment we have to complete our trip successfully. The fewer navigational skills and equipment we utilize, the less likely we will be able to enjoy and complete our journey, much less set our children's generation on a straight, peaceful, happy course of its own.

1. What can be done to stop DWI tragedies? Which solutions do you support as effective ways to stop DWI in New Mexico?

2. Do you think that Mexican gray wolves should be reintroduced in New Mexico? Why or why not?

3. Do you support Indian gaming in New Mexico? Why or why not?

4. Do you favor Mexican immigration restriction in New Mexico and the rest of the United States? Why or why not?

5. Do you favor English Only in New Mexico and the rest of the United States? Why or why not?

6. Do you support public funding for art? Why or why not?

7. Do you support rapid modernization and development in New Mexico? Why or why not?

8. What do you think can be done to solve New Mexico's water problems?

9. What aspects of New Mexico are you most proud of in dealing with our current issues? Why?

10. What aspects of New Mexico are you less proud of in dealing with our current issues? Why?

11. What lessons can we learn from dealing with the many importat issues that face New Mexico?

Photograph and Illustration Credits

Chapter 4

Chapter 5

Index

Page numbers in italic text indicate illustrations.